CONTENTS

FROM
THE
JAWS
OF
DEATH

INTRODUCTION

THROUGHOUT HISTORY, there have been many incredible stories of human survival. Men and women whom, for whatever reason, find themselves stranded in the middle of inhospitable lands or climate, and must reach deep inside themselves to find that strength of will to outlast nature, hunger, and their own frail bodies. They may have to walk dozens of miles through arctic, jungle, or forest terrain, or sail hundreds of miles on the vast, empty ocean before finding help. They may be experienced outdoorsmen camping in the wildest terrain or unprepared tourists out for a day cruise or hike that turns perilous in the span of a few minutes. Perhaps they have some supplies they've managed to salvage from their wrecked boat or crashed plane, perhaps they have none, and must live off whatever they find or catch. Sometimes they start their battle against nature with injuries, which they must deal with as well, and sometimes they come through their immediate brush with death miraculously healthy, only to face the possibility of a slow, agonizing demise in the wild.

There are many factors in what makes a survivor. As mentioned above, the overall health of the person, their level of preparedness, and the equipment they have with them at the time all play a part. However, the key factor, which has been repeated over and over in survival handbooks and outdoor magazines on the subject, is a person's mental preparedness. The abilities to think through difficult or panic situations, to create a plan to survive, and to never give up, even when all hope of rescue seems lost, all play a crucial role in determining whether someone who finds themselves in a survival situation will make it out alive.

As you read the following excerpts, all about or written by the people who experienced these harrowing ordeals, and survived, you may learn tips and tactics that you didn't know before. You may be astonished at the courage and strength these people showed in the face of terrible adversity. But the primary thing to keep in mind is that all of these people, whether they were traveling west to settle America in the nineteenth century or sailing on a modern boat with all the safety accoutrements possible, had one thing in common—the *will* to survive. As many of these excerpts reveal, it is not necessarily the experience or preparedness of a survivor, or their physical health, or their supplies that make the difference, it is a less quantifiable attribute—the sheer determination to survive, that vital ability to push injury, hunger, thirst, and panic to the side and concentrate on that singular goal: to escape their situation and make it back to civilization alive.

I hope you enjoy reading these excerpts as much as I enjoyed collecting them—and that you never, *ever* find yourself in a similar situation. But if you do, then I hope these true stories of human fortitude and resolve will also give you the courage to do what you may have to do to survive.

—BROGAN STEELE

THE VAST OCEANS

There are few things as beautiful as the ocean. The golden rays of the rising sun breaking over an endless expanse of bright blue water, or watching that same red-orange orb sink into the western horizon over a glass-smooth tropical sea can stir emotions like nothing else.

Of course, nature is nothing if not capricious, and that same stretch of calm blue ocean can turn deadly in a matter of hours—sometimes in a matter of minutes, if the conditions are right—going from peaceful and torpid to a raging tempest that obliterates anything caught in it. And that's just the water itself—there are plenty of other dangers out there, from aggressive whales that attack boats, hungry sharks just waiting to make a meal out of an unwary swimmer or diver, hidden, jagged reefs that tear open the keel of a sailboat, even certain areas where the age-old profession of piracy has been resurrected, making unmolested passage less and less likely each year

Despite its dangers, thousands of people take to the oceans around the world every year, whether simply as their job, or looking for adventure. Some find much more than they bargained for, and end up watching those beautiful sunrises and sunsets in a leaky whaleboat or life raft, trapped on the endless expanse of water, sometimes for weeks or even months, subsisting on what they managed to bring aboard and what they can catch from the water until sighting land or being rescued.

The following selections of shipwrecked and castaway men and women spans more than 175 years, and shows that, whether adrift in the eighteenth century or the twentieth, survival at sea has always been a matter of proper mindset, courage, and more than a bit of luck.

ADRIFT ON THE PACIFIC

Owen Chase (1798–1869)

From the *Narrative of the Most Extraordinary and
Distressing Shipwreck of the Whaleship* Essex

*We begin our journey out into the wild ocean with an excerpt from one of the most
famous survival stories ever told. The whaleship* Essex, *while on a two-year voyage
in the Pacific Ocean, was attacked and sunk by a large sperm whale on November
20, 1820. The twenty-one sailors were left in three whaleboats in the middle of the
ocean, with little food or water. So began one of the most incredible journeys of perseverance in the history of mankind. Before it was over, the survivors would resort to
such measures as drinking their own urine and cannibalism to survive. First Mate
Owen Chase's account of the sailors' plight, published in 1821, is still just as gripping
to read today as it must have been at the time. It seems that I'm not the only person to
think so, either, as the narrative was a source of inspiration for Herman Melville to
write his epic novel* Moby-Dick.*

In this excerpt, we pick up the narrative a few days after the sinking of the* Essex,
*and find the men struggling to survive in their leaking boats, with little food and even
less potable water. Although this excerpt seems to have a happy ending, with the survivors reaching an island, if one reads the last few pages carefully, it becomes fairly
obvious that there is more hardship in store for these poor men.*

NOVEMBER 23RD. IN MY CHEST, which I was fortunate enough to preserve, I had several small articles, which we found of great service to us;
among the rest, some eight or ten sheets of writing paper, a lead pencil, a
suit of clothes, three small fishhooks, a jackknife, a whetstone, and a cake
of soap. I commenced to keep a sort of journal with the little paper and
pencil, which I had; and the knife, besides other useful purposes, served
us as a razor. It was with much difficulty, however, that I could keep any
sort of record, owing to the incessant rocking and unsteadiness of the boat,
and the continual dashing of the spray of the sea over us. The boat contained, in addition to the articles enumerated, a lantern, tinderbox, and two
or three candles, which belonged to her, and with which they are kept
always supplied while engaged in taking whale. In addition to all which,

the captain had saved a musket, two pistols, and a canister, containing about two pounds of gunpowder; the latter he distributed in equal proportions between the three boats, and gave the second mate and myself each a pistol. When morning came we found ourselves quite near together, and the wind had considerably increased since the day before; we were consequently obliged to reef our sails; and although we did not apprehend any very great danger from the then violence of the wind, yet it grew to be very uncomfortable in the boats from the repeated dashing of the waves that kept our bodies constantly wet with the salt spray. We, however, stood along our course until twelve o'clock, when we got an observation, as well as we were able to obtain one, while the water flew all over us, and the sea kept the boat extremely unsteady. We found ourselves this day in latitude 0°58' S having repassed the equator. We abandoned the idea altogether of keeping any correct longitudinal reckoning, having no glass, nor log line. The wind moderated in the course of the afternoon a little, but at night came on to blow again almost a gale. We began now to tremble for our little barque; she was so ill calculated, in point of strength, to withstand the racking of the sea, while it required the constant labors of one man to keep her free of water. We were surrounded in the afternoon with porpoises that kept playing about us in great numbers, and continued to follow us during the night.

November 24th. The wind had not abated any since the preceding day, and the sea had risen to be very large, and increased, if possible, the extreme uncomfortableness of our situation. What added more than anything else to our misfortunes was that all our efforts for the preservation of our provisions proved, in a great measure, ineffectual; a heavy sea broke suddenly into the boat, and, before we could snatch it up, damaged some part of it; by timely attention, however, and great caution, we managed to make it eatable and to preserve the rest from a similar casualty. This was a subject of extreme anxiety to us; the expectation, poor enough of itself indeed, upon which our final rescue was founded, must change at once to hopelessness, deprived of our provisions, the only means of continuing us in the exercise, not only of our manual powers, but in those of reason itself; hence, above all other things, this was the object of our utmost solicitude and pains.

We ascertained, the next day, that some of the provisions in the captain's boat had shared a similar fate during the night; both which accidents served to arouse us to a still stronger sense of our slender reliance upon the human means at our command, and to show us our utter depen-. dence on that divine aid, which we so much the more stood in need of.

November 25th. No change of wind had yet taken place, and we experienced the last night the same wet and disagreeable weather of the preceding one. About eight o'clock in the morning we discovered that the water began to come fast in our boat, and in a few minutes the quantity increased to such a degree as to alarm us considerably for our safety; we commenced immediately a strict search in every part of her to discover the leak, and, after tearing up the ceiling or floor of the boat near the bows, we found it proceeded from one of the streaks or outside boards having bursted off there; no time was to be lost in devising some means to repair it. The great difficulty consisted in its being in the bottom of the boat, about six inches from the surface of the water; it was necessary, therefore, to have access to the outside, to enable us to fasten it on again: the leak being to leeward, we hove about, and lay to on the other tack, which brought it then nearly out of water; the captain, who was at the time ahead of us, seeing us maneuvering to get the boat about, shortened sail, and presently tacked, and ran down to us. I informed him of our situation, and he came immediately alongside to our assistance. After directing all the men in the boat to get on one side, the other, by that means, heeled out of the water a considerable distance, and, with a little difficulty, we then managed to drive in a few nails, and secured it, much beyond our expectations. Fears of no ordinary kind were excited by this seemingly small accident. When it is recollected to what a slight vessel we had committed ourselves; our means of safety alone consisting in her capacity and endurance for many weeks, in all probability, yet to come, it will not be considered strange that this little accident should not only have damped our spirits considerably, but have thrown a great gloominess over the natural prospects of our deliverance. On this occasion, too, were we enabled to rescue ourselves from inevitable destruction by the possession of a few nails, without which (had it not been our fortune to save some from the wreck) we would, in all human calculations, have been lost: we were still liable to a recurrence of the same accident, perhaps to a still worse one, as, in the heavy and repeated racking of the swell, the progress of our voyage would serve but to increase the incapacity and weakness of our boat, and the starting of a single nail in her bottom would most assuredly prove our certain destruction. We wanted not this additional reflection, to add to the miseries of our situation.

November 26th. Our sufferings, heaven knows, were now sufficiently increased, and we looked forward, not without an extreme dread, and anxiety, to the gloomy and disheartening prospect before us. We experienced a little abatement of wind and rough weather today, and took the opportunity of drying the bread that had been wet the day previously; to our great joy and satisfaction also, the wind hauled out to ENE and enabled us to hold a much more favorable course; with these exceptions, no circumstance of any considerable interest occurred in the course of this day.

The twenty-seventh of November was alike undistinguished for any incident worthy of note; except that the wind again veered back to E and destroyed the fine prospect we had entertained of making a good run for several days to come.

November 28th. The wind hauled still further to the southward, and obliged us to fall off our course to S and commenced to blow with such violence, as to put us again under short sail; the night set in extremely dark, and tempestuous, and we began to entertain fears that we should be separated. We however, with great pains, managed to keep about a ship's length apart, so that the white sails of our boats could be distinctly discernible. The captain's boat was but a short distance astern of mine, and that of the second mate a few rods to leeward of his. At about eleven o'clock at night, having laid down to sleep, in the bottom of the boat, I was suddenly awakened by one of my companions, who cried out that the captain was in distress and was calling on us for assistance. I immediately aroused myself, and listened a moment, to hear if anything further should be said, when the captain's loud voice arrested my attention. He was calling to the second mate, whose boat was nearer to him than mine. I made all haste to put about, ran down to him, and inquired what was the matter; he replied, "I have been attacked by an unknown fish, and he has stove my boat." It appeared that some large fish had accompanied the boat for a short distance, and had suddenly made an unprovoked attack upon her, as nearly as they could determine, with his jaws; the extreme darkness of the night prevented them from distinguishing what kind of animal it was, but they judged it to be about twelve feet in length, and one of the killer-fish species. After having struck the boat once, he continued to play about her, on every side, as if manifesting a disposition to renew the attack, and did a second time strike the bows of the boat, and split her stem. They had no other instrument of violence but the sprit-pole (a long slender piece of wood, by which the peak of the sail is extended) with which, after repeated attempts to destroy the boat, they succeeded in beating him off. I arrived just as he had discontinued his operations and disappeared. He had made a considerable breach in the bows of the boat, through which the water had began to pour fast; and the captain, imagining matters to be considerably worse then they were, immediately took measures to remove his provisions into the second mate's boat and mine, in order to lighten his own, and by that means, and constant bailing, to keep her above water until daylight should enable him to discover the extent of the damage, and to repair it. The night was spissy* darkness itself; the sky was completely overcast, and it seemed to us as if fate was wholly relentless, in pursuing us with such a cruel complication of disasters. We were not without our fears that the fish might renew his attack some time during the night upon one of the other boats, and unexpectedly destroy us; but they proved entirely groundless, as he was never afterward seen. When daylight came, the wind again favored us a little, and we all lay to, to repair the broken boat; which was effected by nailing on thin strips of boards in the inside; and, having replaced the provisions, we proceeded again on our course. Our allowance of water, which in the commencement merely served to administer to the positive demands of nature, became now to be insufficient; and we began to experience violent thirst from the consumption of the provisions that had been wet with the salt water, and dried in the sun; of these we were obliged to eat first, to prevent their spoiling; and we could not, nay, we did not dare, to make any encroachments on our stock of water. Our determination was to suffer as long as human patience and endurance would hold out, having only in view the relief that would be afforded us when the quantity of wet provisions should be exhausted. Our extreme sufferings here first commenced. The privation of water is justly ranked among the most dreadful of the miseries of our life; the violence of raving thirst has no parallel in the catalog of human calamities. It was our hard lot to have felt this in its extremest force, when necessity subsequently compelled us to seek resource from one of the offices of nature. We were not at first, aware of the consequences of eating this bread; and themselves to a degree of oppression that we could divine the cause of our extreme thirst. But, alas! It was not until the fatal effects of it had shown there was no relief. Ignorant, or instructed of the fact, it was alike immaterial; it composed a part of our subsistence, and reason imposed upon us the necessity of its immediate consumption, as otherwise it would have been lost to us entirely.

---

* Dense.

November 29th. Our boats appeared to be growing daily more frail and insufficient; the continual flowing of the water into them seemed increased, without our being able to assign it to anything else than a general weakness, arising from causes that must in a short time, without some remedy or relief, produce their total failure. We did not neglect, however, to patch up and mend them, according to our means, whenever we could discover a broken or weak part. We this day found ourselves surrounded by a shoal of dolphins; some, or one of which, we tried in vain a long time to take. We made a small line from some rigging that was in the boat, fastened on one of the fishhooks, and tied to it a small piece of white rag; they took not the least notice of it, but continued playing around us, nearly all day, mocking both our miseries and our efforts.

November 30th. This was a remarkably fine day; the weather not exceeded by any that we had experienced since we left the wreck. At one o'clock, I proposed to our boat's crew to kill one of the turtle; two of which we had in our possession. I need not say that the proposition was hailed with the utmost enthusiasm; hunger had set its ravenous gnawings upon our stomachs, and we waited with impatience to suck the warm flowing blood of the animal. A small fire was kindled in the shell of the turtle, and after dividing the blood (of which there was about a gill) among those of us who felt disposed to drink it, we cooked the remainder, entrails and all, and enjoyed from it an unspeakably fine repast. The stomachs of two or three revolted at the sight of the blood, and refused to partake of it; not even the outrageous thirst that was upon them could induce them to taste it; for myself, I took it like a medicine, to relieve the extreme dryness of my palate, and stopped not to inquire whether it was anything else than a liquid. After this, I may say exquisite banquet, our bodies were considerably recruited, and I felt my spirits now much higher than they had been at any time before. By observation, this day we found ourselves in latitude 7°53' S, our distance from the wreck, as nearly as we could calculate, was then about 480 miles.

December 1st. From the first to the third of December, exclusive, there was nothing transpired of any moment. Our boats as yet kept admirably well together, and the weather was distinguished for its mildness and salubrity. We gathered consolation, too, from a favorable slant, which the wind took to NE and our situation was not at that moment, we thought, so comfortless as we had been led at first to consider it; but, in our extravagant felicitations upon the blessing of the wind and weather, we forgot our leaks, our weak boats, our own debility, our immense distance from land, the smallness of our stock of provisions; all which, when brought to mind, with the force which they deserved, were too well calculated to dishearten us, and cause us to sigh for the hardships of our lot. Up to the third of December, the raging thirst of our mouths had not been but in a small degree alleviated; had it not been for the pains which that gave us, we should have tasted, during this spell of fine weather, a species of enjoyment, derived from a momentous forgetfulness of our actual situation.

December 3rd. With great joy we hailed the last crumb of our damaged bread, and commenced this day to take our allowance of healthy provisions. The salutary and agreeable effects of this change was felt at first in so slight a degree as to give us no great satisfaction; but gradually, as we partook of our small allowance of water, the moisture began to collect in our mouths, and the parching fever of the palate imperceptibly left it. An accident here happened to us, which gave us a great momentary spell of uneasiness. The night was dark, and the sky was completely overcast, so that we could scarcely discern each other's boats, when at about ten o'clock, that of the second mate was suddenly missing. I felt for a moment considerable alarm at her unexpected disappearance; but after a little reflection I immediately hove to, struck a light as expeditiously as possible, and hoisted it at the masthead, in a lantern. Our eyes were now directed over every part of the ocean, in search of her, when, to our great joy, we discerned an answering light, about a quarter of a mile to leeward of us; we ran down to it, and it proved to be the lost boat. Strange as the extraordinary interest, which we felt in each other's company may appear, and much as our repugnance to separation may seem to imply of weakness, it was the subject of our continual hopes and fears. It is truly remarked that misfortune more than anything else serves to endear us to our companions. So strongly was this sentiment engrafted upon our feelings, and so closely were the destinies of all of us involuntarily linked together, that, had one of the boats been wrecked and wholly lost, with all her provisions and water, we should have felt ourselves constrained, by every tie of humanity, to have taken the surviving sufferers into the other boats, and shared our bread and water with them, while a crumb of one or a drop of the other remained. Hard, indeed, would the case have been for all, and much as I have since reflected on the subject, I have not been able to realize, had it so happened, that a sense of our necessities would have allowed us to give so magnanimous and devoted a character to our feelings. I can only speak of the impressions, which I recollect I had at the

time. Subsequently, however, as our situation became more straightened
and desperate, our conversation on this subject took a different turn; and
it appeared to be a universal sentiment that such a course of conduct
was calculated to weaken the chances of a final deliverance for some, and
might be the only means of consigning every soul of us to a horrid death
of starvation. There is no question but that an immediate separation, therefore, was the most politic measure that could be adopted, and that every
boat should take its own separate chance: while we remained together,
should any accident happen of the nature alluded to, no other course could
be adopted than that of taking the survivors into the other boats, and giving up voluntarily what we were satisfied could alone prolong our hopes
and multiply the chances of our safety, or unconcernedly witness their
struggles in death, perhaps beat them from our boats, with weapons, back
into the ocean. The expectation of reaching the land was founded upon
a reasonable calculation of the distance, the means, and the subsistence;
all which were scanty enough, God knows, and ill adapted to the probable exigencies of the voyage. Any addition to our own demands, in this
respect, would not only injure, but actually destroy the whole system,
which we had laid down, and reduce us to a slight hope, derived either
from the speedy death of some of our crew, or the falling in with some
vessel. With all this, however, there was a desperate instinct that bound
us together; we could not reason on the subject with any degree of satisfaction to our minds, yet we continued to cling to each other with a strong
and involuntary impulse. This, indeed, was a matter of no small difficulty,
and it constituted, more than anything else, a source of continual watching and inquietude. We would but turn our eyes away for a few moments, during some dark nights, and presently one of the boats would be
missing. There was no other remedy than to heave to immediately and
set a light, by which the missing boat might be directed to us. These pro-
ceedings necessarily interfered very much with our speed, and consequently
lessened our hopes; but we preferred to submit to it, while the consequences
were not so immediately felt, rather than part with the consolation, which
each other's presence afforded. Nothing of importance took place on the
fourth of December; and on the fifth at night, owing to the extreme darkness, and a strong wind, I again separated from the other boats. Finding
they were not to be seen in any direction, I loaded my pistol and fired
it twice; soon after the second discharge they made their appearance a
short distance to windward, and we joined company, and again kept on
our course, in which we continued without any remarkable occurrence

through the sixth and seventh of December. The wind during this period blew very strong, and much more unfavorably. Our boats continued to leak, and to take in a good deal of water over the gunwales.

December 8th. In the afternoon of this day the wind set in ESE and began to blow much harder than we had yet experienced it; by twelve o'clock at night it had increased to a perfect gale, with heavy showers of rain, and we now began, from these dreadful indications, to prepare ourselves for destruction. We continued to take in sail by degrees, as the tempest gradually increased, until at last we were obliged to take down our masts. At this juncture we gave up entirely to the mercy of the waves. The sea and rain had wet us to the skin, and we sat down, silently, and with sullen resignation, awaiting our fate. We made an effort to catch some fresh water by spreading one of the sails, but after having spent a long time, and obtained but a small quantity in a bucket, it proved to be quite as salty as that from the ocean: this we attributed to its having passed through the sail, which had been so often wet by the sea, and upon which, after drying so frequently in the sun, concretions of salt had been formed. It was a dreadful night—cut off from any imaginary relief—nothing remained but to await the approaching issue with firmness and resignation. The appearance of the heavens was dark and dreary, and the blackness that was spread over the face of the waters dismal beyond description. The heavy squalls, that followed each other in quick succession, were preceded by sharp flashes of lightning, that appeared to wrap our little barge in flames. The sea rose to a fearful height, and every wave that came looked as if it must be the last that would be necessary for our destruction. To an overruling Providence alone must be attributed our salvation from the horrors of that terrible night. It can be accounted for in no other way: that a speck of substance, like that which we were, before the driving terrors of the tempest, could have been conducted safely through it. At twelve o'clock it began to abate a little in intervals of two or three minutes, during which we would venture to raise up our heads and look to windward. Our boat was completely unmanageable; without sails, mast, or rudder, and had been driven, in the course of the afternoon and night, we knew not whither, nor how far. When the gale had in some measure subsided we made efforts to get a little sail upon her, and put her head toward the course we had been steering. My companions had not slept any during the whole night, and were dispirited and broken down to such a degree as to appear to want some more powerful stimulus than the fears of death to enable them to do their duty. By great exertions, however, toward morning we again set a double-reefed mainsail and jib upon her, and began to make tolerable progress on the voyage. An unaccountable good fortune had kept the boats together during all the troubles of the night: and the sun rose and showed the disconsolate faces of our companions once more to each other.

December 9th. By twelve o'clock this day we were enabled to set all sail as usual; but there continued to be a very heavy sea running, which opened the seams of the boats, and increased the leaks to an alarming degree. There was, however, no remedy for this but continual bailing, which had now become to be an extremely irksome and laborious task. By observation we found ourselves in latitude 17°40' S. At eleven o'clock at night, the captain's boat was unexpectedly found to be missing. After the last accident of this kind we had agreed, if the same should again occur, that, in order to save our time, the other boats should not heave to, as usual, but continue on their course until morning, and thereby save the great detention that must arise from such repeated delays. We, however concluded on this occasion to make a small effort, which, if it did not immediately prove the means of restoring the lost boat, we would discontinue, and again make sail. Accordingly we hove to for an hour, during which time I fired my pistol twice, and obtaining no tidings of the boat, we stood on our course. When daylight appeared she was to leeward of us, about two miles; upon observing her we immediately ran down, and again joined company.

December 10th. I have omitted to notice the gradual advances, which hunger and thirst for the last six days, had made upon us. As the time had lengthened since our departure from the wreck, and the allowance of provision, making the demands of the appetite daily more and more important, they had created in us an almost uncontrollable temptation to violate our resolution, and satisfy, for once, the hard yearnings of nature from our stock; but a little reflection served to convince us of the imprudence and unmanliness of the measure, and it was abandoned with a sort of melancholy effort of satisfaction. I had taken into custody, by common consent, all the provisions and water belonging to the boat, and was determined that no encroachments should be made upon it with my consent; nay, I felt myself bound, by every consideration of duty, by every dictate of sense, of prudence, and discretion, without which, in my situation, all other exertions would have been folly itself, to protect them, at the hazard of my life. For this purpose I locked up in my chest the whole quantity, and never, for a single moment, closed my eyes without placing some part of my person in contact with the chest; and having loaded my pistol, kept it constantly about me. I should not certainly have put any threats in execution as long as the most distant hopes of reconciliation existed; and was determined, in case the least refractory disposition should be manifested (a thing, which I contemplated not unlikely to happen, with a set of starving wretches like ourselves) that I would immediately divide our substance into equal proportions, and give each man's share into his own keeping. Then, should any attempt be made upon mine, which I intended to mete out to myself according to exigencies, I was resolved to make the consequences of it fatal. There was, however, the most upright and obedient behavior in this respect manifested by every man in the boat, and I never had the least opportunity of proving what my conduct would have been on such an occasion. While standing on our course this day we came across a small shoal of flying fish: four of which, in their efforts to avoid us, flew against the mainsail, and dropped into the boat; one having fell near me, I eagerly snatched up and devoured; the other three were immediately taken by the rest, and eaten alive. For the first time I, on this occasion, felt a disposition to laugh, upon witnessing the ludicrous and almost desperate efforts of my five companions, who each sought to get a fish. They were very small of the kind, and constituted but an extremely delicate mouthful, scales, wings, and all, for hungry stomachs like ours. From the eleventh to the thirteenth of December inclusive, our progress was very slow, owing to light winds and calms; and nothing transpired of any moment, except that on the eleventh we killed the only remaining turtle, and enjoyed another luxuriant repast, that invigorated our bodies, and gave a fresh flow to our spirits. The weather was extremely hot, and we were exposed to the full force of a meridian sun, without any covering to shield us from its burning influence, or the least breath of air to cool its parching rays. On the thirteenth day of December we were blessed with a change of wind to the northward, that brought us a most welcome and unlooked for relief. We now, for the first time, actually felt what might be deemed a reasonable hope of our deliverance; and with hearts bounding with satisfaction, and bosoms swelling with joy, we made all sail to the eastward. We imagined we had run out of the tradewinds, and had got into the variables, and should, in all probability, reach the land many days sooner than we expected. But, alas! Our anticipations were but a dream, from which we shortly experienced a cruel awaking. The wind gradually died away, and at night was succeeded by a perfect calm, more oppressive and disheartening to us from the bright prospects, which had attended us during the day. The gloomy reflections that this hard fortune had given birth to were succeeded by others, of a no less cruel and discouraging nature, when we found the calm continue during the fourteenth, fifteenth, and sixteenth of December inclusive. The extreme oppression of the weather, the sudden and unexpected prostration of our hopes, and the consequent dejection of our spirits, set us again to thinking, and filled our souls with fearful and melancholy forebodings. In this state of affairs, seeing no alternative left us but to employ to the best advantage all human expedients in our power, I proposed, on the fourteenth, to reduce our allowance of provisions one-half. No objections were made to this arrangement: all submitted, or seemed to do so, with an admirable fortitude and forbearance. The proportion, which our stock of water bore to our bread was not large; and while the weather continued so oppressive, we did not think it advisable to diminish our scanty pittance; indeed, it would have been scarcely possible to have done so, with any regard to our necessities, as our thirst had become now incessantly more intolerable than hunger, and the quantity then allowed was barely sufficient to keep the mouth in a state of moisture for about one-third of the time. "Patience and long-suffering" was the constant language of our lips: and a determination, strong as the resolves of the soul could make it, to cling to existence as long as hope and breath remained to us. In vain was every expedient tried to relieve the raging fever of the throat by drinking salt water, and holding small quantities of it in the mouth, until, by that means, the thirst was increased to such a degree, as even to drive us to despairing, and vain relief from our own urine. Our sufferings during these calm days almost exceeded human belief. The hot rays of the sun beat down upon us to such a degree as to oblige us to hang over the gunwale of the boat, into the sea, to cool our weak and fainting bodies. This expedient afforded us, however, a grateful relief, and was productive of a discovery of infinite importance to us. No sooner had one of us got on the outside of the gunwale than he immediately observed the bottom of the boat to be covered with a species of small clam, which upon being tasted, proved a most delicious and agreeable food. This was no sooner announced to us than we commenced to tear them off and eat them, for a few minutes, like a set of gluttons; and, after having satisfied the immediate craving of the stomach, we gathered large quantities and laid them up in the boat; but hunger came upon us again in less than half an hour afterward, within which time they had all disappeared. Upon attempting to get in again, we found ourselves so weak as to require each other's assistance; indeed, had it not been for three of our crew, who could not swim, and who did not, therefore, get overboard, I know not by what means we should have been able to have resumed our situations in the boat.

On the fifteenth our boat continued to take in water so fast from her leaks, and the weather proving so moderate, we concluded to search out the bad places, and endeavor to mend them as well as we should be able. After a considerable search, and, removing the ceiling near the bows, we found the principal opening was occasioned by the starting of a plank or streak in the bottom of the boat, next to the keel. To remedy this, it was now absolutely necessary to have access to the bottom. The means of doing which did not immediately occur to our minds. After a moment's reflection, however, one of the crew, Benjamin Lawrence, offered to tie a rope around his body, take a boat's hatchet in his hand, and thus go under the water, and hold the hatchet against a nail, to be driven through from the inside, for the purpose of clenching it. This was, accordingly, all effected, with some little trouble, and answered the purpose much beyond our expectations. Our latitude was this day 21°42' S. The oppression of the weather still continuing through the sixteenth, bore upon our health and spirits with an amazing force and severity. The most disagreeable excitements were produced by it, which, added to the disconsolate endurance of the calm, called loudly for some mitigating expedient, some sort of relief to our prolonged sufferings. By our observations today we found, in addition to our other calamities, that we had been urged back from our progress, by the heave of the sea, a distance of ten miles; and were still without any prospect of wind. In this distressing posture of our affairs, the captain proposed that we should commence rowing, which, being seconded by all, we immediately concluded to take a double allowance of provision and water for the day, and row, during the cool of the nights, until we should get a breeze from some quarter or other. Accordingly, when night came, we commenced our laborious operations: we made but a very sorry progress. Hunger and thirst, and long inactivity, had so weakened us, that in three hours every man gave out, and we abandoned the further prosecution of the plan. With the sunrise the next morning, on the seventeenth, a light breeze sprung up from the SE and, although directly ahead, it was welcomed with almost frenzied feelings of gratitude and joy.

December 18th. The wind increased this day considerably, and by twelve o'clock blew a gale; veering from SE to ESE. Again we were compelled to take in all sail, and lie to for the principal part of the day. At night, however, it died away, and the next day, the nineteenth, proved very moderate and pleasant weather, and we again commenced to make a little progress.

December 20th. This was a day of great happiness and joy. After having experienced one of the most distressing nights in the whole catalog of our sufferings, we awoke to a morning of comparative luxury and pleasure. About seven o'clock, while we were sitting dispirited, silent, and dejected, in our boats, one of our companions suddenly and loudly called out, "There is land!" We were all aroused in an instant, as if electrified, and casting our eyes to leeward, there indeed, was the blessed vision before us, "as plain and palpable" as could be wished for. A new and extraordinary impluse now took possession of us. We shook off the lethargy of our senses, and seemed to take another, and a fresh existence. One or two of my companions, whose lagging spirits and worn out frames had begun to inspire them with an utter indifference to their fate, now immediately brightened up, and manifested a surprising alacrity and earnestness to gain, without delay, the much wished for shore. It appeared at first a low, white, beach, and lay like a basking paradise before our longing eyes. It was discovered nearly at the same time by the other boats, and a general burst of joy and congratuulation now passed between us. It is not within the scope of human calculation, by a mere listener to the story, to divine what the feelings of our hearts were on this occasion. Alternate expectation, fear, gratitude, surprise, and exultation, each swayed our minds, and quickened our exertions. We ran down for it, and at 11 A.M., we were within a quarter of a mile of the shore. It was an island, to all appearance, as nearly as we could determine it, about six miles long and three broad; with a very high, rugged shore, and surrounded by rocks; the sides of the mountains were bare, but on the tops it looked fresh and green with vegetation. Upon examining our navigators, we found it was Ducie's Island,* lying in latitude 24°40' S, longitude 124°40' W. A short moment sufficed for reflection, and we made immediate arrangements to land. None of us knew whether the island was inhabited or not, nor what it afforded, if anything; if inhabited, it was uncertain whether by beasts or savages; and a momentary suspense was created by the dangers, which might possibly arise by proceeding without due preparation and care. Hunger and thirst, however, soon determined us, and having taken the musket and pistols, I, with

---

* Actually Henderson Island.

three others, effected a landing upon some sunken rocks, and waded thence to the shore. Upon arriving at the beach, it was necessary to take a little breath, and we laid down for a few minutes to rest our weak bodies before we could proceed. Let the reader judge, if he can, what must have been our feelings now! Bereft of all comfortable hopes of life, for the space of thirty days of terrible suffering; our bodies wasted to mere skeletons, by hunger and thirst, and death itself staring us in the face; to be suddenly and unexpectedly conducted to a rich banquet of food and drink, which subsequently we enjoyed for a few days, to our full satisfaction; and he will have but a faint idea of the happiness that here fell to our lot. We now, after a few minutes, separated, and went different directions in search of water; the want of which had been our principal privation, and called for immediate relief. I had not proceeded far in my excursion, before I discovered a fish, about a foot and a half in length, swimming along in the water close to the shore. I commenced an attack upon him with the breach of my gun, and struck him, I believe, once and he ran under a small rock, that lay near the shore, from whence I took him with the aid of my ramrod, and brought him up on the beach, and immediately fell to eating. My companions soon joined in the repast; and in less than ten minutes, the whole was consumed, bones, and skin, and scales, and all. With full stomachs, we imagined we could now attempt the mountains, where, if in any part of the island, we considered water would be most probably obtained. I accordingly clambered, with excessive labor, suffering, and pain, up among the bushes, roots, and underwood, of one of the crags, looking in all directions in vain, for every appearance of water that might present itself. There was no indication of the least moisture to be found, within the distance to which I had ascended, although my strength did not enable me to get higher than about twenty feet. I was sitting down at the height that I had attained, to gather a little breath, and ruminating upon the fruitlessness of my search, and, the consequent evils and continuation of suffering that it necessarily implied, when I perceived that the tide had risen considerably since our landing, and threatened to cut off our retreat to the rocks, by which alone we should be able to regain our boats. I therefore determined to proceed again to the shore, and inform the captain and the rest of our want of success in procuring water, and consult upon the propriety of remaining at the island any longer. I never for one moment lost sight of the main chance, which I conceived we still had, of either getting to the coast, or of meeting with some vessel at sea; and felt that every minute's detention, without some equivalent object, was lessening those chances, by a consumption of the means of our support. When I had got down, one of my companions informed me, that he had found a place in a rock some distance off, from which the water exuded in small drops, at intervals of about five minutes; that he had, by applying his lips to the rock, obtained a few of them, which only served to whet his appetite, and from which nothing like the least satisfaction had proceeded. I immediately resolved in my own mind, upon this information, to advise remaining until morning, to endeavor to make a more thorough search the next day, and with our hatchets to pick away the rock, which had been discovered, with the view of increasing, if possible, the run of the water. We all repaired again to our boats, and there found that the captain had the same impressions as to the propriety of our delay until morning. We therefore landed; and having hauled our boats up on the beach, laid down in them that night, free from all the anxieties of watching and labor, and amid all our sufferings, gave ourselves up to an unreserved forgetfulness and peace of mind, that seemed so well to accord with the pleasing anticipations that this day had brought forth. It was but a short space, however, until the morning broke upon us; and sense, and feeling, and gnawing hunger, and the raging fever of thirst then redoubled my wishes and efforts to explore the island again. We had obtained, that night, a few crabs, by traversing the shore a considerable distance, and a few very small fish; but waited until the next day, for the labors of which, we considered a night of refreshing and undisturbed repose would better qualify us.

Having exhausted the resources of Henderson Island, Chase and several of his party opt to continue onward, leaving three men behind (who were later rescued as well). Chase and the two other surviving sailors in his boat were rescued ninety-three days after the Essex went down. Only eight of the twenty-one sailors lived through the gruesome ordeal after the sinking of the whaleship Essex. The event haunted Chase for the rest of his life; he suffered from nightmares and terrible headaches, and often cached food in his lodgings, even when safe on dry land.

SHIPWRECKED OFF THE AFRICAN COAST

Captain James Riley (1777–1840)

From *Authentic Narrative of the Loss of the American Brig Commerce*

What's worse than running a merchant sailing ship aground off the western coast of Africa in 1815? How about surviving the wreck, only to be taken captive, sold into slavery, and marched through the inhospitable Sahara desert by the natives? That is exactly what happened to the good captain and several of his crew members, all of which was recounted by Captain Riley in his narrative, published in 1817. This book also had a profound effect on those who read it—President Abraham Lincoln said that Riley's account was one of the main influences (along with the Bible and Pilgrim's Progress*) on his political thinking.*

The following excerpt chronicles the shipwreck itself, the escape to the shore, and Riley's and his men's first encounter with the locals, which doesn't go remotely well. To be fair, the deck was stacked against the good captain from the start—marooned on a desolate coastline with their provisions and equipment scattered to hell and gone, facing hostile natives with no way to truly communicate with them, and working with a fairly undisciplined crew (one of their first actions upon going ashore was to break out the wine, a big mistake in any survival situation). And from there things go from very bad to much worse, as you'll soon read.

WE SET SAIL FROM THE BAY OF GIBRALTAR on the twenty-third of August, 1815, intending to go by way of the Cape de Verde Islands, to complete the lading of the vessel with salt. We passed Cape Spartel on the morning of the twenty-fourth, giving it a birth of from ten to twelve leagues, and steered off to the WSW. I intended to make the Canary Islands, and pass between Teneriffe and Palma, having a fair wind; but it being very thick and foggy weather, though we got two observations at noon, neither could be much depended upon. On account of the fog, we saw no land, and found, by good meridian altitudes on the twenty-eighth, that we were in the latitude of 27°30' N having differed our latitude by the force of current, 120 miles; thus passing the Canaries without seeing any of them. I concluded we must have passed through the intended

21

passage without discovering the land on either side, particularly, as it was in the night, which was very dark, and black as pitch; nor could I believe otherwise from having had a fair wind all the way, and having steered one course ever since we took our departure from Cape Spartel. Soon after we got an observation on the twenty-eighth, it became as thick as ever, and the darkness seemed (if possible) to increase. Toward evening I got up my reckoning, and examined it all over, to be sure that I had committed no error, and caused the mates to do the same with theirs. Having thus ascertained that I was correct in calculation, I altered our course to SW, which ought to have carried us nearly on the course I wished to steer, that is, for the easternmost of the Cape de Verde; but finding the weather becoming more foggy toward night, it being so thick that we could scarcely see the end of the jibboom, I rounded the vessel to, and sounded with 120 fathoms of line, but found no bottom, and continued on our course, still reflecting on what should be the cause of our not seeing land (as I never had passed near the Canaries before without seeing them, even in thick weather or in the night). I came to a determination to haul off to the NW by the wind at 10 P.M. as I should then be by the log only thirty miles north of Cape Bojador. I concluded on this at nine, and thought my fears had never before so much prevailed over my judgment and my reckoning. I ordered the light sails to be handed, and the steering sail booms to be rigged in snug, which was done as fast as it could be by one watch, under the immediate direction of Mr. Savage.

We had just got the men stationed at the braces for hauling off, as the man at helm cried "ten o'clock." Our trysail boom was on the starboard side, but ready for jibing; the helm was put to port, dreaming of no danger near. I had been on deck all the evening myself; the vessel was running at the rate of nine or ten knots, with a very strong breeze, and high sea, when the main boom was jibed over, and I at that instant heard a roaring; the yards were braced up—all hands were called. I imagined at first it was a squall, and was near ordering the sails to be lowered down; but I then discovered breakers foaming at a most dreadful rate under our lee. Hope for a moment flattered me that we could fetch off still, as there were no breakers in view ahead: the anchors were made ready; but these hopes vanished in an instant, as the vessel was carried by a current and a sea directly toward the breakers, and she struck! We let go the best bower anchor; all sails were taken in as fast as possible: surge after surge came thundering on, and drove her in spite of anchors, partly with her head onshore. She struck with such violence as to start every man from the deck. Knowing there was no possibility of saving her, and that she must very soon bilge and fill with water, I ordered all the provisions we could get at to be brought on deck, in hopes of saving some, and as much water to be drawn from the large casks as possible. We started several quarter casks of wine, and filled them with water. Every man worked as if his life depended upon his present exertions; all were obedient to every order I gave, and seemed perfectly calm. The vessel was stout and high, as she was only in ballast trim. The sea combed over her stern and swept her decks; but we managed to get the small boat in on deck, to sling her and keep her from staving. We cut away the bulwark on the larboard side so as to prevent the boast from staving when we should get them out; cleared away the longboat and hung her in tackles, the vessel continuing to strike very heavy, and filling fast. We, however, had secured five or six barrels of water, and as many of wine, three barrels of bread, and three or four salted provisions. I had as yet been so busily employed, that no pains had been taken to ascertain what distance we were from the land, nor had any of us yet seen it; and in the meantime all the clothing, chests, trunks, were got up, and the books, charts, and sea instruments, were stowed in them, in the hope of their being useful to us in future.

The vessel being now nearly full of water, the surf making a fair breach over her, and fearing she would go to pieces, I prepared a rope, and put it in the small boat, having got a glimpse of the shore, at no great distance, and taking Porter [the second mate] with me, we were lowered down on the larboard or lee side of the vessel, where she broke the violence of the sea, and made it comparatively smooth; we shoved off, but on clearing away from the bow of the vessel, the boat was overwhelmed with a surf, and we were plunged into the foaming surges: we were driven along by the current, aided by what seamen call the undertow (or recoil of the sea), to the distance of three hundred yards to the westward, covered nearly all the time by the billows, which, following each other in quick succession, scarcely gave us time to catch a breath before we were again literally swallowed by them, till at length we were thrown, together with our boat, upon a sandy beach. After taking breath a little, and ridding our stomachs of the salt water that had forced its way into them, my first care was to turn the water out of the boat, and haul her up out of the reach of the surf. We found the rope that was made fast to her still remaining; this we carried up along the beach, directly to leeward of the wreck, where we fastened it to sticks about the thickness of handspikes, that had drifted on the shore from the vessel, and which we drove into the sand by the help of other pieces of wood. Before leaving the vessel, I had directed that all the chests, trunks, and everything that would float, should be hove overboard: this all hands were busied in doing. The vessel lay about one hundred fathoms from the beach, at high tide. In order to save the crew, a hawser was made fast to the rope we had onshore, one end of which we hauled to us, and made it fast to a number of sticks we had driven into the sand for the purpose. It was then tautened on board the wreck, and made fast. This being done, the longboat (in order to save the provisions already in her) was lowered down, and two hands steadied her by ropes fastened to the rings in her stem and stern posts over the hawser, so as to slide, keeping her bow to the surf. In this manner they reached the beach, carried on the top of a heavy wave. The boat was stove by the violence of the shock against the beach; but by great exertions we saved the three barrels of bread in her before they were much damaged; and two barrels of salted provisions were also saved. We were now, four of us, onshore, and busied in picking up the clothing and other things, which drifted from the vessel, and carrying them up out of the surf. It was by this time daylight, and high water; the vessel careened deep offshore, and I made signs to have the mast cut away, in the hope of easing her, that she might not go to pieces. They were accordingly cut away, and fell on her starboard side, making a better lee for a boat alongside the wreck, as they projected considerably beyond her bows. The masts and rigging being gone, the sea breaking very high over the wreck, and nothing left to hold on by, the mates and six men still on board, though secured, as well as they could be, on the bowsprit and in the larboard fore-channels, were yet in imminent danger of being washed off by every surge. The long-boat was stove, and it being impossible for the small one to live, my great object was now to save the lives of the crew by means of the hawser. I therefore made signs to them to come, one by one, on the hawser, which had been stretched taut for that purpose. John Hogan ventured first, and having pulled off his jacket, took to the hawser, and made for the shore. When he had got clear of the immediate lee of the wreck, every surf buried him, combing many feet above his head; but he still held fast to the rope with a death-like grasp, and as soon as the surf was passed, proceeded on toward the shore, until another surf, more powerful than the former, unclenched his hands, and threw him within our reach; when we laid hold of him and dragged him to the beach; we then rolled him on the sand, until he discharged the salt water from his stomach, and revived. I kept in the water up to my chin, steadying myself by the hawser, while the surf passed over me, to catch the others as they approached, and thus, with the assistance of those already onshore, was enabled to save all the rest from a watery grave.

All hands being now landed, our first care was to secure the provisions and water, which we had so far saved, knowing it was a barren thirsty land; and we carried the provisions up fifty yards from the water's edge, where we placed them, and then formed a kind of a tent by means of our oars and two steering sails. I had fondly hoped we should not be discovered by any human beings on this inhospitable shore, but that we should be able to repair our boats, with the materials we might get from the wreck, and by taking advantage of a smooth (if we should be favored with one), put to sea, where by the help of a compass and other instruments, which we had saved, we might possibly find some friendly vessel to save our lives, or reach some of the European settlements down the coast, or the Cape de Verde Islands.

Being thus employed, we saw a human figure approach our stuff, such as clothing, which lay scattered along the beach for a mile westward of us. It was a man! He began plundering our clothing. I went toward him with all the signs of peace and friendship I could make, but he was extremely shy, and made signs to me to keep my distance, while he all the time seemed intent on plunder. He was unarmed, and I continued to approach him until within ten yards.

He appeared to be about five feet seven or eight inches high, and of a complexion between that of an American Indian and negro. He had about him, to cover his nakedness, a piece of coarse woolen cloth, that reached from below his breast nearly to his knees; his hair was long and bushy, resembling a pitch mop, sticking out every way six or eight inches from his head; his face resembled that of an orangutan more than a human being; his eyes were red and fiery; his mouth, which stretched nearly from ear to ear, was well lined with sound teeth; and a long curling beard, which depended from his upper lip and chin down upon his breast, gave him altogether a most horrid appearance, and I could not but imagine that those well-set teeth were sharpened for the purpose of devouring human flesh! Particularly as I conceived I had before seen in different parts of the world, the human face and form in its most hideous and terrific shape. He appeared to be very old, yet fierce and vigorous; he was soon joined by two old women of similar appearance, whom I took to be his wives. These looked a little less frightful, though their two eye-teeth stuck out like hogs' tusks, and their tanned skins hung in loose plaits on their faces and breasts; but their hair was long and braided. A girl of from eighteen to twenty, who was not ugly, and five or six children, of different ages and sexes, from six to sixteen years were also in company. These were entirely naked. They brought with them a good English hammer, with a rope-lanyard through a hole in its handle. It had no doubt belonged to some vessel wrecked on that coast. They had also a kind of ax with them, and some long knives slung on their right sides, in a sheath suspended by their necks. They now felt themselves strong, and commenced a bold and indiscriminate plundering of everything they wanted. They broke open trunks, chests, and boxes, and emptied them of their contents, carrying the clothing on their backs upon the sandhills, where they spread them out to dry. They emptied the beds of their contents, wanting only the cloth, and were much amused with the flying of the feathers before the wind from my bed. It appeared as though they had never before seen such things.

I had an adventure of silk laced veils and silk handkerchiefs, the former of which the man, women, and children tied around their heads in the form of turbans; the latter around their legs and arms, though only for a short time, when they took them off again, and stowed them away among the other clothing on the sandhills. They all seemed highly delighted with their good fortune, and even the old man's features began to relax a little, as he met with no resistance. We had no fire- or sidearms, but we could easily have driven these creatures off with handspikes, had I not considered that we had no possible means of escaping either by land or water, and had no reason to doubt but they would call others to their assistance, and in revenge destroy us. I used all the arguments in my power to induce my men to endeavor to conciliate the friendship of these natives, but it was with the greatest difficulty. I could restrain some of them from rushing on the savages and putting them to death, if they could have come up with them; but I found they could run like the wind, while we could with difficulty move in the deep sand. Such an act I conceived would cost us our lives as soon as we should be overpowered by numbers, and I therefore permitted them to take what pleased them best, without making any resistance; except our bread and provisions, which, as we could not subsist without them, I was determined to defend to the last extremity. On our first reaching the shore I allowed my mates and people to share among themselves one thousand Spanish dollars, for I had hauled my trunk onshore by a rope, with my money in it, which I was induced to do in the hope of its being useful to them in procuring a release from this country in case we should be separated, and in aiding them to reach their homes. We had rolled up the casks of water and wine, which had been thrown overboard and drifted ashore. I was now determined to mend the longboat, as soon and as well as possible, in order to have a retreat in my power (or at least the hope of one), in case of the last necessity. The wind lulled a little in the afternoon, at low water, when William Porter succeeded in reaching the wreck and procured a few nails and a marlinespike; with these he got safe back to the shore. I found the timbers of the boat in so crazy a state, and the nails, which held them together, so eaten off by the rust, that she would not hold together, nor support her weight in turning her up in order to get at her bottom. I tacked her timbers together, however as well as I could, which was very imperfectly, as I had bad tools to work with, and my crew, now unrestrained by my authority, having broached a cask of wine, and taken copious draughts of it, in order to dispel their sorrows, were most of them in such a state, that instead of assisting me, they tended to increase my embarrassment. We, however, at last, got the boat turned up, and found that one whole plank was out on each side, and very much split. I tacked the pieces, assisted by Mr. Savage, Horace, and one or two more. We chinked a little oakum into the seams and splits with our knives, as well as we could, and worked upon her until it was quite dark. I had kept sentinels walking with handspikes, to guard the tent and provisions during this time, but the Arabs had managed to rob us of one of our sails from the tent, and to carry it off, and not content with this, they tried to get the other in the same way. This I would not permit them to do. They then showed their hatchets and their arms, but finding it of no effect they retired for the night, after promising as near as I could understand them, that they would not molest us further till morning, when they would bring camels down with them. We had previously seen a great many camel tracks in the sand, and I of course believed there were some near. One of the children had furnished us with fire, which enabled us to roast a fowl that had been drowned, and driven onshore from the wreck, on which, with some salt pork, and a little bread and butter, we made a hearty meal, little thinking that this was to be the last of our provisions we should be permitted to enjoy. A watch was set of two men, who were to walk guard at a distance from the tent, to give an alarm in case of the approach of the natives and keep burning a guard fire. This we were enabled to do by cutting up some spars we found on the beach, and which must have belonged to some vessel wrecked there before us.

Night had now spread her sable mantle over the face of nature, the savages had retired, and all was still, except the restless and unwearied waves, which dashed against the deserted wreck, and tumbled among the broken rocks a little to the eastward of us, where the high perpendicular cliffs, jutting out into the sea, opposed a barrier to their violence, and threatened, at the same time, inevitable and certain destruction to every ill-fated vessel and her crew that should, unfortunately, approach too near their immovable foundations: these we had escaped only by a few rods. From the time the vessel struck to this moment, I had been so entirely engaged by the laborious exertions, which our critical situation demanded, that I had no time for reflection; but it now rushed like a torrent over my mind, and banished from my eyes that sleep, which my fatigued frame so much required. I knew I was on a barren and inhospitable coast; a tempestuous ocean lay before me, whose bosom was continually tossed and agitated by wild and furious winds, blowing directly onshore; no vessel or boat sufficient for our escape, as I thought it impossible for our shattered longboat to live at sea, even if we should succeed in urging her through the tremendous surges that broke upon the shore with such violence, as to make the whole coast tremble; behind us were savage beings, bearing the human form indeed, but in its most terrific appearance, whose object I knew, from what had already passed, would be to rob us of our last resource, our provisions; and I did not doubt, but they would be sufficiently strong in the morning, not only to accomplish what they meditated, but to take our lives also, or to seize upon our persons, and doom us to slavery till death should rid us of our miseries.

This was the first time I had ever suffered shipwreck. I had left a wife and five young children behind me, on whom I doted, and who depended on me entirely for their subsistence. My children would have no father's, and perhaps no mother's care, to direct them in the paths of virtue, to instruct their ripening years, or to watch over them, and administer the balm of comfort in time of sickness; no generous friend to relieve their distresses, and save them from indigence, degradation, and ruin. These reflections harrowed up my soul, nor could I cease to shudder at these imaginary evils, added to my real ones, until I was forced mentally to exclaim, "Thy ways, great Father of the universe, are wise and just, and what am I? An atom of dust, that dares to murmur at thy dispensations."

I next considered, that eleven of my fellow sufferers, who had en-trusted themselves to my care, were still alive and with me, and all but two of them (who were on the watch) lying on the ground, and wrapped in the most profound and apparently pleasing sleep; and as I surveyed them with tears of compassion, I felt it was a sacred duty assigned me by Providence, to protect and preserve their lives to my very utmost. The night passed slowly and tediously away; when daylight at length began to dawn in the eastern horizon, and chased darkness before it, not to usher to our view the cheering prospect of approaching relief, but to unfold new scenes of suffering, wretchedness, and distress. So soon as it was fairly light, the old man came down accompanied by his wives and two young men of the same family—he was armed with a spear of iron, having a handle made with two pieces of wood spliced together, and tied with cords: the handle was about twelve feet long. This he held balanced in his right hand, above his head, making motions as if to throw it at us; he ordered us off to the wreck, pointing, at the same time, to a large drove of camels that were descending the heights to the eastward of us, his women run-ning off at the same time whooping and yelling horribly, throwing up sand in the air, and beckoning to those who had charge of the camels to approach. I ran toward the beach, and seized a small spar that lay there, to parry off the old man's lance, as a handspike was not long enough. He in the meantime came to the tent like a fury, where the people still were, and by slightly pricking one or two of them, and pointing at the same time toward the camels, he succeeded in frightening them, which was his object, as he did not wish to call help, lest he should be obliged to di-vide the spoil. The crew all made the best of their way to the small boat, while I parried off his spear with my spar, and kept him at a distance. He would doubtless have hurled it at me, but for the fear of losing it.

The small boat was dragged to the water, alongside our hawser, but the people huddling into her in a confused manner, she was filled by the first sea, and bilged. I now thought we had no resource, except trying to get eastward or westward. Abandoning, therefore, our boats, provisions, etc., we tried to retreat eastward, but were opposed by this formidable spear, and could not make much progress; for the old man was very active. He would fly from us like the wind, and return with the same speed. The camels were approaching very fast, and he made signs to inform us, that the people who were with them had firearms, and would put us instantly to death; at the same time opposing us every way with his young men, with all their weapons, insisting on our going toward the wreck, and refusing to receive our submission, while the women and children still kept up their yelling. We then laid hold of the longboat, turned her over, and got her into the water; and as I would suffer only one at a time to get on board, and that, too, over her stern, we succeeded at length, and all got off safe alongside the wreck, which made a tolerable lee for the boat, though she was by this time half filled with water.

All hands got on board the wreck except myself and another, we kept bailing the boat and were able to keep her from entirely filling, having one bucket and a keg to work with. The moment we were out of the way, all the family ran together where our tent was; here they were joined by the camels and two young men, which we had not before seen, apparently about the ages of twenty and twenty-six. They were armed with scimitars, and came running on foot from the eastward. The old man and women ran to meet them, hallooing to us brandishing their naked weapons and bidding us defiance. They loaded the barrels of bread on their camels, which kneeled down to receive them; the beef and all the other provisions, with the sail that the tent was made of, etc., etc., and sent them off with the children who drove them down. The old man next came to the beach; with his ax stove in all the heads of our water casks and casks of wines, emptying their contents into the sand. They then gathered up all the trunks, chests, sea instruments, books and charts, and consumed them by fire in one pile. Our provisions and water being gone, we saw no other alternative but to try to get to sea in our leaky boat, or stay and be washed off the wreck the next night, or to perish by the hands of these barbarians, who we expected would appear in great force, and bring firearms with them, and they would besides soon be enabled to walk to the wreck, on a sand bar that was fast forming inside of the vessel, and now nearly dry at low water. The tide seemed to ebb and flow about twelve feet. We had now made all the preparations in our power for our departure, which amounted to nothing more than getting from the wreck a few bottles of wine and a few pieces of salt pork. No water could be procured, and the bread was completely spoiled by being soaked in salt water. Our oars were all lost except two that were onshore in the power of the natives. We had split a couple of plank for oars, and attempted to shove off, but a surf striking the boat, came over her bow, and nearly filling her with water, drifted her again alongside the wreck. We now made shift to get on board the wreck again, and bail out the boat; which when done, two hands, were able to keep her free, while two others held her steady by ropes, so as to prevent her from dashing to pieces against the wreck.

The sight of our deplorable situation seemed to excite pity in the breasts of the savages who had driven us from shore. They came down to the water's edge, bowed themselves to the ground, beckoning us, and particularly me whom they knew to be the captain, to come onshore; making at the same time all the signs of peace and friendship they could. They carried all their arms up over the sandhills, and returned without them. Finding I would not come onshore, one of them ran and fetched a small goat or dog skin, which by signs, they made me understand was filled with water, and all retiring to a considerable distance from the beach, except the old man who had it: he came into the water with it up to his armpits, beckoning me to come and fetch it and drink. He was nearly naked, and had no weapons about him. Being very thirsty, and finding we could not get at any water, and no hope remaining of our being able to get out through the surf to sea, I let myself down by the hawser, and went by means of it to the beach, where the old man met me and gave me the skin of water, which I carried off to the wreck, and the people hauled it up on board. This done, he made me understand that he wished to go on board, and me to remain on the beach until his return.

Seeing no possible chance of escaping or of preserving our lives in any other way but by their assistance, and that that was only to be obtained by conciliating them—telling my men my mind, I went again to the shore. The young men, women, and children were now seated unarmed on the beach, near the water—the grown people nearly, and the children entirely naked. They made all the signs of peace they knew of, looking upward, as if invoking heaven to witness their sincerity. The old man advancing, took me by the hand, and looking up to heaven, said, "Allah K. Beer." I knew that Allah was the Arabic name for the Supreme Being, and supposed K. Beer meant "our friend or father." I let him pass to the wreck, and went and seated myself on the beach with the others, who seemed very friendly, interlacing their fingers with mine; putting my hat on one another's head and returning it to me again; stroking down my trousers, feeling my head and hands, examining my shoes, and feeling into my pockets, etc.

When the people had hauled the old man on board, I endeavored to make them understand that they must keep him until I was released, but they did not comprehend my meaning, owing to the noise of the surf; and after he had satisfied his curiosity by looking attentively at everything he could see, which was nothing more than the wreck of the contents of the hold floating in her, inquiring for baftas, for firearms, and for money, as I afterward learned, and finding none he came onshore. When he was near the beach, and I about to rise to meet him, I was seized by both arms by the two stoutest of the young men, who had placed themselves on each side of me for the purpose of safekeeping. They grasped my arms like lions, and at that instant the women and children presented their daggers, knives, and spears to my head and breast. To strive against them was instant death; I was therefore obliged to remain quiet, and determined to show no concern for my life or any signs of fear. The countenance of everyone around me now assumed the most horrid and malignant expressions; they gnashed their teeth at me, and struck their daggers within an inch of every part of my head and body. The young men still held me fast, while the old one seizing a sharp scimitar, laid hold of my hair at the same instant, as if to cut my throat, or my head off. I concluded my last moments had come, and that my body was doomed to be devoured by these beings, whom I now considered to be none other than cannibals, that would soon glut their hungry stomachs with my flesh. I could only say, *Thy will be done,* mentally, and felt resigned to my fate, for I thought it could not be prevented. But this conduct on their part, it soon appeared, was only for the purpose of frightening me, and as I had not changed countenance, the old man, after drawing his scimitar lightly across the collar of my shirt, which he cut a little, released my head, bidding me by signs to order all the money we had on board to be brought directly on shore.

My mates and people then on the wreck, had witnessed this scene, and had agreed, as they afterward informed me, that if I was massacred, which they did not doubt from appearances would soon be the case, to rush on-shore in the boat, armed in the best manner they were able, and revenge my death by selling their lives as dearly as possible.

When the old man had quit his hold, and I hailed my people, their hopes began to revive, and one of them came on the hawser to know what they should do. I told him all the money, which they had on board must be instantly brought onshore. He was in the water at some distance from me, and could not hear, on account of the noise occasioned by the surf, what I added, which was for them not to part with the money until I should be fairly released. He went on board, and all hands hoping to procure my release, put their money, which they still had about them, to the amount of about one thousand dollars into a bucket, and slinging it on the hawser, Porter shoved it along before him near the beach, and was about to bring it up to the place where I sat. With considerable difficulty, however I prevented him, as the surf made such a roaring, that he could not hear me, though he was only a few yards distant; but he at last understood my signs, and stayed in the water until one of the young men went and received it from him. The old man had taken his seat alongside of me, and held his scimitar pointed at my breast.

The bucket of dollars was brought and poured into one end of the old man's blanket, when he bid me rise and go along with them, he and the young men urging me along by both arms, with their daggers drawn before, and the women and children behind with the spear, and their knives near my back. In this manner they made me go with them over the sand drifts to the distance of three or four hundred yards, where they seated themselves and me on the ground. The old man then proceeded to count and divide the money. He made three heaps of it, counting into each heap by tens, and so dividing it exactly, gave the two young men one-third or heap, to his two wives one-third, and kept the other to himself. Each secured his and their own part, by wrapping and tying it up in some of our clothing. During this process, they had let go of my arms, though they were all around me. I thought my fate was now decided, if I could not by some means effect my escape. I knew they could outrun me, if I should leap from them, and would undoubtedly plunge their weapons to my heart if I attempted, and failed in the attempt. However I resolved to risk it, and made a slight movement with that view at a moment when I thought all eyes were turned from me; but one of the young men perceiving my maneuver, made a lounge at me with his scimitar. I eluded the force of his blow, by falling backward on the ground; it however pierced my waistcoat. He was about to repeat it, when the old man bade him desist.

The money being now distributed and tied up, they made me rise with them, and were all going together from the beach, holding me by the arms with naked daggers all around me. There appeared now no possible means of escape, when the thought suddenly occurred to me, to tempt their avarice. I then, by signs, made them understand that there was more money in the possession of the crew. This seemed to please them, and they instantly turned themselves and me about for the beach, sending the money off by one of the young men and a boy. When they approached to within one hundred yards of the beach, they made me seat myself on the sand, between two of them, who held me by the arms, bidding me order the money onshore. I knew there was none on board the wreck, or in the boat, but I imagined if I could get Antonio Michel on-shore, I should be able to make my escape. I hailed accordingly and made signs to my people to have one of them come near the shore; but as they saw, by every movement of the natives, that my situation was dreadfully critical, none of them were inclined to venture, and I waited more than an hour, was often threatened with death, and made to halloo with all my might, until I became so hoarse as scarcely to make myself heard by those around me. The pity of Mr. Savage at last overcame his fears. He ventured on the hawser, and reaching the beach in safety was about to come up to me, where he would have been certainly seized on as I was, when I endeavored to make him understand, by signs, that he must stay in the water, and keep clear of the natives, if he valued his life; but not being able to hear me, my guards, who supposed I was giving him orders to fetch the money, obliged me to get up and approach him a little, until I made him understand what I wanted: he then returned on board the wreck, and I was taken back to my former station.

Antonio came to the shore, as soon as he knew it was my wish, and made directly toward me. The natives expecting he would bring more money, flocked about him to receive it, but finding he had none, struck him with their fists and the handles of their daggers, and stripped off all his clothing; the children at the same time pricking him with their sharp knives, and all seemed determined to torment him with a slow and cruel death. He begged for his life upon his knees, but they paid no regard to his entreaties. In hopes of saving him from the fury of these wretches, I told him to let them know by signs that there were dollars and other things buried in the sand near where our tent had stood, and to endeavor to find them by digging. A new spyglass, a handsaw, and several other things had been buried there, and a bag containing about four hundred dollars at a short distance from them. He soon made them undersand that something was buried, and they hurried him to the spot he had pointed out, and he began to dig. I had imagined that if this man would come onshore, I should be enabled to make my escape; yet I knew not how, nor had I formed any plan for effecting it.

I was seated on the sand, facing the sea, between the old man on my left, with his spear uplifted in his left hand, pointing to my breast, and the stoutest young man on my right, with a naked scimitar in his right hand, pointing to my head—both weapons were within six inches of me, and my guards within a foot on each side. I considered at this time, that so soon as anything should be found by those who were digging, they would naturally speak and inform those who guarded me of it (these had let go of my arms sometime before); and as I was pretty certain that both of them would look around as soon as the discovery of any treasure should be announced, I carefully drew up my legs under me, but without exciting suspicion in order to be ready for a start. The place where they were digging was partly behind us on our right, and upon their making a noise, both my guards turned their heads and eyes from me toward them, when I instantly sprang out from beneath their weapons, and flew to the beach. I was running for my life, and soon reached the water's edge: knowing I was pursued, and nearly overtaken, I plunged into the sea, with all my force, head foremost, and swam underwater as long as I could hold my breath; then rising to the surface, I looked around on my pursuers. The old man was within ten feet of me, up to his chin in water, and was in the act of darting his spear through my body, when a surf rolling over me, saved my life, and dashed him and his comrades on the beach. I was some distance westward of the wreck; but swimming as fast as possible toward her, while surf after surf broke in towering heights over me, I was enabled by almost superhuman exertion to reach the lee of the wreck, when I was taken into the boat over the stern by the mates and people.

I was so far exhausted that I could not immediately witness what passed onshore, but was informed by those who did, that my pursuers stood motionless on the beach, at the edge of the water, until I was safe in the boat: that they then ran toward poor Antonio, and plunging a spear into his body near his left breast downward, laid him dead at their feet. They then picked up what things remained, and made off altogether. I saw them dragging Antonio's lifeless trunk across the sandhills, and felt an inexpressible pang, that bereft me for a moment of all sensation, occasioned by a suggestion that to me alone his massacre was imputable; but on my recovery, when I reflected there were no other means whereby my own life could have been preserved, and under Providence, the lives of ten men, who had been committed to my charge, I concluded I had not done wrong, nor have I since had occasion to reproach myself for being the innocent cause of his destruction, nor did any of my surviving shipmates, though perfectly at liberty so to do, ever accuse me on this point; from which I think I have an undoubted right to infer, that their feelings perfectly coincided with mine on this melancholy occasion.

Hostilities had now commenced, and we could not doubt but these merciless ruffians would soon return in force, and when able to overpower us

would massacre us all as they had already done Antonio. The wind blowing strong, and the surf breaking outside and on the wreck twenty or
thirty feet high, the hope of getting to sea in our crazy longboat was indeed but faint. She had been thumping alongside the wreck, and on a
sand bank all day, and writhed like an old basket, taking in as much water
as two men constantly employed with buckets could throw out. The deck
and outside of the wreck were fast going to pieces, and the other parts
could not hold together long. The tide, (by being low) together with the
sand bar that had been formed by the washing of the sea from the bow of
the wreck to the beach, had very much lessened the danger of communicating with the shore during this day; but it was now returning to sweep
everything from the wreck, aided by the wind, which blew a gale on
shore every night. To remain on the wreck, or go onshore was almost
certain death; the boat could no longer be kept afloat alongside, and being without provisions or water, if we should put to sea, we must soon
perish. We had neither oars nor a rudder to the boat; no compass nor a
quadrant to direct her course; but as it was our only chance, I resolved
to try and get to sea; expecting, nevertheless, we should be swallowed up
by the first surf, and launched into eternity all together.

I, in the first place, sent Porter onshore to get the two broken oars
that were still lying there, while I made my way through the water into the
hold of the wreck, to try once more if any fresh water could be found.
I dove in at the hatchway, which was covered with water, and found, after coming up under the deck on the larboard side, as I expected, just room
enough to breathe, and to work among the floating casks, planks, and wreck
of the hold. After much labor I found a water cask, partly full, and turning
it over, discovered that its bung was tight. This gave me new courage, and
after upheading it, I came up and communicated the circumstance to my
shipmates, and we then made search for some smaller vessel to fill from the
cask. After much trouble, a small keg was found in the after hold; it might
probably hold four gallons—the head of the water cask was stove in, and
with the help of Mr. Savage and Clark I got the keg full of water, and a
good drink for all hands besides, which was very much needed. The others
were in the meantime employed in rigging out spars, which we had lashed
together over the stern of the wreck with a rope made fast to their outer
ends, in order to give the boat headway, and clear her from the wreck,
when we should finally shove off. Porter had returned with the oars, and
also brought the bag of money that had been buried, containing about four
hundred dollars: this he did of his own accord.

We had got the small boat's sails, consisting of a jib and mainsail, into the boat, with a spar that would do for a mast, and the brig's fore-topmast staysail; the keg of water, a few pieces of salt pork, a live pig, weighing about twenty pounds, which had escaped to the shore when the vessel struck, and which had swam back to us again when we were driven from the shore; about four pounds of figs, that had been soaking in salt water ever since the brig was wrecked, and had been fished out of her cabin; this was all our stock of provisions.

Everything being now ready, I endeavored to encourage the crew as well as I could; representing to them that it was better to be swallowed up all together, than to suffer ourselves to be massacred by the ferocious savages; adding, that the Almighty was able to save, even when the last ray of hope was vanishing; that we should never despair, but exert ourselves to the last extremity, and still hope for his merciful protection.

As we surveyed the dangers that surrounded us, wave following wave, breaking with a dreadful crash just outside of us, at every instant, our hearts indeed failed us, and there appeared no possibility of getting safely beyond the breakers, without a particular interference of Providence in our favor. The particular interference of Providence in any case I had always before doubted. Everyone trembled with dreadful apprehensions, and each imagined that the moment we ventured past the vessel's stern, would be his last. I then said, "Let us pull off our hats, my shipmates and companions in distress." This was done in instant; when lifting my eyes and my soul toward heaven, I exlaimed, "Great Creator and preserver of the universe, who now seest our distresses; we pray thee to spare our lives, and permit us to pass through this overwhelming surf to the open sea; but if we are doomed to perish, thy will be done; we commit our souls to the mercy of thee our God, who gave them: and Oh! Universal Father, protect and preserve our widows and children."

The wind, as if by divine command, at this very moment ceased to blow. We hauled the boat out; the dreadful surges that were nearly bursting upon us, suddenly subsided, making a path for our boat about twenty yards wide, through which we rowed her out as smoothly as if she had been on a river in a calm, while on each side of us, and not more than ten yards distant, the surf continued to break twenty feet high, and with unabated fury. We had to row nearly a mile in this manner; all were fully convinced that we were saved by the immediate interposition of divine Providence in this particular instance, and all joined in returning thanks to the Supreme Being for this mercy. As soon as we reached the open sea,

and had gained some distance from the wreck, we observed the surf rolling behind us with the same force as it had on each side the boat. We
next fitted the mast, and set the small boat's mainsail. The wind now
veered four points to the eastward, so that we were enabled to fetch past
the point of the Cape, though the boat had neither keel nor rudder, it was
sunset when we got out, and night coming on, the wind as usual increased to a gale before morning, and we kept the boat to the wind by
the help of an oar, expecting every moment to be swallowed up by the
waves. We were eleven in number on board; two constantly bailing were
scarcely able to keep her free, changing hands every half hour. The night
was very dark and foggy, and we could not be sure of fetching clear of the
land, having nothing to guide us but the wind. In the morning we sailed
back again for the land, and had approached it almost within reach of the
breakers without seeing it, when we put about again. It had been my intention after we had got to sea, to run down the coast in the hope of finding some vessel, or to discover the mouth of some river, in order to
obtain a supply of water. But now the dangers and difficulties we should
have to encounter in doing this, were taken into consideration. If we tried
to navigate along the coast, it was necessary to know our course, or we
should be in imminent danger of being dashed to pieces on it every dark
day, and every night. The thick foggy weather would prevent our seeing
the land in the daytime; while the wind, blowing almost directly on the
land, would force us toward it, and endanger the safety of both the boat
and our lives at every turn or point. We had no compass to guide us either by day or night; no instrument by which to find our latitude; no rudder to steer our boat with; nor were we in possession of materials wherewith
it was possible to make one; she had no keel to steady her, nor was there
a steering place in her stern, where an oar could be fixed by any other
means than by lashing to the stern ring, which afforded a very unsteady
hold. On the other hand, we considered that if we escaped the danger of
being driven onshore or foundering at sea, and should succeed in reaching the cultivated country south of the desert, we should have to encounter the ferocious inhabitants who would not fail, in the hope of plunder,
to massacre us, or doom us to slavery. On the other hand, we reflected
that we had escaped from savages who had already killed one of our shipmates, had gained the open sea through divine mercy, and could stand
off to the westward without fear of being driven onshore. In this direction we might meet with some friendly vessel to save us, which was our

only hope in that way; and the worst that could happen to us was to sink altogether in the sea, or gradually perish through want of sustenance.

Having considered, and represented to my companions the dangers that beset us on every side, I asked their opinions one by one, and found they were unanimously in favor of committing themselves to the open sea in preference to keeping along the coast. The dangers appeared to be fewer, and all agreed that it was better to perish on the ocean, if it was God's will, than by the hands of the natives. There being a strong breeze, we stood off by the wind had at length arrived, and expecting that every approaching surge would bury us forever in a watery grave.

The boat racked like an old basket, letting in water at every seam and split; her timbers working out or breaking off; the nails I had put in while last onshore were kept from entirely drawing out, merely by the pressure of the water acting on the outside of the boat. Sharp flashes of lightning caused by heat and vapor shot across the gloom, rendering the scene doubly horrid. In this situation some of the men thought it was no longer of use to try to keep the boat afloat, as they said she must soon fill in spite of all their exertions. Having prayed to the Almighty and implored pardon for our transgressions, each one seemed perfectly resigned to his fate: this was a trying moment, however, and my example and advice could scarcely induce them to continue bailing; while some of them, by thrusting their heads into the water, endeavored to ascertain what the pains of death were, by feeling the effects the water would produce on their organs. Thus passed this night; all my exertions were necessary to encourage the men to assist me in bailing the boat, by reminding them of our miraculous escape from the savages, and through the surf to the open sea, and enforcing on their minds the consideration that we were still in the hands of the same disposing power, escaping from the shore by a miracle, to be abandoned here and swallowed up by the ocean; and that for my own part I still entertained hopes of our preservation; at any rate that it was a duty we owed to God and ourselves to strive to the latest breath to prevent our own destruction. Day came on amid these accumulated horrors; it was the first of September; thirst pressed upon us, which we could only allay by wetting our mouths twice a day with a few drops of wine and water, and as many times with our urine.

The wind continued to blow hard all this day, and the succeeding night with great violence, and the boat to work and leak in the same manner as before. Worn down with fatigues and long continued hunger and thirst, scorched by the burning rays of the sun, and no vessel appearing to save us, our water fast diminishing, as well as our strength, every hope of succor by meeting with a vessel entirely failed me, so that in the afternoon of the second of September, I represented to my companions, that as we were still alive, after enduring so many trials, it was my advice to put about, and make toward the coast again; that if we continued at sea, we must inevitably perish, and that we could but perish in returning toward the land; that we might still exist four or five days longer, by means of the water and provisions that remained, and that it might be the will of Providence to send us on the coast where our vessel had been wrecked, and where means were perhaps prepared to bring about our deliverance and restoration to our country and our families. All seemed convinced that it was so, and we immediately put about with a kind of cheerfulness I had not observed in any countenance since our first disaster.

From this time all submitted to their fate with tolerable patience, and kept the boat free, though we had continual bad weather, without murmuring. We wetted our lips with wine and water twice every day, and ate the bones and some of the raw flesh of our pig, with its skin; but at length we became so faint as to be unable to take our turns in bailing, while the boat labored so much as to work off nearly all the nails that kept the planks to her timbers above water.

By the sixth of September, at night, we had not made the land, and could not hope to make the boat hold together in any manner above another day. I expected we should have found the land that day, but was disappointed, and some of the people began again to despair. Impelled by thirst, they forgot what they owed to their shipmates, and in the night got at, and drank off one of the two bottles of wine we had remaining. When I mentioned the loss of the wine on the morning of the seventh, all denied having taken or drank it, adding that it was an unpardonable crime, and that those who did it ought to be thrown overboard instantly. From the heat observable in their conversation, I guessed the offenders, but the wine was gone, and no remedy remained but patience, and stricter vigilance for the future.

In a short time we discovered land at a great distance ahead, and to leeward. This gave all hands new spirits; hope again revived for a moment; the land appeared perfectly smooth in the distant horizon; not the smallest rising or hill was to be seen, and I concluded we must be near a desert coast, where our sufferings would find no relief, but in death. We continued to approach the land, driving along to the southward by a swift current, roaring like a strong tide in a narrow rocky passage, until near sunset.

The coast now appeared to be formed of perpendicular and overhanging cliffs, rising to a great height, with no shelving shore to land on, or way by which we might mount to the top of the precipices. My opinion was, that we should endeavor to keep to sea this night also, and steer along down the coast, until by the help of daylight, we might find a better place to land, and where we should not be in such danger of being overwhelmed by the surf; but in this I was opposed by the united voice of the mates and all the people.

The surf was breaking high among the rocks, near the shore: we were now very near the land, and seeing a small spot that bore the appearance of a sand beach, we made for it, and approaching it with the help of our oars, we were carried on the top of a tremendous wave, so as to be high and dry, when the surf retired, on a little piece of sand beach, just large enough for the boat to lie on. Without us, and in the track we came, numerous fragments of rocks showed their craggy heads over which the surf foamed as it retired, with a dreadful roaring, which made us feel we had once more escaped instant destruction, by what appeared a miraculous interference of Providence.

We got out of the boat, and carried up the little remains of our water and pork, among the rocks beyond the reach of the surf. The remains of the pig had been previously consumed; our boat was now stove in reality; over our heads pended huge masses of broken and shattered rocks, extending both ways as far as the eye could reach: our limbs had become stiff for the want of exercise; our flesh had wasted away for the want of sustenance, and through fatigue our tongues were so stiff in our parched mouths, that we could with great difficulty speak so as to be understood by each other, though we had finished our last bottle of wine between us for fear of losing it, just before we ventured to the shore through the surf.

Being thus placed on dry land, we had yet to discover how we were to reach the surface above us—so taking Mr. Savage with me, we clambered over the rocks to the westward (for the coast running here from ENE to WSW induced me to think we were near Cape Blanco, which indeed afterward proved to be the case), but we searched in vain, and as there appeared to be no access to the summit in that direction, we returned (it being then dark) to our shipmates, who had been busied in preparing a place on the sand, between rocks, to sleep on. We now wet our mouths with water, ate a small slice of the fat of salt pork, and after pouring out our souls before the universal Benefactor, in prayers and thanksgiving for his mercy and his long continued goodness (as had constantly been our custom), we laid down to rest, and notwithstanding our dreadful situation, slept soundly till daylight.

Captain Riley's bad luck was to continue through his journey. Just when he and his men thought they'd escaped the savages, they were captured by slavers, split up, and marched on a tortuous journey through the Sahara desert. I imagine that they probably often thought of the ocean on that particular journey. Riley kept his head, however, and was able to ransom his men and himself when they came across civilization in the form of the city known as Mogador (now named Essaouira) and were able to free themselves with the help of a sympathetic British merchant and consul named William Wilshire.

Ironically, Riley had so impressed his owner, a man named Seti Hamet, with his loyalty to his crew members that after Riley was free, Hamet promised to return to the desert to find his other crew members. Two of the men were later released, but Riley received word that two Arabs had been stoned to death in the desert, and he assumed it was Hamet, killed while trying to fulfill his promise.

Apparently in the African desert, no deed—good or bad—goes unpunished.

THE BOAT JOURNEY

Sir Ernest Shackleton (1874–1922)

From *South*

From the searing heat of the African desert, we go to almost the opposite end of the planet, to the frozen, windswept plains of Antarctica. In the early twentieth century, men raced to be the first to reach the top and bottom of the world, respectively. Sir Ernest Shackleton came close in 1909, man-hauling a sledge to within ninety-seven miles of the South Pole before he had to turn back. He was thwarted in his goal when Roald Amundsen became the first man to stand at the South Pole in 1911 and return alive (a second expedition, led by Robert Scott, perished on the way back from the Pole).

Shackleton had always expressed a desire to return to Antarctica to attempt a complete crossing of the continent. However, during his next trip south in 1914, his ship, the Endurance, *became trapped by ice floes, and was crushed after ten months of drifting along the Antarctic coast. The twenty-eight man crew camped on the ice for five months before reaching Elephant Island, located in the South Shetland Islands, about one hundred miles away from the Antarctic continent, and six hundred miles away from the southernmost tip of Argentina, South America.*

In this excerpt, Shackleton has decided to take five men with him on a hazardous, eight hundred-mile crossing through open seas to South Georgia Island to get help. Not only are they risking their own lives, but Shackleton knows that if they fail, the rest of the crew will suffer a slow death from starvation and exposure on the barren. Not to mention that the journey ahead of them will be through some of the most dangerous seas on earth, with high waves that could swamp the boat in one pass to nasty ice floes that would lay the keel open in an instant. Regardless, the six men set out, embarking on a classic voyage of survival at sea.

THE INCREASING SEA MADE IT NECESSARY for us to drag the boats farther up the beach. This was a task for all hands, and after much labor we got the boats into safe positions among the rocks and made fast the painters to big boulders. Then I discussed with Wild and Worsley the chances of reaching South Georgia before the winter locked the seas against us.

Some effort had to be made to secure relief. Privation and exposure had left their mark on the party, and the health and mental condition of several men were causing me serious anxiety. Blackborrow's feet, which had been frostbitten during the boat journey, were in a bad way, and the two doctors feared that an operation would be necessary. They told me that the toes would have to be amputated unless animation could be restored within a short period. Then the food supply was a vital consideration. We had left ten cases of provisions in the crevice of the rocks at our first camping place on the island. An examination of our stores showed that we had full rations for the whole party for a period of five weeks. The rations could be spread over three months on a reduced allowance and probably would be supplemented by seals and sea elephants to some extent. I did not dare to count with full confidence on supplies of meat and blubber, for the animals seemed to have deserted the beach and the winter was near. Our stocks included three seals and two-and-a-half skins (with blubber attached). We were mainly dependent on the blubber for fuel, and, after making a preliminary survey of the situation, I decided that the party must be limited to one hot meal a day.

A boat journey in search of relief was necessary and must not be delayed. That conclusion was forced upon me. The nearest port where assistance could certainly be secured was Port Stanley, in the Falkland Islands, 540 miles away, but we could scarcely hope to beat up against the prevailing northwesterly wind in a frail and weakened boat with a small sail area. South Georgia was over 800 miles away, but lay in the area of the west winds, and I could count upon finding whalers at any of the whaling stations on the east coast. A boat party might make the voyage and be back with relief within a month, provided that the sea was clear of ice and the boat survive the great seas. It was not difficult to decide that South Georgia must be the objective, and I proceeded to plan ways and means. The hazards of a boat journey across 800 miles of stormy sub-Antarctic ocean were obvious, but I calculated that at worst the venture would add nothing to the risks of the men left on the island. There would be fewer mouths to feed during the winter and the boat would not require to take more than one month's provisions for six men, for if we did not make South Georgia in that time we were sure to go under. A consideration that had weight with me was that there was no chance at all of any search being made for us on Elephant Island.

The case required to be argued in some detail, since all hands knew that the perils of the proposed journey were extreme. The risk was justified solely by our urgent need of assistance. The ocean south of Cape Horn in the middle of May is known to be the most tempestuous storm-swept area of water in the world. The weather then is unsettled, the skies are dull and overcast, and the gales are almost unceasing. We had to face these conditions in a small and weather-beaten boat, already strained by the work of the months that had passed. Worsley and Wild realized that the attempt must be made, and they both asked to be allowed to accompany me on the voyage. I told Wild at once that he would have to stay behind. I relied upon him to hold the party together while I was away and to make the best of his way to Deception Island with the men in the spring in the event of our failure to bring help. Worsley I would take with me, for I had a very high opinion of his accuracy and quickness as a navigator, and especially in the snapping and working out of positions in difficult circumstances—an opinion that was only enhanced during the actual journey. Four other men would be required, and I decided to call for volunteers, although, as a matter of fact, I pretty well knew which of the people I would select. Crean I proposed to leave on the island as a right-hand man for Wild, but he begged so hard to be allowed to come in the boat that, after consultation with Wild, I promised to take him. I called the men together, explained my plan, and asked for volunteers. Many came forward at once. Some were not fit enough for the work that would have to be done, and others would not have been much use in the boat since they were not seasoned sailors, though the experiences of recent months entitled them to some consideration as sea-faring men. McIlroy and Macklin were both anxious to go but realized that their duty lay on the island with the sick men. They suggested that I should take Blackborrow in order that he might have shelter and warmth as quickly as possible, but I had to veto this idea. It would be hard enough for fit men to live in the boat. Indeed, I did not see how a sick man, lying helpless in the bottom of the boat, could possibly survive in the heavy weather we were sure to encounter. I finally selected McNeish, McCarthy, and Vincent in addition to Worsley and Crean. The crew seemed a strong one, and as I looked at the men I felt confidence increasing.

The decision made, I walked through the blizzard with Worsley and Wild to examine the *James Caird*. The twenty-foot boat had never looked big; she appeared to have shrunk in some mysterious way when I viewed her in the light of our new undertaking. She was an ordinary ship's whaler, fairly strong, but showing signs of the strains she had endured since the crushing of the *Endurance*. Where she was holed in leaving the pack was, fortunately, about the waterline and easily patched. Standing beside her, we glanced at the fringe of the storm-swept, tumultuous sea that formed our path. Clearly, our voyage would be a big adventure. I called the carpenter and asked him if he could do anything to make the boat more seaworthy. He first inquired if he was to go with me, and seemed quite pleased when I said "Yes." He was over fifty years of age and not altogether fit, but he had a good knowledge of sailing boats and was very quick. McCarthy said that he could contrive some sort of covering for the *James Caird* if he might use the lids of the cases and the four sledge-runners that we had lashed inside the boat for use in the event of a landing on Graham Land at Wilhelmina Bay. This bay, at one time the goal of our desire, had been left behind in the course of our drift, but we had retained the runners. The carpenter proposed to complete the covering with some of our canvas, and he set about making his plans at once.

Noon had passed and the gale was more severe than ever. We could not proceed with our preparations that day. The tents were suffering in the wind and the sea was rising. We made our way to the snow-slope at the shoreward end of the spit, with the intention of digging a hole in the snow large enough to provide shelter for the party. I had an idea that Wild and his men might camp there during my absence, since it seemed impossible that the tents could hold together for many more days against the attacks of the wind; but an examination of the spot indicated that any hole we could dig probably would be filled quickly by the drift. At dark, about 5 P.M., we all turned in, after a supper consisting of a pannikin of hot milk, one of our precious biscuits, and a cold penguin leg each.

The gale was stronger than ever on the following morning (April 20th). No work could be done. Blizzard and snow, snow and blizzard, sudden lulls and fierce returns. During the lulls we could see on the far horizon to the northeast bergs of all shapes and sizes driving along before the gale, and the sinister appearance of the swift-moving masses made us thankful indeed that, instead of battling with the storm amid the ice, we were required only to face the drift from the glaciers and the inland heights. The gusts might throw us off our feet, but at least we fell on solid ground and not on the rocking floes. Two seals came up on the beach that day, one of them within ten yards of my tent. So urgent was our need of food and blubber that I called all hands and organized a line of beaters instead of simply walking up to the seal and hitting it on the nose. We were prepared to fall upon this seal en masse if it attempted to escape. The kill was made with a pick-handle, and in a few minutes five days' food and six days' fuel were stowed in a place of safety among the boulders above high-water mark. During this day the cook, who had worked well on the floe and throughout the boat journey, suddenly collapsed. I happened to be at the galley at the moment and saw him fall. I pulled him down the slope to his tent and pushed him into its shelter with orders to his tent-mates to keep him in his sleeping bag until I allowed him to come out or the doctors said he was fit enough. Then I took out to replace the cook one of the men who had expressed a desire to lie down and die. The task of keeping the galley fire alight was both difficult and strenuous, and it took his thoughts away from the chances of immediate dissolution. In fact, I found him a little later gravely concerned over the drying of a naturally not over-clean pair of socks, which were hung up in close proximity to our evening milk. Occupation had brought his thoughts back to the ordinary cares of life.

There was a lull in the bad weather on April 21st, and the carpenter started to collect material for the decking of the *James Caird*. He fitted the mast of the *Stancomb Wills* fore and aft inside the *James Caird* as a hog-back and thus strengthened the keel with the object of preventing our boat "hogging"—that is, buckling in heavy seas. He had not sufficient wood to provide a deck, but by using the sledge-runners and box-lids he made a framework extending from the forecastle aft to a well. It was a patched-up affair, but it provided a base for a canvas covering. We had a bolt of canvas frozen stiff, and this material had to be cut and then thawed out over the blubber-stove, foot by foot, in order that it might be sewn into the form of a cover. When it had been nailed and screwed into position it certainly gave an appearance of safety to the boat, though I had an uneasy feeling that it bore a strong likeness to stage scenery, which may look like a granite wall and is in fact nothing better than canvas and lath. As events proved, the covering served its purpose well. We certainly could not have lived through the voyage without it.

Another fierce gale was blowing on April 22nd, interfering with our preparations for the voyage. The cooker from No. 5 tent came adrift in a gust, and, although it was chased to the water's edge, it disappeared for good. Blackborrow's feet were giving him much pain, and McIlroy and Macklin thought it would be necessary for them to operate soon. They were under the impression then that they had no chloroform, but they found some subsequently in the medicine chest after we had left. Some cases of stores left on a rock off the spit on the day of our arrival were retrieved during this day. We were setting aside stores for the boat journey

and choosing the essential equipment from the scanty stock at our disposal. Two ten-gallon casks had to be filled with water melted down from
ice collected at the foot of the glacier. This was a rather slow business.
The blubber-stove was kept going all night, and the watchmen emptied the
water into the casks from the pot in which the ice was melted. A working
party started to dig a hole in the snow-slope about forty feet above sea
level with the object of providing a site for a camp. They made fairly good
progress at first, but the snow drifted down unceasingly from the inland
ice, and in the end the party had to give up the project.

The weather was fine on April 23rd, and we hurried forward our preparations. It was on this day I decided finally that the crew for the *James
Caird* should consist of Worsley, Crean, McNeish, McCarthy, Vincent,
and myself. A storm came on about noon, with driving snow and heavy
squalls. Occasionally the air would clear for a few minutes, and we could
see a line of pack-ice, five miles out, driving across from west to east.
This sight increased my anxiety to get away quickly. Winter was advancing, and soon the pack might close completely around the island and stay
our departure for days or even for weeks, I did not think that ice would
remain around Elephant Island continuously during the winter, since the
strong winds and fast currents would keep it in motion. We had noticed
ice and bergs going past at the rate of four or five knots. A certain amount
of ice was held up about the end of our spit, but the sea was clear where
the boat would have to be launched.

Worsley, Wild, and I climbed to the summit of the seaward rocks and
examined the ice from a better vantage point than the beach offered. The
belt of pack outside appeared to be sufficiently broken for our purposes,
and I decided that, unless the conditions forbade it, we would make a
start in the *James Caird* on the following morning. Obviously the pack
might close at any time. This decision made, I spent the rest of the day
looking over the boat, gear, and stores, and discussing plans with Worsley
and Wild.

Our last night on the solid ground of Elephant Island was cold and uncomfortable. We turned out at dawn and had breakfast. Then we launched
the *Stancomb Wills* and loaded her with stores, gear, and ballast, which
would be transferred to the *James Caird* when the heavier boat had been
launched. The ballast consisted of bags made from blankets and filled with
sand, making a total weight of about 1,000 pounds. In addition we had
gathered a number of round boulders and about 250 pounds of ice, which
would supplement our two casks of water.

The stores taken in the *James Caird*, which would last six men for one month, were as follows:

30 boxes of matches
6½ gallons paraffin
1 tin methylated spirit
10 boxes of flamers
1 box of blue lights
2 Primus stoves with spare parts and prickers
1 Nansen aluminum cooker
6 sleeping bags
A few spare socks
A few candles and some blubber-oil in an oil-bag

Food:
3 cases sledging rations = 300 rations
2 cases nut food = 200"
2 cases biscuits = 600 biscuits
1 case lump sugar
30 packets of Trumilk
1 tin of Bovril cubes
1 tin of Cerebos salt
36 gallons of water
112 pounds of ice

Instruments:

Sextant	Sea anchor
Binoculars	Charts
Prismatic compass	Aneroid

The swell was slight when the *Stancomb Wills* was launched and the boat got under way without any difficulty; but half an hour later, when we were pulling down the *James Caird*, the swell increased suddenly. Apparently the movement of the ice outside had made an opening and allowed the sea to run in without being blanketed by the line of pack. The swell made things difficult. Many of us got wet to the waist while dragging the boat out—a serious matter in that climate. When the *James Caird* was afloat in the surf she nearly capsized among the rocks before we could get her clear, and Vincent and the carpenter, who were on the deck, were thrown into the water. This was really bad luck, for the two men would have small chance of drying their clothes after we had got under way. Hurley, who had the eye of the professional photographer for "incidents," secured a picture of the upset, and I firmly believe that he would have liked the two unfortunate men to remain in the water until he could get a "snap" at close quarters; but we hauled them out immediately, regardless of his feelings.

The *James Caird* was soon clear of the breakers. We used all the available ropes as a long painter to prevent her drifting away to the northeast, and then the *Stancomb Wills* came alongside, transferred her load, and went back to the shore for more. As she was being beached this time the sea took her stern and half filled her with water. She had to be turned over and emptied before the return journey could be made. Every member of the crew of the *Stancomb Wills* was wet to the skin. The water casks were towed behind the *Stancomb Wills* on this second journey, and the swell, which was increasing rapidly, drove the boat on to the rocks, where one of the casks was slightly stove in. This accident proved later to be a serious one, since some seawater had entered the cask and the contents were now brackish.

By midday the *James Caird* was ready for the voyage. Vincent and the carpenter had secured some dry clothes by exchange with members of the shore party (I heard afterward that it was a full fortnight before the soaked garments were finally dried), and the boat's crew was standing by waiting for the order to cast off. A moderate westerly breeze was blowing. I went ashore in the *Stancomb Wills* and had a last word with Wild, who was remaining in full command, with directions as to his course of action in the event of our failure to bring relief, but I practically left the whole situation and scope of action and decision to his own judgment, secure in the knowledge that he would act wisely. I told him that I trusted the party to him and said good-bye to the men. Then we pushed off for the last time, and within a few minutes I was aboard the *James Caird*. The crew of the *Stancomb Wills* shook hands with us as the boats bumped together and offered us the last good wishes. Then, setting our jib, we cut the painter and moved away to the northeast. The men who were staying behind made a pathetic little group on the beach, with the grim heights of the island behind them and the sea seething at their feet, but they waved to us and gave three hearty cheers. There was hope in their hearts and they trusted us to bring the help that they needed.

I had all sails set, and the *James Caird* quickly dipped the beach and its line of dark figures. The westerly wind took us rapidly to the line of pack, and as we entered it I stood up with my arm around the mast, directing the steering, so as to avoid the great lumps of ice that were flung about in the heave of the sea. The pack thickened and we were forced to turn almost due east, running before the wind toward a gap I had seen in the morning from the high ground. I could not see the gap now, but we had come out on its bearing and I was prepared to find that it had been influenced by the easterly drift. At four o'clock in the afternoon we found the channel, much narrower than it had seemed in the morning but still navigable. Dropping sail, we rowed through without touching the ice anywhere, and by 5:30 P.M. we were clear of the pack with open water before us. We passed one more piece of ice in the darkness an hour later, but the pack lay behind, and with a fair wind swelling the sails we steered our little craft through the night, our hopes centered on our distant goal. The swell was very heavy now, and when the time came for our first evening meal we found great difficulty in keeping the Primus lamp alight and preventing the hoosh splashing out of the pot. Three men were needed to attend to the cooking, one man holding the lamp and two men guarding the aluminum cooking pot, which had to be lifted clear of the Primus whenever the movement of the boat threatened to cause a disaster. Then the lamp had to be protected from water, for sprays were coming over the bows and our flimsy decking was by no means watertight. All these operations were conducted in the confined space under the decking, where the men lay or knelt and adjusted themselves as best they could to the angles of our cases and ballast. It was uncomfortable, but we found consolation in the reflection that without the decking we could not have used the cooker at all.

The tale of the next sixteen days is one of supreme strife amid heaving waters. The sub-Antarctic Ocean lived up to its evil winter reputation. I decided to run north for at least two days while the wind held and so get into warmer weather before turning to the east and laying a course for South Georgia. We took two-hourly spells at the tiller. The men who were not on watch crawled into the sodden sleeping bags and tried to forget their troubles for a period; but there was no comfort in the boat. The bags and cases seemed to be alive in the unfailing knack of presenting their most uncomfortable angles to our rest-seeking bodies. A man might imagine for a moment that he had found a position of ease, but always discovered quickly that some unyielding point was impinging on muscle or bone. The first night aboard the boat was one of acute discomfort for us all, and we were heartily glad when the dawn came and we could set about the preparation of a hot breakfast.

This record of the voyage to South Georgia is based upon scanty notes made day by day. The notes dealt usually with the bare facts of distances, positions, and weather, but our memories retained the incidents of the passing days in a period never to be forgotten. By running north for the first two days I hoped to get warmer weather and also to avoid lines of pack that might be extending beyond the main body. We needed all the advantage that we could obtain from the higher latitude for sailing on the great circle, but we had to be cautious regarding possible ice-streams. Cramped in our narrow quarters and continually wet by the spray, we suffered severely from cold throughout the journey. We fought the seas and the winds and at the same time had a daily struggle to keep ourselves alive. At times we were in dire peril. Generally we were upheld by the knowledge that we were making progress toward the land where we would be, but there were days and nights when we lay hove to, drifting across the storm-whitened seas and watching, with eyes interested rather than apprehensive, the uprearing masses of water, flung to and fro by Nature in the pride of her strength. Deep seemed the valleys when we lay between the reeling seas. High were the hills when we perched momentarily on the tops of giant combers. Nearly always there were gales. So small was our boat and so great were the seas that often our sail flapped idly in the calm between the crests of two waves. Then we would climb the next slope and catch the full fury of the gale where the wool-like whiteness of the breaking water surged around us. We had our moments of laughter— rare, it is true, but hearty enough. Even when cracked lips and swollen mouths checked the outward and visible signs of amusement we could see a joke of the primitive kind. Man's sense of humor is always most easily stirred by the petty misfortunes of his neighbors, and I shall never forget Worsley's efforts on one occasion to place the hot aluminum stand on top of the Primus stove after it had fallen off in an extra heavy roll. With his frostbitten fingers he picked it up, dropped it, picked it up again, and toyed with it gingerly as though it were some fragile article of lady's wear. We laughed, or rather gurgled with laughter.

The wind came up strong and worked into a gale from the northwest on the third day out. We stood away to the east. The increasing seas discovered the weaknesses of our decking. The continuous blows shifted the box-lids and sledge-runners so that the canvas sagged down and accumulated water. Then icy trickles, distinct from the driving sprays, poured fore and aft into the boat. The nails that the carpenter had extracted from cases at Elephant Island and used to fasten down the battens were too short to make firm the decking. We did what we could to secure it, but our means were very limited, and the water continued to enter the boat at a dozen points. Much baling was necessary, and nothing that we could do prevented our gear from becoming sodden. The searching runnels from the canvas were really more unpleasant than the sudden definite douches of the sprays. Lying under the thwarts during watches below, we tried vainly to avoid them. There were no dry places in the boat, and at last we simply covered our heads with our Burberrys and endured the all-pervading water. The baling was work for the watch. Real rest we had none. The perpetual motion of the boat made repose impossible; we were cold, sore, and anxious. We moved on hands and knees in the semi-darkness of the day under the decking. The darkness was complete by 6 P.M. and not until 7 A.M. of the following day could we see one another under the thwarts. We had a few scraps of candle, and they were preserved carefully in order that we might have light at mealtimes There was one fairly dry spot in the boat, under the solid original decking at the bows, and we managed to protect some of our biscuit from the salt water; but I do not think any of us got the taste of salt out of our mouths during the voyage.

The difficulty of movement in the boat would have had its humorous side if it had not involved us in so many aches and pains. We had to crawl under the thwarts in order to move along the boat, and our knees suffered considerably. When a watch turned out it was necessary for me to direct each man by name when and where to move, since if all hands had crawled about at the same time the result would have been dire confusion and many bruises. Then there was the trim of the boat to be considered. The order of the watch was four hours on and four hours off, three men to the watch. One man had the tiller-ropes, the second man attended to the sail, and the third baled for all he was worth. Sometimes when the water in the boat had been reduced to reasonable proportions, our pump could be used. This pump, which Hurley had made from the Flinders bar case of our ship's standard compass, was quite effective, though its capacity was not large. The man who was attending the sail could pump into the big outer cooker, which was lifted and emptied overboard when filled. We had a device by which the water could go direct from the pump into the sea through a hole in the gunwale, but this hole had to be blocked at an early stage of the voyage, since we found that it admitted water when the boat rolled.

While a new watch was shivering in the wind and spray, the men who had been relieved groped hurriedly among the soaked sleeping bags and tried to steal a little of the warmth created by the last occupants; but it was not always possible for us to find even this comfort when we went off watch. The boulders that we had taken aboard for ballast had to be shifted continually in order to trim the boat and give access to the pump, which became choked with hairs from the moulting sleeping bags and finneskoe. The four reindeer-skin sleeping bags shed their hair freely owing to the continuous wetting, and soon became quite bald in appearance. The moving of the boulders was weary and painful work. We came to know every one of the stones by sight and touch, and I have vivid memories of their angular peculiarities even today. They might have been of considerable interest as geological specimens to a scientific man under happier conditions. As ballast they were useful. As weights to be moved about in cramped quarters they were simply appalling. They spared no portion of our poor bodies. Another of our troubles, worth mention here, was the chafing of our legs by our wet clothes, which had not been changed now for seven months. The insides of our thighs were rubbed raw, and the one tube of Hazeline cream in our medicine chest did not go far in alleviating our pain, which was increased by the bite of the salt water. We thought at the time that we never slept. The fact was that we would doze off uncomfortably, to be aroused quickly by some new ache or another call to effort. My own share of the general unpleasantness was accentuated by a finely developed bout of sciatica. I had become possessor of this originally on the floe several months earlier.

Our meals were regular in spite of the gales. Attention to this point was essential, since the conditions of the voyage made increasing calls upon our vitality. Breakfast, at 8 A.M., consisted of a pannikin of hot hoosh made from Bovril sledging ration, two biscuits, and some lumps of sugar. Lunch came at 1 P.M., and comprised Bovril sledging ration, eaten raw, and a pannikin of hot milk for each man. Tea, at 5 P.M., had the same menu. Then during the night we had a hot drink, generally of milk. The meals were the bright beacons in those cold and stormy days. The glow of warmth and comfort produced by the food and drink made optimists of us all. We had two tins of Virol, which we were keeping for an emergency; but, finding ourselves in need of an oil lamp to eke out our supply of candles, we emptied one of the tins in the manner that most appealed to us, and fitted it with a wick made by shredding a bit of canvas. When this lamp was filled with oil it gave a certain amount of light, though it was easily blown out, and was of great assistance to us at night. We were fairly well off as regarded fuel, since we had six-and-a-half gallons of petroleum.

A severe southwesterly gale on the fourth day out forced us to heave to. I would have liked to have run before the wind, but the sea was very high and the James Caird was in danger of broaching to and swamping. The delay was vexatious, since up to that time we had been making sixty or seventy miles a day; good going with our limited sail area. We hove to under double-reefed mainsail and our little jigger, and waited for the gale to blow itself out. During that afternoon we saw bits of wreckage, the remains probably of some unfortunate vessel that had failed to weather the strong gales south of Cape Horn. The weather conditions did not improve, and on the fifth day out the gale was so fierce that we were compelled to take in the double-reefed mainsail and hoist our small jib instead. We put out a sea anchor to keep the James Caird's head up to the sea. This anchor consisted of a triangular canvas bag fastened to the end of the painter and allowed to stream out from the bows. The boat was high enough to catch the wind, and, as she drifted to leeward, the drag of the anchor kept her head to windward. Thus our boat took most of the seas more or less end on. Even then the crests of the waves often would curl right over us and we shipped a great deal of water, which necessitated unceasing baling and pumping. Looking out abeam, we would see a hollow like a tunnel formed as the crest of a big wave toppled over onto the swelling body of water. A thousand times it appeared as though the James Caird must be engulfed; but the boat lived. The southwesterly gale had its birthplace above the Antarctic Continent, and its freezing breath lowered the temperature far toward zero. The sprays froze upon the boat and gave bows, sides, and decking a heavy coat of mail. This accumulation of ice reduced the buoyancy of the boat, and to that extent was an added peril; but it possessed a notable advantage from one point of view. The water ceased to drop and trickle from the canvas, and the spray came in solely at the well in the after part of the boat. We could not allow the load of ice to grow beyond a certain point, and in turns we crawled about the decking forward, chipping and picking at it with the available tools.

When daylight came on the morning of the sixth day out we saw and felt that the James Caird had lost her resiliency. She was not rising to the oncoming seas. The weight of the ice that had formed in her and upon her during the night was having its effect, and she was becoming more like a log than a boat. The situation called for immediate action. We first broke away the spare oars, which were encased in ice and frozen to the sides of the boat, and threw them overboard. We retained two oars for use when we got inshore. Two of the fur sleeping bags went over the side; they were thoroughly wet, weighing probably forty pounds each, and they had frozen stiff during the night. Three men constituted the watch below, and when a man went down it was better to turn into the wet bag just vacated by another man than to thaw out a frozen bag with the heat of his unfortunate body. We now had four bags, three in use and one for emergency use in case a member of the party should break down permanently. The reduction of weight relieved the boat to some extent, and vigorous chipping and scraping did more. We had to be very careful not to put ax or knife through the frozen canvas of the decking as we crawled over it, but gradually we got rid of a lot of ice. The *James Caird* lifted to the endless waves as though she lived again.

About 11 A.M. the boat suddenly fell off into the trough of the sea. The painter had parted and the sea anchor had gone. This was serious. The *James Caird* went away to leeward, and we had no chance at all of recovering the anchor and our valuable rope, which had been our only means of keeping the boat's head up to the seas without the risk of hoisting sail in a gale. Now we had to set the sail and trust to its holding. While the *James Caird* rolled heavily in the trough, we beat the frozen canvas until the bulk of the ice had cracked off it and then hoisted it. The frozen gear worked protestingly, but after a struggle our little craft came up to the wind again, and we breathed more freely. Skin frostbites were troubling us, and we had developed large blisters on our fingers and hands. I shall always carry the scar of one of these frostbites on my left hand, which became badly inflamed after the skin had burst and the cold had bitten deeply.

We held the boat up to the gale during that day, enduring as best we could discomforts that amounted to pain. The boat tossed interminably on the big waves under gray, threatening skies. Our thoughts did not embrace much more than the necessities of the hour. Every surge of the sea was an enemy to be watched and circumvented. We ate our scanty meals, treated our frostbites, and hoped for the improved conditions that the morrow might bring. Night fell early, and in the lagging hours of darkness we were cheered by a change for the better in the weather. The wind dropped, the snow squalls became less frequent, and the sea moderated. When the morning of the seventh day dawned there was not much wind. We shook the reef out of the sail and laid our course once more for South Georgia. The sun came out bright and clear, and presently

Worsley got a snap for longitude. We hoped that the sky would remain clear until noon, so that we could get the latitude. We had been six days out without an observation, and our dead reckoning naturally was uncertain. The boat must have presented a strange appearance that morning. All hands basked in the sun. We hung our sleeping bags to the mast and spread our socks and other gear all over the deck. Some of the ice had melted off the *James Caird* in the early morning after the gale began to slacken, and dry patches were appearing in the decking. Porpoises came blowing around the boat, and Cape pigeons wheeled and swooped within a few feet of us. These little black-and-white birds have an air of friendliness that is not possessed by the great circling albatross. They had looked gray against the swaying sea during the storm as they darted about over our heads and uttered their plaintive cries. The albatrosses, of the black or sooty variety, had watched with hard, bright eyes, and seemed to have a quite impersonal interest in our struggle to keep afloat amid the battering seas. In addition to the Cape pigeons an occasional stormy petrel flashed overhead. Then there was a small bird, unknown to me, that appeared always to be in a fussy, bustling state, quite out of keeping with the surroundings. It irritated me. It had practically no tail, and it flitted about vaguely as though in search of the lost member. I used to find myself wishing it would find its tail and have done with the silly fluttering.

We reveled in the warmth of the sun that day. Life was not so bad, after all. We felt we were well on our way. Our gear was drying, and we could have a hot meal in comparative comfort. The swell was still heavy, but it was not breaking and the boat rode easily. At noon Worsley balanced himself on the gunwale and clung with one hand to the stay of the mainmast while he got a snap of the sun. The result was more than encouraging. We had done over 380 miles and were getting on for halfway to South Georgia. It looked as though we were going to get through.

The wind freshened to a good stiff breeze during the afternoon, and the *James Caird* made satisfactory progress. I had not realized until the sunlight came how small our boat really was. There was some influence in the light and warmth, some hint of happier days, that made us revive memories of other voyages, when we had stout decks beneath our feet, unlimited food at our command, and pleasant cabins for our ease. Now we clung to a battered little boat, "alone, alone, all, all alone, alone on a wide, wide sea." So low in the water were we that each succeeding swell cut off our view of the skyline. We were a tiny speck in the vast vista of the sea—the ocean that is open to all and merciful to none, that threatens even when it seems to yield, and that is pitiless always to weakness. For a moment the consciousness of the forces arrayed against us would be almost overwhelming. Then hope and confidence would rise again as our boat rose to a wave and tossed aside the crest in a sparkling shower like the play of prismatic colors at the foot of a waterfall. My double-barreled gun and some cartridges had been stowed aboard the boat as an emergency precaution against a shortage of food, but we were not disposed to destroy our little neighbors, the Cape pigeons, even for the sake of fresh meat. We might have shot an albatross, but the wandering king of the ocean aroused in us something of the feeling that inspired, too late, the Ancient Mariner. So the gun remained among the stores and sleeping bags in the narrow quarters beneath our leaking deck, and the birds followed us unmolested.

The eighth, ninth, and tenth days of the voyage had few features worthy of special note. The wind blew hard during those days, and the strain of navigating the boat was unceasing, but always we made some advance toward our goal. No bergs showed on our horizon, and we knew that we were clear of the ice fields. Each day brought its little round of troubles, but also compensation in the form of food and growing hope. We felt that we were going to succeed. The odds against us had been great, but we were winning through. We still suffered severely from the cold, for, though the temperature was rising, our vitality was declining owing to shortage of food, exposure, and the necessity of maintaining our cramped positions day and night. I found that it was now absolutely necessary to prepare hot milk for all hands during the night, in order to sustain life till dawn. This meant lighting the Primus lamp in the darkness and involved an increased drain on our small store of matches. It was the rule that one match must serve when the Primus was being lit. We had no lamp for the compass and during the early days of the voyage we would strike a match when the steersman wanted to see the course at night; but later the necessity for strict economy impressed itself upon us, and the practice of striking matches at night was stopped. We had one watertight tin of matches. I had stowed away in a pocket, in readiness for a sunny day, a lens from one of the telescopes, but this was of no use during the voyage. The sun seldom shone upon us. The glass of the compass got broken one night, and we contrived to mend it with adhesive tape from the medicine chest. One of the memories that comes to me from those days is of Crean singing at the tiller. He always sang while he was steering, and nobody ever discovered what the song was. It was devoid of tune and as monotonous as the chanting of a Buddhist monk at his prayers; yet somehow it was cheerful. In moments of inspiration Crean would attempt "The Wearing of the Green."

On the tenth night Worsley could not straighten his body after his spell at the tiller. He was thoroughly cramped, and we had to drag him beneath the decking and massage him before he could unbend himself and get into a sleeping bag. A hard northwesterly gale came up on the eleventh day (May 5th) and shifted to the southwest in the late afternoon. The sky was overcast and occasional snow squalls added to the discomfort produced by a tremendous cross-sea—the worst, I thought, that we had experienced. At midnight I was at the tiller and suddenly noticed a line of clear sky between the south and southwest. I called to the other men that the sky was clearing, and then a moment later I realized that what I had seen was not a rift in the clouds but the white crest of an enormous wave. During twenty-six years' experience of the ocean in all its moods I had not encountered a wave so gigantic. It was a mighty upheaval of the ocean, a thing quite apart from the big white-capped seas that had been our tireless enemies for many days. I shouted, "For God's sake, hold on! It's got us!" Then came a moment of suspense that seemed drawn out into hours. White surged the foam of the breaking sea around us. We felt our boat lifted and flung forward like a cork in breaking surf. We were in a seething chaos of tortured water; but somehow the boat lived through it, half-full of water, sagging to the dead weight and shuddering under the blow. We baled with the energy of men fighting for life, flinging the water over the sides with every receptacle that came to our hands, and after ten minutes of uncertainty we felt the boat renew her life beneath us. She floated again and ceased to lurch drunkenly as though dazed by the attack of the sea. Earnestly we hoped that never again would we encounter such a wave.

The conditions in the boat, uncomfortable before, had been made worse by the deluge of water. All our gear was thoroughly wet again. Our cooking stove had been floating about in the bottom of the boat, and portions of our last hoosh seemed to have permeated everything. Not until 3 A.M., when we were all chilled almost to the limit of endurance, did we manage to get the stove alight and make ourselves hot drinks. The carpenter was suffering particularly, but he showed grit and spirit. Vincent had for the past week ceased to be an active member of the crew, and I could not easily account for his collapse. Physically he was one of the strongest men in the boat. He was a young man, he had served on

North Sea trawlers, and he should have been able to bear hardships better than McCarthy, who, not so strong, was always happy.

The weather was better on the following day (May 6th), and we got a glimpse of the sun. Worsley's observation showed that we were not more than a hundred miles from the northwest corner of South Georgia. Two more days with a favorable wind and we would sight the promised land. I hoped that there would be no delay, for our supply of water was running very low. The hot drink at night was essential, but I decided that the daily allowance of water must be cut down to half a pint per man. The lumps of ice we had taken aboard had gone long ago. We were dependent upon the water we had brought from Elephant Island, and our thirst was increased by the fact that we were now using the brackish water in the breaker that had been slightly stove in in the surf when the boat was being loaded. Some seawater had entered at that time.

Thirst took possession of us. I dared not permit the allowance of water to be increased since an unfavorable wind might drive us away from the island and lengthen our voyage by many days. Lack of water is always the most severe privation that men can be condemned to endure, and we found, as during our earlier boat voyage, that the salt water in our clothing and the salt spray that lashed our faces made our thirst grow quickly to a burning pain. I had to be very firm in refusing to allow anyone to anticipate the morrow's allowance, which I was sometimes begged to do. We did the necessary work dully and hoped for the land. I had altered the course to the east so as to make sure of our striking the island, which would have been impossible to regain if we had run past the northern end. The course was laid on our scrap of chart for a point some thirty miles down the coast. That day and the following day passed for us in a sort of nightmare. Our mouths were dry and our tongues were swollen. The wind was still strong and the heavy sea forced us to navigate carefully, but any thought of our peril from the waves was buried beneath the consciousness of our raging thirst. The bright moments were those when we each received our one mug of hot milk during the long, bitter watches of the night. Things were bad for us in those days, but the end was coming. The morning of May 8th broke thick and stormy, with squalls from the northwest. We searched the waters ahead for a sign of land, and though we could see nothing more than had met our eyes for many days, we were cheered by a sense that the goal was near at hand. About ten o'clock that morning we passed a little bit of kelp, a glad signal of the proximity of land. An hour later we saw two shags sitting on a big mass of kelp, and knew then that we must be within ten or fifteen miles of the shore. These birds are as sure an indication of the proximity of land as a lighthouse is, for they never venture far to sea. We gazed ahead with increasing eagerness, and at 12:30 P.M., through a rift in the clouds, McCarthy caught a glimpse of the black cliffs of South Georgia, just fourteen days after our departure from Elephant Island. It was a glad moment. Thirst-ridden, chilled, and weak as we were, happiness irradiated us. The job was nearly done.

We stood in toward the shore to look for a landing place, and presently we could see the green tussock-grass on the ledges above the surf-beaten rocks. Ahead of us and to the south, blind rollers showed the presence of uncharted reefs along the coast. Here and there the hungry rocks were close to the surface, and over them the great waves broke, swirling viciously and spouting thirty and forty feet into the air. The rocky coast appeared to descend sheer to the sea. Our need of water and rest was well-nigh desperate, but to have attempted a landing at that time would have been suicidal. Night was drawing near, and the weather indications were not favorable. There was nothing for it but to haul off till the following morning, so we stood away on the starboard tack until we had made what appeared to be a safe offing. Then we hove to in the high westerly swell. The hours passed slowly as we waited the dawn, which would herald, we fondly hoped, the last stage of our journey. Our thirst was a torment and we could scarcely touch our food; the cold seemed to strike right through our weakened bodies. At 5 A.M. the wind shifted to the northwest and quickly increased to one of the worst hurricanes any of us had ever experienced. A great cross-sea was running, and the wind simply shrieked as it tore the tops off the waves and converted the whole seascape into a haze of driving spray. Down into valleys, up to tossing heights, straining until her seams opened, swung our little boat, brave still but laboring heavily. We knew that the wind and set of the sea was driving us ashore, but we could do nothing. The dawn showed us a storm-torn ocean, and the morning passed without bringing us a sight of the land; but at 1 P.M., through a rift in the flying mists, we got a glimpse of the huge crags of the island and realized that our position had become desperate. We were on a dead lee shore, and we could gauge our approach to the unseen cliffs by the roar of the breakers against the sheer walls of rock. I ordered the double-reefed mainsail to be set in the hope that we might claw off, and this attempt increased the strain upon the boat. The James Caird was bumping heavily, and the water was pouring in everywhere. Our thirst was

forgotten in the realization of our imminent danger, as we baled unceasingly, and adjusted our weights from time to time; occasional glimpses
showed that the shore was nearer. I knew that Annewkow Island lay to
the south of us, but our small and badly marked chart showed uncertain
reefs in the passage between the island and the mainland, and I dared not
trust it, though as a last resort we could try to lie under the lee of the
island. The afternoon wore away as we edged down the coast, with the
thunder of the breakers in our ears. The approach of evening found us
still some distance from Annewkow Island, and, dimly in the twilight,
we could see a snow-capped mountain looming above us. The chance of
surviving the night, with the driving gale and the implacable sea forcing
us onto the lee shore, seemed small. I think most of us had a feeling that
the end was very near. Just after 6 P.M., in the dark, as the boat was in the
yeasty backwash from the seas flung from this ironbound coast, then, just
when things looked their worst, they changed for the best. I have marveled often at the thin line that divides success from failure and the sudden
turn that leads from apparently certain disaster to comparative safety. The
wind suddenly shifted, and we were free once more to make an offing.
Almost as soon as the gale eased, the pin that locked the mast to the
thwart fell out. It must have been on the point of doing this throughout
the hurricane, and if it had gone nothing could have saved us; the mast
would have snapped like a carrot. Our backstays had carried away once
before when iced up and were not too strongly fastened now. We were
thankful indeed for the mercy that had held that pin in its place throughout the hurricane.

We stood offshore again, tired almost to the point of apathy. Our
water had long been finished. The last was about a pint of hairy liquid,
which we strained through a bit of gauze from the medicine chest. The
pangs of thirst attacked us with redoubled intensity, and I felt that we
must make a landing on the following day at almost any hazard. The night
wore on. We were very tired. We longed for day. When at last the dawn
came on the morning of May 10th there was practically no wind, but a high
cross-sea was running. We made slow progress toward the shore. About
8 A.M. the wind backed to the northwest and threatened another blow.
We had sighted in the meantime a big indentation which I thought must
be King Haakon Bay, and I decided that we must land there. We set the
bows of the boat toward the bay and ran before the freshening gale. Soon
we had angry reefs on either side. Great glaciers came down to the sea
and offered no landing place. The sea spouted on the reefs and thundered

against the shore. About noon we sighted a line of jagged reef, like black-
ened teeth, that seemed to bar the entrance to the bay. Inside, comparatively smooth water stretched eight or nine miles to the head of the bay.
A gap in the reef appeared, and we made for it. But the fates had another
rebuff for us. The wind shifted and blew from the east right out of the
bay. We could see the way through the reef, but we could not approach it
directly. That afternoon we bore up, tacking five times in the strong wind.
The last tack enabled us to get through, and at last we were in the wide
mouth of the bay. Dusk was approaching. A small cove, with a boulder-
strewn beach guarded by a reef, made a break in the cliffs on the south
side of the bay, and we turned in that direction. I stood in the bows directing the steering as we ran through the kelp and made the passage of
the reef. The entrance was so narrow that we had to take in the oars, and
the swell was piling itself right over the reef into the cove; but in a minute
or two we were inside, and in the gathering darkness the *James Caird* ran in
on a swell and touched the beach. I sprang ashore with the short painter
and held on when the boat went out with the backward surge. When the
James Caird came in again three of the men got ashore, and they held the
painter while I climbed some rocks with another line. A slip on the wet
rocks twenty feet up nearly closed my part of the story just at the moment
when we were achieving safety. A jagged piece of rock held me and at the
same time bruised me sorely. However, I made fast the line, and in a few
minutes we were all safe on the beach, with the boat floating in the surging water just off the shore. We heard a gurgling sound that was sweet
music in our ears, and, peering around, found a stream of fresh water almost at our feet. A moment later we were down on our knees drinking
the pure, ice-cold water in long draughts that put new life into us. It was
a splendid moment.

The next thing was to get the stores and ballast out of the boat, in order that we might secure her for the night. We carried the stores and gear
above high-water mark and threw out the bags of sand and the boulders
that we knew so well. Then we attempted to pull the empty boat up the
beach, and discovered by this effort how weak we had become. Our
united strength was not sufficient to get the *James Caird* clear of the water.
Time after time we pulled together, but without avail. I saw that it would
be necessary to have food and rest before we beached the boat. We made
fast a line to a heavy boulder and set a watch to fend the *James Caird* off
the rocks of the beach. Then I sent Crean around to the left side of the
cove, about thirty yards away, where I had noticed a little cave as we

were running in. He could not see much in the darkness, but reported
that the place certainly promised some shelter. We carried the sleeping
bags around and found a mere hollow in the rock-face, with a shingle
floor sloping at a steep angle to the sea. There we prepared a hot meal, and
when the food was finished I ordered the men to turn in. The time was
now about 8 P.M., and I took the first watch beside the *James Caird,* which
was still afloat in the tossing water just off the beach.

Fending the *James Caird* off the rocks in the darkness was awkward
work. The boat would have bumped dangerously if allowed to ride in
with the waves that drove into the cove. I found a flat rock for my feet,
which were in a bad way owing to cold, wetness, and lack of exercise in
the boat, and during the next few hours I labored to keep the *James Caird*
clear of the beach. Occasionally I had to rush into the seething water. Then,
as a wave receded, I let the boat out on the alpine rope so as to avoid a
sudden jerk. The heavy painter had been lost when the sea anchor went
adrift. The *James Caird* could be seen but dimly in the cove, where the
high black cliffs made the darkness almost complete, and the strain upon
one's attention was great. After several hours had passed I found that my
desire for sleep was becoming irresistible, and at 1 A.M. I called Crean. I
could hear him groaning as he stumbled over the sharp rocks on his way
down the beach. While he was taking charge of the *James Caird* she got
adrift, and we had some anxious moments. Fortunately, she went across
toward the cave and we secured her unharmed. The loss or destruction of
the boat at this stage would have been a very serious matter, since we
probably would have found it impossible to leave the cove except by sea.
The cliffs and glaciers around offered no practicable path toward the head
of the bay. I arranged for one-hour watches during the remainder of the
night and then took Crean's place among the sleeping men and got some
sleep before the dawn came.

The sea went down in the early hours of the morning (May 11th), and
after sunrise we were able to set about getting the boat ashore, first bracing ourselves for the task with another meal. We were all weak still. We
cut off the topsides and took out all the movable gear. Then we waited
for Byron's "great ninth wave," and when it lifted the *James Caird* in we
held her and, by dint of great exertion, worked her around broadside to
the sea. Inch by inch we dragged her up until we reached the fringe of the
tussock-grass and knew that the boat was above high-water mark. The rise
of the tide was about five feet, and at spring tide the water must have
reached almost to the edge of the tussock-grass. The completion of this

job removed our immediate anxieties, and we were free to examine our surroundings and plan the next move. The day was bright and clear.

King Haakon Bay is an eight-mile sound penetrating the coast of South Georgia in an easterly direction. We had noticed that the northern and southern sides of the sound were formed by steep mountain ranges, their flanks furrowed by mighty glaciers, the outlets of the great ice-sheet of the interior. It was obvious that these glaciers and the precipitous slopes of the mountains barred our way inland from the cove. We must sail to the head of the sound. Swirling clouds and mist-wreaths had obscured our view of the sound when we were entering, but glimpses of snow-slopes had given us hope that an overland journey could be begun from that point. A few patches of very rough, tussocky land, dotted with little tarns, lay between the glaciers along the foot of the mountains, which were heavily scarred with scree-slopes. Several magnificent peaks and crags gazed out across their snowy domains to the sparkling waters of the sound.

Our cove lay a little inside the southern headland of King Haakon Bay. A narrow break in the cliffs, which were about a hundred feet high at this point, formed the entrance to the cove. The cliffs continued inside the cove on each side and merged into a hill, which descended at a steep slope to the boulder beach. The slope, which carried tussock-grass, was not continuous. It eased at two points into little peaty swamp-terraces dotted with frozen pools and drained by two small streams. Our cave was a recess in the cliff on the left-hand end of the beach. The rocky face of the cliff was undercut at this point, and the shingle thrown up by the waves formed a steep slope, which we reduced to about one in six by scraping the stones away from the inside. Later we strewed the rough floor with the dead, nearly dry underleaves of the tussock-grass, so as to form a slightly soft bed for our sleeping bags. Water had trickled down the face of the cliff and formed long icicles, which hung down in front of the cave to the length of about fifteen feet. These icicles provided shelter, and when we had spread our sails below them, with the assistance of oars, we had quarters that, in the circumstances, had to be regarded as reasonably comfortable. The camp at least was dry, and we moved our gear there with confidence. We built a fireplace and arranged our sleeping bags and blankets around it. The cave was about eight-feet deep and twelve-feet wide at the entrance.

While the camp was being arranged, Crean and I climbed the tussock slope behind the beach and reached the top of a headland overlooking the sound. There we found the nests of albatrosses, and, much to our delight, the nests contained young birds. The fledgelings were fat and lusty, and we had no hesitation about deciding that they were destined to die at an early age. Our most pressing anxiety at this stage was a shortage of fuel for the cooker. We had rations for ten more days, and we knew now that we could get birds for food; but if we were to have hot meals we must secure fuel. The store of petroleum carried in the boat was running very low, and it seemed necessary to keep some quantity for use on the overland journey that lay ahead of us. A sea elephant or a seal would have provided fuel as well as food, but we could see none in the neighborhood. During the morning we started a fire in the cave with wood from the topsides of the boat, and though the dense smoke from the damp sticks inflamed our tired eyes, the warmth and the prospect of hot food were ample compensation. Crean was cook that day, and I suggested to him that he should wear his goggles, which he happened to have brought with him. The goggles helped him a great deal as he bent over the fire and tended the stew. And what a stew it was! The young albatrosses weighed about fourteen pounds each fresh killed, and we estimated that they weighed at least six pounds each when cleaned and dressed for the pot. Four birds went into the pot for six men, with a Bovril ration for thickening. The flesh was white and succulent, and the bones, not fully formed, almost melted in our mouths. That was a memorable meal. When we had eaten our fill, we dried our tobacco in the embers of the fire and smoked contentedly. We made an attempt to dry our clothes, which were soaked with salt water, but did not meet with much success. We could not afford to have a fire except for cooking purposes until blubber or driftwood had come our way.

The final stage of the journey had still to be attempted. I realized that the condition of the party generally, and particularly of McNeish and Vincent, would prevent us putting to sea again except under pressure of dire necessity. Our boat, moreover, had been weakened by the cutting away of the topsides, and I doubted if we could weather the island. We were still 150 miles away from Stromness whaling station by sea. The alternative was to attempt the crossing of the island. If we could not get over, then we must try to secure enough food and fuel to keep us alive through the winter, but this possibility was scarcely thinkable. Over on Elephant Island twenty-two men were waiting for the relief that we alone could secure for them. Their plight was worse than ours. We must push on somehow. Several days must elapse before our strength would be sufficiently recovered to allow us to row or sail the last nine miles up to the head of the bay. In the meantime we could make what preparations were possible and dry our clothes by taking advantage of every scrap of heat from the fires we lit for the cooking of our meals. We turned in early that night, and I remember that I dreamed of the great wave and aroused my companions with a shout of warning as I saw with half-awakened eyes the towering cliff on the opposite side of the cove.

Shortly before midnight a gale sprang up suddenly from the northeast with rain and sleet showers. It brought quantities of glacier-ice into the cove, and by 2 A.M. (May 12th) our little harbor was filled with ice, which surged to and fro in the swell and pushed its way onto the beach. We had solid rock beneath our feet and could watch without anxiety. When daylight came rain was falling heavily, and the temperature was the highest we had experienced for many months. The icicles overhanging our cave were melting down in streams and we had to move smartly when passing in and out lest we should be struck by falling lumps. A fragment weighing fifteen or twenty pounds crashed down while we were having breakfast. We found that a big hole had been burned in the bottom of Worsley's reindeer sleeping bag during the night. Worsley had been awakened by a burning sensation in his feet, and had asked the men near him if his bag was all right; they looked and could see nothing wrong. We were all superficially frostbitten about the feet, and this condition caused the extremities to burn painfully, while at the same time sensation was lost in the skin. Worsley thought that the uncomfortable heat of his feet was due to the frostbites, and he stayed in his bag and presently went to sleep again. He discovered when he turned out in the morning that the tussock-grass, which we had laid on the floor of the cave had smoldered outward from the fire and had actually burned a large hole in the bag beneath his feet. Fortunately, his feet were not harmed.

Our party spent a quiet day, attending to clothing and gear, checking stores, eating and resting. Some more of the young albatrosses made a noble end in our pot. The birds were nesting on a small plateau above the right-hand end of our beach. We had previously discovered that when we were landing from the boat on the night of May 10th we had lost the rudder. The *James Caird* had been bumping heavily astern as we were scrambling ashore, and evidently the rudder was then knocked off. A careful search of the beach and the rocks within our reach failed to reveal the missing article. This was a serious loss, even if the voyage to the head of the sound could be made in good weather. At dusk the ice in the cove was rearing and crashing on the beach. It had forced up a ridge of stones close to where the *James Caird* lay at the edge of the tussock-grass. Some pieces of ice were driven right up to the canvas wall at the front of our cave. Fragments lodged within two feet of Vincent, who had the lowest sleeping place, and within four feet of our fire. Crean and McCarthy had brought down six more of the young albatrosses in the afternoon, so we were well supplied with fresh food. The air temperature that night probably was not lower than thirty-eight or forty degrees Fahrenheit, and we were rendered uncomfortable in our cramped sleeping quarters by the unaccustomed warmth. Our feelings toward our neighbors underwent a change. When the temperature was below twenty degrees Fahrenheit we could not get too close to one another—every man wanted to cuddle against his neighbor; but let the temperature rise a few degrees and the warmth of another man's body ceased to be a blessing. The ice and the waves had a voice of menace that night, but I heard it only in my dreams.

The bay was still filled with ice on the morning of Saturday, May 13th, but the tide took it all away in the afternoon. Then a strange thing happened. The rudder, with all the broad Atlantic to sail in and the coasts of two continents to search for a resting place, came bobbing back into our cove. With anxious eyes we watched it as it advanced, receded again, and then advanced once more under the capricious influence of wind and wave. Nearer and nearer it came as we waited on the shore, oars in hand, and at last we were able to seize it. Surely a remarkable salvage! The day was bright and clear; our clothes were drying and our strength was returning. Running water made a musical sound down the tussock slope and among the boulders. We carried our blankets up the hill and tried to dry them in the breeze 300 feet above sea level. In the afternoon we began to prepare the *James Caird* for the journey to the head of King Haakon Bay. A noon observation on this day gave our latitude as 54°10'47" S, but according to the German chart the position should have been 54°12' S. Probably Worsley's observation was the more accurate. We were able to keep the fire alight until we went to sleep that night, for while climbing the rocks above the cove I had seen at the foot of a cliff a broken spar, which had been thrown up by the waves. We could reach this spar by climbing down the cliff, and with a reserve supply of fuel thus in sight we could afford to burn the fragments of the *James Caird's* topsides more freely.

During the morning of this day (May 13th) Worsley and I tramped across the hills in a northeasterly direction with the object of getting a view of the sound and possibly gathering some information that would be useful to us in the next stage of our journey. It was exhausting work, but after covering about two-and-a-half miles in two hours, we were able to look east, up the bay. We could not see very much of the country that we would have to cross in order to reach the whaling station on the other side of the island. We had passed several brooks and frozen tarns, and at a point where we had to take to the beach on the shore of the sound we found some wreckage—an eighteen-foot pine-spar (probably part of a ship's topmast), several pieces of timber, and a little model of a ship's hull, evidently a child's toy. We wondered what tragedy that pitiful little play-thing indicated. We encountered also some gentoo penguins and a young sea elephant, which Worsley killed.

When we got back to the cave at 3 P.M., tired, hungry, but rather pleased with ourselves, we found a splendid meal of stewed albatross chicken waiting for us. We had carried a quantity of blubber and the sea elephant's liver in our blouses, and we produced our treasures as a surprise for the men. Rough climbing on the way back to camp had nearly persuaded us to throw the stuff away, but we had held on (regardless of the condition of our already sorely tried clothing), and had our reward at the camp. The long bay had been a magnificent sight, even to eyes that had dwelt on grandeur long enough and were hungry for the simple, familiar things of everyday life. Its green-blue waters were being beaten to fury by the northwesterly gale. The mountains, "stern peaks that dared the stars," peered through the mists, and between them huge glaciers poured down from the great ice-slopes and -fields that lay behind. We counted twelve glaciers and heard every few minutes the reverberating roar caused by masses of ice calving from the parent streams.

On May 14th we made our preparations for an early start on the fol-lowing day if the weather held fair. We expected to be able to pick up the remains of the sea elephant on our way up the sound. All hands were recovering from the chafing caused by our wet clothes during the boat journey. The insides of our legs had suffered severely, and for some time after landing in the cove we found movement extremely uncomfortable. We paid our last visit to the nests of the albatrosses, which were situated on a little undulating plateau above the cave amid tussocks, snow-patches, and little frozen tarns. Each nest consisted of a mound over a foot high of tussock-grass, roots, and a little earth. The albatross lays one egg and very rarely two. The chicks, which are hatched in January, are fed on the nest by the parent birds for almost seven months before they take to the sea and fend for themselves. Up to four months of age the chicks are beautiful white masses of downy fluff, but when we arrived on the scene their plumage was almost complete. Very often one of the parent birds was on guard near the nest. We did not enjoy attacking these birds, but our hunger knew no law. They tasted so very good and assisted our recuperation to such an extent that each time we killed one of them we felt a little less remorseful.

May 15th was a great day. We made our hoosh at 7:30 A.M. Then we loaded up the boat and gave her a flying launch down the steep beach into the surf. Heavy rain had fallen in the night and a gusty northwesterly wind was now blowing, with misty showers. The *James Caird* headed to the sea as if anxious to face the battle of the waves once more. We passed through the narrow mouth of the cove with the ugly rocks and waving kelp close on either side, turned to the east, and sailed merrily up the bay as the sun broke through the mists and made the tossing waters sparkle around us. We were a curious-looking party on that bright morning, but we were feeling happy. We even broke into song, and, but for our Robinson Crusoe appearance, a casual observer might have taken us for a picnic party sailing in a Norwegian fjord or one of the beautiful sounds of the west coast of New Zealand. The wind blew fresh and strong, and a small sea broke on the coast as we advanced. The surf was sufficient to have endangered the boat if we had attempted to land where the carcass of the sea elephant was lying, so we decided to go on to the head of the bay without risking anything, particularly as we were likely to find sea elephants on the upper beaches. The big creatures have a habit of seeking peaceful quarters protected from the waves. We had hopes, too, of finding penguins. Our expectation as far as the sea elephants were concerned was not at fault. We heard the roar of the bulls as we neared the head of the bay, and soon afterward saw the great unwieldy forms of the beasts lying on a shelving beach toward the bayhead. We rounded a high, glacier-worn bluff on the north side, and at 12.30 P.M. we ran the boat ashore on a low beach of sand and pebbles, with tussock growing above high-water mark. There were hundreds of sea elephants lying about, and our anxieties with regard to food disappeared. Meat and blubber enough to feed our party for years was in sight. Our landing place was about a mile and a half west of the northeast corner of the bay. Just east of us was a glacier-snout ending on the beach but giving a passage toward the head of the bay, except at high water or when a very heavy surf was running. A cold, drizzling rain had begun to fall, and we provided ourselves with shelter as quickly as possible. We hauled the *James*

Caird up above high-water mark and turned her over just to the lee or east side of the bluff. The spot was separated from the mountainside by a low morainic bank, rising twenty or thirty feet above sea level. Soon we had converted the boat into a very comfortable cabin *à la* Peggotty, turfing it around with tussocks, which we dug up with knives. One side of the *James Caird* rested on stones so as to afford a low entrance, and when we had finished she looked as though she had grown there. McCarthy entered into this work with great spirit. A sea elephant provided us with fuel and meat, and that evening found a well-fed and fairly contented party at rest in Peggotty Camp.

Our camp, as I have said, lay on the north side of King Haakon Bay near the head. Our path toward the whaling stations led around the seaward end of the snouted glacier on the east side of the camp and up a snow-slope that appeared to lead to a pass in the great Allardyce Range, which runs northwest and southeast and forms the main backbone of South Georgia. The range dipped opposite the bay into a well-defined pass from east to west. An ice-sheet covered most of the interior, filling the valleys and disguising the configuration of the land, which, indeed, showed only in big rocky ridges, peaks, and nunataks. When we looked up the pass from Peggotty Camp the country to the left appeared to offer two easy paths through to the opposite coast, but we knew that the island was uninhabited at that point (Possession Bay). We had to turn our attention farther east, and it was impossible from the camp to learn much of the conditions that would confront us on the overland journey. I planned to climb to the pass and then be guided by the configuration of the country in the selection of a route eastward to Stromness Bay, where the whaling stations were established in the minor bays, Leith, Husvik, and Stromness. A range of mountains with precipitous slopes, forbidding peaks, and large glaciers lay immediately to the south of King Haakon Bay and seemed to form a continuation of the main range. Between this secondary range and the pass above our camp a great snow-upland sloped up to the inland ice-sheet and reached a rocky ridge that stretched athwart our path and seemed to bar the way. This ridge was a right-angled offshoot from the main ridge. Its chief features were four rocky peaks with spaces between that looked from a distance as though they might prove to be passes.

The weather was bad on Tuesday, May 16th, and we stayed under the boat nearly all day. The quarters were cramped but gave full protection from the weather, and we regarded our little cabin with a great deal of satisfaction. Abundant meals of sea elephant steak and liver increased our contentment. McNeish reported during the day that he had seen rats feeding on the scraps, but this interesting statement was not verified. One would not expect to find rats at such a spot, but there was a bare possibility that they had landed from a wreck and managed to survive the very rigorous conditions.

A fresh west-southwesterly breeze was blowing on the following morning (Wednesday, May 17th), with misty squalls, sleet, and rain. I took Worsley with me on a pioneer journey to the west with the object of examining the country to be traversed at the beginning of the overland journey. We went around the seaward end of the snouted glacier, and after tramping about a mile over stony ground and snow-coated debris, we crossed some big ridges of scree and moraines. We found that there was good going for a sledge as far as the northeast corner of the bay, but did not get much information regarding the conditions farther on owing to the view becoming obscured by a snow squall. We waited a quarter of an hour for the weather to clear but were forced to turn back without having seen more of the country. I had satisfied myself, however, that we could reach a good snow-slope leading apparently to the inland ice. Worsley reckoned from the chart that the distance from our camp to Husvik, on an east magnetic course, was seventeen geographical miles, but we could not expect to follow a direct line. The carpenter started making a sledge for use on the overland journey. The materials at his disposal were limited in quantity and scarcely suitable in quality.

We overhauled our gear on Thursday, May 18th, and hauled our sledge to the lower edge of the snouted glacier. The vehicle proved heavy and cumbrous. We had to lift it empty over bare patches of rock along the shore, and I realized that it would be too heavy for three men to manage amid the snow-plains, glaciers, and peaks of the interior. Worsley and Crean were coming with me, and after consultation we decided to leave the sleeping bags behind us and make the journey in very light marching order. We would take three days' provisions for each man in the form of sledging ration and biscuit. The food was to be packed in three socks, so that each member of the party could carry his own supply. Then we were to take the Primus lamp filled with oil, the small cooker, the carpenter's adze (for use as an ice ax), and the alpine rope, which made a total length of fifty feet when knotted. We might have to lower ourselves down steep slopes or cross crevassed glaciers. The filled lamp would provide six hot meals, which would consist of sledging ration boiled up with biscuit. There were two boxes of matches left, one full and the other partially used. We left the full box with the men at the camp and took the second box, which contained forty-eight matches. I was unfortunate as regarded footgear, since I had given away my heavy Burberry boots on the floe, and had now a comparatively light pair in poor condition. The carpenter assisted me by putting several screws in the sole of each boot with the object of providing a grip on the ice. The screws came out of the *James Caird*.

We turned in early that night, but sleep did not come to me. My mind was busy with the task of the following day. The weather was clear and the outlook for an early start in the morning was good. We were going to leave a weak party behind us in the camp. Vincent was still in the same condition, and he could not march. McNeish was pretty well broken up. The two men were not capable of managing for themselves and Mc-Carthy must stay to look after them. He might have a difficult task if we failed to reach the whaling station. The distance to Husvik, according to the chart, was no more than seventeen geographical miles in a direct line, but we had very scanty knowledge of the conditions of the interior. No man had ever penetrated a mile from the coast of South Georgia at any point, and the whalers I knew regarded the country as inaccessible. During that day, while we were walking to the snouted glacier, we had seen three wild ducks flying toward the head of the bay from the eastward. I hoped that the presence of these birds indicated tussock-land and not snowfields and glaciers in the interior, but the hope was not a very bright one.

We turned out at 2 A.M. on the Friday morning and had our hoosh ready an hour later. The full moon was shining in a practically cloudless sky, its rays reflected gloriously from the pinnacles and crevassed ice of the adjacent glaciers. The huge peaks of the mountains stood in bold relief against the sky and threw dark shadows on the waters of the sound. There was no need for delay, and we made a start as soon as we had eaten our meal. McNeish walked about 200 yards with us; he could do no more. Then we said good-bye and he turned back to the camp. The first task was to get around the edge of the snouted glacier, which had points like fingers projecting toward the sea. The waves were reaching the points of these fingers, and we had to rush from one recess to another when the waters receded. We soon reached the east side of the glacier and noticed its great activity at this point. Changes had occurred within the preceding twenty-four hours. Some huge pieces had broken off, and the masses of mud and stone that were being driven before the advancing ice showed

movement. The glacier was like a gigantic plow driving irresistibly toward
the sea.

Lying on the beach beyond the glacier was wreckage that told of many
ill-fated ships. We noticed stanchions of teakwood, liberally carved, that
must have come from ships of the older type; iron-bound timbers with
the iron almost rusted through; battered barrels and all the usual debris
of the ocean. We had difficulties and anxieties of our own, but as we passed
that graveyard of the sea we thought of the many tragedies written in the
wave-worn fragments of lost vessels. We did not pause, and soon we were
ascending a snow-slope, heading due east on the last lap of our long trail.

The snow surface was disappointing. Two days before we had been
able to move rapidly on hard, packed snow; now we sank over our ankles
at each step and progress was slow. After two hours' steady climbing we
were 2,500 feet above sea level. The weather continued fine and calm, and
as the ridges drew nearer and the western coast of the island spread out
below, the bright moonlight showed us that the interior was broken tremendously. High peaks, impassable cliffs, steep snow-slopes, and sharply
descending glaciers were prominent features in all directions, with stretches
of snow-plain overlaying the ice-sheet of the interior. The slope we were
ascending mounted to a ridge and our course lay direct to the top. The
moon, which proved a good friend during this journey, threw a long
shadow at one point and told us that the surface was broken in our path.
Warned in time, we avoided a huge hole capable of swallowing an army.
The bay was now about three miles away, and the continued roaring of a
big glacier at the head of the bay came to our ears. This glacier, which we
had noticed during the stay at Peggotty Camp, seemed to be calving almost continuously.

I had hoped to get a view of the country ahead of us from the top of
the slope, but as the surface became more level beneath our feet, a thick
fog drifted down. The moon became obscured and produced a diffused
light that was more trying than darkness, since it illuminated the fog without guiding our steps. We roped ourselves together as a precaution against
holes, crevasses, and precipices, and I broke trail through the soft snow.
With almost the full length of the rope between myself and the last man
we were able to steer an approximately straight course, since, if I veered
to the right or the left when marching into the blank wall of the fog, the
last man on the rope could shout a direction. So, like a ship with its "port,"
"starboard," "steady," we tramped through the fog for the next two hours.

Then, as daylight came, the fog thinned and lifted, and from an elevation of about 3,000 feet we looked down on what seemed to be a huge frozen lake with its farther shores still obscured by the fog. We halted there to eat a bit of biscuit while we discussed whether we would go down and cross the flat surface of the lake, or keep on the ridge we had already reached. I decided to go down, since the lake lay on our course. After an hour of comparatively easy travel through the snow we noticed the thin beginnings of crevasses. Soon they were increasing in size and showing fractures, indicating that we were traveling on a glacier. As the daylight brightened the fog dissipated; the lake could be seen more clearly, but still we could not discover its east shore. A little later the fog lifted completely, and then we saw that our lake stretched to the horizon, and realized suddenly that we were looking down upon the open sea on the east coast of the island. The slight pulsation at the shore showed that the sea was not even frozen; it was the bad light that had deceived us. Evidently we were at the top of Possession Bay, and the island at that point could not be more than five miles across from the head of King Haakon Bay. Our rough chart was inaccurate. There was nothing for it but to start up the glacier again. That was about seven o'clock in the morning, and by nine o'clock we had more than recovered our lost ground. We regained the ridge and then struck southeast, for the chart showed that two more bays indented the coast before Stromness. It was comforting to realize that we would have the eastern water in sight during our journey, although we could see there was no way around the shoreline owing to steep cliffs and glaciers. Men lived in houses lit by electric light on the east coast. News of the outside world waited us there, and, above all, the east coast meant for us the means of rescuing the twenty-two men we had left on Elephant Island.

Perhaps the most incredible fact about Shackleton's epic feat of endurance is that he didn't lose a single man during the various trials they suffered—all twenty-eight men survived to be rescued.

What struck me most as I read this excerpt was the calm, matter-of-fact tone that Shackleton had while recounting this particular adventure, as if everything he and his men had endured was nothing out of the ordinary—just what they had to put up with from the fates while they battled for their very lives. Stiff upper lip and all that, chaps.

This unflappability in the face of seemingly insurmountable odds is why Shackleton's heroic reputation has risen to new heights in the last few decades. One of his contemporaries, Apsley Cherry-Garrard, a member of Scott's ill-fated Terra Nova

Expedition, put it best in his preface to his book The Worst Journey in the World, *chronicling his own adventure with Scott at the bottom of the world:* "For a joint scientific and geographical piece of organization, give me Scott; for a winter journey, Wilson; for a dash to the Pole and nothing else, Amundsen: and if I am in the devil of a hole and want to get out of it, give me Shackleton every time."

Hear, hear.

ALONE ON THE PACIFIC

John Caldwell (1919–1998)

From *Desperate Voyage*

The author of our next seafaring excerpt, John Caldwell, is a man after my own heart more or less. He possessed that incredible strength of will necessary for any person who, when they find themselves in a survival situation, to retain the clarity of thought and focus necessary to ensure that they do survive. Caldwell had that internal willpower—after all, how else does one describe a man who sets out on a nine thousand-mile ocean voyage from Panama to Sydney, Australia, aboard a twenty-foot sailboat in 1946, with only two kittens (Flotsam and Jetsam), a gannet (Gawky), and a stowaway rat (named, of course, Stowaway) for company?

However, it is how *Caldwell prepares for this trip that makes me think he tended to plunge into situations headlong first and actually think about the consequences of his decision later. Wishing to rejoin his wife, Mary, whom he hadn't seen in a year, he set sail despite having no hands-on knowledge of sailing and studying navigation and the art of sailing from books for a week-and-a-half before starting his journey. Not what I would call the most prepared of men. But with equal parts courage, determination, and foolhardiness, Caldwell accomplished his goal, and afterward wrote* Desperate Voyage, *which has since become a classic among true nautical stories.*

Despite the recklessness of his challenge of the unpredictable Pacific Ocean, as I read this excerpt, I couldn't help but be taken with Caldwell's disarming charm as he recounts his triumphs and mistakes (his recounting of a close encounter with a shark for its teeth is a classic of "look but don't touch" literature), but also his easygoing acceptance of everything that happened to him, good and bad. Say what you want about the man, but he sure could spin a yarn.

He reminds me of other adventurers who were more than ready to tackle whatever the world could throw at them, and doing so with unruffled calm and ability, learning as they go, and even making mistakes along the way.

Hell, he reminds me of . . . well, me.

FROM PERLAS TO GALÁPAGOS there are 900 miles of ocean to cross. I had been told in Panama that sailing craft had taken anywhere from

seven days to eternity to make it. That was about all the actual information I had.

Even men who had sailed over this vexatious stretch of water couldn't
lay their finger on anything much that could help me. When they talked
about it they looked off at the ocean and frowned. "Work into the Galápagos from the east," they said, "don't get west of them; you can't fight
back against the trades and the current."

So that was my plan: work south till I could shape up for the Galápagos by steering into them to westward. Someone said that once I got to
the Galápagos, the rest of the voyage to Australia was all "downhill."
The trade winds were the thing. It was the trade winds I was after, and as
vexations piled up on themselves I looked toward the trades as a salvation
worth fighting to.

To limit the conditions of weather in the area between Panama and
the southeast trades to such a simple word as bad or terrible is crass un-
derstatement. What makes it bad here is that disturbances are general
rather than particular. No type of weather is dominant. Rather, one encounters every conceivable annoyance—not to mention their combination.

I had been in one gale, and a squall in the Perlas. And I had thought
them bad at the time. But when I nosed out into Panama Gulf and farther,
Pandora's box threw wide its lid and hell was a-poppin' from the start.

I didn't meet any really severe weather conditions—that is, harsh
storms. But I should rather have the weather flay me a week at a time,
then waft me along for a day of sailing, than do what it did.

Almost every night I was double-reefed at the main and hove to. Otherwise I was in a flat calm or in a wind too gentle to enable me to make
effective headway against the current. Sandwiched between these three
perplexing weather habits was the unpredictable appearance of tropical
squalls. Usually their only indication was the whir of wind or the cry of
a rent sail.

These waters are undoubtedly the sharpest bone a sailor can have in
his throat. Three uncongenial ocean currents meet here and claw at each
other under the keel. There is the Mexican current dropping in from the
north with its cool flood from Unalaska and the coasts of Japan. Out of
the west comes the equatorial countercurrent, torrid and forceful, bringing tropic warmth and tropic life with it. Up from the Antarctic, along
the South American coast, flows the cold stream called the Humboldt Current. When these varying waters meet the same thing happens that can

only happen when brunette, redhead, and blonde come seeking the same man!

In the midst of these variant upsets an unsteady, one-minute-vicious and one-minute-calm, southwest wind added the final touch of mayhem. For it was to the southwest that I wanted to ply . . . straight into the eye of the wind. So I had to tack; first to south and then to west, fighting the current, which was trying to suck me back to Panama—and it was succeeding at times. Some days found me hours on end in nerve-racking calms. Then a gale of wind would prod me in the ribs, causing me to heave to and fall back for most of the night. The morning would find me in a dead calm beneath a deluge of rain and rumbling clouds, or in an electric storm, the sky frightful with lightning.

On the first afternoon out I was in a rising south wind with one reef tucked in and pondering whether I should drop sail and tie in the other, when suddenly the wind dropped away to a void. Great smooth rollers ran under me and away to sternward. In twenty minutes a behemoth of a cloud swept down on me from directly behind. I could hear it talking as it came. By rights I should have doused all sail and gone below. But I was too desperate to make a few feet of southwesting. All day I had beaten to and fro across the same acre of water, into the same forceless head wind. A stern wind was a boon. I held to my hat and sat tight. The squall roared up and very crassly gave me the equivalent of a kick in the pants. In a moment I was flying before it at about seven knots! It was just what I wanted.

Imagine footing it at that clip and plowing head on into the oncoming rollers? *Pagan* was flying off the top of one into the center of another, a great spray cannonading upward and wetting the rigging to the masthead. Waves of water sluiced along the decks and spilled over the stern. A thump would herald her fall from the back of a smoking wave, and a thud would tell me that she was plowing into the base of another. At one stage I grew a little apprehensive and determined to bring her about and shorten all sail. "Nuts to it, we're going somewhere," I called out; and let her fly.

The squall lasted about forty minutes, then fell away to nothing, leaving me in a highly confused sea.

The next day I saw my first tide rip. In a moment—out of nowhere—the sea became an acreage of numberless cone shaped bouncing wavelets. It rose and fell in an endless dance, licking at the sky with unnumbered fingers. I sat looking at something I had never seen before. It was amazing to see the uncanny epilepsy. It actually jumped aboard, but ran harm-lessly out of the self-bailing cockpit. Under the keel two contrary currents had met; and redhead and blonde were tearing out each other's hair.

Another incident was unique in its way. The day had been one of weak and vacillating ladies' winds. I had used the engine several hours during the long hot day, in a futile search for a breeze. In midafternoon I gave up and decided to do with what I had. But as night drew on I found myself quite suddenly in a gale—in fact so suddenly as to be unable to pull down sail immediately. By the time the mainsail was reefed and double reefed the storm was down around my ears in earnest. Frothy seas were piling up, and *Pagan* was pitching savagely. The time had come and gone to hazard the bowsprit and doff the jib.

Staying atop a heaving bowsprit in a gale is like balancing on a rolling barrel. Every time the sprit goes down, you are past your knees in swirl-ing water. About every fourth time, you come up with water in your pockets—your vest pockets!

You cling like grim death to the topmast stay and work at the sail with your free hand. On a dark and stormy night it doesn't pay to fall off. So you hold tight and work fast—but not too fast. You get careless. That's what I did!

I had been out on the bowsprit several times in the Perlas and I was approaching the jaunty stage. But sailboats are marvelous devices for im-pressing the need of constant vigilance. *Pagan,* in her own inimical way, heeled over, pitched full down and then came up, tossing her bowsprit at the sky. With the grace of a circus clown I floundered end over end into the reaching dark waves.

I fought instantly for the surface. A series of seas clouted me, knocking me sternward somewhere behind the transom. The bumkin was a bare foot out of reach—and I knew I must soon get hold of it, or something, or the next heavy roller would sweep me down wind. My fiercest swim-ming was barely enough to enable me to hold my own against *Pagan's* slow slog to windward. Seawater was impairing my vision and stifling my breath. In this desperate moment I struck something: at first I thought it the rudder edge, but it was a pair of pants I was dragging astern to wash in the wake. I pulled myself by them up to the rail and clung to it for a moment while I rested.

The sea gave tremendous pulls—impressing me with its unlimited power. In four years of the Merchant Service I had not realized its infinite strength. From the decks of great freighters one is on the seas but not of it. One is cradled between sturdy bulkheads of steel. One just sees the sea. When a merchant seaman gets a salt spray on his lips, it's an adventure.

As I trailed in *Pagan*'s spuming wake, too spent to pull myself aboard, I learned the need for some sort of line dragging from the stern, something to grab onto if I fell over again. After I got aboard I went to the bowsprit and wrestled in the jib. But before doing so I lay on the poop, staring soberly at the retreating columns of the sea. Like brutes they ran from under *Pagan,* growling into the night. It's natural that I reflected on what could have happened. The danger for the lone sailor is what I had just escaped. I had been lucky. Next time I might not be so lucky. I felt a close part of my boat, an inseparable part of it in the battle with the hungry sea.

I wondered if I would have begun this trip had I known of the actual uncertainties to be facing me, as I was seeing them now. Yes I would, I concluded. What I was doing was fun, it had thrills. Despite the danger, I loved it. There was an appeal that every man feels—the appeal to adventure. And besides, it was taking me to the one girl in the world.

The morning of the fourth day out was like any other, except for one thing. Daylight found me standing east of south, bent slightly before the wind, making laggard time. As usual there was something untoward about the sky—but that was nothing more than I was learning to expect. I had been deep-reefed the night before. To make the most of the day I had risen early and hoisted full sail. But it was useless; the wind was falling steadily off to a calm under a leaden sky.

I cranked up my talkative engine and ran her for two hours before I came upon a light breeze. It was southwest as usual and mild enough to fill my sails but faintly.

During these first five days I was in the process of learning celestial navigation, which heretofore I had been too crowded with tasks to get to. While learning the celestial, I figured my daily progress by dead reckoning, using the bubbles rushing off the end of the keel as an indication of my speed through the water. So far I had estimated my gait to be a modest seven knots!—placing me approximately halfway to the Galápagos.

At 10 A.M. I found a new interest.

A great blunt-faced shark was lazing alongside *Pagan*. He eyed me with tiny pig's eyes and sidled quickly in to thwack the bilge strakes with his ponderous body.

Seeing and hearing this activity of sharks was an old story to me. Many times in the night or day I have heard them thump the planking. They do it to scratch themselves—or maybe they are vengeful. The first time I ever heard it was when I was sailing in the Perlas. It was night. I was hove-to near Saboga and down below asleep. I was awakened by a sinister thump, which shivered the boat. I bolted to deck thinking it had struck a reef, because I wasn't sure of my position. My first thought was that I had come about and run back in to shore. But mostly I thought of a reef. On deck I could discern nothing. The air was static and overcast. *Pagan* was scarcely swaying. For a long time I was perplexed. Then from an oblique angle a silver wake of phosphorus marked the track of an approaching object. At my very feet it banged into the side, scraped eerily a few feet, and slithered away. It was a shark.

I couldn't have that. *Pagan*'s planks were only one-inch oak and they were twenty-six years old. Too many back scratchings by hulking sharks and I would be swimming in my bunk. I broke out a spear and when the big shark lumbered in, I reefed it into him. With a startled twist he broke my hold and plunged speedily. Lost: one good spear. After that I tied a bowie knife to an oar—and when they ranged near I gave them a tweak in the ribs with six inches of cold steel.

But to return: the shark, which filliped *Pagan*'s hull that morning of the twenty-third was a whopper. I couldn't help but marvel at him. He was all shark. He had the swagger of a brute bully; he was half the length of *Pagan,* and had teeth the size of fingers.

When I saw those staggered twisted teeth I wanted them . . . to show what I had seen. I wanted Mary to see that crushing jawbone, to hold it in her hand.

I brought my heavy sport reel and pole on deck, and attached my largest steel shark hook. I baited it with a fat yellowjack partly gnawed at by Flotsam and Jetsam. When the shark came near I dangled it before him and dragged it away before he could look it over, a simple bit of classroom psychology, which, as it whetted him, angered him. Next time he nuzzled it, and arrogantly swept it into his jagged mouth.

I heaved back with all the strength I had. The hook lodged unmistakably in his bold jaw, and with the burn of cold steel he tensed, then, slashing about with a startled suddenness, roiling the water, sent a wave against the planking and made off to beamward.

Threshing in agitation with his slow main strength, he battled away from the boat, making the reel hum. When he ended his run of sixty yards he turned on the hook and flailed the surface, gleaming silvery as he twisted in foam.

I braced myself against the lashed tiller for a ringside view of the most fascinating struggle I had ever seen.

The massive thing tore at the surface of the water, bending violently, from U shape to S shape, champing viciously. Sometimes he appeared astern, then on the bow, always with a smear on the quiet sea. He turned on his back and threshed fitfully, or spun in great full circles abeam and close aboard, followed by his pilot fish.

At one time he was more than a hundred feet down straight under me—so deep in fact I could see nothing in the limpid water. His most spectacular effort came about a half hour after he had been hooked. He had fought the line to its end, dead astern. With dorsal fin cleaving the surface he sped in fury full around the boat, threshing mightily as he went. Spray shot above him and a long wake rolled away behind him. He ended his circular run, paused a second, then sped fifty feet toward the quarter, swirled about, and raced away as though he would wrench his head off with the impending shock at the line's end. Barely before he reached the line's end he thrust himself from the water, and twisting on his back he sent a shiver from head to tail that, had the line grown taut—even if it were boltrope—would have snapped it like spaghetti. After that his defiance fell completely away. He struggled only pettily as I towed him to the rail.

The teeth I saw were unbelievable. They lay in two uneven rows, each two inches long and thicker than a pencil. They jutted at rakish angles, looked unmercifully sharp, and were wielded by a jaw mammoth enough to crush bone. My envy of his power, coupled with the animal instincts of the victor, induced me to lean over the rail and punch him in the nose. I found it about as hard as *Pagan*'s decks.

The great jaw, the jagged teeth—they were fascinating. But how to get them? My wicked intuition that all was well prodded me. Pull him aboard; cut his head off; boil the flesh away—it's simple.

Flotsam and Jetsam, with paws on the rail, could smell the fishy stench of the beast's breath and were fidgeting and mewing eagerly for a feast. I decided to pull him aboard.

First, I naïvely tried to lift him by direct pull, but only budged him scantily. He weighed hundreds of pounds. I fastened the main halyard to the gaff hook fitted in his gill and with desperate heaves dragged him an inch at a time over the transom, into the cockpit. What a monster. His head lay in the cockpit and his tail hung over the stern. He stirred faintly. I took the hatchet and buried it in his spine to end his tremors. A spurt of blood sprayed over me.

At the same moment the big body quivered violently. Flotsam and Jetsam went racing to the bow. I watched them. I heard a resounding scuffle and saw my tiller, splintered loose at the rudderpost, go flying into the sea.

All hell broke loose around me. The great shark came completely to life, threw himself in wild assault. With great sweeps of his tail and butts of his head he swept my legs from under me, almost knocking me overboard.

The great tail was pounding up and down like a sledgehammer, splintering, slamming, erasing. The gas-tank hatch disintegrated in a flash and the brazed copper tank went flat, spilling its load into the bilge. I clung to the rail, horror-stricken. The cockpit coaming rumbled, shattered, and flew at me, and if I hadn't ducked it would have gone down my throat.

In the meantime the hatchway sliding door had been popped through to the cabin floor and the rear porthole cracked. The bottom of the cockpit was giving way. *Pagan* was bouncing as though pounded by great fist blows.

I darted as close as I dared, grabbed up my hatchet, and chopped away at the heaving spine. Again he set to beating with sinuous motions. The partition between the engine compartment and cockpit screamed and split away. The cockpit deck itself broke through, the gasoline drums rumbled into the engine compartment, and the shark lay head down on the motor. I jumped in and struck again, burying the blade, and burying it again.

The destruction went on.

Pagan was being blasted apart before my eyes. I hacked with the hatchet like a wild woodcutter. I opened gashes in the head, and in the back. I had chopped his dorsal fin half away. Still he mauled my boat. I was afraid he would work his way into the cabin and rip it down or endanger the mast. I struck the harder. I went after him like a madman—blood bespattered and desperate.

He mangled the engine with side movements of his head, bending the sparkplugs down and tearing the wiring away. He fell beside the motor, threw himself around athwartships, and lying on the propeller shaft throbbed till it bent out of line. I was terrified lest he should work his way against the ribbing and smash the hull open. I lay on my side atop the engine, eased close, and notched a great hole in his stomach and lower jaw.

He jumped spasmodically. I moved after him, lost in the bloody, death-dealing strokes. I cut his eye completely out and opened a hole from his gill to his shorn dorsal fin; still he lashed like a whip.

I sidled closer, drawing my legs up so that I could fit into the confined space, and turned more on my side to apply all my strength. Aiming for his nose—a supposed Achilles' heel—I laid it open bone and all, as far back as his front teeth. Still he throbbed dangerously. Moving closer—inches from him—I hacked into his vital stomach organs.

I was so far gone I was hardly nicking him. But it suddenly didn't matter; he gaped at the mouth and lay still. I lay for a long time beside him, watching him, hoping he wouldn't move, because if he had, I would have been in his way and too tired to shift. Everything about me was either smashed or coated red. I was caked with blood.

Before I could consider getting the battered carcass over the side, I had a few jobs to do. I had to pump gallons of gasoline, battery acid, and clotted blood from the bilges. Then I washed the gore from the decks, cabin, planking, and ribbing inside. After that I cleared away the splintered and broken lumber, piling it in the cabin.

The cockpit was a gaping hole. In the midst of it, the kittens were growling hungrily over the shark; chewing tastily with the corners of their mouths. I cut them a sizable meal and placed them with it on the fore scuttle.

Cutting into the shark's stomach, I found a motley of tragic creatures which had wholly or partly contributed themselves to his meals: two whole squid, a large Spanish mackerel, a mass of predigested small fry, the yellowjack I had baited him with, and several chunks of flesh and bone torn evidently from a very large fish.

After such a contest to subdue the shark, I considered his jawbone more a prize than ever. I cut his head off and later cleaned and scraped the bones and yellow teeth—a gruesome sight.

To heave the carcass over the side I had to cut it into two pieces and tussle with it by main strength. As to the wreckage—most of my spare time for the next two weeks was spent in rebuilding the stern.

Because of the shark I added another moral to my list: don't haul sharks aboard!

The engine was useless unless I turned back to Panama to have it repaired. As I look back now, I realize I should have turned back and put in at the Mechanical Division in Balboa for the work. In the long run I would have saved time. Too, I probably would have had a much hastier and most uneventful and dull trip across the Pacific.

The principal reason I didn't do an about-face was the state of my exchequer—it was low; only twenty-five dollars. And that wouldn't pay the docking fee. Also, my navigation by dead reckoning indicated I was making from eighty to a hundred miles a day. I expected to be in the Galápagos in a week—once there I wouldn't need an engine. The southeast trade winds, I was told, begin there, and with their power and constancy, motor power is unneedful.

So I bore on, strictly under sail.

There is one great hazard above all in singlehanded sailing, as I had learned, and that is, if you should topple over, there is no one to turn the boat about and pick you up. This was always before my mind, and I was forever cautious to guard against it.

The day after the shark battle I rigged a lifeline of about sixty feet, which I dragged astern—something to grab onto if I should fall over. Sometimes I bent a hook to its end baited with a stripping of white rag, and caught a fresh meal for the crew and me. Or I tied on a dirty pair of pants or a shirt to launder themselves in the wake. I used it also for a log line to indicate my speed. Primarily, though, its purpose was that of lifesaver in case I should fall over.

But one morning even my lifesaver nearly left me afloat on the sea.

The sun was barely up before a tumult of wind was down on me from the southwest. The sea picked up into a churlish, slapping hand, and I was banging into the teeth of it. The mainsail and staysail were reefed. I hesitated about pulling the jib, thinking conditions would abate.

Getting dunked and even dragged off the bowsprit now and then wasn't discouraging any longer. *Pagan's* bowsprit was too long—about seven feet—and very small around.

Taking in the jib in a gale was an activity for which I was never able to formulate an exact process. Never once did I doff it satisfactorily—so to the end I was practicing with it. But to get it in I usually proceeded something like this: First I crawled out and loosened the lanyard. I crawled back and slacked the halyard a foot or two, dropping the sail. Out again to snap loose a couple of hanks, pull the clew in, and pack it behind the

rail at the forepeak. Slack away at the halyard again; unsnap several clips
and pull in more of the sail from the grasping water, and stow it on deck.

Invariably I always left the jib to the last minute before tugging it in.
Because it was clumsy to handle, it made little difference whether I grappled
with it in a mild gale or a full one.

On this morning of high wind I was preparing myself for a bout with
the jib by the usual cursing and swearing beforehand. When I got out on
the bowsprit, I found that the turnbuckle of the stay was almost unscrewed.
I twisted it by hand to tighten it, but must have turned it backward—
suddenly it parted. I grabbed a handful of the sail, and hung to it as the
wind filled it.

The next moment I was in mid-air dangling from the billowed sail. I
was fifteen feet up and the same distance off the beam. I had a death's
grip on the sail luff and I was wondering if I would be thrown too far out
to swim back if I should let go. I decided to hang on.

Suddenly the sail spilled its wind and I swung inboard, crashing into the
mast. Before I could think to let go I was blown back into the air again.
The wind was whipping at the sail. I was being shaken back and forth as a
terrier shakes a rat. Then the sail slipped loose from the stay, lost its wind,
and folded as it splashed onto the sea.

The knotted halyard end caught in the block and I was towed astern. I
was clinging to the stiff sail and wrestling with it as I clung; trying to gather
it into a bundle, hoping I could somehow save it by gaining the deck with
it. The canvas resisted stubbornly. Then the halyard slipped through, leaving me adrift: I had only the sail to hold to. *Pagan* moved away. I had the
sail in a close grip, and swam to the lifeline astern. But sea slime and small
rubbery sea animals had grown to it; and hanging to it, while clinging to
the sail, was like holding on in a slippery pig contest.

I was determined to save the jib. My spare jib had been blown out in
the storm off San José. The one I was fighting to save was my last. I
needed it badly. A jib is a vital sail when working to windward.

In a minute I knew that fighting my way up the slimy rope with the
sail still in hand was impossible. I managed to edge a few feet ahead, only
to be thrown back by the wash of a swell.

I was deeply mindful of the cruel steel shark hook at the line's end.
When I stopped to rest, I found that the line was slipping steadily through
my hands. Not all the pressure of my grasp would counter the drag. The
hook was near my feet, and threatening to snag them. I was slipping helplessly. The sea, pulling on the sail, was sliding me back and back.

The sail was bundled loosely on my stomach. I freed my hold on it and let the water devour it. I hated to do it, but what could I do?

Pagan, double-reefed and heeling deeply as she pushed into the teeth of the rising wind, had a plucky look about her partly denuded spars and exposed hull as her trim lines battered the rough edges of the swelling seas, thirty feet ahead of me. She was wreathed in spray. I could hear the bow cleave the oncoming rollers.

I started the long haul up the slimed-over line from handhold to handhold, fighting each sea and the bubbling wake.

I crawled onto deck and lay watching the churning seas, crested with foam, racing away to the horizon, rumbling like trains as they went.

Lying there thinking morbidly over what might have happened, I noticed, as my eyes wandered astern with each sea, a ripple on the water's surface. I could see that it was my sail, and that somehow it was fouled with the end of my life line, and towing behind.

I gathered in the line, hoping the sail wouldn't disentangle. It didn't. When it neared the transom I saw that the shark hook had barbed the sail at the boltrope. One chance in hundreds.

I later entered the occurrence in the log as "taking in the jib the hard way."

Those first nine days I figured my speed by approximation. Each evening I plotted an estimated position on the chart. It was marvelous the distance I had covered. The water was sweeping beneath the keel at a rate of at least seven knots, I figured. According to my dead reckoning I was hard by the Galápagos; but was I? I wondered. Someone in Panama had said, "Don't go to Galápagos by dead reckoning; it's suicide." I was beginning to get uneasy the day I tried my first sextant shot.

It was a shoddy affair. I spent the day capturing the shifty sun in terms of an angle, and working out a questionable noon sight from a maze of figures. Late that evening, after juggling ciphers and sights all afternoon, I arrived at a position, which put me somewhere inland in Central Panama. I gave up for the night.

On the next two days I arrived at consistent figures—but what figures! My wearisome computations, no matter what number of times I checked and rechecked them, came up always with the same result: they placed me only some 350 bare miles from Panama. The figures said I was near a barren isolated rock called Malpelo Isle. I refused to believe the figures. I stuck with my dead reckoning estimate, which put me some 900 miles from Panama.

But as the morning wore on I rechecked the figures. Unfailingly they established me as somewhere near Malpelo. Finally I scaled the mast and searched the horizon, and saw nothing more than the monotonous sea. It was dirty in the southwest. A hazy curtain hung over the water.

There were birds around and they led me to believe land was near. But there couldn't be land; the Galápagos were a day away . . . unless . . . it could be Malpelo. Then, as midday rolled around, from out of the sea eased the loom of land. Dead ahead the crag floated, about ten miles off, barren, solitary, unmistakable.

This meeting of boat and sea-swept rock out on the pathless ocean came as a sort of miracle to me. For eleven days I had sailed and searched and had lifted no more than a steamer's smoke. Then suddenly figurings and jottings on a squared sheet of paper said land would raise itself across the bows now . . . and it did! The land was before me in the form of an indistinct blob of rock, small, and frothed at its base where the sea charged.

Seeing it there brought a flood of relief. Navigation suddenly became a game of fun, all the uncertainty I had felt over it glimmered, and I quickly looked upon it as simple, where for years I had fidgeted in awe at the mere thought of it.

Before I bought *Pagan* I used to think one had to know differential calculus to navigate a peanut across a dishpan. Too, I had looked at Bowditch, Dutton, and Cugle's and walked away blubbering to myself in a navigational fog. That's the way it was when I first went aboard *Pagan*. In the front of my mind was the prospective trip out onto the sea and in the back, haunting me, was my ignorance of navigation.

The devil of it was, while in port before I sailed I hadn't a spare hour to study it, the whole two weeks I owned *Pagan*. I had such a high respect for its complexities that I didn't want to put forth from Panama knowing the little I did of it, which was only visual pilotage from flying. But what could I do? Time was against me . . . I had to get across the Pacific before the hurricane season set in over the Coral and Tasman Seas. There was no time, as I saw it, to attend a fortnight of navigation school. The moment cried that I go.

When I sailed, I had exactly this navigating equipment aboard: one sextant, given to me by Captain Baverstock of Balboa. A pocket watch, exceedingly reliable. A cheap compass, that came with the boat. A hand lead line. A copy of Bowditch, given to me, though I didn't need it; I used it once—to light my Primus stove. A copy of Warwick Tompkins's *The Offshore Navigator,* $1.50, and worth its weight in gold. A copy of Hydrographic Office Publication No. 211, 90 cents. A small cardboard protractor, 10 cents. A six-inch rule, 10 cents. Good charts of likely island groups along the way, $4.00. Sailing directions and light lists for the waters I was to cross, $2.30. Total cost, $8.90.

If you will navigate, take what is listed here and sail away. When, after ten days of study and stars, you can't fix your position, turn back and take up harbor sailing, for you will never navigate. Any sensible person who can see the sun or horizon plainly can use these tools to go around the world.

To me Malpelo meant nothing. I was not on a sightseeing trip. But if I had been, I would not have come there for scenery. The isle is so wind-, rain-, and sea-swept that not even the guano from its host of birds will cling to it. Around its base are a few toothlike rocks. Otherwise it is sheer and uninviting. I was glad to see it for what it meant to me as a check on my navigation, but it was a setback to learn that in eleven days I had traversed only some 350 miles.

I laid my slow progress to inexperience and the host of frustrating weather conditions, which had beset me. Also there was no certainty regarding the speed and exact set of the currents. But the main factor in my poor showing was the loss of the engine. The use of an engine in a calm, even for an hour, can often move the craft into an area of wind.

By nightfall I had made a good offing from Malpelo into the south. But a little later it fell calm. I dropped the main to avoid hearing it slat aimlessly and went below for the night. At daylight . . . I found that the current during the night had pulled me off to the northeast of Malpelo. The calm still held, and I fished from the deck to while away the time till a bold young breeze should whip me past the lonely rock for the second time.

Around midmorning a lusty breeze sprang up. I stood away to the west till I had cleared Malpelo, then shoved around to south and beat away toward the equator. Through the afternoon I bounded into a making wind till at nightfall I was deeply reefed and ready to heave to. Malpelo was far behind. In the face of a line squall I doused the main and put her in stops, and heaved to for a stormy night. Before I went below, out of the weather, I had what I thought to be a last look at Malpelo.

Dawn came with rain pelting the cabin like bird shot. I got up to as morbid a bit of weather as I have seen. Visibility was nil; the wind high; a lump of sea running. It was a day of perpetual dusk. Not even the ubiquitous sea birds were out. I didn't dare put up a stitch of cloth. I stayed below.

Though I couldn't see it I knew the deformed island was somewhere near. For three days now I had been in its vicinity, and I grew sober whenever I thought of my helplessness before the weather.

At noon sea and air were still unchanged, except that off to starboard I could catch the recurrent hollow boom of pounding seas. At first I thought a ship was somewhere about. But there was no blast of foghorn. After a while I realized I was falling back before the storm, past Malpelo.

Deep in the night the winds abated. I climbed out of the warm sack and showed on deck. Stars blinked in patches; the sea was still rolling in heavily; the air was both bold and weak as it is in moments of change. But it looked as if some sail could stand. I tied a reef into the mainsail and ran her up. In a few hours I passed Malpelo for the third time, looking gray in the early dawn.

The breeze freshened as the sun climbed. Late in the morning I tied in the last reefs and pulled down the jib. In the early afternoon the wind veered to a little north of west. A heavy swell set in from the south. Shortly cross-seas were at work and *Pagan* was rolling and yawing wildly. Malpelo hid herself in the falling clouds. By dark I was hove-to properly.

The cats were tottering weakly on the bunk with *mal de mer*. I tucked their drooping little bodies close by me where they would be warm, and made them feel in their misery that they had an understanding friend.

The wind was backing slowly to its wonted position. Cross-seas were worsening. Above the noise of wind in the rigging and rumbling of sea crests I could hear occasional proofs of seas breaking on Malpelo.

Long after I had bedded down I was awakened by the nearer crash of seas on a shore. I knew before I uncovered myself that it was Malpelo. Damn this island; wouldn't I ever get past it? On deck I reached with eye and ear into the wet night of drizzle and made the crash and hiss of the surf dead astern more or less. I couldn't risk falling back farther, so I strung up the staysail to see if *Pagan* could stand off a lee shore.

In an hour the roar was louder. It was no longer difficult to hear or make out its bearing. *Pagan* could hold her own with the wind, but it was the current that was sucking her back. I reefed the staysail and put up the double-reefed main. For the remainder of the night she held her own.

At daylight—five days after sighting the island—I found Malpelo leering at me a hundred yards down wind, and the wind was stiffening! She was directly in my wake, and reaching closer with each squall and gust. I was gravely in need of the engine. A scathing wind was on. *Pagan* had no business with sail up—still, I didn't dare take in a stitch.

At times it looked as though she might ride clear of the isle if I should drop sail and let her drift. I was tempted to back her around and risk clearing the island by running before the wind. But in such a sea I was afraid of being broached-to by veering too sharply into the wind, or pooped by shipping a wave over the stern. With *Pagan*'s cockpit still not fully repaired from the battle with the shark, I didn't dare hazard it. The more I watched the jagged spire the more ominous it became.

A cold wind swept the clouds from the air. The blue dome of the sky, across which a cool sun worked up to high noon, looked down over me as I grew furrowed at the brow. There was no need for a noon sight; my exact position was impressed on me by every minute.

I could easily have tossed a sea biscuit onto the closest rocks. The roar quite suddenly grew deafening. It's a wonder Malpelo isn't toppled right over by force of driving seas, so greatly do they slam against her. I slipped as close to her weather-worn sides as I dared, still hoping the wind would abate, or that *Pagan* would work away.

At this juncture I did the only thing I could possibly have done. But first I pushed my little pneumatic life raft off the foredeck and led it aft to secure it to the bumkin, in readiness against the moment I might need it. I tied the cork blocks to Flotsam and Jetsam and stuck them in a corner of the cockpit. Then, knife in hand, I cut the lashings and reef points away along the boom, freeing the sail, and jerked the strained canvas hastily up. It filled, and *Pagan* shivered. The lee rail went under the sea and a froth swirled against the deckhouse.

I jumped to the tiller and pointed *Pagan* as far off the wind as I could without broaching her to. She heeled more steeply and the rudder kicked. She breasted each sea jerkily. Holding the tiller was real work. Great lumps of sea bombarded the windward rail. Spray landed on the cliff face close abeam.

I knew the sail wouldn't hold long, but a few minutes' sailing would drive me far enough to clear the rocks. If the sail flew out at the seams right away—I had only one resort, the rubber raft. Flotsam and Jetsam were unmindful of my weighted concerns. They sat close together like a furry ball, looking calmly ahead.

In five minutes I peered down wind and thought that even then I could clear the isle. Then the slides ripped from the luff of the sail. They screeched and the sail pounded at loose ends. I shoved the tiller down. *Pagan* rounded to into the wind, and fell before it. I knew she would pass close to the rocks if she passed at all. And close it was. Spray from the battered stone fell over us. It reminded me of Punta de Cocos. Flotsam and Jetsam shivered and crawled up to my lap.

The same night I drifted far to northeastward of Malpelo. At dawn the wind was still high, a lumpy sea was still rolling—and *Pagan,* under staysail and jib, was hove-to far to leeward of the horny rock. Overhead was the clearest sky I have seen on the Pacific; not a cloud showed, only a depthless blue. A fierce unvarying wind blew the full day, driving cresting seas onto the decks. I was seated in the chill cabin at work with palm and needle on the tattered mainsail. She had pulled loose at the seams, and had frayed a bit at the ends. Here and there was a rip, which demanded a little attention. I noted that only the seams sewed by machine had split; those which I had stitched in at San José were good.

As I worked I thought, *Why go on fighting uselessly against the fitful winds overhead and the redheads and blondes at loggerheads around the keel?* Six days on one small field of water. I was for turning back to Panama, for a rest and repairs and a new start. The more I thought of doing it, the more sensible it sounded. Then my wicked intuition lulled me, telling me the trade winds were hard by, and coaxing me to push on. Mug that I am, I listened.

Late in the afternoon I completed the job and spent the time to dusk fretting before a porthole. Through the night the wind held, and only with the dawn did it moderate to where I could put on the sails and start the long beat into the wind toward Malpelo for the fourth time. All morning I worked sail and tiller. At noon I was close by the rock.

Throughout the afternoon I sailed under a halcyon sky, hoping the friendly wind would hold till the night. I was beginning to think of Malpelo as a jinx. If only I could pass out of sight of her once, my troubles would be over. As I passed her I stood at the shrouds and loathed the sight of her hornlike crags in the belated twilight. At ten o'clock, with wind still holding fair, I tied the proper angle on the rudder and called it a day.

For the first few hours of the next morning I could see a tuft of rock on the horizon astern. What an unburdening it was to imagine not seeing that grotesque shape again. Late in the forenoon, I saw again what I had not seen for eight tiring days—a landless expanse of sea.

Amazingly, Caldwell survived his transoceanic journey (and both kittens made it through as well, although he gave them to some islanders he encountered along the way), reunited with his wife, and spent his days operating a hotel on Palm Island in the Grenadines until his death in 1998. He was one of the last of a vanishing breed of adventurers, the likes of whom we don't see too often nowadays.

SETTLING IN FOR SURVIVAL
Maurice Bailey and Maralyn Bailey (1941–2002)
From *117 Days Adrift*

_____

Stories of whales attacking boats aren't limited to the nineteenth century. One of the most amazing stories of survival after a whale attack comes to us in this next excerpt, told from the different perspectives of a husband-and-wife sailing team marooned in the Pacific Ocean after a wounded whale sank their sailboat, the Au-ralyn. Evacuating with whatever they could carry in two small rafts, they embark on a journey of endurance for the next 117 days. Although they were in a well-traveled part of the Pacific Ocean, rescue wouldn't come for a long time. They saw several ships during their voyage, one even approaching to within a half mile of their location, but apparently none saw their tiny rafts. They were picked up by a Korean fishing trawler more than three months after their accident.

Afterward, Maurice credited his wife with helping him combat the depression and hopelessness that threatened to overwhelm them both during the ordeal. The following excerpt is from right after the boat has sunk, and Maurice and Maralyn have to take stock of what they have to subsist on until they are rescued. Keep in mind that they estimate they have enough food for twenty days, not for the next three-and-a-half months.

MARALYN

MARCH 4TH

We settled into the raft as comfortably as possible and before the sun rose too high we had our breakfast, which consisted of four biscuits each spread thickly with margarine and a smear of marmalade. At lunch time we had a small handful of peanuts each and our evening meal was one tin of food between us.

At the last moment as I left the yacht I had grabbed our small Camping Gaz butane stove. Unfortunately, the gas canister was part used and we had no spare cartridges, but by careful use I reckoned it would last out our supply of tins. I put the contents of a tin in a small saucepan we had managed to salvage and heated the food for three or four minutes. I took

95

one spoonful then handed the pan to Maurice who also took one spoonful. We shared it like this until the food had gone. At mealtimes all conversation ceased and we concentrated on our food. When the last mouthful had disappeared we were both still very hungry and occasionally for "afters" we would raid the biscuit tin and have one each, or sometimes a date, and drool over its sweetness.

In our emergency kit I had placed two plastic bottles each holding two pints of water and one of these bottles would be our day's ration. When it was empty we would fill it from the main supply kept in the dinghy. For breakfast we would stir approximately three spoons of Coffee-mate into a cup of water and the rest of the day we would take turns and have sips from the bottle, finishing the rest after our evening meal. We learned later that our thirst might have been better satisfied if we had drunk our ration at one go.

On leaving the yacht I had rescued two books, one was Eric Hiscock's *Voyaging,* which he had kindly autographed for me one day on the Hamble River. The second book was a historical volume, *Richard III* by Paul Kendall Murray. We passed many hours remembering the books we had left behind and usually by starting with the words, "Did you read . . . ," we would tell each other the story in minute detail. I remembered one story of the life of Eleanor of Aquitaine; she was imprisoned for sixteen years by her husband and the way in which she kept her mind occupied during that time was fascinating. Another story was of an American soldier captured during the Korean War who was kept in solitary confinement yet retained his sanity by designing and building in his mind his future home. It was this last story that gave us the idea of designing and planning our next boat in every detail.

MAURICE

The sun rose higher and the heat became intense and with it a state of languor pervaded the raft. I opened the chart and plotted our dead reckoning position. We were, in fact, quite close to the shipping lane. I estimated our position to be 1°30' N 85°47' W, 250 miles north of Ecuador and 300 miles east of the Galápagos Islands, which was too far north to allow the west-going current to drift us on to the islands.

The wind blew from the southeast and, although light in strength, would drive us even farther north. Could we, perhaps, row the hundred or so miles south to the latitude of the Galápagos? It would take us about twelve days to reach the longitude of the Galápagos drifting at twenty-five miles per day. We would then have to row ten miles per day south to offset the wind and current and to reach their latitude at the same time as attaining the longitude. These calculations depended a lot on the wind and current remaining constant. Were we capable of rowing the dinghy ten miles each day with the raft in tow? Should we abandon the raft to give ourselves a better chance?

I stopped thinking about this problem and contented myself with the knowledge that in the next few days we should be drifting in a shipping lane. Nevertheless, I would have to mention the possibility of rowing to Maralyn. But later; not now.

We noticed a slight loss of pressure in the raft during the afternoon, and I pumped air into the tubes with the pump provided in the raft's emergency kit. This made me aware of the appalling vulnerability of our position; only our two small craft to keep us afloat on that vast ocean.

The raft consisted principally of two superimposed circular inflated tubes giving four-and-a-half-feet internal diameter. A floor was attached around the lower perimeter of the bottom tube. Below the raft was fixed a CO_2 bottle and three stabilizing pockets. A semicircular inflated tube that bridged the raft was fixed to the top tube and this supported a bright, orange colored canopy covering the whole raft.

There was a flap to cover the entrance and opposite this was a ventilation and lookout aperture protected by a skirt. Two nonreturn topping-up valves were situated just inside the entrance, one for the lower tube, the other for the upper and "bridge" tubes. Lifelines were fixed around the raft on the outside. The raft was made of black natural-rubber-proofed material. Apart from the pump the raft was equipped with two paddles, a repair kit, a length of orange polythene line, and a quoit.

The dinghy, made of heavier gray, rubberized fabric, was boat-shaped, about nine feet overall, and was divided into two separate flotation chambers with an inflated seat or thwart attached amidships. It had two fixed rubber rowlocks, two oars, and a bellows-type pump.

During the late afternoon I explained to Maralyn the desperate half-formed plan to row south to reach the latitude of the Galápagos Islands.

"We'll have to do the rowing at night," she said, "it would be impossible in the heat of the day."

I was depressed by the seriousness of our position and reluctant to make any decision. I found myself renouncing all pretence of leadership, and with her flair for organization Maralyn was taking command. "If it is too dark to see the compass we can steer by the stars," she said simply.

Maralyn appeared undaunted. "We'll start rowing immediately after supper. Two-hour spells will be enough." I hated the idea of rowing and asked, "How far do you think you can row in two hours?" She would not be discouraged. "We must try," she said.

The day wore on and the sun slid toward the clear horizon bringing the refreshing coolness we longed for. After our evening meal I argued a case for deferring rowing until the next evening. It was not just laziness that made me argue like this. We were drifting toward the shipping lane, which runs to the south of the Galápagos. In another twenty-four hours we should be in the center of this lane and we might just see a ship.

Of course this was wrong, we should have started rowing straightaway. The longer we delayed, the more we would have to row on subsequent nights. We settled down for our first night adrift, making ourselves as comfortable as possible. Unable to lie down in the raft together, one of us would curl up on the floor and sleep, while the other keeping watch, would sit hunched up in the little remaining space. We would change over every three hours. Maralyn had the worst of the arrangement because, whether sleeping or watch-keeping, I would take up the most room. We found this arrangement satisfactory only when the raft was inflated hard. The watchkeeper therefore had to pump the raft frequently to replace any slight loss of pressure. When several weeks later the raft became damaged and it was impossible to keep fully inflated, we abandoned this system and slept fitfully where we sat.

Dawn arrived and heralded another scorching day. We used some of our precious food, but hardly enough to sustain us, and sipped our daily one-pint ration of water carefully. Even then we found our thirst intolerable but hunger, up to then, was bearable. I examined the water containers in the dinghy and was horrified to discover that four gallons had been contaminated by seawater. It was obvious that we had to have rain soon to replace this foul water.

MARCH 5TH

That night after retrieving the drogue we started rowing. The task of towing the unwieldy bulk of the raft was slow, painful, and laborious; we strained our bodies and badly blistered our hands. At each stroke the dinghy would be propelled forward at a good pace, only to be brought up short when the painter between the two craft tautened, thus braking any further progress. The raft, responding to the momentum, would then slowly, oh! so slowly and sluggishly, move forward for a short distance. Hour followed laborious hour.

When the moon was up we checked our course with the compass, afterward we used the stars, using principally the constellations of Orion, Crux, and the Plough, with the Pole Star low on the northern horizon.

Eight hours rowing had exhausted us and we found that even though we doubled our water ration we did not find any relief from our thirst. This was indeed a bad thing. I doubted our ability to row enough each night to attain the right latitude before our water ran out. Although she had suffered through this strenuous activity, Maralyn did not complain and I could not disillusion her.

During the day I took sextant altitude sights of the sun from the dinghy; a morning sight for a position line and a noon sight for our latitude. The continual movement of the dinghy, the ocean swell, and the horizon being under two miles distant because my eye was only three feet above the sea, made accurate observations impossible. The declination of the sun was daily getting farther north and within a few more days it would be in the proximity of our latitude and would be useless for finding our position because the sextant angle would be too wide. The northern summer was fast approaching and with it, Maralyn reminded me, the wet season.

MARCH 6TH

My calculations showed that we had only gained a little over four miles to the south, while our westerly drift had been nearly thirty miles. I could say nothing to Maralyn; she was very optimistic. In fact, later in the day, when a layer of cumulus cloud appeared on the horizon to the southwest, she was convinced that it lay over the Galápagos Islands.

I kept a check on the accuracy of my wristwatch by frequent comparisons with the compass and ensuring that the sun's maximum altitude coincided with the hands showing twelve o'clock. The accuracy of the watch helped me a lot when waiting to take a noon latitude sextant sight.

This watch, a Rotary Incabloc, was hung on the electric cable of the emergency light, which itself was out of action because the battery was broken, and Maralyn would sometimes catch her hair on the winder, which pulled it out and stopped the watch. This was frustrating as our day was organized around the time taken from this watch. Although it was nearly nine years old and repeatedly saturated with water, it kept remarkably good time. To start the watch again I would wait until the sun attained its maximum altitude, which I found with the sextant, and then set the hands of the watch to twelve o'clock and start it again. Although we placed little reliance on its absolute accuracy, we were indeed surprised to discover that it was only two minutes slow when we were rescued.

During the day we would get an idea of our drift or the wind direction by using the watch as a compass. This was especially helpful after we later lost the boat's compass when the dinghy capsized.

MARCH 7TH–8TH

Our efforts at rowing were continued on the third and fourth nights and then, having fixed our position at noon on the fifth day, I explained to Maralyn my misgivings about rowing any more. Surprisingly she agreed, saying that the sooner we drifted into a shipping lane the better.

"You will not find these lanes full of shipping like the English Channel," I said. "Months may pass before a ship will be seen."

"But there will be a chance," Maralyn replied emphatically.

MARALYN

For three nights we had rowed in turn, two hours each throughout the coolness of the evening until the sun rose the next morning. We had taken the ship's compass from the cockpit and Maurice had wedged it between the water carriers and we followed a compass course when there was enough light from the moon. After that we steered by the stars.

At the end of this time we were both exhausted and had blisters on our hands. A feature of this exercise was our alarming consumption of water. I had laid down the ration as one pint of water each per day, as I knew that one of the most dangerous things to do was to let the body dehydrate and this was about the least amount our bodies would need. However, we found that during these three days we were exceeding our ration. It was then that Maurice explained the true position to me. We had only managed by rowing to gain ten miles south and we would have to row for, at least, another ten to twelve days to attain sufficient southing to keep on the same latitude as the Galápagos Islands—but the current was taking us west faster than we rowed south. This, in simple terms, meant that however hard we rowed we would still pass north of the Galápagos Islands.

MAURICE

MARCH 9TH

Maralyn brooded for some time and left the raft and clambered into the dinghy. Picking up the oars she thrust them upright down each side of the thwart and guyed them fore and aft with a thin line. Between these two "masts" she rigged a sail bag as a sail.

In the light southeast wind the sail worked well. "You'll be driving us northwest," I said.

"And toward a shipping lane—and toward the American coast!" Maralyn retorted.

What could I say? It was no use explaining that once we were out of the doldrum belt we would meet the northeast trade winds again and these would drive us southwest away from the American continent. There was only one thing that I could really hope for and that was to meet a possible counter current running east just north of the cold Humboldt current.

Soon after Maralyn had fixed the sail we encountered an electrical storm; more picturesque than violent. The sky was lit by momentary flashes of light charging from the tall and majestic cumulo-nimbus clouds that now towered above us. Thunder rolled over us like loud and tumultuous gunfire. Yet there was no rain. The display soon finished and left us fractionally cooler.

The four days that followed were even hotter; the sun shining from an almost cloudless sky; there was no wind. We wilted during the hottest part of the day under the raft's canopy, trying to keep cool by means of evaporation, draping our bodies with our spare clothes soaked in seawater. Drop by drop we conserved our depleting water supply.

Our main hope of survival now was to meet a ship. We kept a strict watch, two hours each throughout the day and night and reasoned that, with the colossal amount of shipping going through the Panama Canal, at least one ship would pass our way.

What I had failed to comprehend was the vastness of that ocean and the fact that we were a mere speck of human flotsam.

MARALYN

So the first week drew to a close. The days had gone fairly quickly as we had managed to keep ourselves occupied and everything was new and strange.

We had seen many prehistoric-looking turtles and it amazed us how unafraid of us they were. They would swim in a leisurely fashion around the raft and then disappear underneath. They rubbed and bumped the bottom and emerged again on the other side. After our initial surprise and delight at their presence we began to worry about damage to the raft from the barnacles and, in the case of young turtles, the spines on their backs. Surely continual rubbing would chafe and puncture the thin floor of the raft? Next time one approached we turned it around and pushed it off in the opposite direction. But they were very persistent and returned time and time again. Eventually, of course, we became angry and frustrated and we gave them a clout on the head with one of the raft paddles. This treatment surprised them and kept them at bay for a while but ten minutes later they would return, so it turned out to be a constant running battle between us and the turtles.

MARCH 12TH

I mentioned to Maurice the possibility of catching one and eating it, but as we still had a stock of tinned food, albeit very small, Maurice decided to spare them until it was absolutely necessary to kill.

MAURICE

We could not think why turtles should find our raft so congenial. Was it to shelter from the sun, or just to rub themselves on the fabric, ridding themselves of parasites? In the early afternoon when we heard a gasp that invaded the silent world around us, we prepared ourselves for what was usually a very uncomfortable time. Sure enough there was a bump, which lifted the sextant case several inches out of place. Followed by another bump toward the center of the raft, and another. . . . It went on with such frequency that our bodies inevitably received a number of blows. Then there was another gasp as a turtle surfaced to breathe.

Almost simultaneously we both now decided to capture this one for its meat.

MARALYN

We were having breakfast in the raft when I saw a ship! I shouted excitedly to Maurice; rescue was at hand! It was about two miles away and closing. In the thin light of the early morning it appeared like a dream ship; only eight days and our ordeal was over!

Maurice climbed into the dinghy and shortened the lines between the two craft. As he was doing this I collected all our flares together and laid them out ready for use. The ship appeared to be a small fishing boat or maybe a private yacht, and, on her present course, she would pass about one mile away.

As she drew level with us Maurice asked for the first flare—a smoke flare—and with mounting excitement I handed it to him. He tore off the tape and struck the top with the igniter—nothing happened. For long seconds we stared at the useless object and it was with a cry of exasperation that Maurice threw it into the sea. "It's a dud. A bloody dud!" I handed him a second flare and this time we both heaved a sigh of relief as it ignited. As the glow began to diminish I handed him a second red flare. There was no answering signal from the ship and she still maintained her course. A third flare was used—our hopes were fading rapidly.

"How many flares are left?"

"Three: two white and one red."

"Hand me another one—she must see us!" I could see the boat going further and further away. We hadn't been seen. It was pointless using the other two flares.

While Maurice sat dejectedly in the dinghy I began to wave my oil-skin jacket although I knew it was no use. After a few minutes Maurice asked me to stop and save my energy and reluctantly I did so. By now the ship's funnel was only visible in the swells on the horizon and before many more minutes had passed the ocean was ours again.

MAURICE

I think for the first time in my life I felt true compassion as I saw the disappointment and sadness in Maralyn's eyes. Our morale at this stage took a further plunge, there was nothing to alleviate our despair. We finished our meal in silence. Our position was becoming daily more critical—our food was running low and, if rain did not come soon, water would have to be restricted to about half a pint each per day.

MARALYN

As we rested during the heat of the day we discussed the ship and the reason why she had not seen us and I came to the conclusion that as it was early (8 A.M.) the crew must have been at breakfast, possibly leaving the vessel on autopilot.

Then the subject got around to food and inevitably the turtle we still had in the dinghy. Our gas had run out and I had only just managed to warm the tin the previous night. The remaining tins of food would have to be eaten cold. I suggested using the turtle's meat as bait to catch fish to supplement our diet, but unfortunately we had failed to repack the fish hooks and line into our emergency pack at Panama.

That evening over our cold meal we agreed that if we wanted to survive we had to kill the turtle and decided the best time was next morning before the sun got too high.

MAURICE

MARCH 13TH

At dawn the following morning Maralyn and I sat in the dinghy and planned the killing. Our instruments were simple—a blunt stainless steel mariner's knife, a mild steel penknife honed to some degree of sharpness on a leather sheath, and a pair of stainless steel scissors.

The reptile lay on the floor of the dinghy in a very docile manner. Both of us felt sick at heart, but we had to kill it if we were to live.

"I'll try knocking it out," I said. If it was unconscious I felt it would not struggle and the slaughter might not be too bad.

I lifted the turtle on to the side tube so that its head protruded over the side. I remember my surprise at discovering that, unlike its shore-based brother, the tortoise, its head did not fully retract into the heart-shaped carapace. The head, ugly yet fascinating, had no teeth. Sadly I wished that it would have been possible to have studied the various tortoise species under better circumstances.

Lifting a paddle over my head I brought it down with a resounding crash on to the turtle's skull. Then again, and again. The turtle ceased its movement, it was unconscious. It had not uttered a sound; to our ears it was mute.

MARALYN

I knew the only way to kill it was to cut its throat, or decapitate it, and I also knew that I would have to do it as Maurice would have to hold it still. I didn't want to kill it, either; it was so friendly and helpless, but we had to be practical and ruthless if we wanted to live. We knew we couldn't put off the deed any longer and I agreed to do the butchery if Maurice could somehow immobilize it.

Maurice stunned the turtle by hitting it over the head with a paddle. It was then held upside down on the dinghy thwart, its head hanging down over a bowl. I then began the gruesome task of slitting its throat. The first stroke of the knife made no impression at all and it took many minutes to hack a small gash in its throat. I expected its skin to be tough but this thick, rubbery, leathery skin was a surprise and our knife totally inadequate for the job.

It was at this point that the turtle came to life again and began to struggle, flailing around with its flippers and claws. I felt an unreasonable anger against the creature for making a difficult job more so and Maurice had a hard task to hold it in place. It took a lot of effort to keep the neck stretched and when the head was half severed I dug deep for the arteries and, as the rich blood spurted over my hands, the turtle ceased its struggle.

The bowl filled with thick red blood and although we had read of people drinking turtle blood, the idea was so revolting that it was emptied into the sea. Immediately, hordes of fish converged on the dinghy and began eating the congealed blood, making loud sucking noises as they greedily devoured the contents of the bowl. I had great difficulty washing my hands as they swarmed toward my fingers as soon as they entered the water.

The next part of the butchery was to remove the lower shell or plastron. After scoring the perimeter deeply, Maurice cut through it with the penknife and eventually we could prize both halves of the shell away leaving the rich white meat exposed. I hacked about four large steaks from each shoulder blade and we slipped the rest of the carcass over the side glad to be rid of the bloody mess and relieved it was all over.

MAURICE

Hundreds of fish seized the remaining meat and the blood, and began to devour it all with a terrifying haste.

"We *must* fish," Maralyn said, excited by the sight of so many fish. "And I think I know of a way to do it." She climbed into the raft and after some little time rummaging about, returned to the dinghy clutching the pliers and several stainless steel safety pins. Without another word she cut away the clip portion of one pin and bent it into a small hook. She then threaded thin cord through the spring hoop and tied it with a single-loop Turle knot.

"There," she said triumphantly. Once more Maralyn had displayed her genius at improvization. I asked, "Where did you find those pins?" She began making another hook, and without looking up answered, "In the first-aid kit. I remembered seeing them when I sorted everything out."

"Do you think they will work?" I asked, immediately regretting the uselessness of the question.

"We'll soon find out," Maralyn replied and began baiting the hook with a small piece of turtle meat. She dropped the line into the water and the meat was immediately seized by several fish who tore it away from the hook. The meat was so soft that it would not stay on. Maralyn tried again but with no more success. "The meat isn't tough enough," she said in an exasperated voice, "Let's look for some tougher steaks." Our search among the meat revealed no coarse flesh, but I noticed that several of the steaks were lined with a membrane.

"Try this," I said, handing Maralyn a piece of meat cut with the membrane attached. Maralyn carefully baited the hook once more, ensuring that the membrane was securely pierced. This time, although the fish pounced upon the meat, it stayed on the hook, and in a very short time Maralyn pulled the line on board with a beautiful silver fish firmly attached to it.

I grabbed the wriggling slippery creature and hit it repeatedly on the back of the head with the mariner's knife until it died. The fish were now in fact taking the hook. Maralyn, without stopping would bait the hook, throw it over the side and land a fish on board. This did not succeed every time, but the fish came in quickly enough to supply us with ample for our morning meal.

The most abundant variety was the flat, somewhat ugly, purple-gray trigger fish, six-to-nine-inches long and oval in shape. Its head occupied nearly half the body, and it had two retractable spines toward the back of the head. The teeth protruded from a relatively small mouth. These fish were to become our main source of food. They were easy to catch and simple to cut up and fillet, although we suffered bites from their teeth and numerous cuts and scratches from their spines. One or two of these scratches caused septic wounds on my thumbs.

While Maralyn fished, I would gut the fish and separate the livers, and hard and soft roes from the females and males respectively. By the time I had finished, Maralyn had started cutting away the heads: then I would slit the underside of each toward the tail. Maralyn followed me by cutting the flesh away from the backbone so that I could strip the fillets away from the skin and tail. Finally only one more thing had to be done. We gouged the eyes out of the head and, sometimes when fish were scarce and we were hungry, we took the heart and anything edible out of the head. For our meal we then had the white-meat steaks, delicacies which we called "sweetmeats," or "poops," as Maralyn would call them, and the eyeballs, which we found full of thirst-satisfying liquid.

To enable us to catch fish for our morning and evening meals we had to make sure several fish steaks were kept from each catch for bait. We therefore seized every opportunity to keep this bait fresh, replacing it whenever we could.

MARALYN

I chopped the fillets into smallish pieces and placed an equal amount in two bowls. We then returned to the raft and sat facing each other, our raw meal between us, each waiting for the other to begin eating. Maurice was the first to take a bite and tried to encourage me to eat the raw flesh. I ate one fillet but I couldn't face eating any more. I knew I would have to conquer the revulsion I felt.

That evening we used the rest of the turtle meat to catch more fish and this time I managed to eat a little more but not enough to survive on, but gradually my intake of raw fish increased until I could almost match Maurice.

MAURICE

The weather changed soon after our first fishing episode. The wind came boisterously from the southeast, piling the sea into short, steep waves, which gave an uncomfortable motion to the raft. All around us the clouds increased. Dare we hope that they would bring rain? None came and our daily wearisome routine of fishing and gutting continued. Our ration of water was barely adequate, and we tried sucking the fish flesh and bones for additional moisture.

It was at this time that Maralyn devised a game of dominoes.

MARALYN

To keep ourselves occupied during the day we read our books, each taking a turn at reading a page out loud. We would then stop and discuss various aspects, which would lead often to talking about other things. "Cat's cradle" amused us for a short time using an odd piece of string. When we tired of this we played word games. Each of us in turn would select a word and using the letters contained in the word we would quietly list all the words of four or more letters we could discover. This kept our minds active and occupied us for several hours, but how I wished I had had the presence of mind to take our pocket chess set. We had no means of making any improvised chess men but we first made dominoes using blank pages out of the logbook. The dominoes were cut from

strips of paper about one inch by two inches and folded into four. We had
to play in an unorthodox manner as it was impossible to play correctly by
placing each domino end to end; they would have either blown away or
been soaked. We each took six pieces representing dominoes and wrote
each move on a piece of paper: for instance, I would write down "2–" (2/
blank) and hand Maurice the piece of paper; he would write "–6" (blank/6)
and so we would continue until the game was completed.

MARCH 14TH

During the first two weeks we observed many whales, both sperm and
killer whales. Usually they were in pairs and the sperm whales were always closer to us passing about twenty to thirty feet away. I sat anxiously
until they had passed.

Our closest contact with a whale while adrift was quite remarkable and
I can now look back on the occasion and realize it was a unique meeting
that very few people have unintentionally experienced. Strangely enough
this time the whale was alone, perhaps it was looking for a mate! A huge
sperm whale surfaced about twenty feet behind us. I heard the *whoosh*
of air being expelled and put my head through the vent and shouted to
Maurice. We stumbled to the entrance to watch the brute's slow advance.
It was not going to pass by like all the others. We could find no words to
speak, but sat entranced together wondering how the monster would react.

Maurice was very calm and said that there was nothing we could do.
He sat by the raft doorway while I knelt beside him and I gazed in fascinated horror at this huge creature. It was now so very close; within
touching distance. The small round blow-hole looked wet and moist like
a dog's nose; it opened slowly and a jet of moisture-laden air, so fine it
gave the appearance of steam, shot into the air and fell like a shower of
rain on the raft.

Maurice tightened his grip on my hand and quietly explained that if
the whale tipped the raft over it might be difficult for him to rescue me. He
told me to hold on to the dinghy ropes and not to let go. I nodded agreement but I don't think his advice really sank in. I think this was the first
time that Maurice was worried about my inability to swim.

We held on to each other as the enormous creature became stationary
alongside. I was biting my lip to stop myself crying and I remember hearing Maurice saying quietly—"Why doesn't he go away and leave us in
peace?" The portion of its body opposite the doorway was the back and I
remember thinking how cow-like it was—jet black shining with mois-

ture its ribs showing through the skin. The leviathan maintained this position for what seemed to us an incredibly long time, in fact, it was probably no longer than ten minutes but we expected its fluke to cleave us in two any moment.

At last, as no response was forthcoming to its advances, the whale started moving away from us and began to sink below the surface. "Don't dive now," I whispered in the tenseness of the moment but with a sudden movement its tail was perpendicular and it disappeared below the surface of the sea in a near vertical dive with hardly a splash. Our last view of it was a huge black fan-shaped tail starkly outlined against a brilliant blue sky. Then it was gone deep into the ocean and I was left speechless and trembling with the raft rocking gently as the ripples in the sea subsided.

When whales appeared after this incident I kept a wary eye on them until we knew they had passed. I would not like to have a repeat performance!

MAURICE

We sat for some minutes looking at the spot where the whale had vanished. "What a pity we didn't take a photograph. No one will believe us when we talk about it," Maralyn said eventually. Her confidence in our survival surprised and also depressed me, and I started hauling the dinghy alongside. "I think it's time to start fishing for supper," I said. This time we reversed our roles and I fished.

It was interesting to note the contrast in opinions between Maurice and Maralyn. Whereas one might consider the man to be the person to take charge and figure out how best to proceed in this situation, Maralyn is the one who constantly shows her ingenuity and optimism in the face of hardship and setbacks. This observation is not meant to be denigrating in any way to Mr. Bailey—a prolonged survival situation can be most perilous to a person's mental state, draining them of initiative and willpower when they need it most. He was a lucky man to have the person who was best able to help him get through this ordeal with his mind and body intact—his wife.

Maralyn Bailey passed away in 2002. A diligent search for more information on Mr. Bailey turned up no recent data.

A FAMILY AGAINST THE OCEAN

Dougal Robertson (1924–1992)

From *Survive the Savage Sea*

At approximately 10 A.M. on June 15, 1972, two hundred miles away from the Galápagos Islands, the thirty-nine-foot schooner Lucette *was rammed and sunk by a pod of killer whales, leaving its crew, consisting of the Robertson family (parents Dougal and Lyn, and their children Douglas, Neil, and Sandy) and a friend of theirs named Robin Williams, adrift on the Pacific Ocean with a fiberglass dinghy and a life raft their only protection against the ocean. For the next thirty-seven days, this intrepid group would battle weather and the ocean to save themselves. Their adventure was made into a television movie in 1991, starring Robert Urich and Ali McGraw.*

In this case, it is not only a matter of survival that haunts our narrator, but the fact that he and his wife also have three of their children to look after as well. The following excerpt covers the first six days after being set adrift, and as is soon discovered, there are different problems for six people in a small boat than there are for one or two.

FIRST DAY

We sat on the salvaged pieces of flotsam lying on the raft floor, our faces a pale bilious color under the bright yellow canopy, and stared at each other, the shock of the last few minutes gradually seeping through to our consciousness. Neil, his teddy bears gone, sobbed in accompaniment to Sandy's hiccup cry, while Lyn repeated the Lord's Prayer, then, comforting them, sang the hymn "For Those in Peril on the Sea." Douglas and Robin watched at the doors of the canopy to retrieve any useful pieces of debris, which might float within reach and gazed with dumb longing at the distant five-gallon water container, bobbing its polystyrene lightness ever further away from us in the steady trade wind. The dinghy *Ednamair* wallowed, swamped, nearby with a line attached to it from the raft and our eyes traveled over and beyond to the heaving undulations of the horizon, already searching for a rescue ship even while knowing there would not be one. Our eyes traveled fruitlessly across the limitless waste of sea and sky, then once more ranged over the scattering debris. Of the killer whales, which had so recently shattered our very existence, there was no sign. Lyn's sewing basket floated close and it was brought aboard followed by a couple of empty boxes, the canvas raft cover, and a plastic cup.

I leaned across to Neil and put my arm around him, "It's alright now, son, we're safe and the whales have gone." He looked at me reproachfully. "We're not crying 'cos we're frightened," he sobbed, "we're crying 'cos Lucy's gone." Lyn gazed at me over their heads, her eyes filling with tears. "Me, too," she said, and after a moment added, "I suppose we'd better find out how we stand."

This was the question I had been dreading; feelings of guilt, that our present predicament was not only due to my unorthodox ideas on educating our children (there had been plenty of critics to object that I was needlessly jeopardizing the children's lives) but also that I had failed to foresee this type of disaster, now engulfed me, and this, added to the fact that we had lost almost everything we possessed as well as *Lucette,* depressed me to the depths of despair. How could I have been so foolish as to trust our lives to such an old schooner! Then I saw, once again, in my mind's eye that damage under the floorboards of *Lucette.* Not only had the frames withstood the impact of the blow, but the new garboard strake of inch and a half pitchpine, fitted in Malta at the surveyor's recommendation, had been one of the hull planks, which had been smashed inward. Her hull had taken a full minute to sink below the waves, but a modern boat, constructed with less regard to brute strength than *Lucette,* would have sustained much heavier damage and sunk even more quickly, with more terrible results.

I looked at Douglas, he had grown to manhood in our eighteen months at sea together; the twins, previously shy, introspective farm lads, had become interested in the different peoples we had met and their various ways of life, and were now keen to learn more; I tried to ease my conscience with the thought that they had derived much benefit from their voyage and that our sinking was as unforeseeable as an earthquake, or an airplane crash, or anything to ease my conscience.

We cleared a space on the floor and opened the survival kit, which was part of the raft's equipment, and was contained in a three-foot-long polythene cylinder; slowly we took stock: ·

Vitamin-fortified bread and glucose for ten men for two days.

Eighteen pints of water, eight flares (two parachute, six hand).

One bailer, two large fishhooks, two small, one spinner and trace, and a twenty-five pound breaking strain fishing line.

A patent knife, which would not puncture the raft (or anything else for that matter), a signal mirror, torch, first-aid box, two sea anchors, instruction book, bellows, and three paddles.

In addition to this there was the bag of a dozen onions, which I had given to Sandy, to which Lyn had added a one-pound tin of biscuits and a bottle containing about half a pound of glucose sweets, ten oranges, and six lemons. How long would this have to last us? As I looked around our meager stores my heart sank and it must have shown on my face for Lyn put her hand on mine; "We must get these boys to land," she said quietly. "If we do nothing else with our lives, we must get them to land!" I looked at her and nodded, "Of course, we'll make it!" The answer came from my heart but my head was telling me a different story. We were over two hundred miles down wind and current from the Galápagos Islands. To try to row the small dinghy into two hundred miles of rough ocean weather was an impossible journey even if it was tried by only two of us in an attempt to seek help for the others left behind in the raft. The fact that the current was against us as well only put the seal of hopelessness on the idea. There was no way back.

The Marquesas Islands lay 2,800 miles to the west but we had no compass or means of finding our position; if, by some miraculous feat of endurance, one of us made the distance, the chances of striking an island were remote.

The coast of Central America, more than a thousand miles to the northeast, lay on the other side of the windless Doldrums, that dread area of calms and squalls, which had inspired Coleridge's

Water, water, everywhere,
And all the boards did shrink;
Water, water, everywhere,
Nor any drop to drink.

I was a Master Mariner, I thought ruefully, *not an ancient one, and could count on no ghostly crew to get me out of this dilemma!*

What were our chances if we followed the textbook answer, "Stay put and wait for rescue?" In the first place we wouldn't be missed for at least five weeks and if a search was made, where would they start looking in three thousand miles of ocean? In the second place the chance of seeing a passing vessel in this area was extremely remote and could be discounted completely, for of the two possible shipping routes from Panama to Tahiti and New Zealand, one lay four hundred miles to the south and the other three hundred miles to the north. Looking at the food, I estimated that six of us might live for ten days and since we could expect no rain in this area for at least six months, apart from an odd shower, our chances of survival beyond ten days were doubtful indeed. It seemed to me that we stood a very good chance of becoming one of Robin's statistics.

My struggle to reach a decision, gloomy whichever way I looked at it, showed on my face, and Lyn leaned forward. "Tell us how we stand," she said, looking around, "we want to know the truth." They all nodded, "What chance have we?" I could not tell them I thought they were going to die so I slowly spelled out the alternatives, and then suddenly I knew there was only one course open to us; we must sail with the trade winds to the Doldrums four hundred miles to the north. We stood a thin chance of reaching land but the only possible shipping route lay in that direction, our only possible chance of rain water in any quantity lay in that direction even if it was four hundred miles away, and our only possible chance of reaching land lay in that direction, however small that chance might be. We would work and fight for our lives at least; better than dying in idleness! "We must get these boys to land," Lyn had said. I felt the reality of the decision lifting the hopelessness from my shoulders and looked around; five pairs of eyes watched me as I spoke, Lyn once again with her arms round the twins, Douglas and Robin each at their lookout posts watching for any useful debris that might come within reach. "We have no alternative," I said, "we'll stay here for twenty-four hours to see if any other wreckage appears, then we must head north and hope to find rain in the Doldrums." I looked around, "We might also find an easterly current there, which will help us to the coast of Central America, if we've not been picked up by then." The lifting of my depression communicated and as I talked of the problems and privations, which confronted us, I saw the resolve harden on Douglas's face. Robin nodded and fired a question about shipping lanes, Lyn smiled at me, not caring that I was offering her torture from thirst, starvation, and probably death if we were not rescued, just so long as we had a working chance. The twins dried their tears and eyed the sweets; we were in business again.

With one of the sea anchors streamed we set to work, clearing the raft floor of the debris we had collected: the huge genoa sail, two hundred feet of nylon fishing line (breaking strain one hundred pounds), three gallons of petrol, two oars, two empty boxes. Lyn's sewing basket was a treasure beyond wealth for not only did it contain the usual threads and needles, but also two scalpel blades, four knitting needles, a blanket pin, hat pin, three plastic bags, a ball of string, buttons, tinfoil, a shoehorn, two small plastic cups, two plastic boxes, two small envelopes of dried yeast, a piece of copper wire one foot long, some elastic, a bottle of soluble aspirin, a pencil, and a biro pen. (What else could one possibly expect to find in a sewing basket!) We also had a half pint of copal varnish, a very sodden edition of a West Indies pilotage book, and one cracked and saturated smoke flare. My watch, a twenty-year-old Rolex Oyster, gave us the time and the first-aid box contained artery forceps and scissors, but otherwise we had no compass, no charts, no instruments of any kind in fact, that would aid our navigation or measure our distance run.

We stowed the mountain of debris as best we could then set to work, our first task being to strip out the long luff wire from the genoa so that it could be used to join the dinghy to the raft. It was at this point that we met our first real drawback for first Robin, then Neil started being seasick, the undulating motion of the raft in the high swell and breaking seas finding them unable to settle to the strange movement. Lyn administered seasick pills from the first-aid box as soon as she thought the boys able to retain them, but they had already lost precious quantities of body fluid. Lyn and I continued to work on the sail while Douglas checked and restowed the rations and equipment. In one of the raft pockets he found two sponges and plugs, with a repair kit for holes, but the glue had completely dried out, rendering the repair kit useless. In another pocket he found the instruction book, which gave little intelligent information on how to preserve one's life in mid-ocean, but gave a lot of superfluous jargon about morale, leadership, and rescue, finishing up with the two most sensible words in the whole book in capital letters, GOOD LUCK!! (The exclamation marks are mine.)

At last we freed the luff wire, about forty feet long and covered with white plastic, then set about cutting a sail for the dinghy, after which we could use the surplus for sheets and covers for warmth at night, since we were all clad in swimming shorts and shirts with the exception of Lyn, who was wearing a nylon housecoat. The wire would make an excellent towrope for the dinghy and I fastened it to the outside of the raft to give us a little more space in which to settle down for the night. As evening drew in we had one biscuit and a sip of water, one orange between six, and a glucose sweet each, generally speaking a pretty sumptuous banquet

in the light of things to come, but meager enough rations for us at that
time.

Lyn sang "The Lord Is My Shepherd," and then prayed most earnestly for our safety. As the sun set, the wind grew suddenly colder and
we shivered as we drew our terylene sailcloth sheets about us. Lyn suddenly laughed "Well, tell us," we urged. "When I was swimming to the
raft," she said, "and it was making that funny noise with the extra gas,
Douglas thought the raft was leaking and blocked the pipes with his
fingers; he shouted to me to give him a patch; in the middle of the Pacific!" She chuckled again. "He kept on so I gave him an orange and
said, 'Will this do?'"

The raft's flotation chambers had gone soft with the cooling of the air,
so while Douglas pumped them firm again, Lyn saw to Neil and Robin,
both still seasick, and I closed the windward door of the canopy, leaving
a peephole for both lookout and ventilation. Robin insisted that he take
his share of the adults' two-hour lookout watches in spite of his sickness,
and as darkness fell we curled around the boxes and tins, legs and bodies
overlapping in places, and tried to rest. The raft was still plunging and lifting in the long fifteen-feet-high swells, while the shorter crested waves,
built up under the force of the local winds, surged heavily around us,
causing the raft to jerk into the troughs as she brought up sharply on the
sea anchor. As we turned and twisted around seeking ease for our aching
limbs, we began to experience curious bumps and sharp nudges through
the inflated floor of the raft; at first I thought something sharp had wedged
under the raft and worried lest it should puncture the flotation chambers,
then I heard Lyn give a faint shriek as she, too, was nudged from below.
Douglas, on lookout, said that he could see large fish swimming under
the raft, dorado, he thought, and they seemed to be after some smaller fish
close under the raft floor.

The bumps and nudges occurred at frequent intervals as the dorado
performed their endless gyrations under the raft, often several times in the
space of a minute. The severity of the bump depended on the speed and
angle of the dorado's impact but generally speaking they were mild compared with the blows from sharks, and quite distinctive from the hard
bump of a turtle's shell under the floor, which we were to experience later.
Turtles were also to bite us through the floor of the raft (no doubt an en-
dearing courtship practice) but never hard enough to penetrate the double
skin, although they were probably responsible for the leaks, which developed in the air chambers of which the raft floor was composed, destroying

the buffered effect, which the air chambers rendered against the assaults
of the fish. There didn't seem to be any shortage of fish around, I thought
hopefully; perhaps we wouldn't find it so difficult to supplement our rations after all, but nonetheless the experience of being poked sharply in
the sit-upon when drowsing, or worse, bitten on sit-upon while asleep,
was quite startling and we never became accustomed to these assaults during our occupation of the raft.

As we settled down again my mind ranged over the events of the last
week for I was trying to remember the distance between the islands in
an attempt to arrive at the coordinates for the position in which we had
sunk. I knew that our latitude was 1°15' S of the equator, from the course
line on the chart, but I could not remember the longitude of Cape
Espinosa although I did remember that Wreck Bay on Chatham Island
had a longitude of about 89°30' W. If only I'd worked out that dead reckoning position a little sooner, but then, if only a lot of things, and one
doesn't normally pay a great deal of attention to terrestrial coordinates
when known land is in sight.

Hood Island, I thought, had been roughly on the same longitude as
Chatham Island, and we had sailed from there at midnight traveling west
by north to Charles Island at about four knots, arriving off Post Office
Bay around three in the afternoon, say sixty miles, and had then turned
west-northwest to round the south point of Isabela Island the following
morning. Allowing for calms and current, I reckoned on a departure of
about 120 miles before we had turned north for Fernandina Island. My
mind came back to the present as the raft floor shuddered under the
assault of a dorado and hearing the mumble of voices I turned sideways, lifting on my elbow to see if Robin, taking over the watch from
Douglas, was fit enough to keep a good lookout; he fumbled around on
the floor of the raft, looking for his glasses, then finding them, leaned out
of the raft and vomited emptily at the sea. "You alright, Robin?" I asked.
He muttered something about being as right as you can be when you're
stranded on a raft in the middle of the Pacific with no food or water and
very seasick; he put his glasses on, "But if there's a ship about, I'll find it!"
He looked at me owlishly in the faint light. "Let me know if you're in
doubt about anything, and don't hesitate to wake me," I said. I turned on
my back again, watching Robin's silhouette moving against the doorway
of the canopy as he scanned the horizon; his six-foot frame was thin, but
he was tough.

My mind switched back to my longitude calculation. We had stopped at the south end of Fernandina where after an exhausting exploration of the lava beds Neil had been so glad to get back to *Lucette*. "Good old Lucy" had been home to him.

I glanced over to where Neil lay asleep, his limbs entangled under Sandy's and on top of Lyn's; he was a very loving child, with unorthodox views and a stubborn streak of determination, which would stand him in good stead in the days to come. Lyn was worried about his seasickness for his young body would not stand up to the loss of fluid as well as Robin's. Douglas grunted as a dorado collided with the raft under him. "We'll have to do something about these fish, Dad," he mumbled, half asleep, "like catching them."

Doggedly I returned to the problem of longitude. We had made a little easting, say fifteen miles, to travel to the northern side of Fernandina Island then about half that distance west to arrive at Cape Espinosa. So with a departure of 112 miles from Wreck Bay the longitude of Espinosa would be roughly 91°20' W.

"Two o'clock!" I jerked awake from my doze to see Robin bending toward me in the darkness. "Aye aye! Everything alright?" I crawled across to the doorway to take over the watch; the stars twinkled brightly in the arch of darkness beyond the sweep of the sea. Robin gagged at the water; "No ships," he muttered and crawled to his place beside Douglas. I peeped around the canopy of the raft at the dinghy; the *Ednamair* lay disconsolately awash at the end of her painter, her white gunwale just visible above the surface of the water. She was helping the sea anchor, I supposed, but we'd have to bail her out first thing in the morning, for the wooden thwarts, which contained the polystyrene flotation reserve, would loosen and come adrift if they became waterlogged.

The water exploded as a thirty-pound dorado leaped high in the air after a flying fish, landing with a slap on its side in a shower of luminescence. I glanced down to where several large fish swam under the raft, constantly rising to skim the underside of the raft's edge, sometimes hitting it a heavy blow with their high jutting foreheads. Douglas was right, we should have to do something about these fish!

SECOND DAY

The long night paled into the beautiful dawn sky of the South Pacific; slowly we collected our scattered wits for already our dreams of being elsewhere than on the raft had taken on the vivid reality of hallucination. Wretched with cramp and discomfort it had been such a simple solution to go next door and there I would find my childhood bed, so clear in every forgotten detail, waiting for me.

The pressure in the raft's flotation chambers had dropped drastically during the night so our first task was to top up with air. We connected the bellows pipe to the non-return valve and started pumping, taking turns to keep the bellows going; after fifteen minutes we could see no improvement in the pressure so we disconnected the bellows and tested them for leaks; there weren't any bad ones, but the air intake didn't close properly and most of the air escaped the way it went in. Douglas and I looked at each other; we knew the answer to this one for the bellows we had used for our old inflatable dinghy had similarly served us. We cut the pipe from the bellows, not without difficulty, for the curve of the knife prevented any sawing action, then placing the pipe in his mouth Douglas blew mightily. We took turns for about a few minutes and the raft was soon back to normal, but we knew even then that we had not seen the last of this particular trouble.

I looked across at Lyn, rubbing the cramp out of the twins' legs. "We'll see to the *Ednamair* after breakfast"; I looked hopefully at the water jar, but it was nearly empty. We had emptied the glucose sweets out of their glass jar so that it could be used to hold drinking water as it was decanted from the tin, for although we had discussed the issue of equal rations of water (there wasn't enough to do that) we had decided simply to pass the jar around, each person limiting him or herself to the minimum needed to carry on; at the same time, the visible water level in the jar enabled everyone to see there was no cheating. Breakfast consisted of one quarter-ounce biscuit, a piece of onion, and a sip of water, except for Robin and Neil who could not eat and were with difficulty persuaded to take some extra water with a seasick pill. We had used two pints of water in one day between six, hardly a maintenance ration under a tropic sun, which I remembered had been placed as high as two pints per person per day! We ate slowly, savoring each taste of onion and biscuit with a new appreciation and, although we hardly felt as if we had breakfasted on bacon and eggs, we were still sufficiently shocked at our altered circumstances not to feel hunger.

Breakfast over, Lyn, with Sandy helping, sorted out the various pieces of sail, which were to be used for bedding, chatting quietly all the while to Neil and Robin. Douglas and I went to the door of the raft and, pulling the dinghy alongside, first attempted to bail it out as it lay swamped, but the waves filled it as fast as we bailed. We turned its stern toward us and, lifting slowly, allowed the bow to submerge, then when we could lift it no higher, I called "Let go!" The dinghy flopped back in the water with three inches of freeboard, we bailed desperately with small bailers, then Douglas took one of the wooden boxes and with massive scoops bailed enough water out to allow him to board the dinghy and bail it dry. We were all cheered by the sight of little *Ednamair* afloat again, and with a cry of delight Douglas held up his Timex watch; it had been lying in the bottom of the dinghy all this time and was still going! He also found what was to prove our most valuable possession, the stainless-steel kitchen knife, which I had thrown in after the fruit.

After a segment of orange each for elevenses we loaded the oars, a paddle, the empty boxes, the petrol can, the hundred-foot raft painter, and the piece of the genoa designated for the dinghy sail, then climbing into the dinghy started work on the jury rig that was to turn the *Ednamair* into a tugboat for our first stage of the journey north. Douglas, in the meantime, helped Lyn to reorganize the inside of the raft now that there was much more room, and topped up the flotation chambers with air.

I rigged one oar in the mast step with appropriate fore and back stays (I had rigged *Ednamair* as a sailing dinghy in Colon, but leeboards, mast and sail had been stowed below in *Lucette* for the ocean passage and had of course been lost), then cutting notches in the raft paddle, bent the head of the sail onto it to form a square sail. I had previously taken the precaution of making the luff wire, shackled to the towing straps of the raft, fast to the ringbolt in the bow of the dinghy, in case the nylon painter had frayed. I had decided the dinghy would have to perform her function of towing by proceeding stern first, for her cutaway stern could not be exposed to the overtaking waves without danger of swamping. The paddle was made fast to the top of the oar, and the sail foot secured to the two ends of the other oar, placed athwartships across the rowlock sockets. A violent jerk sent me sprawling into the bottom of the boat and I realized that we were operational.

I climbed back aboard the raft for a lunch of a small piece of fortified bread, of which there was about a pound and a half in the emergency rations along with eight ounces of glucose, and a mouthful of water; I felt very thirsty after my exertions in the raft. *Ednamair* was now straining at the leash so I called to Douglas to trip the sea anchor and haul it aboard; the time was two o'clock in the afternoon and we had started our voyage to the Doldrums, and, I shuddered at the thought of the alternative, rain. I estimated our position at latitude 1° S and longitude 94°40' W or, more accurately, two hundred miles west of Cape Espinosa.

The white plastic-covered luff wire was now snapping taut with considerable force as *Ednamair* yawed at the end of her towrope, so having little use for the petrol I lashed the can to the center of the towing wire to act as a tension buffer, which it did quite effectively. We now turned our attention to the flotation chambers of the raft to see if we could find any leaks. The raft, an old model, had been a gift from our friend Captain Siggi Thorsteinsson of the Icelandic rescue craft *Bonnie*; Siggi with his wife Etta and their family had run parallel to our voyage on *Lucette* from Falmouth to Miami; we remembered, with deep gratitude, his concern when our previous inflatable had become such a doubtful asset that he had presented us with one of the two, which they carried. I had expressed my hope at the time that we would never find occasion to use it, thanked him warmly for it, cursed its unwieldy bulk many a time on our cramped coach roof and felt comforted by its presence thereon, nevertheless. Now? Well, you never can tell, but we probably owed our lives to it. The double canopy alone was worth a gallon of water a day to us in keeping out the heat of the sun, and its emergency rations were available to us now only because they were already stowed inside the raft.

We examined the raft's flotation chambers as well as we could, pouring water over all the exposed surface areas, but could find no leaks, although there were one or two repair patches, and finally put down the loss of air to seepage through the treated fabric of the raft. We arranged a regular routine of topping up on each watch to keep the raft as rigid as possible, for the continuous flexing of the softened chambers by the waves was bound to cause wear. The double floor in the after section of the raft, which was divided by a central flotation piece, had been holed from below and a tiny hole in the upper skin was allowing the seawater to seep through to our bedding and required us to perform mopping up operations at fairly frequent intervals. We tried to repair the leak with sticking plaster but with no success. The sun now dipping toward the horizon, our attention was turned to other things, which had to be checked before nightfall. The lashings on the towing wire, the sail and the rigging on the dinghy were inspected and made secure where they looked in need of attention. I tripped the two small drogues at the forward end of the raft to increase our speed, which I estimated to be about one knot, plus a set from the current of one knot, all in a nor' nor'westerly direction.

We gathered around for "tea," and our meal of a one-and-a-half square inch biscuit each, a small piece of glucose and a mouthful of water was shared by all, Neil and Robin having regained their sea legs with the help of the pills. As dusk drew in, Lyn settled the twins to sleep after playing "I Spy," and singing to them. Robin was more cheerful and chatted about his travels across the continent of America by bus, working casually for his keep, and as we listened, we wondered if we would ever see land again. During the day Lyn had cut pieces of sail for the twins and Douglas to write letters, telling their friends in England and America what had happened, while she had written a loving farewell letter to our nineteen-year-old daughter Anne who had left us in the Bahamas to follow her own destiny. Robin had written to his mother, and I added a footnote to Anne's letter sending her my best wishes for her happiness in life with my love. In the footnote to Robin's I apologized for having been instrumental in bringing his life to such an untimely end. These farewell notes were placed in a waterproof wrapping and tucked in one of the pockets of the raft, for we knew that when the time came to write such farewell letters, we would be unable, both in mind and body, to cope with the effort. We all felt a little sad and depressed at the prospect of our imminent demise especially Neil, who, I felt, could visualize more clearly the privations, which lay ahead of us without knowing the possibilities of the ways in which they could be avoided. He had looked a very sad and forlorn little boy, lying in his mother's arms gazing, unblinking, into space and seeing heaven knows what terrors in his mind's eye, but now tucked in beside Sandy under sheets of sailcloth, chatted quietly about friends in Miami and Colon.

Robin had first watch tonight and I warned him which points needed watching on the dinghy which, in the increasing wind, was pulling hard on the towrope and yawing widely as the pull on her sail swung the stern around. (The dinghy, as explained, was proceeding stern first to permit her to ride the seas without swamping.) As I settled down beside Lyn she leaned across and whispered, close to tears, "If Neil 'goes' I shall not allow him to go alone." I felt shocked that she could even be thinking in terms of death, even though we had just completed our farewell letters "in case." I put my hand out and clasped hers; "I don't think it will come to that," I said steadily, "but if it did, you could help more by staying." Lyn was one of the most competent people I have ever met to have helping in an emergency, and my deep respect for her capabilities as a nurse and as a wife and mother had grown steadily over our twenty years of married life. I feared that she was holding back on something in Neil's medical condition that I did not know of, to make her so despondent, but as she talked it became clear to me that the shock of the last thirty-six hours was catching up on her, as it had with me, so I talked of our chances of being picked up and if we weren't, of the possibility of reaching the coast of Central America, maintaining ourselves on fish, which I felt we could catch, and rainwater to drink. "And the rain our drink," she murmured (Han Suyin had worked for a while as a doctor in the Hong Kong hospital where Lyn had been sister) and I knew she was no longer thinking of death, or for that matter of Malaya, but of the happy days we had spent sailing together in Hong Kong where we were married. "I'll draw you a map tomorrow," I said, wriggling around to find a comfortable place for my head; there wasn't one. Neil's and Sandy's legs were crossed over the top of my body and I could feel the pool of seawater, which had seeped through the hole in the floor, gathering under my bottom. "Pass me the sponge and the bailer," I muttered to Lyn, as she got ready to go on watch, and silently she passed them to me, our hands touching and understanding in the darkness. Dry underneath again, I lay down to think in the long hours of the night of how long it would take us to reach the Doldrums and of our chances of finding rain there; an exercise that was to occupy my nights with increasing urgency as our meager store of water cans gradually dwindled. Robin had puffed rather ineffectually at the inflating tube before he went off watch, but the raft was still pretty soft, so I stuck the end in my mouth and gave it a good blow at both ends; Robin would get better at it as he got used to the idea.

THIRD DAY

My watch, in the dawn hours of the morning, started with a clear sky, but, as the sun tinted the clouds, the wind freshened again from the south and the tall flowery cumulus, pink peaked with gray bases, seemed heavy enough to give rain. As soon as it was light I pulled in the dinghy and climbed aboard to inspect the sail fastenings and stays, one of which had worked loose in the night. While I was securing the stay I caught sight of a small black shape under the wooden box by the thwart; I stooped and lifted our first contribution from the sea, a flying fish of about eight inches. I gutted and descaled it, then passed it over to Lyn, now awake, for her to marinate it in a squeeze of lemon juice, which acted as a cooking agent. We breakfasted at seven, an hour later, each savoring our tiny piece of fish done to a turn in the lemon juice, followed by a crunchy piece of onion and a mouthful of water. The raft had begun pitching heavily again, surging on the crests of the breaking sea and dropping steeply into the troughs. To our disappointment, both Neil and Robin started being seasick again and though we offered them seasick pills they decided to do without and try to get used to the motion of the raft instead.

The waves began to break over the stern of the raft, and with swells of up to twenty feet high, it looked as if we were in for a bad day. *Ednamair* yawed violently as the wind gusted in her sail and she pulled hard on the towrope, lifting it clear of the water at times. I decided to take a reef in the sail to ease the strain on the towing straps of the raft, so Douglas hauled the dinghy alongside the raft and held her while I balanced precariously on the seat. To reef her, I simply tied a rope around the belly of the sail, giving it an hourglass effect and reducing its effective pulling power by half. I had just completed the operation and was standing up again to return when a large breaker surged around the raft and caught the dinghy broadside. As she tilted, I lost balance and fell, grabbing at the mast to prevent myself falling into the sea; *Ednamair* tilted sharply with the increased leverage and the sea rushed in over the gunwale in a wave. Before I could let go the mast and drop to the floor of the dinghy, it was swamped. Luckily we retained about three inches of freeboard and before the next wave could complete the damage, I dived through the door of the canopy into the raft, and the dinghy, relieved of my weight, floated a little higher. We bailed desperately for several minutes from the raft and then, gaining on the influx of water slopping over the gunwale, we finally got enough freeboard to allow me to return to the *Ednamair* and bail it dry again. In the night, I had thought of the possibility of us taking to the dinghy altogether and leaving the raft, but this incident served to highlight the difficulty of any such move; the subject of trim with a very small freeboard would be of paramount importance and now I doubted if the dinghy could take the six of us and remain afloat in the open sea.

After our exhausting morning, we rested awhile, lunching on a mouthful of water and a few "crumbs" of a type of fortified bread which, although made up in tablet form, disintegrated at the first touch and made the conveyance of the crumbs from container to mouth an operation that required great care to avoid spilling and usually resulted in some waste, even when we licked the stray crumbs off our clothes. This was followed by a piece of orange.

The clouds thickened as the day advanced and the high cumulus began to drop rain in isolated showers. The wind freshened still further and with the surf of breaking waves slopping through the canopy door at the rear of the raft, we closed the drawstrings on the flaps as much as was possible without cutting off all ventilation. With the large blanket pin I punched bigger holes in the empty water cans and made plugs to fit them in case a shower should cross us and give us water, while Douglas blew lustily into the pipe to make the raft as rigid as possible in the heavy seas. *Ednamair* bounced around at the end of her towrope like a pup on a leash and I was considering taking the sail down altogether when the patter of raindrops on the canopy warned us that we were about to get rain. A pipe led down from the center of the rain catchment area on the roof and, pulling this to form a depression in the roof, we prepared to gather our first rainwater. With fascinated eyes we gazed at the mouth of the pipe, at the liquid that dribbled from the end, bright yellow, and saltier than the sea. As soon as the salt had been washed off the roof, we managed to collect half a pint of yellowish rubbery-tasting liquid before the shower passed over. I looked at the jar of fluid (one could hardly call it water) sadly; we would need to do a lot better than that if we were to survive.

The raft, now pitching heavily, required blowing up every hour to keep it rigid, and the undulations and jerks did nothing to ease the spasms of seasickness, which Neil and Robin were suffering; they both looked drawn and pale, refusing even water in spite of Lyn's pleading. As the raft slid up the twenty-foot swells to the breaking combers at the top, Lyn prayed desperately for calm weather and for rain, urging that the rest of us should join her in prayer with such insistence that I had to remind her that freedom of thought and religion was a matter of individual choice and no one should be coerced. Lyn looked at me, startled, and continued praying aloud while Robin, on the verge of making a facetious remark, stilled his tongue with it half said; although he described himself as a non-practicing Christian the religious fervor with which Lyn had appealed to us embarrassed him. Silence, interrupted only by the hiss and roar of the breaking waves, followed Lyn's praying, then quietly she sang "The Lord Is My Shepherd" to the twins as I put away the still-empty cans and the jar containing the foul-tasting yellow stuff; it was better than seawater.

I passed the water jar around for "sippers" before our meager ration of biscuit, reminding everyone that our supplies were now very low and that only minimal amounts should be taken. "We must try to drink less than two pints per day between us," I said. "We have only twelve tins left and we still have over three hundred miles to go." A quart of water each for the next three hundred miles, it didn't sound much.

As darkness closed in and the first watchkeeper settled to his two-hour vigil, I could feel the bump and bite of the dorado fish through the bottom of the raft and resolved to try to catch one in the morning. Neil and Sandy were sleeping soundly after helping to blow up the raft and mop up the water, which was now coming through the floor at a greater rate than before. They looked so vulnerable that my heart turned over at the prospect of what lay ahead for them; death by thirst, or starvation, or just a slow deterioration into exhaustion. I heard Lyn's voice many times that night, in my mind: "We must get these boys to land," and sleep would not come to ease the burden of my conscience.

FOURTH DAY

During the night the wind fell to a gentle breeze and seas calmed to tolerable conditions, which allowed the raft to move easily in the seaway. Dawn brought a clear sky and the promise of a hot day, but at least the calmer weather would allow Neil and Robin to make a recovery from their seasickness. The cry of "pissoir" for the bailing jar, which we used for urinating in, to avoid the necessity of the persons relieving themselves to get to the doorway over sleeping bodies, was heard less often now and our urine had taken on a very dark color. I had contemplated tasting some to find out if it was at all palatable but Lyn said that she had already tried hers. "It was very salty," she said rather sadly. "I understand from an article I once read by some professor that we might derive some benefit from drinking each other's." "Would you like to try some of mine?" I said. We both burst out laughing; "Not yet, thanks." Douglas looked at us disgustedly from the doorway. "For God's sake!" he said. "What's for breakfast?"

I climbed over to *Ednamair* to shake the reef out of the sail, and to my delight found a large and a small flying fish in the bottom of the boat. They were duly dressed, then divided with much ceremony, and the heads saved for bait. Robin and Neil looked better now and were able to eat their share with a little extra water. I watched Lyn carefully to see that she took her sip of water, and when she didn't, insisted that she should do so, for we could not afford to have her sick, anyway not that way; if we were going to die from dehydration, we'd do it together. We chewed our piece of onion and segment of orange slowly, doing without the biscuit this morning, for the dry food was going too quickly. "We shall have to try to catch some fish," I said. "We put the line out yesterday morning," Lyn called, "when you were working with the dinghy, but when we pulled it in the hook had gone." She looked across at Sandy. "Did you try again?" Sandy shook his head. "No bait, we only had one fish head." He looked questioningly at me and I wondered what could have taken the hook (probably a shark in view of the absence of any struggle) but said nothing. "I'll try the spinner from the dinghy; if that doesn't work we'll try some more bait."

I climbed back into *Ednamair* to try my hand at catching a dorado. Since they are game fish and feed mostly on flying fish, I would either have to use live bait or a spinner, and since I had a spinner I decided to try that. I looked doubtfully at the wire trace, wondering if it would be strong enough, then fixing some weights to it, ran out a length of line. Before casting I took a couple of turns around the mast with the line and then, swinging the spinner, cast it thirty feet to the lee side, pulling in smartly to make the spinner travel. To my surprise three dorado dashed for the spinner, but turned away before striking; they were big fish and would surely break the line if I did catch one. I looked around, perhaps I could cast at a smaller one. I stretched out more line and made a few tentative casts in the direction of some smaller fish, rather like small jacks, but they ignored the flash of the spinner though once again the big dorado followed but did not strike. Three small female dorado suddenly swam near, and excited, I cast the spinner well out and ahead of them. To my utter dismay I watched the spool curve outward in a gentle arc after the spinner, land in the water and sink quietly into the depths. The line had gone. I was tempted to go after it but a lively deterrent in the shape of a large triangular fin belonging to a white-tipped shark appeared on the other side of the raft and I cursed my stupidity in frustrated anguish. How could I have been so careless as to leave the line unfastened to the mast? Our only spinner and our only wire trace, chucked over the side as if I were a kid at a Sunday school picnic. My knuckles beat at my brow; if I was going to make stupid mistakes like this now, what would it be like later? This was the sort of carelessness that cost lives at sea and if I was making these mistakes now what could I reasonably expect from newcomers to the sea like Robin, or youngsters like Neil and Sandy? I resolved to examine every move before I made it, and every decision before we acted upon it, for sooner or later, because I had overlooked something, someone would die.

I made my apologies to the others for losing the line and set to work immediately, made another spinner from the tinfoil on the lid of the "crumbs box," attached hook and weight to the nylon line and was ready to cast again by midday. The twins had spruced up with Mum's help and had actually combed their hair; they looked ready to go ashore! Returning to the dinghy, I cast in all directions for nearly an hour, trolling at different speeds, trying variations of red and white bunting on the spinner and flying fish heads on the hook, but all to no avail, the dorado would follow the line with interest but would not strike. I gave up, exhausted, my mouth dry with thirst under the noonday sun, and tumbled back into the raft, depressed but glad to be in the cool again. Douglas, on watch for ships, motioned me to the door of the raft and pointed to the sinister triangular fin approaching and we gazed in dumb awe as the ten-foot-long torpedo-shaped shark glided quietly under the raft, its attendant bevy of pilot fish in perfect arrowhead formation across its back. We looked at each other and made a silent pact not to tell the twins of our unwelcome company.

Lunch, consisting of a piece of orange (we now ate the peel as well) and a half biscuit, followed by a small mouthful of water, was over all too soon and we settled down in the afternoon to rest during the heat of the day. The twins were finishing a sketch of "*Lucette* and the whales" with pencil on sailcloth and Lyn was embroidering a message on some blue cotton in case our written letters were obliterated by immersion in seawater. It seemed a good time to draw my chart, so I fetched a piece of wood from the dinghy as a table and taking a dried-out chart reference map, which we had saved from the now pulped *West Indies Pilot,* marked in the coordinates from the Panama Canal to the Marquesas Islands, with the Galápagos, and as many of the islands as I could remember to the north. I then drew in the rhumb line route from the Marquesas to the Canal and our own position and projected route to the Doldrums. "We should start crossing our next possible shipping route in a couple of days' time," I remarked. Robin leaned over and studied my tiny squiggles of positions. "How far to land?" he queried. "I'll have to draw that on a different scale," I said, "but you can see from this that if we don't see anything on the route from the Canal westward our next chance won't come until we cross the route from North America to Peru or Chile and we'll have to get east of the Galápagos for that."

I marked out a larger scale and drew in the square from the American coast through the Galápagos to the position where we were sunk then northward to take in the whole of the Doldrums area, which at this time

of the year stretched from about 5° N to 15° N, spreading out at each limit
to about 20° of latitude as it neared the Central American coast. Then,
more difficult, I lightly penciled in the route, which I thought we might
take for the coast, northwest to the Doldrums, then east-by-north or
northeasterly to the coast. I had difficulty remembering which country
started where on that stretch of coastline but I knew it ran in a northwesterly direction all the way to Mexico, and Robin although he had
traveled down the isthmus by bus, was unable to help me much, but he
could see that we would land several hundred miles north of Panama,
"Perhaps around Nicaragua," he thought. I drew in our position, on the
larger scale chart, which I now estimated to be about 1°30' N and 220 miles
west of Espinosa (about 95° W) and measured our distance from the Doldrums limit. "About two hundred and fifty miles to go before we get
rain," I murmured, "two hundred and fifty miles at fifty miles a day, five
days and we have"—I looked over to where the cans of water lay on the
raft floor—"ten tins of water left, we'll just make it."

I tried to sound cheerful and, while we could see that we had already
grown thinner, we weren't exactly emaciated; indeed, although Neil and
Robin could ill afford to lose any weight from their already thin frames,
I had been putting on weight before the disaster, Sandy and Douglas
were well fleshed, and Lyn had a pound or two of fat, which she could afford to lose. We had good body reserves to live on if only we could reach
the rain area and if the wind held, but that was the rub, the wind would
die away before we reached the Doldrums, so would the northwesterly
current, and our margin for error was lamentably small, how long we
would drift between trade winds and the rain area was anybody's guess.
Robin looked at my little map and pointed questioningly to some squig-
gly arrows I had drawn on it. "Those represent the countercurrent, which
runs through the Doldrums, and when we get into that we'll be getting
a lift in the right direction. I don't think I've seen an estimate of the drift
of the countercurrent, but it should be half a knot anyway." I hoped it
would be more, but it would be a bad blow to our morale if at the end of
many weeks of agonizing struggle we did not find land when we expected it. I measured up the distance in the curved courseline I expected
us to take, with a can opener—"About a thousand miles, fifty days at
twenty miles a day; it doesn't sound bad if you say it quickly." *If we already
looked thin after four days,* I thought, *what sort of condition would we be in after
fifty?* It was a grim prospect. "Of course, we could reasonably expect
to be picked up before then," I said confidently. "If nowhere else then

most certainly on the busy coastal shipping routes to the Panama Canal."
Robin now looked a bit more cheerful, and he chatted happily to Lyn
about his experiences as a porter in various hotels in Wales and Ireland
during the university holidays. I had said nothing of the tiny islands, one,
perhaps two, which lay between us and the mainland; it would be nice if
we could land on one of them, but that would be a matter of luck, not
navigation.

The raft now required topping up with air at much shorter intervals, three or four times a watch, and though we looked again for a leak, it
wasn't until Lyn went on watch in the evening that she spotted the telltale
bubbles rising from under the towing straps. We spread out the puncture
outfit to see if we could use any of the patches with the remains of the rubber solution, which had a consistency of chewing gum. The patches were
old ones, too, and didn't have the sealing compound on them, which one
finds in a good modern outfit. We had four rubber plugs, some patches of
ordinary rubberized fabric, and a bit of emery paper. We would have to try
something in the morning.

As the evening drew in and we had supped our morsels of food and
water, we were talking about ways in which we might catch the dorado.
I had said that, if we plunged our hands downward as they skimmed under the edge of the raft, there was bound to come a time when we could
grip them where the body of the fish narrows to the tail, the only place
where it is possible to grasp and hold the slippery, streamlined body of
the dorado. We might have to try hundreds of times but, since we had
nothing else to do at night except look for ships and blow up the raft, we
could try in our spare moments. Sandy's voice piped up as he asked casually if nobody else had seen the sharks around; he'd just seen another
two, and he'd wondered if they were the big fish we'd been talking about
to Mum. "They're maneaters, too!" he said interestedly. We looked at each
other and laughed at our secrecy when we found out that Neil and Sandy
had been talking about them all evening. It would take more than a rotten old shark to frighten them.

During the night watch Lyn told me how she could sometimes see her
sisters Edna and Mary, after whom the dinghy was named, in the dinghy
pulling us toward safety and she often talked with them in the long lonely
hours of watchkeeping. (Lyn often took an extra watch to allow Douglas
or Robin a little more sleep.) That night, however, the task of topping up
became an exhausting fifteen-minute interval marathon, the forward flotation chambers losing pressure rapidly as soon as we stopped blowing.

FIFTH DAY

Dawn brought a beautiful sunrise. The sea, now quiet in the gentle southerly breeze, reflected the beautiful colors of the Pacific with incredibly intense blues and reds ranging into delicate tints of green and pink, the whole sky a blaze of glorious color.

Another two flying fish this morning, one from the dinghy, the other had flown through the door of the raft during Robin's watch with so much flap-and-slap it sounded like a twenty-pound fish. These provided us with breakfast of a two-inch strip of fish each. Pacific flying fish are much smaller than their Atlantic brethren, and in the Galápagos area the number of predators, which live on flying fish, among other things, gives one occasion to marvel at the fact that there are any left at all.

After breakfast we allowed the raft to deflate at the towing end, where we had located the leak under the towing strap at about three inches below the water line. Then with Douglas holding the strain of the dinghy on the towrope, we doubled the floor back and managed to bring the damaged area into the raft. Three small holes leaked air in an area of torn fabric under the strap (*Ednamair*'s pull on the towrope had been too vigorous in the strong breeze). The surface was cleaned and allowed to dry in the hot sunshine, then after roughening the surface with the emery paper I tried to get the dried-out solution to stick in and around the small holes, with no success. We decided to try varnish; the coats of varnish took half an hour to become tacky in the strong sun, and after applying three coats to the raft and the patches, we stuck them together and waited a further hour for the varnish to harden, but not so that it was brittle. Blown up, the raft deflated even more quickly than before, and puzzled, I lifted the towing straps clear again. The patches seemed alright. I called to Robin to inflate the damaged area again while I held it up and as the pressure built up the hiss of escaping air came from further along the side of the flotation chamber. I leaned over the doubled-up raft and found the hole, a quarter of an inch in diameter, worn in the fabric by one of the drogue trip ropes. No wonder we'd had to keep blowing! I plugged this one with a rubber stopper, and lashed the paper-thin fabric tight around the plug with nylon thread, then noting that the varnished patches had started peeling off, I stripped them off altogether. I enlarged the pinholes in the fabric enough to insert rubber plugs in them and we blew up the chamber again, turn about, sitting in a row like the three wise monkeys. It stayed up this time and we relaxed, happily relieved of our blowing routine for a while anyway. Robin's blowing prowess was growing by leaps and bounds, and he was filling his lungs and blowing with great gusto, improving his technique daily. I felt the exercise must be doing him a lot of good!

During the afternoon we played Twenty Questions; Neil was particularly good at guessing the object, especially when Sandy had chosen it, before many questions had been asked; whereas Robin was masterful at tracking down the objective with shrewd questions. I worked out our noon position at 2°06' N, 230 miles west of Espinosa (I had decided to stick to a longitude relative to the Galápagos for it saved explaining our position in terms of land) and announced that we were now entering an area in which there just might be a ship. (Robin had worked out that there should be one passing through the area every two days if 25 percent of the French and New Zealand traffic took the rhumb line route north of Galápagos, but his basis of information came from my guesswork, which was none too knowledgeable in shipping volumes.) Cumulus cloud built up again during the day but the only visible shower of rain falling from the base of the cloud in a gray curtain missed us by miles. I wondered if Robin would be interested in a statistical exercise of shower probability but he declined on the grounds that he would have to be supplied with necessary data over a period of years. I made a mental note that statistics, unless based on local data, was a dead duck, and that a theoretical education could only supply a man with a theoretical living, the thirst that we suffered at that moment being anything but theoretical.

The rain came just after dark, a heavy shower of short duration from which we collected half a pint of brackish yellow rubber-smelling water, and a pint of ordinary yellow rubber-smelling water in that order. As our excitement subsided with the passing of the shower, we settled down again in our now continuously wet clothing, though hardly to sleep, for I rarely slept at all now, listening all the time to the sounds of the raft, the sea, the fish, the dinghy, and thinking of ways of catching fish, of the possibility of straining plankton from the sea, and of covering the raft canopy with sail-cloth to exclude the filthy yellow dye from the water; of what would happen to us when the raft became untenable as it would do in time to come. I knew that Lyn, too, lay awake at night, and that her thoughts were never far away from methods of getting food and water into the twins' bodies, and of helping them and us to survive in this alien environment. We now welcomed our call to go on watch, if only to relieve the burden of our minds in action, and to stop having to pretend to rest.

At about ten o'clock a strange new sound like a giant breath exhaled intruded on the usual noises; we listened with bated breath as it came closer, Douglas, on watch, grunted from the door of the raft, "Whale." This time Lyn and the children were frightened (I was none too happy myself!) for the memory of the killer whales had grown more terrible with the passing of time and their fear that the raft would now be attacked was shared in some degree by us all. We soon identified it as a large, slow-moving Sei whale, one of the types that is preyed upon by the killers, and though I tried to reassure Lyn that this one would not harm us for it lives by straining tiny plankton organisms from the sea, she prayed with desperate appeal that we be spared a second attack. The whale surfaced many times around us during the following thirty minutes, often coming quite close. Sandy had fallen asleep again and now the whale's blowing coincided so accurately with Sandy's snoring that we all ended up laughing at the duet.

A water leak developed in the forward compartment of the raft later in the night although the buoyancy compartment in the floor seemed undamaged; the influx of water seemed to come from the area where the dorado struck the raft most, between floor and side compartments, and made for more discomfort in the already trying circumstances. The after flotation compartment had started going soft for no apparent reason and I resolved to look for more leaks in the morning.

The Robertsons and their friend were eventually picked up by a Japanese fishing ship after more than a month on the open sea. Their story is another excellent example of people working together to insure everyone's survival in some of the most adverse conditions possible. However, even the vastness of the Pacific Ocean pales in comparison to the danger encountered in this next story of survival at sea.

SURVIVING THE *ST. PATRICK*

Spike Walker

From *Working on the Edge*

There are few jobs more dangerous in the world than crab fishing in the North Bering Sea off the coast of Alaska. Yet every year hundreds of men and women head north for what they think is the ultimate adventure. Yes, it's the chance to make some big money, if you get aboard the right ship and make a good haul, but it's also endless days and nights of backbreaking labor that might result in coming back into port with empty pockets. And for some, a fishing trip on the wild Bering Sea turns out to be a lot more than they bargained for.

ON THE GRAY AND WINTRY MORNING OF NOVEMBER 29, 1981, the 158-foot fishing vessel *St. Patrick* slipped her Kodiak moorings and slid east through the narrow passage of Near Island channel and moved out into the Gulf of Alaska. For the majority of the ten men and one woman on board, it would be a journey of no return.

On board was twenty-three-year-old Wallace Thomas. A few weeks earlier, he had ventured north to Alaska from his home in balmy St. Augustine, Florida. Like thousands of naïve and adventurous hopefuls before him, he'd come in search of a berth on one of the fleet's high-paying crab boats. Unlike most, he had managed to land a job as a full-share deckhand on the *St. Patrick,* a scalloper that had arrived several months before from the east coast by way of the Panama Canal.

That night, Thomas lay uneasily in one of the crew bunks housed forward in the bow of the ship. The *St. Patrick* had begun to plunge and leap beneath him. He could hear heavy seas crashing across the deck overhead, and each time the ship's bow buried itself in a wave, Thomas felt himself being pressed heavily into his mattress. Then as the bow rebounded, soaring high over the crest of the next wave, he would float upward, entirely free of his bedding.

Sensing that the storm was building, Thomas left his bunk, slipped into his rain gear, and in the chilling spray and darkness made his way across the deck to the wheelhouse mounted astern.

It was nearly midnight when Thomas entered the comforting warmth and light of the galley. What he saw stunned him. The kitchen was in shambles. The new tightly secured microwave oven had broken free and lay smashed on the floor. The cupboard doors were swinging open and a combination of catsup, pickles, grape juice, strawberry jam, buttermilk, and sugar was sliding this way and that with the G forces of the rolling ship, in a sticky, scrambled, flowing mass. Arthur "Art" Simonton, a former logger from the state of Washington (the most experienced deckhand on board), was standing with his back to the sink, clutching its edges as he stared at the demolished kitchen. Other crew members were leaving as Simonton turned white-faced to Thomas. "We're going to put on our survival suits. This storm is getting out of hand."

Thomas felt sick with fright. He didn't own a survival suit! And he knew he didn't stand a chance in the thirty-nine-degree seas without one. Though he had never worn one in his short career at sea, he knew about their buoyant, heat-saving qualities.

The life raft! remembered Thomas. If the ship went down, it would be his only chance! He grabbed a flashlight and ran out on the back deck, where he managed to locate the tightly packaged self-inflating raft. He read the instructions.

Looks simple enough, he thought.

Thomas made his way back inside, where he ran into the ship's newly hired cook, twenty-three-year-old Vanessa Sandin. The blonde-haired, green-eyed daughter of a Kodiak salmon fisherman was carrying her survival suit, an older variety that looked in poor shape. It didn't have a built-in flotation device or life vest attached. The normally cheerful Vanessa was terrified. "Wally! What should I do?" she asked.

"The wheelhouse would be the best place to be if the ship was to get in trouble," he told her. "I'll take you up there."

Thomas climbed the stairs into the wheelhouse, then jerked to a stop. Nearly the entire crew stood before him. Most were wearing survival suits.

There was thirty-four-year-old Jack Taylor and thirty-three-year-old Curt Nelson, both from the state of Virginia. It was only Taylor's second trip out as skipper of the *St. Patrick*. Nelson was his engineer. Then there was John Blessing, a hard-working youngster from Oregon. He'd come north to help finance his college education. And there was Harold Avery, Jim Harvey, and Ben Pruitt. All three of these tough, scrappy crewmen were from Virginia. Also there at the time was Robert Kidd. This incredibly strong and sinewy deckhand was from Rhode Island. And there was Paul Ferguson, a husky lad and former football player from Nebraska. Not in the room, but also on board at the time, was a youngster named Larry Sanders, as well as Arthur "Art" Simonton.

When Thomas looked out the wheelhouse window, he saw a mountainous wave rise out of the darkness and slam heavily into the *St. Patrick*'s port side, lifting and shaking the entire ship. Wave after wave broke over the tall handrailings and collapsed across the deck below him with a thundering crash.

The black foam-streaked waves looked mammoth in the far-reaching beams of the mast lights. Some of the waves towered above the wheel house windows, more than twenty-five feet above the deck below.

To aid vision, the light at night in the wheelhouse was always kept to a minimum. In the near darkness, Thomas turned and looked at the others. Their wide eyes were filled with fear. The faces peering out from the sealed openings of the hoods of their survival suits looked bloated.

If anything happens to the St. Patrick, he thought, *I'll have only the life raft to save me.*

Back inside, Wallace Thomas helped Vanessa Sandin slip her legs into her survival suit. Then he rushed below to look for a suit for himself. The knot in the pit of his stomach continued to tighten. As he searched below, he felt a monstrous wave strike the *St. Patrick*. The boat shifted sharply and Thomas staggered against the wall.

Thomas crossed the floor at the bottom of the stairs and started down the next gangway into the engine room. He had gone only a few steps when another wave drove into the ship. In a steady motion, the engine room rotated before him, and suddenly he found himself lying on his back on what had been the wall. Stored canned goods, oil filters, tools, and supplies fell noisily from their shelves. Several fuel lines broke and diesel fuel began to spew everywhere. Then the *St. Patrick* partially righted herself.

Thomas struggled to his feet and raced back toward the wheelhouse. His heart pounded as he crossed the sloping galley floor. The entrance to the wheelhouse stairway was marked by two full-length swinging doors. As he approached, the doors burst open and were ripped from their hinges as a wall of rushing seawater exploded through them. The broad and powerful current carried with it charts and navigational equipment. The seawater slammed Thomas against the wall. When the hallway below quickly flooded, the waist-deep water began to empty down the second stairwell, which lead into the engine room.

Even before the torrent of water had finished draining from the wheelhouse, Wallace Thomas raced up the stairs. The scene there horrified him. A giant rogue wave had smashed through the St. Patrick's "stormproof" windows, tearing most of the ship's navigational equipment from its mounts. Equipment hung from the dripping ceiling, swaying from the ends of strands of wiring, while much of the ship's electronics lay broken and scattered across the flooded floor. A bone-chilling wind was gusting in through the holes where the windows had been.

The St. Patrick was listing about fifteen degrees to starboard at the time, making the wheelhouse floor slick and difficult for Thomas to cross. He spied his skipper lying amid the strewn equipment and broken window glass. Then he turned to Vanessa Sandin. She'd been only partially protected when the rogue wave shattered the windows and exploded into the room, and now she stood drenched and shaking.

Thomas had just finished helping Vanessa into her suit when the fuel-pressure alarm went off, clanging like an incessant fire bell. Then the main engines died and the lights aboard ship flickered, dimmed, and went dead. In the ghostly silence, a moaning wail became audible as winds approaching eighty knots howled through the steel cables of the mist rigging overhead and into the wheelhouse through the gaping window openings.

Jack Taylor found himself adrift at sea without steering or power. The only light aboard ship came from several battery-powered lamps two flights below. Then a second huge breaker drove into the side of the ship, rocking her sharply, and two crewmen were thrown to the floor. Thomas heard Taylor yell. "Hey! We've got to get off this damned thing! Let's get into the life raft before she goes down!"

An icy spray drenched them as they fled from the wheelhouse. Moving out in single file, they crawled along through the wet, cold darkness, climbing over the twisted, wave-bent handrailings and through tangles of rope and gear.

When Thomas reached the stern, he groped for the raft. "It's gone! The raft's gone!" he screamed above the howl of the wind. A few disbelieving groans met the news and then the group slipped into stunned silence. Thomas heard the skipper yell again. "We've got to get off this thing before it sinks! It'll flip over and suck us all down with her!"

A half-formed wave crashed against the far side of the St. Patrick and threw a wall of icy water over the crew. Those in survival suits paid scant attention. Clad only in his work clothes, Wallace Thomas was soaked and already ached with cold, however. He felt Vanessa grab him and heard her scream above the wind. "What are we going to do?" At that moment, Thomas spotted an amber beacon rising and failing off the stern. "It's the life raft!" he yelled. "It's got to be! Maybe we can swim for it!"

A crewman found a long length of rope and suggested that they tie themselves together to prevent getting separated once they were adrift in the ocean. The skipper agreed. Someone had located a waterproof flashlight, and periodically a voice would call out "Could you give me some light over here? I can't see!"

Suddenly, the realization of what he was about to do struck Thomas. The time twenty minutes pounded in his head. From his instruction in wilderness survival, he knew that a man without a survival suit seldom lasted longer than twenty minutes in seas of this temperature. *If you go into that water without a survival suit,* he thought to himself, *you'll be dead in twenty minutes!*

The stern deck grew steeper as the unrelenting velocity of the storm rolled the *St. Patrick* further on its side. Like the rest of the crew, Thomas was sure the ship was sinking. For one long moment, he stood on the stern at the water's edge, and as the water licked up the sloping deck and over his feet, he grappled with the insanity of panic. He pictured himself alone in the darkness of the wheelhouse, stretching for air as the wintery Gulf of Alaska seas rose slowly over his head.

Soon, the crew members finished tying themselves together. They were about to abandon ship, and, irrespective of logic, Thomas felt drawn to follow. As his skipper and crew edged closer to the water and prepared to jump, Thomas bolted, however.

"Taylor!" he shouted to his skipper. "I can't go in with you! I've got to stay with the ship as long as I can! I'll die if I go in that water!"

The skipper seemed dazed. "What?" he shouted back.

"I don't have a survival suit and I'm not going in that water without one! I'll stay aboard until the ship goes down and call out more Maydays!"

"I think there's another suit in the captain's cabin!" the skipper yelled back.

Thomas shook with fear as he hurried back toward the wheelhouse. He was frantic, and his legs drove him forward faster than his numbed hands could interpret the shape of things. But the suit meant life to him and he scarcely noticed the skinned shins and bruises he acquired as he stumbled along. Entering by the rear wheelhouse door, he crawled along the wall through the rubble, feeling his way to the captain's cabin.

Thomas was on the verge of hysteria. It was the prospect of being abandoned alone on board the sinking ship that terrified him. He wanted to get back to the others waiting on the stern before they became too fearful and left without him. His hands slapped frantically against the walls as he crawled through the darkness. He realized he was in the bathroom and quickly backed out. His hands shook uncontrollably as they fumbled through scattered socks, shirts, boots, pillows, a suitcase, and supplies that lay strewn about the room.

"Where is it? Where is it?" he yelled aloud.

Then as he groped in the darkness, he felt the distinctive shape of a survival-suit bag. There was nothing in it! The suit had been taken! His mind raced. Was the skipper mistaken? Could there possibly be another suit in all this junk? Had there ever been an extra suit in the first place?

He plodded ahead blindly, bumping into one wall and then another. He tore through a jumble of bedding and clothes. Reaching some cabinet doors, he jerked them open. Inside, he felt the soft bulk of another long vinyl bag. There was a survival suit inside.

Thomas wiggled into the suit and felt his way back to the stern, where he raced to tie himself between Vanessa Sandin and John Blessing. John was one of three crewmen without a survival suit. He had slipped on every piece of clothing he could wear and yet still fit into a bulky life jacket. "We've got to get off this thing!" yelled the skipper again. "She could go down any minute!"

As they prepared to jump, Thomas looked around him and caught brief glimpses of the crew in the flickering flashlight beams. Their slick, wet figures looked ghostly.

Then Chief Engineer Curt Nelson yelled a warning. "When the water hits those batteries, they're going to explode!" Just then, a loud *bang* sounded from below in the engine room. A massive wave rolled by, passing as a black hulk just off the stern. Water swept up the slanting deck and over the crew's feet.

As the stern of the *St. Patrick* dipped and swayed, the youthful six-foot-four-inch frame of Art Simonton arrived. He had just returned from the bow. "Two guys just jumped overboard off the front deck!" he screamed, his eyes wide with terror. "We're going to capsize!"

"Okay," the skipper yelled. "Let's get off this thing!"

With the back deck constantly awash, Thomas could feel the ankle-deep water pulling at his legs. *We're going down,* he thought. *We've got no choice but to abandon ship.*

Bound together—around the waist and under the arms—by loosely tied loops for easy movement, the crew shuffled down the steep deck. The railing before them had been torn away and now, timing their move with the downward roll of the ship, the crew stepped off the stern deck.

As they struck the water, the crew went under briefly. When Thomas's head bobbed clear, he gulped in the precious air. *I'm all right!* he thought, his mind racing. *I can breathe! I'm not dead!*

In the next moment, the massive steel hull of the *St. Patrick* flashed before his eyes as it plunged down beside him, narrowly missing crushing the entire crew. Thomas screamed, "Paddle! Paddle!" and the group stroked furiously to get clear of the ship's deadly stern.

They were afloat in the stormy darkness and except for the fragile beam of a lone flashlight, vision was impossible Looking back, only a few yards into their journey, not a hint of the ship's outline remained. Yet distinctly visible in the battering night were two small portholes. Power still generating from the engine-room batteries filled the round windows with warm light, and now the circles soared and dived in the blackness. Moments later, the porthole lights disappeared. *She finally sank,* thought Thomas. *We got off just in time.*

No sooner had the nine drifting crewmen of the *St. Patrick* swum clear of her deadly stern than a wave began to lift them. Up and up it carried them. Thomas was certain they had neared the top of the steep, sloping wave when he heard a loud thundering roar coming from behind him and far overhead. He turned toward the booming rumble just as the first monstrous wave top collapsed down upon them.

The body of the wave carried whole fathoms of sea over them. It drove the struggling crew under and tossed them end over end. Like Thomas, some of the crew members had turned toward the wave when it overtook them and caught the full force of its fury directly in their faces.

No one could have imagined such a wave. Some in the party were washed out of their rope loops. They bobbed to the surface, gasping for air, and fought to remain upright as they groped blindly for the rope.

Hundreds of feet of floating excess line had become tangled around them. And seventy-knot winds whipped an icy spray across the water, blinding those who had forgotten to turn away and stinging any face not protected with a sheltering hand.

Wallace Thomas soon discovered that two people were hanging on to him. Vanessa clung to an arm and John Blessing was hugging him around a thigh. Blessing was already shaking violently from the effects of the cold.

Thomas shouted to him.

"You're going to be all right, buddy! Just hang on!"

"Count off! Count off!" someone screamed.

Some of the crew seemed too disoriented to obey, while others were perhaps unable to hear the command.

Thomas felt another wave begin to lift him. It swept him up into the wind-torn blackness, ever higher and higher. Then he heard one end of the wave begin to roar as it folded over and collapsed through the darkness toward him.

"Look out! Look out!" he screamed. "It's another big one!"

The gigantic breaker rolled over the crew, submerging and tumbling them upside down as it passed. A few in the group had prepared for the approaching swell. Holding their breaths, they had turned their backs to it. Though they still found themselves tossed and wrenched violently about, their recovery, once the wave had passed, was surprisingly rapid. Suffering repeated dunkings, others of the drifting crew soon adapted—except, that is, for those without survival suits.

Thomas could feel John Blessing shivering violently as he clung to his leg. Less than twenty minutes had passed when his friend became delirious, moaning and speaking irrationally.

"It's cold! It's so cold!" he gasped in a painful rasping voice.

Thomas tried to encourage him. "Hang on, John! You've got to ride it out!"

But the mountainous waves continued to sweep them high. And each time the wave crests folded over, they smashed down upon the ragged group of fishermen like concrete walls.

Then one of the crewmen cried out above the noise of the storm.

"So you guys think we should pray?"

Thomas was quick to respond.

"Now is the time if there ever was one!"

They recited the Lord's Prayer then, their voices dissipating quickly in the storm-lashed night.

"Our Father, who art in heaven, hallowed be Thy name; Thy kingdom come, Thy will be done, on earth . . ."

They had completed less than half of the prayer when, without warning, another enormous wave broke directly over their heads, driving them deep beneath the surface

The moment their heads again cleared the surface, there was heavy retching and gagging. Those tangled in the excess line fought frantically to free themselves before the next wave found them.

Wallace Thomas could see that John Blessing was in serious trouble. He wrapped his arm around the shaking man.

"Come on, John! Stay with us," he begged.

John stammered out his reply.

"My legs . . . arms . . . stiff . . . so cold."

John's moaning increased. Several times, Thomas felt his friend's quivering body go limp. When another large wave struck them, John was swept from Thomas's tiring grip and began to drift off. Stretching behind him in the wet darkness, Thomas managed to snag John with one hand. Then as he drew him near, he saw a small beacon attached to John's life jacket. He worked hard in the clumsy two-fingered gloves of his survival suit to grip the beacon and yank it alive. His aching arm muscles told him he couldn't carry his friend much longer.

The tiny beacon had just begun flashing when John spasmodically flailed his arms and floundered out of control. Almost immediately, the wind and current swept him away. Thomas was horrified to realize he could no longer reach him. He watched helplessly as the tiny amber beacon light weaved off into the darkness and disappeared.

Someone yelled, "Was that John?"

"My God, yes!" Thomas answered.

As he watched John disappear, Thomas felt Vanessa reattach herself to his arm. From the outset, Vanessa's suit had leaked steadily. It was becoming an ever-increasing struggle for her to keep her head above water. Together, they floated up and over the endless series of waves.

Vanessa Sandin prided herself in never getting seasick, even in the toughest weather. Several of her predecessors had lasted but a single trip. When Vanessa came on board, she was confronted by a galley that was dingy, dirty, and disorganized. She scrubbed the place from floor to ceiling. She emptied the cupboards and completely reorganized them. Then came the burned pots and pans, the oven interior, covered with burned grease and food, and finally the kitchen table, some twenty feet long.

She soon became known for having a good heart, and mischievous sense of humor. When Wallace Thomas had his twenty-third birthday shortly before shoving off on their fateful final journey, Vanessa had prepared him a huge birthday cake. When he tried to cut into it, however, his knife chinked to a stop. Vanessa had taken a twelve-pack of beer, wrapped it in cardboard, and camouflaged it with a thick spread of canned frosting.

She could also cook. Each summer, she fished right along with her father on his gillnet boat in Bristol Bay. One day, when she had decided to prepare a dinner of sockeye salmon, her father, a long-time Alaskan fisherman, made the mistake of trying to tell her how to go about cooking it.

"You run the boat," she scolded him, "and I'll fry the fish. Now get out of here!"

The salmon proved to be the best he had ever eaten.

Vanessa, her father recalled, could not only cook but also tie knots, mend webbing, make a drift set, pick tangled salmon out of the gillnet, and navigate. One day, it came to him that she learned more quickly and with greater ease than he had as a young man. But now this adventurous young woman could only cling to Thomas through the night and pray to be rescued at first light.

As they passed over the top of another immense swell, Thomas felt something bump heavily into his back. Fearful that a log had drifted up on them out of the night, he shouted, "Get that light over here! Something just hit me!"

Thomas searched the darkness with the dim beam of light. Suddenly, he reeled in the water. There, adrift beside him, floated the body of Larry Saunders, another crewman who had abandoned ship without a survival suit. He was still tied to the crew's rope line. "Turn off the light and save it!" shouted Thomas. The light flicked off.

Close by, Thomas overheard the muffled conversation between Ben Pruitt and Jim Harvey. Harvey had been on his first voyage to sea in Alaska. He was the last of the original three without survival suits. Now he turned numbly to his crewmate and pleaded.

"Ben! Ben, I'm so cold! Could I borrow your suit for a little while?"

"Jim, I'm cold, too! And the suit's leaking, anyway! Just try to hang on!"

"Ben! What am I going to do? Help me! Please, help me, Ben!"

Thomas knew that there was nothing anyone could do. Hypothermia was the dangerous lowering of one's body temperature; more specifically, the temperature of one's core, comprised of the heart, lungs, and brain. The moment the three frantic young men jumped from the stern of the St. Patrick without survival suits, they were doomed. Under such conditions, no man could live more than an hour.

A short time later, Jim Harvey began to moan and jabber incoherently. Eventually, he grew motionless and, still bound to the group by the rope line, his body drifted among them.

Eight hours after they had first abandoned ship, dawn slowly replaced the smothering black veil of darkness. In the dim gray light, Wallace Thomas could finally take in the unbelievable size of the massive seas. Raw winds whipped thin white streaks of foam across the moss green water. The waves moved under a bleak ceiling of sky, and he could make out blue-black rain squalls, squatting low as they moved across the horizon.

Each time he passed over the crest of another wave, his eyes swept the desolate expanse of water. Then something caught his eye.

"I can see somebody swimming over there!" he yelled. The six remaining crew members soon spotted him, too.

"Hey, it's the skipper!"

They yelled and waved and blew metal whistles that came attached to their suits, but Jack Taylor showed no sign of having heard them. He backstroked slowly away from them and was lost from sight.

Then Vanessa began to yell excitedly.

"I can see land! I can see it! I'm sure of it!"

As he crested another twenty-five-foot wave, Thomas caught sight of it, too. Before long, he was able to make out two separate points of land. The spirits of the numb, pain-racked crew soared.

"When I get back," promised Vanessa, "I'm going to eat the biggest pizza I can order!"

Hours later, when the low-lying clouds cleared adequately, a steep rock coastline loomed large before them. Its uppermost slopes were covered with rich shades of winter-browned grass and crowned with dark green stands of spruce trees.

The crew members decided to paddle for the nearest outcropping of land but wave after wave struck them from the side, throwing them off course, and fog intermittently obliterated all sight of land.

"We're never going to make it this way!" Thomas called out. "We've got to swim more in line with the way the waves are moving! Then we can angle a little bit at a time in toward land!"

Swimming with the waves, they made steady progress, but soon Ben began to speak in fragmented phrases and suddenly collapsed facedown. The two crewmen on either side rolled him over.

"Come on, Ben! You've got to swim!" they screamed at him. "You've got to help us! We're not going to make it if you don't swim!"

Ben Pruitt tried. He flopped one weak arm and then the other out in front of him, but he was nearly unconscious. His two friends continued to encourage him as they pulled him along between them, kicking their numb legs and stroking with one hand while clutching Ben by the arm with the other.

Vanessa, too, was nearing the point of exhaustion. With her leaking survival suit now nearly full of the icy seawater, her body ached with cold. If she was to survive, she would need constant help.

Then Wallace Thomas and Harold Avery devised a method. One of them would paddle on his back, carrying Vanessa on top of him, while the other trailed the pair, watching for land and verbally guiding them.

Paul Ferguson and Curt Nelson soon adopted this technique to carry Ben. Gradually, they grew weaker and their progress slowed appreciably. Their bodies were chilled from nearly fourteen hours in the near-freezing water. Hunger cramped their stomachs and they were becoming dehydrated.

The survivors had decided to save the bodies for decent burial. But then, under the sinking weight of the body of Larry Sanders, Thomas saw how Ferguson was struggling to remain afloat.

"We've got to untie him!" he yelled.

Thomas swam forward through a tangle of floating lines and loosened the rope line. The corpse quickly sank from sight. Without comment, the six remaining crew members regrouped and pushed on.

Ever since they had first spotted land that morning, the struggling crew had been swimming. Now, some eight hours later, the coastline seemed much closer. Thomas could see the black flat faces of cliffs, perhaps a hundred feet high, lining the shore, but he could not see an accessible or calm stretch of beach. As they closed to within perhaps two miles, Thomas spotted the white explosions of waves bursting along the cliff bottoms.

The sight petrified him. He knew the deadly power of coastal breakers from years of surfing in Florida. Such seas were frightening enough, but to become entangled with one another in the rope lines in a heavy breaking surf would be suicidal.

"Before we try to go in, we've got to untie!" he called out to the others. "It's too dangerous! We won't make it this way!" The exhausted, floundering members numbly agreed.

Now Ben Pruitt seemed on the edge of collapse. The two who had carried him no longer appeared to be able to do so. Thomas left Vanessa with Harold Avery and swam to Ben and held his blue face out of the frigid water. He was still breathing.

Then off to his right, Thomas caught a flash of something white on the water. As it rose over the crest of the next wave, he saw it clearly. "There's a ship!"

Those who were able began to wave wildly and blow their whistles. They swung their shivering arms back and forth till they could no longer hold them aloft. Thomas wore his tongue raw whistling and the taste of blood filled his mouth. The ship closed toward them for nearly a half hour. Wallace and the rest of the crew members were sure it was coming for them.

Then they watched in disbelief as their rescue ship began to turn away. As it changed course, Thomas could see the distinct lines of the ship's wooden hull.

"No! No!" he cried. "Why can't they see us? Please, please see us!"

But the vessel was soon lost from sight.

The collective disappointment was almost too much. Wallace Thomas was the first to break the silence.

"We've got to get swimming again, you guys. He didn't see us."

With disappointment showing in every stroke, the remnant crew once again began to plod ahead toward shore. They had hardly begun, however, when Ben Pruitt rolled facedown in the water. Paul Ferguson and Curt Nelson summoned all their remaining strength to roll him back over and give him mouth-to-mouth resuscitation, but there was no response.

"Come on, you two!" Thomas finally called, his voice breaking. "You've got to let him go now. You've got to save yourselves. We've done everything we could. We've got to take care of the living now!"

The remaining survivors of the *St. Patrick* were too exhausted to untie Ben's body, so they left it in tow and resumed swimming.

Less than an hour later, the five remaining survivors closed to within what they believed was a half mile of the shoreline. "I'll go on in," yelled Harold Avery, "and if it's all right, I'll wave for you to follow on in after me! I've got some waterproof matches and I'll get a warm fire going. So just watch for my signal and then follow me in!"

Thoughts of a crackling-hot fire lifted the spirits of the four remaining crewmen. Vanessa was shaking constantly from the cold water seeping into her suit. She was growing visibly weaker. With Vanessa lying across his lap, Thomas shuddered as he watched Harold swim away.

They were able to stop paddling then and, sighing with relief, settled back to await the signal from shore. As they drifted nearer to shore, they decided to untie themselves from each other in preparation for the swim in through the surf. Freed from the rope line, Vanessa and Thomas found themselves drifting away from Paul Ferguson and Curt Nelson. But the two couples were too fatigued to reunite.

Shortly, Thomas saw the two men drop into a hollow in the sea and disappear. That afternoon, he caught his last brief glimpse of them. They appeared to have stopped swimming.

Now, with Vanessa completely dependent upon him for her survival, Thomas drifted and waited in anticipation for a signal from Harold Avery. Each time, as he rose up and over another wave, he would search for his good friend and deckmate's wave from the distant banks. Drifting ever nearer, he studied the soaring rock precipices. He could see the ghastly black form of the cliffs, slickened with spray and rising abruptly from out of a pounding misty-gray surf, with fog rolling across its sheer granite face.

He contemplated that perhaps he had underestimated the size of the surf and cliffs along the shore.

Suddenly, he caught the flicker of something tiny and orange in the thundering surf. It looked toylike, about the size of a petite orange buoy as it was lifted up and tossed against the wet face of the rock cliffs. He watched it being swept out by the surf, only to be gathered by another massive wave and flung high against the stone walls.

Then as he drifted nearer, the true dimensions of the terrain ahead finally struck Thomas. The rock cliffs were not a mere one hundred feet high, as he had estimated, but in frightening reality towered more than a thousand feet overhead!

When he spotted the minute orange object again, it was suspended in a wave and being swept some thirty feet up the face of the cliffs, with spray exploding far above it. And at that moment, it dawned on him— the object he had been studying so intently as it surged back and forth against the cliffs was not a buoy. It was the lifeless body of Harold Avery.

The sight took his breath. His heart felt like lead. All seemed lost and utterly hopeless. The safety they had associated with the first sighting of land had been only another cruel illusion. Vanessa hadn't seen the body. Thomas decided not to tell her.

"We can't get in here!" he yelled to her.

But what if there isn't any accessible beach on this island's entire shoreline? he worried secretly.

As Vanessa lay across his lap, Thomas noticed that her condition was worsening. She could no longer move her legs, the feeling had gone out of her arms, and her lips had turned a dark blue. As he paddled on his back over the waves, he tried to parallel the coastline.

He, too, had begun to shake uncontrollably, and his legs felt stiff and weighted. Toward evening, Wallace Thomas's back and arms began to cramp badly. He felt he couldn't carry Vanessa much longer. As he lay back, he thought he'd close his eyes and doze for a moment. It seemed only seconds before Vanessa rattled him awake.

"Wally! Wally, are you all right? You're looking pretty bad!"

"I'm fine, Vanessa," he reassured her. "I was just trying to relax for a few minutes."

Then a loud thumping noise began to pound in their ears. As if out of nowhere, an orange and white helicopter roared past them, close by overhead. In an adrenaline-pumping rush of excitement, Thomas waved his arms wildly; Vanessa raised one quivering hand.

"It's the Coast Guard! My God, they've finally come for us! They knew we're here! We've done it! We're going to be rescued! We're going to live!"

The helicopter sped out of sight, though. A few minutes later, they saw it making another pass in the distance.

Vanessa was too exhausted to wave.

"Did he spot us?" she asked in a weak voice.

"No. And he's too far away now."

He'd hardly finished speaking when another helicopter flew directly over them. As it passed, the side door slid open and Thomas could see a crewman standing in the doorway. He appeared to be looking right at them.

Thomas tried to rock forward, thereby rising slightly in the water, but Vanessa lay heavily across his lap. He screamed and waved frantically.

"Come on, Vanessa! We've got to signal to them! This might be the one time they see us!"

"I don't think I can anymore, Wally," she replied weakly.

The helicopter flew on out of sight.

"They didn't see us, did they?"

Thomas answered with silence.

"I don't think I'm going to make it, Wally," said Vanessa, her voice straining with pain and fatigue.

"Come on, Vanessa. We can still get out of this mess alive. We can float a good while longer if we have to."

"Oh, Wally," she replied in a disheartened voice, "I don't know. I'm awfully cold and there's a lot of water getting into my suit."

"Look over there," argued Thomas. "See that point of rock? Look past it. The waves aren't even breaking. There's a cove. We'll swim in around there somewhere."

Suddenly, Vanessa began to cough roughly. Then she jerked forward out of his arms and rolled facedown in the water.

Thomas was horrified. He jerked her back upright and shook her violently.

"Vanessa! Wake up! Say something to me! Answer me!"

There was no response. Her face was chalk blue. Her eyes were glassy. She hacked deeply then and again wrenched free of Thomas's grip. Summoning what little strength he could, Thomas paddled to her side. He lifted her head and held her close. Her eyes were closed. Her body hung limply in his arms. She was no longer breathing. Vanessa was gone.

Thomas turned and slowly swam away. He was weary and heart-broken, and darkness was closing fast. His entire body ached with cold and now shook uncontrollably. He had been awake for more than thirty-six hours, twenty of them spent battling the stormy Alaskan seas. Now he wanted only to close his eyes and be done with it. His movements had grown sluggish to the point of immobility, but he fought to keep his tired mind on the task at hand.

I'm dead! I'm going to die! he concluded.

Shortly after nightfall, Wallace Thomas spotted a ship's mast lights. He did not grow overly excited. The lights were miles off. Each time, as he rose over another wave top, he caught glimpses of them. They appeared to be headed in his direction.

As the ship drew closer, Thomas tried to gather his failing strength. He lifted his leaden arms and began waving, drawing an arm back down to rest now and again. Occasionally, he called out, hoping his voice would somehow carry to those on board the ship. Then the vessel pulled up even with Thomas, and he screamed, "My God, I'm here! I'm right here!"

He fumbled for his whistle and began blowing it frantically. Then he held his breath and listened for a reply. He could hear the sounds of men's voices above the low rumble of the diesel engines. He could see the figures of crewmen working outside under the back deck lights. Yet the ship slowly lunged past him and disappeared into the night.

I'm dead, a goner. I'm going to die, he thought.

He struggled to come to terms with the finality of his predicament. He thought of his parents—how sad and wasteful losing their son this way would seem to them.

I'm sorry, Mom! I'm sorry, Dad! he thought, picturing them now in his mind. *Such a lousy way to die,* he pondered.

Thomas's shuddering body throbbed with cold. Then as he rode over the crest of a wave, he spotted tiny lights flickering in the distance. Only a few hours before, Thomas would have known that they represented another ship miles away, but his thinking had become disoriented. He was sure they were the lights of Kodiak. "I'll swim in there," he decided. But seconds later, he'd forgotten the idea and paddled numbly ahead.

Thomas knew he had to get out of the water. His body was just too cold to remain in it much longer. Several times, his legs grew so stiff that he was sure he no longer could use them. He knew he would soon pass out from the relentless cold. His wilderness training in hypothermia flashed through his mind. *If you got cold, you didn't try to ignore it,* he remembered. *You act!*

He crouched up into the fetal position then, and as he drifted in the darkness, he tucked his mouth down into his suit and for a time breathed heavily into it. His debilitating numbness and shivering seemed to diminish slightly.

Then, as he came off the peak of a big loping wave, Thomas saw something large in the moon-tinted darkness. It was floating beside him. It looked like a huge buoy, partially covered with dark green blotches of algae or seaweed, but its dimensions puzzled Thomas.

Maybe I can hang on to that and get some rest, he reasoned. *I'll just float along for a little while.*

He paddled toward the object, but oddly, he didn't seem to be getting any closer. A moment later, Thomas drew back, frightened of the thing. Now it looked like a whale, and, retreating, he splashed water at the massive creature in an attempt to frighten it away.

Eventually, Thomas came to realize that the whale he had feared was actually a point of land less than a half mile away. *Maybe it's not your time,* he thought hopefully. *You've got to at least try to swim for it! At least you can do that!* He turned then and using the breaststroke headed in toward land.

"It's not your turn. It's not your time," he chanted to himself. "Going to die if you stay out here any longer. May be the last thing you ever do. Might as well swim for it. Got to try."

Shortly, Thomas found his movement impeded. A swaying tangle of slimy fingers was bobbing about him, while others wrapped themselves around his arms and legs. Fear began to build. *Oh, kelp,* he realized suddenly. *Must be getting closer. Must be.*

He struggled on toward the shore, and on either side of him, in the faint light, he spied tall pillars of blue-gray rock and moon-silvered breakers fanning out and bursting high against them. When he heard the roar of the breakers exploding along the shore, he grew sick with fear. The vision of Harold Avery's body as it washed up against the cliff kept shooting through his groggy mind. *Aim yourself in between those two pillars,* he told himself. *It's your only chance.*

Wallace Thomas had no sooner decided upon his new course than he felt an immense wave pick him up and hurl him forward through the night. The wind blew sharply in his face and the water churned beneath him as it heaved him along toward shore. Then, without warning, the wave crest he was riding curled forward.

He felt suspended in air as he fell down its folding face. When he landed, the tremendous force of the pounding water shoved him under the surface and held him there. The boiling torrent of ocean surf pulled and pounded on him as if nothing short of his total destruction would satisfy it. It twisted him upside down, jerked him sideways, and rolled him about. The smothering black surf seemed to pull at his suit from all directions, and he could feel icy rivulets of water jetting in around the facial opening of his hood.

Thomas fought to right himself and return to the surface. His lungs burned for air. He had already begun the involuntary inhalation of the icy salt water when his head finally cleared the surface. Thomas choked violently and gasped in a lungful of the damp sea air. Then another huge wave caught him and once again launched him swiftly forward through the night.

He threw his battered arms out in front of him and attempted to swim along with the thrusting power of the wave. Then he thought he felt a hand strike a rock, and the foaming rush of water that had carried him there seemed to disappear from beneath him.

Thomas found himself lying facedown on the steep face of a solid rock bank. He clung to the steely cold surface in disbelief, his chest heaving for air. He felt too weak to move, but he knew if the next mammoth wave was to catch him still lying there, it might very well crush him with a single paralyzing blow.

In his mind, he stood to run, but his legs refused to move. It was as if they were no longer part of him! "Oh God! Dear God, help me!" he cried, pawing wildly at the slick bare rock of the bank.

Thomas had managed to crawl only a single body length up the surf-slickened bank when the next wave exploded at his feet, drenching him.

A bitter cold wind was gusting along the shoreline and soon it chilled Thomas to his core. The short stretch of rock he had lucked upon was only a few yards wide. Too weak to stand, and shivering uncontrollably, he pulled himself along with his hands, and, lucking upon a shallow rock crevice, he instinctively rolled into it. There, out of the direct assault of the wind, Thomas closed his weighted eyes and almost instantly fell asleep.

Yet it was a fitful rest. The surf pounded loudly only a few yards away, and even in the naturally protected chasm, the razor-sharp wind found him.

Wallace Thomas awoke with a start, to see the figure of Art Simonton standing close by and staring at him. His former crewmate and friend wore street clothes and seemed unaffected by the arctic wind racing along the shore. Was it the visible apparition of a dead and departed friend, or had he survived?

"Art!" he called out. "What are you doing here?"

When no answer came, Thomas took a moment to reposition himself and draw closer. But when he looked again, the figure had disappeared. He slumped back down and slipped into unconsciousness, lost in a merciful slumber.

The excruciating pain in his hands awakened him next. The arms of his suit were bloated with salt water forced in by the pummeling surf. He rolled onto his back, lifted his arms, drained the stinging water into the lower half of his suit, and fell back to sleep. When he awoke later, he found his hands had warmed to a point where he could at least open them.

The Coast Guard was finally able to verify that twelve crewmen had been aboard the fishing vessel *St. Patrick*. At first light, U.S. Coast Guard helicopter pilot Lt. Jimmy Ng lifted off from his base on Kodiak Island. Along with several other helicopters, C-130 SAR planes, and the Coast Guard cutter *Boutwell,* they began searching the area off Afognak Island for signs of survivors.

Lt. Ng worked his way around the steep rock shoreline of Marmot

Island (positioned approximately four miles from the shores of Afognak Island). Some of the shoreline cliffs he encountered rose up in a sheer vertical climb more than 1,200 feet above the water. A short time later, Lt. Ng located the first body. It was floating facedown in a small cliff-encircled cove. Oddly, the man wore neither rain gear nor a survival suit. The cliffs were too high and the cove too small to maneuver safely, so Lt. Ng hovered approximately fifty feet away and watched for signs of life. There were none, so he resumed his search around Marmot Island, and he soon came upon several more bodies.

"One body was off in the surf," he recalled. "He was bouncing around in the rocks. And two others were lying up on the beach. All were dead."

With the discovering of the first body, the Coast Guard search for the missing crew of the *St. Patrick* intensified. Soon, USCG helicopters, planes, and cutters were scanning the waters and shoreline from Whale Island, just offshore from Kodiak, to Marmot Bay, to Iszuit Bay, and completely around the northern tip of Afognak Island, all in the hope of finding someone still alive.

Shortly after dawn, Wallace Thomas propped himself upright on a boulder. He sat shivering and studied the world around him. Overhead, rock walls rose as sheer and apparently inaccessible as those of a prison. More than one thousand feet above him, Thomas could see convoluted outcroppings of bare granite rock jutting into the sky, and beyond that, clinging to thin layers of soil, weather-stunted spruce trees bent in the wind. On either side of him, short stretches of narrow shoreline cut into the cliff rock and were strewn with boulders the size of dump trucks.

The cloud ceiling appeared to have lifted slightly but the freezing thirty-knot winds continued to blow without pause. The sea rushing up at him wore a blinding silver sheen. His pain-wracked legs still refused to support him, so he rubbed them furiously in an effort to restore circulation.

Thomas felt groggy and exhausted, miserably cold and hungry. But it was a maddening thirst that drove him finally to rise on wobbly legs and stagger stiff-legged along the cliff bottoms in search of fresh water. With water sloshing about inside, his survival suit hung heavily on him. He wanted to shed the suit but knew that to stand exposed to the Siberian-born winds in soaked clothing would mean death within hours.

Maybe I'll make it if I stay in the suit, he reasoned.

Thomas could find no fresh water close at hand. Walking only a few steps exhausted him.

If I'm going to survive, I've got to locate water, he told himself.

But there appeared to be no escaping the cliffs lining the beach. The sharp-crested outcroppings of rock extended well out into the surf. They loomed impossibly steep and dangerous to climb.

The pounding surf before him, which had taken the lives of so many of his companions and nearly his own, now petrified him. He would remain trapped on the shore and take his chances with hunger and thirst and exposure before he would return to the ocean again.

Then as the surf receded to near-dead low tide, he saw an opportunity. The tide had receded enough to allow passage around the base of the jutting column on his left. Wallace did not hesitate. Leaning against the rock walls, he hurried around them as quickly as his buckling legs would carry him.

He discovered an even shorter stretch of enclosed shoreline. Large boulders covered most of it. He stumbled forward and fell on the bank, panting. Slowly, a faint dribbling sound struck his consciousness. He spun and his eyes caught the movement of a tiny stream of water trickling off the face of a vertical rock bluff.

He rose staggering and fell. He crawled the last few feet but found a small pond formed where the droplets had landed. He dipped his glove-covered hands anxiously into the clear pool and sipped the bounty. The water tasted salty and he spit it back out. His heart fell.

Damn! A tide pool! he thought angrily.

Then he sampled the pool again.

It was fresh water!

Thomas felt foolish. The salt he had tasted had come from the gloves of his survival suit. The water in the pool was fresh and cold. He drank down a few eager swallows and then stopped abruptly. He could feel the water cool him and he wanted to allow his body time to catch up.

Even with fresh water, Thomas doubted he could make it through another night in his wet clothes without food or a fire. It had been nearly forty-five hours since his last meal and he was sick with hunger.

In an effort to hide from the painful and life-sapping cold of the December winds, Thomas hunched down between two huge boulders. From there, he could still command a view of a good portion of the ocean. As he waited, he shook so hard it felt as if all the bones in his body were rattling. Gradually, he thought he could make out the faint rumble of an engine. The noise dimmed, then grew stronger, only to fade once more.

He debated whether to stand and look, exposing himself fully to the draining cold of the wind.

He had to try, he decided. His body was fast growing colder. He wavered as he stood, and his eyes squinted into the wind and swept quickly over the ocean before him. He was about to crouch back down when he spotted movement. It was the bow of a ship nosing its way through heavy seas off a point of land on his far right. Almost crippled with cold yet frantic with excitement, Thomas struggled up the side of a large boulder and began flailing his weary arms.

"They must be out looking for me! They've got to spot me! They've just got to see me now!" he cried out loud.

The one-hundred-foot ship drove nearly halfway across the open stretch of water in front of him before Thomas thought he saw it slow. Through watering eyes, he saw quick flashes of light coming from the wheelhouse.

Were those really signals? Have they actually spotted me? Or am I only imagining things again?

Every few seconds, the ship would crest the top of another swell and then slide into a deep trough, and then, except for the radar scanner spinning steadily atop the wheelhouse, it would disappear as if swallowed whole.

The waving seemed to take the last of Thomas's strength. A sudden gust of wind staggered him, nearly toppling him from the rock. He dropped to his knees to maintain his balance. *If they did see me, what will they do next? What could they do?* his fuzzy mind puzzled.

On the horizon, Thomas caught sight of a small black dot moving directly toward him low over the water. Moments later, a four-engined C-130 U.S. Coast Guard plane roared by overhead. Its deep, growling engines shook his insides like the blast from a cannon. Thomas was ecstatic. He blew kisses and screamed excitedly. "Yes! Yes, they've seen me! Thank God, at least they know where I am!"

Soon, he spied a U.S. Coast Guard helicopter moving toward him. "I'm here! I'm alive!" he called out.

The wind was blowing hard against the one-thousand-foot cliffs behind him. The helicopter flew in twice over Thomas and hovered, only to clack noisily away.

Dear God, he can't get to me! he thought. *I'm too cold! I've got to get out of here!*

Then the bright orange, black, and white helicopter returned and hovered not fifty feet above him. The ten-knot wind churned up by the copter's blades whipped a mist off the water.

Thomas was thrilled when he saw the large steel body basket descend from out of the side door. But it landed well out in the breaking surf, and the pilot seemed reluctant to move in closer to the cliffs.

Gradually, the helicopter pilot maneuvered the craft closer, resting the basket in the surf on the edge of the shoreline. Though terrified of the water, Thomas shuffled down the embankment and fell into the basket. Fear that the next wave would catch him and batter him to death now that he was so near to being rescued raged in his mind. Yet almost instantly, the helicopter plucked Thomas up and out of the surf.

Thomas watched the shoreline grow minute in the distance. A cutting wind whipped over him as the upward acceleration of the helicopter pressed his body hard against the wire-meshed basket's bottom. Then the helicopter leveled off and stood away from the shore, hovering noisily. Thomas could feel himself being lifted toward the door.

Far below, he could see the ship that had first spotted him and radioed his location. It was the *Nelle Belle.* She was throwing off heavy sheets of bow spray as she plowed through the waves.

The helicopter crew hoisted him in through the door and checked him for serious injuries. Next a radio headset was fitted over his head, and Thomas heard the voice of the chief pilot.

"Are you all right, young man?"

"Yes. I think so."

"How do you feel?"

"Well, you got me out of there! I feel so much better now."

"Look, you've got hypothermia! Do you understand that?"

"I kind of figured as much."

"Okay, so now listen to what I'm telling you! Do not relax! Keep yourself charged up until we can get you into the hospital. You could go into shock right now and you could die before we could get you there! That has happened to us before."

The helicopter pilot was worried about a dangerous phenomenon called "after drop," the process in which a hypothermia victim's core temperature continues to plunge even after he has been rescued and wrapped in wool blankets. If not halted, this downward slide will continue until the victim suffers a heart attack from the cool blood circulating through his heart.

"Have you found anyone else besides me?" asked Thomas.

"No. You're the only one so far," answered the pilot.

The somber news shook Thomas. He had hoped that Paul Ferguson or Curt Nelson had somehow found a way safely ashore. He wondered about Bob Kidd and Arthur "Art" Simonton, whom he'd seen in his dreams the night before. Bob Kidd had jumped overboard with Simonton from up near the bow minutes before Thomas and the rest of the crew had abandoned the *St. Patrick* off the stern.

When Wallace Thomas arrived at the hospital, his body temperature was ninety-three degrees Fahrenheit. Death can occur from heart failure at ninety degrees. The medical staff placed heated blankets and hot towels across his body and forced him to breathe heated oxygen. But it took little coaxing. The warm devices felt wonderful to Thomas's numb, sea-ravaged body.

The next day, Thomas learned that one other crewmate had survived the ordeal. As he lay recovering in a Kodiak hospital bed, nurses wheeled in Bob Kidd for a visit. "I can't believe it," Thomas finally confided to his good friend.

"I would never have believed that a ship built like the *St. Patrick* could have gone down as quickly as she did!"

Bob Kidd sat upright and turned and looked at Wally Thomas in astonishment. "Wally," said Kidd, "it didn't go down. It didn't sink. They found the *St. Patrick* floating the day after we abandoned ship. They're towing it in right now!"

The sea is a harsh mistress, alternately capricious and cruel, depending on her whim. And every man and woman on every boat that sets sail on her knows, deep down in the depths of their soul, that this trip may be the very last one.

The definition of irony couldn't be made more clear by the St. Patrick's *survival while the majority of its crew perished. Although it is easy to read about this scenario from the comfort of dry land, I can certainly tell you that faced with this situation, I would have done the same thing those brave souls did when they abandoned the* St. Patrick *to take their chances in the unforgiving sea. Would I have survived? I assure you that I would have done everything in my power to, that's for sure.*

RESCUE ON SITKA SOUND

Spike Walker

From *Coming Back Alive*

Despite the dangers of the Bering Sea at just about any time, there are plenty of men and women that make their living from its treacherous waters. And when those people get in trouble, there is a very special group of men and women who go out and try to rescue them—the members of the U.S. Coast Guard.

The following chapters from Spike Walker's spine-tingling nonfiction book Coming Back Alive *details just one of these white-knuckle helicopter rides into hell, wherein five men risk their own lives to save a fisherman and his six-year-old son. They would perform this hazardous mission with barely a thought to their own safety—and pull it off like true heroes.*

IN 1986, DURING THE TURBULENT MONTH OF DECEMBER, a local man named Jim Blades and his six-year-old son Clint, both close friends of Dug Jenson's today, became key players in a desperate encounter while fishing commercially out on Sitka Sound. This tale of fatherly love and Coast Guard heroics has taken on a kind of legendary status over the years.

In 1982, Jim Blades, who had been felling timber in Wyoming, decided to quit his job and set out for Alaska. The early 1980s were special times in the Big Bear State. If an able-bodied man stepped off the ferryboat just into port from Seattle, people were literally waiting there to hire him. They were, in fact, quite desperate to find laborers. Some employers even went as far as walking back and forth along the rows of seats in Ketchikan's movie theater, soliciting help.

Blades found work near Whale Pass, in a logging camp run and owned by a man named Gildersleeve, one of the last of the staunch, never-give-an-inch independents. Some of the old-growth trees they felled were nine feet thick at the stump.

As it turned out, Jim Blades was handy, the kind of man Alaska has always welcomed. Master of but a few trades, he nevertheless possessed a sound working knowledge of many. By laboring side by side with people who knew their crafts, he had become an accomplished stonemason. He had acquired a solid understanding of the principles of both plumbing and electrical wiring, and he knew how to pour concrete, frame and roof a house, and put up Sheetrock. He could fell timber, drive heavy equipment, and repair the machines he ran, as well.

Since Alaskan residents are allowed the right to salvage ten thousand board feet of free timber per person each year (more than enough to build an ordinary house, and have firewood galore), Jim Blades would eventually construct a sawmill and cut his own lumber, all he might need.

During those robust days, Blades often found each year at tax preparation time that he'd accumulated as many as fourteen W-2 forms during the previous twelve months.

It was during a trip back home to Wyoming that Jim Blades met and proposed to his future wife, Jill. Giving her a hard time, he told the ebony-haired, God-fearing young woman that she had good teeth and that she would be quite useful at softening the hides of any animals he might trap. Three months later, they were married in the First Baptist Church of Pinedale, seventy miles south of Jackson Hole.

Jim Blades didn't want his wife to be disappointed when she got to Alaska, so he billed the place as one where there was much hardship, bad weather, and privation. He made it clear that there weren't any igloos where they were going, and that it rained all the time—the only difference in the seasons being the temperature of the rain.

When Jill finally arrived in southeast Alaska, Jim was pleased to find that she liked it. During their first few years together, they lived on False Island up in Peril Strait, some fifty miles from Sitka. With an abundant supply of halibut, salmon, codfish, and trout close by, and with game laws allowing the harvesting of six deer per person per year, there was never any shortage of either fish or venison in the Blades's home.

While Jim hunted for Sitka deer, trapped for martin, or fished for salmon and halibut, Jill lived the life of a self-sufficient frontier woman. She eventually gave birth to two boys, Clint and Curt. During the tiring, but contented, years that followed, she home-schooled her kids. Raising them in a place surrounded by a burgeoning population of free-roaming brown bears, she always kept a loaded rifle close at hand.

They had the entire island to themselves. And with bald eagles nesting nearby and killer whales and sea lions cruising past, it proved to be an idyllic beginning to a devoted partnership and a successful marriage. From the living room of their floating home, they could watch brown bears feeding on the roots of the swamp grass at the head of the bay. One morning, the Blades awoke to find five land otters playing on their front deck. For several hours, the whole family watched the otters preening one another's fur in the morning sun. Several dove off the deck, caught fish, dragged them back to the deck and ate them. Others took turns peering through the bottom of the sliding glass door at the strange human creatures inside the house.

Given how idyllic their life was, Jim Blades would shrug off questions when pressed as to why someone would choose to home-school their little ones forty miles from town, in a place with almost no radio contact, no neighbors, and no emergency medical care. "Oh, we were young," he says. "We didn't worry about that stuff."

The raft supporting their home was a rectangular creation of lumber twenty-five feet wide and forty feet long, composed of logs bound together with cable. Also perched on the raft and tied securely in place were a little shop, a sauna that ran off of freshwater piped down from a nearby creek, and a generator shed. Jim Blades built them all on skids (timbers with tapered ends), the house, included, so that if he desired, he could drag them off the raft and ashore anywhere the landscape permitted.

Jim's boat, the F/V *Bluebird,* was only twenty-six feet long—small by commercial salmon-trolling standards—but it had a deep draft and, when under way, drew close to four feet of water. Eventually, when the family did decide to move in closer to town, they tied their home to the stern of the *Bluebird* and towed it along behind them as they made their way through Peril Strait.

Ten miles from Sitka, five miles from the nearest road, they discovered a quiet cove shrouded in old-growth timber that pushed right down to the uppermost edge of the high-water line. It offered near-total protection from the notorious southeast winds that often strike the region.

Checking further, they found that the pristine anchorage had fresh running water, plenty of game, and a deep channel that allowed passage during even the most severe tidal fluctuations. And they could soak in the warmth of the sun during its rare appearances and gaze upon the famous Alaskan sunsets to the west. So they dropped anchor in the heavily forested arm of that wild and solitary bay and, once again, set out to make it home.

During the summer months, Jim Blades made a good living trolling commercially from the *Bluebird* for both king and coho salmon. During the rest of the year, whenever the weather permitted, he long-lined for bottom-feeders offshore, specifically codfish and red snapper.

The boat's trolling poles were twenty-five feet long and made of spruce wood. When the boat was under way, the poles were stored upright, tucked in tightly against the wheelhouse. When fishing, Jim lowered the poles, secured them, and extended them out on either side of the *Bluebird* at a forty-five-degree angle, providing stability to the small vessel, in much the same way a balancing pole aids a gymnast during a tightrope walk. Over the years, Blades had become so sensitive to the feel of his boat that, while trolling, he could often determine the weight of the salmon striking the lure by the trembling transmitted to the hull through the poles.

Jim Blades often took his son Clint on fishing excursions. Though only six years old at the time, the youngster could already be counted on to contribute to the work effort in a meaningful way.

Just before Christmas, while fishing for codfish near Cape Edgecumbe on the far edge of Sitka Sound, only a dozen or so wilderness miles from home, Blades and his son encountered the exceptional.

From the outset, the fishing that day had been excellent, and Clint and his father were quickly caught up in the excitement and steady action of pulling fish after fish aboard. They hooked, landed, cleaned, and iced some six hundred pounds of ling cod. At $1.70 a pound, Blades would pocket about $1,000 for the day's work. With Christmas only two weeks away, such a profit would be a welcome boon.

It was only 3 P.M. when another long December's night in the far north fell upon them. The advancing darkness and the lucrative day of fishing set Jim Blades to figuring. *I should run back in now,* he thought. It was a judgment call, but with two intimidating reefs, Low Island and Vitskari Rocks, lying between him and home, he hesitated.

Smooth swells twenty to thirty feet high had been rolling through the area all day, but with no wave tops capping them, riding over them had been no problem.

Fatigued as he was, and with no working radar on board, he decided not to attempt the two-hour run back into town. He and Clint would catch up on their sleep and pick up where they'd left off on the fine fishing first thing the next morning.

I'll just ride it out here in the lee of St. Lazaria Island tonight, he decided finally.

Jim Blades radioed his wife and told her of his decision. He might have trouble with his anchor dragging on the rock bottom there, but he wanted to sit out the night behind St. Lazaria Island anyway and wait for dawn.

Jill wasn't exactly crazy about the idea but said she would leave the final decision in the matter to her husband.

"Okay, then, take care," she radioed. "Love ya! Talk to you in the morning," she added, signing off.

Jill switched off the radio, shut off the lights, and climbed up into the loft of their one-room A-frame cabin. Then, as her three-year-old son, Curt, quietly crayoned in his picture book on the bed beside her, she sat and read.

"Daddy will be home in the morning," she told him.

Blades would have been hard-pressed to pick a more picturesque spot. Located on the farthest edge of Sitka Sound, St. Lazaria Island is a bird sanctuary, the breeding ground of literally millions of seabirds and a National Wildlife Refuge since 1909. The protected anchorage behind it is a favorite of local fishermen.

As he dropped anchor in the lee of the island, countless gulls and murres and comical-looking tufted puffins looped noisily out from their cliffside dwellings before returning again to their precarious perches. St. Lazaria is only a few miles from Cape Edgecumbe and the Fuji-like form of Mount Edgecumbe rising up on the island of Kruzof.

Generally, Blades knew, there were telltale signs that warned a fisherman of an approaching storm as much as a day in advance. Usually, he would detect some cat's-paws, the strange moving islands of rippling water where gusts of wind touch down as if pawing at the ocean's surface. Under such circumstances, one might expect a storm by the following morning.

On this night, however, there was little evidence of approaching danger. It looked to be a decent night to lay up and ride it out. But several hours later, sudden thirty-mile-per-hour gusts of wind arrived without so much as a hint of warning. They, in turn, were followed by punishing gusts of thirty-five and then forty miles per hour. Within minutes, a blast of wind approaching seventy miles per hour came hurtling around the island's granite cliffs, roaring through the spruce trees and imprinting the water before whistling off through the *Bluebird*'s rigging.

As the seas rose into breakers, the *Bluebird* began to shift restlessly at anchor. Jim Blades found himself surrounded by the close yellow glow of the ship's cabin light; beyond that lay a larger theater, a seamless curtain of impenetrable darkness.

Now the swirling wind began making bizarre course changes. Blinding volleys of jetting snow shot past them. Jim knew then that he'd been caught out in the open by an intense little storm cell, the type Alaskan meteorologists often refer to as "bombs."

This doesn't look good, he thought as the abrupt rock formations of St. Lazaria Island rose and fell before him. Then Blades turned to his son. "Clint, go put on your survival suit," he said.

Working the hydraulics from inside the *Bluebird,* he winched his anchor back aboard and got under way. He wanted to escape the gnarly breakers now surging up and down on the cliffs before him. Following his compass, he idled slowly past the cliffs and through the slapping seas in the lee of the island.

As the storm intensified, the craggy rock shoreline of the island in front of him disappeared altogether in the blinding blizzard. Amid the disorienting flurries, Jim Blades tried to calculate where the protruding rocks had been and to navigate accordingly.

Caught in outside waters, without radar, running in the blind, Jim Blades fixed his eyes on the only dependable navigation device he had left—the little red compass light mounted on the panel in front of him.

He was feathering the throttle, trying to maintain his course, going the way that he thought he should be going, when the pitching *Bluebird* crunched down on a pinnacle of rock. The pointed crown of the Volkswagen-sized boulder pierced the wooden hull of the boat. Then came the echoing crunch of wood rending, much like the sound of a sledgehammer striking a watermelon. Blades threw her into reverse and floored it. Pivoting, he bolted anew. Seconds later, seeking his escape through the vision-obliterating snow squall in the opposite direction, his beloved *Bluebird* plowed bow-first into the cliff face of St. Lazaria Island. Bringing the boat around once more, Blades once again reversed his course. He was now certain that he knew the way out. As he motored ahead, waves exploded against the cliffs on one side and roared in among upright pillars of rock on the other. Passing nervously by the rock upon which his boat had previously been impaled, Blades slipped gladly into deeper waters.

With the destructive sounds of the impact still echoing in his ears, Jim Blades didn't even bother going below for a closer inspection. He knew that the ship was sinking and that they had very little time. As if to reaffirm this belief, the automobile horn that he'd cleverly rigged to his bilge alarm sounded. He grabbed the wire and tore it free, silencing the blaring noise. Then he grabbed his radio mike and called for assistance.

"Mayday! Mayday!" he called. "This is the fishing vessel *Bluebird*! The fishing vessel *Bluebird*! Mayday! Mayday! Mayday!"

"Fishing vessel *Bluebird,* this is the U.S. Coast Guard, Sitka," came the quick reply. "Sir, please give us your name, your location, and the condition of your vessel."

"Sitka Coast Guard, this is the fishing vessel *Bluebird*," he replied. "My name is Jim Blades, and you had better send someone out to get us, because I'm sinking fast here off St. Lazaria Island. I hit a rock pretty hard. I've got my six-year-old boy on board with me here. I don't know how long we'll be able to remain afloat. Over."

As the Coast Guard gathered information and rushed to prepare for the mission ahead, an anonymous voice of a fellow fisherman sounded over Jim Blades's CB radio.

"Hang in there, Jim!" encouraged the voice. "You're going to be all right. Just keep jockeying."

Blades found comfort in those words.

To rescue swimmer Jeff Tunks, on duty at the USCG base in Sitka at the time, the Mayday sounded urgent. The situation was obviously critical. Pilot John Whiddon informed Tunks that they would debrief while en route to the scene.

With thirteen years of aviator experience under his belt, Cmdr. John Whiddon would do the flying, while Lt. Greg Breithaupt would ride shotgun as his copilot. Tunks would go as the mission's rescue swimmer. Carl Saylor would run the hoist, and Mark Mylne would ride along as their avionics man.

It took Tunks and his crewmates just eighteen minutes to roll out the H-3 helo, fuel it up, load it up, and prepare for liftoff.

The model HH-3F "Pelican" helicopter (or just H-3, as most Coasties refer to it) is a large, powerful, and very dependable workhorse of an aircraft. It has two jet engines and a semiamphibious hull that can be used to land on water to facilitate a rescue, so long as the weather and conditions are relatively calm. If the rotor blades plow into a wave in heavy seas, however, the aircraft will flip over and fill with water as quickly as a capsized canoe.

That night, it was raining furiously outside. A building wind blowing in off the sound was driving the inch-an-hour rainfall horizontally. Sheets of it were inundating the area, tumbling across the airfield's apron and out across the ramp.

While the helicopter's jet engines were warming up, and before her main rotor blades were engaged, Tunks sat in the rear cabin, looking out through the side door of the H-3. From there, he could see the long rotor blades extending out from directly overhead. Now, in the gusting winds, the long, flat blades began leaping up and down like diving boards bouncing in the wind.

The blades of the helicopter had only just begun to turn, when a gust of wind rolled in off Sitka Sound, pounding against the metal sides of the hangar nearby and scooting the eleven-ton helicopter several yards across the runway.

"We've got a boat sinking off St. Lazaria Island," said Cmdr. Whiddon, climbing into the pilot's seat and strapping himself in. "We're going to go out and see how we can help."

Sitka Sound in winter, Tunks knew, is a brutal place. The seas are often short, choppy, and unforgiving. Should a mechanical failure force them down on this night, there would be no backup. Of the three choppers stationed at the Sitka base, one was currently down for repairs, and another was on patrol well north of them, outside of Cordova. Only theirs remained.

They had hardly risen clear of the circular helicopter pad when their loran-C computer shut down. Whiddon rose to the standard altitude of three hundred feet, where, in the cooler atmosphere, he encountered a wall of swirling snow. He found it both disorienting and hypnotizing, and, ultimately, blinding. Nevertheless, Whiddon continued on, closing determinedly on their destination. As he did so, he encountered fierce storm winds tearing around Cape Edgecumbe and accelerating down off the steep slopes of Mount Edgecumbe itself. They were closing on St. Lazaria Island when they were beseiged by the battering ninety-mile-per-hour gusts.

Under favorable conditions, a pilot might hover within fifty feet or so of the ocean's surface and those he hoped to rescue. But on this night, at an altitude of seventy-five feet, Whiddon found that he was being pelted not only with blowing snow but freezing sea spray, as well. Shortly, the face of the radar screen outside became so coated in ice, it ceased functioning altogether. Worse yet, the gale-force winds were driving into them with such velocity, and in such irregular bursts, Whiddon knew it would be impossible to maintain anything like a stationary hover. With his navigational equipment now dead and only his altimeter and horizon-leveler instruments to guide him, Whiddon flew on.

"*Bluebird!*" radioed John Whiddon as his eyes searched the inky void all around. "This is Coast Guard rescue helicopter one four eight six. Do you read me?"

"Yes, I hear you," replied Jim Blades.

"*Bluebird,* I need you to key your mike and count backward for me from ten to one. And keep counting. As you do, we'll try to track you down using our DF [direction finding] equipment. Over."

"Roger that," said Blades. "Ten, nine, eight, seven, six, five, four . . ."

Glancing outside, Blades noticed seawater creeping up his back deck. *This is not looking good,* he thought.

"Well, guys—we're here. Where you at?" Blades radioed finally.

"We're doing our best to find you," replied John Whiddon.

"Give me another DF count," Whiddon radioed.

Whiddon could tell by the interference—the amount of static caused by the surprising power of the storm cell—whether they were gaining or losing ground.

At first he sounded close, then he seemed to fade away.

Jim Blades knew that his always-dependable *Bluebird* was sinking. Dying partnership or not, he hated the idea of going back inside the ship's cabin, each time, to answer the radio; like any fisherman, he abhorred the idea of getting entombed inside the sinking hull.

Wind-whipped flurries of cascading snow were tumbling unabated out of the coal black night when Blades opened the back door and shined his handheld spotlight downwind of the boat.

"Do you see that?" he radioed Whiddon. "Do you see my light?"

With their visibility limited to just a few hundred feet, none of the searching eyes on board the helicopter could see a thing. Then Carl Saylor spotted a tiny glint of light shining through the swirling snowfall off to their right. But as he watched, it soon disappeared. Jim Blades's spotlight had shown itself as the foundering *Bluebird* crested over a wave, but the seas were so large that each time it did, the F/V *Bluebird* would disappear entirely into the yawning pit of the wave troughs, taking the light with it.

"Pilot, this is the flight mech. I think I see a flashing light," radioed Saylor.

"I don't see it yet," shot back Whiddon. "Give me a heading."

As they drew closer, copilot Greg Breithaupt spotted it, too.

"We've spotted you, *Bluebird*!" said copilot Greg Breithaupt. "Yes, we see you!" He paused. "We'll be on scene in two minutes!"

Using full power, Whiddon motored upwind toward the foundering vessel. Drawing nearer, he could see that she was riding low in the stern, with wave after wave pummeling her. The *Bluebird* was pitching wildly as she drifted up and over the long-rising swells. With her bow banked at a forty-five-degree angle and her stern constantly awash, Whiddon could see a man and a small child in orange survival suits snuggled in close to each other, clinging tenaciously to the back of the wheelhouse.

From the chopper's side door overhead, rescue swimmer Jeff Tunks could see that Jim and Clint Blades and their beloved *Bluebird* were getting the "hell beat out of them," as he put it. The fishing boat looked minuscule amid the burly storm waves lifting and tossing her. The waves themselves were covered with gray-white streaks of windblown foam, stretching in thin layers across the slate black surface. Yet wherever the chopper's floodlight touched down on the otherwise black face of the surrounding sea, it illuminated the world below in a brilliant circular swath of color and life—the green of the water glowing with an almost phosphorescent intensity.

Tunks could feel Whiddon fighting to maintain an even flight plain. Lowering the rescue basket from their wind-jousted helicopter onto the tiny gyrating rectangle of the *Bluebird*'s back deck looked impossible.

The gusts were williwaw blasts of cold mountain air roaring down off the slopes of Mount Edgecumbe. Cooled well below freezing by the altitude, gathering tremendous energy and speed as they descended, the accelerating winds struck the helicopter and shook it to its rivets. At one point, the H-3 helicopter dipped so low that it nearly impaled itself on the twenty-five-foot-high cedar trolling poles that rose up on either side of the wheelhouse.

Whiddon, Tunks could tell, kept putting forward and up control commands into the flight stick, but the helo kept sliding back and down. Tipping as far as twenty degrees from side to side, they were often forced to hold on, as if riding a bucking bronco.

Then an exceptionally powerful gust of wind, well in excess of 110 miles per hour, struck the helicopter, driving them back. Whiddon fought to bring the nose down and regain control, using all the power the aircraft possessed.

"You're backing down!" shouted Carl Saylor.

As they plummeted toward the water, Whiddon and Breithaupt glanced over at each other, exchanging a look that said, *This is it!* Whiddon was certain that they were about to crash. It was one of those instinctive feelings. They were going in.

Yet John Whiddon felt too caught up in his duties to be scared. Oddly, a sense of peace and calm settled over him, and the message he internalized was one of acceptance, one that said, *This is just the way it is.*

Whiddon had three boys and a loving wife, to whom he was devoted, waiting at home just across the bay. They were all safely ashore now—a world apart. Then his mind seized upon the memory of his good friend and flying partner Pat Rivas. Pat was a superb pilot and a wonderful human being. Back in the early 1980s, they had flown alongside each other on a number of missions in Alaska. And they had made a difference. Their most notable effort was being part of the largest medivac operation in U.S. Coast Guard history. Working with their airborne comrades, they employed a relay system and were able to pluck more than five hundred survivors off the cruise ship M/V *Prinsendam* when it caught fire and began sinking far out in the Gulf of Alaska. Just ten months later, Pat Rivas and his entire crew were killed in that infamous crash in Prince William Sound, when their tail rotor chipped a wave, toppling them from the sky.

So this is how it all ended for Pat thought Whiddon as he, his crew, and the weather-beaten helicopter carrying them careened out of control:

Both Whiddon and Breithaupt were yanking up, pulling "full-collective," on the horizontal arms mounted on the sides of their seats. Waiting for the H-3 to respond was a painfully slow process. They were just fifteen feet from striking the water itself when the wind gust released them.

Heart in throat, Whiddon turned to Breithaupt. "Boy, let's never do *that* again," he said, forcing out a chuckle.

For the rest of the crew, Whiddon's comment proved to be an aptly timed tension breaker.

"Let's get back up there and get these guys," he told them.

"Damn straight!" replied Jeff Tunks from the rear cabin.

Now Whiddon found that he nearly had to max out the engine to move ahead at all. Slowly, however, flying into winds that fluctuated between 90 and 115 miles per hour, he inched the helicopter forward.

Hoist operator Carl Saylor worked to conn Whiddon back over the sinking *Bluebird*. "Forward and right three hundred," he said. "Forward and right two hundred. Forward and right one hundred. Hold."

The floodlight shining down on the *Bluebird* created an amphitheater effect. The boat was taking on water and riding ever lower; then, as Jeff Tunks watched, a storm wave broke against the boat, sending up an almost dazzling light-filled spray over the *Bluebird*'s entire length.

Jim Blades hurried back inside and grabbed his mike. "How do you want to do this?" he radioed.

"Sir," replied Breithaupt, "the only way we're going to be able to execute this SAR operation is if you get your son and get off the boat."

To Tunks, Jim Blades's voice sounded so concerned with saving his son's life that he was sure the man would have gladly eaten a bucket of nails if that would have helped.

"Okay," said Blades.

"Hang on, Clint," Jim Blades told his son. "We're going to have to get in the water now."

The elder Blades found that he couldn't get the zipper on his survival suit to work properly. Some months before, he'd broken that very zipper and had gone to great effort to have it replaced. The person who had repaired it, however, had failed to put back the two-inch whistle that had always served as a handle and was normally attached to the tiny metal zipper flap itself. Now, wearing the the suit's clumsy two-fingered Gumby gloves, Blades found that despite all his efforts to prepare for just such an emergency, he was unable to pull the zipper the entire way up and lock it into the all-essential position directly beneath his chin.

As Jeff Tunks watched from the side door of the helicopter above, Jim Blades gathered up his son and walked out onto the pitching back deck of his boat. Clipping his son's suit harness to his own, he then stepped off the vessel's stern and into the tossing sea.

Their predicament, Tunks could readily see, soon went from bad to worse. For although Jim Blades and his son had dutifully abandoned ship, the prevailing winds quickly blew them in against the hull of the *Bluebird*, pinning them there.

After a half-dozen more attempts, Whiddon became convinced that the plan to basket-hoist the pair from the water unassisted would not work. When their efforts to lower the basket failed once more, Whiddon turned to rescue swimmer Jeff Tunks, who was seated behind him in the rear cabin.

"Jeff, we're not going to be able to complete this rescue without you. Do you want to give it a go?"

"Yes, sir. I'll give it a try," replied Tunks without hesitation.

"Do you think that you can get them?"

"Yah, I think I can. Let's give it a shot."

"Okay, then, Jeff, why don't you go ahead and get ready."

Hardly a year old at the time, the Coast Guard's rescue-swimmer program was still in its infancy. A swimmer wore the basics: two fins, a mask, a snorkel, a wet suit, a harness, and a knife.

Tunks was still prepping for the into-the-water deployment at hand when the F/V *Bluebird*'s bow rose sharply into the air and slipped stern-first into the waiting sea. With little Clint Blades still riding on his chest, Jim Blades lay on his back and stroked urgently away from the boat and any possible entanglements.

Jeff Tunks followed the lights of the ship's cabin as it descended perhaps twenty, even thirty feet below the surface. It was, Tunks said, "Just blazing all the way down." Tunks found it quite dramatic, even touching, to see the Bladeses' entire living and everything they were about sink out from under them.

Little Clint Blades had said nothing as his father carried him down the sloping deck and stepped off into the water. Clint's suit had arms but only a single mummylike compartment for his legs. He was lying on his back on top of his dad's chest, sea-otter-style, when the first breaking wave rolled in over them.

"Clint, keep your mouth closed and hold your breath!" Jim Blades yelled to his son. "Hold your breath until the wave passes!"

Then everything went black. Jim Blades felt the cold wash of the wave water stinging his face, and the invisible currents pulling at them. As they tumbled through the surging space, the elder Blades was certain that had he not strapped his son Clint to himself, he would surely have lost him.

Back on the surface again, Blades could feel the chilling seawater flooding in through the neck opening of his suit. He was quite aware of the advancing stages of hypothermia and the paralyzing immobility that ultimately accompanies it. Though he would not go down without a fight, Blades was certain that he had a limited amount of time. If the rescue team didn't get to them quickly, he'd soon be dead, and his son Clint would drown, too, strapped to him as he was.

Then, as he waited, he glanced to one side and caught sight of his boat careening down the face of a wave, white smoke trailing from her stack.

Jim Blades could already feel the cold robbing him of his strength and his ability to resist. He studied the chopper struggling overhead and soon realized that the erratic and unpredictable winds were making rescue virtually impossible. "God," he prayed, "could you please slow the winds down just a little? We're in a real jam here. I don't believe my son and I are going to survive this without your help."

After a quick but precise final run-through of the rescue swimmers' checklist, flight mechanic Carl Saylor signaled Tunks forward. Tunks took a seat in the doorway and snapped on his gunner's belt (safety strap) to keep him from tumbling out. Then he slid the four-inch-wide, four-foot-long loop strap down over his head, shoulders, and arms. Theoretically, the strap would allow Tunks to extend his arms overhead and slip free of it whenever he chose. He then pulled his mask snugly into place and bit down on his snorkel's mouthpiece. With finned feet dangling out into space, he gathered himself for what looked to be a wild descent.

Barely three years prior to this, on a bitter cold night, during a driving winter storm off Cape Hatteras, North Carolina, thirty-six crew members were left to survive as best they could in the icy seas after being forced to abandon the sinking freighter *Marine Electric*.

When the pilot of an H-3 Pelican finally located them, he found the waves too high to attempt a landing on the water, and dozens of seamen scattered across the crowning seas. Though the flight mech was repeatedly able to place the rescue basket in close proximity to those struggling in the water, in the end, he and the others aboard the helicopter could only watch as, one by one, no less than thirty-three of the severely hypothermic survivors fell unconscious and died.

Ultimately, Alaska's own LCMD Kenneth Coffland (now retired) would play an instrumental role in helping wrestle something redeeming from the ruins of this tragedy and others. Subsequent hearings, investigations, and inquiries into this deadly incident explored the key shortcoming in the link between the Coast Guard crews in the air, and those imperiled souls in the water below.

As a result of the efforts of Coffland and many others, Jeff Tunks knew, just ten months before, the U.S. Coast Guard had gone "operational" with the rescue-swimmer program.

"Prepare to deploy the swimmer," ordered Whiddon.

"Okay, deploying the swimmer," replied Saylor.

Then came the token signal for which Jeff Tunks had so intensively trained—Carl Saylor's one tap on the chest. In response, Tunks released his gunner's belt and gave Saylor the standard response, a thumbs-up.

Jeff Tunks could feel the harness tighten under his arms as Saylor, working the hoist controls, lifted him into the air. As he swung out the door, Tunks heard the log-shredding power of the mammoth storm waves exploding along the shore of Kruzof Island, several thousand feet away.

"Swimmer going down," radioed Saylor.

"Swimmer going down," reiterated Whiddon.

Now Tunks took in the panoramic scene one hundred or so feet below him and saw precisely what he was "fixin' to get into."

He could see Jim and Clint almost directly beneath him, and he found himself thinking, *This is going to be fairly simple. I'm going to disconnect, and then I'm going to gather them up and drag them to the basket and put them inside. Once they're safely aboard, they'll drop the basket back down to me and I'll crawl in myself, and we'll be out of here.*

But in what seemed no more than a snap of a finger, Tunks found himself being dragged backward through the waves as another gust swept the chopper downwind. With so much tension suddenly seizing him under his arms, he quickly discovered that he had no way of releasing himself from the harness strap now holding him fast.

Whiddon gunned the engines, bringing the reverse odyssey to a halt, but not before dragging Tunks close to a hundred yards from the Bladeses. Finally able to slip free of the body strap, he free-fell into the sea, submerged briefly, then resurfaced and glanced quickly around. The Bladeses were nowhere in sight.

Above him, Tunks took in the "magnificent" vision of the H-3 aircraft "exuding power" and the large black USCG letters stenciled across the helo's white belly. He could see that, for all her power, the H-3 was being buffeted—its nose up, then down—and was shimmying from side to side, as if its 22,000-pound weight was inconsequential.

Tunks tried to call out to the Bladeses, wherever they were, hoping that in spite of the roar of the helicopter above and the breaking seas, they would hear him. Strangely, however, he couldn't make a sound. Tunks had never experienced anything like this. Perhaps it was the tremendous surge of adrenaline coursing through his system. Regardless, Tunks was forced to accept that he was unable to express so much as a "single blessed word."

Tunks performed a frantic 360-degree turn, searching for the man and his son, but it was pitch-black out, and the waves rolling through the area were so high that he was unable to visually hit upon them.

From the uncertain position of the helicopter overhead, it was clear to Whiddon that Tunks had become disoriented and that he no longer had any idea where the Bladeses were. Then Whiddon struck on an idea. He swung the searchlight away from Tunks and shone it down on the Bladeses.

Tunks took in the powerful column of the aircraft's floodlight as it swung to point somewhere in the distance. The shaft of light seemed to imply that Jim Blades and his son were several hundred feet away. Though Tunks could not see them, or communicate with Whiddon, he was certain that the end of that light was where he needed to be, and he began to move in that direction.

It was not a previously choreographed signal. "He didn't know to do that," John Whiddon later recalled. "It was one of the miraculous things that happened that night."

Moving along, his head completely above the water, Tunks used his arms only to steer him and his flipperlike fins into the oncoming storm waves. He swam up to the top of one wave and down to the bottom of the next. En route, he was roughed up severely when several of the waves broke over him. Peering intently as he passed over the top of one wave, he saw the searchlight beam bang off the reflective tape as the Bladeses simultaneously crested over a distant wave.

Feeling both grateful and relieved, Tunks urgently sprinted ahead in order to prevent any possibility of losing them again. When he finally closed on them, he swam up behind the drifting pair, grasped Jim Blades by the back of his suit, and swung him around. And suddenly he found himself staring into the youthful face of six-year-old Clint Blades. The boy possessed a serenity that Tunks had not expected, a kind of grace under pressure, which, given the present set of circumstances, seemed inexplicable.

Tunks would forever remember the moment. The boy seemed very peaceful. Tunks had a little boy, too, and he realized that he had to do everything that he could to get the boy and his father out of there.

"How are you doing?" shouted Tunks.

"We're hanging in there," Jim Blades replied, even though he was certain that he wouldn't be able to get into the basket under his own power. "Do you think they're going to be able to get us out of here?"

"Not to worry. We do this all the time," replied Jeff Tunks reassuringly, stretching the truth more than a little.

"Okay, now," explained Tunks. "We're going to get the basket over here, we're going to put you in the basket, we're going to hoist you up into the aircraft, and everything's going to be fine."

Several minutes later, the rescue basket landed in the water, well off from them. Immediately, Tunks grabbed the Bladeses and started dragging them toward it. They were closing fast on it, when the helicopter struggling to hover overhead was abruptly blown back off the site. The basket sprang from the water and shot into the sky like a missile being launched.

For the next few minutes, each time Tunks saw the basket land in the water in anything like a stationary position, he'd immediately start hustling toward it, towing the Bladeses along behind him.

Half a dozen similar attempts ensued before the gyrations of both basket and man finally coincided. Tunks could feel another sudden surge of adrenaline flooding his system. He grabbed Jim Blades by the back of his body harness, pulled the basket close with the other, and floated the Bladeses near. Then, just as he had been trained, he rolled them up and over his hip and set them down inside the basket in one seemingly effortless movement.

Tunks could see the hoist operator, Carl Saylor, crouched in the side doorway of the helo. He was waiting for Tunks to climb into the basket, as well. There was no room left, however, so Tunks pushed the basket away, lifted his right arm, and gave Saylor the thumbs-up sign.

Jim and Clint Blades sprang from the water as if weightless as Carl Saylor "two-blocked" the hoist, bringing the basket up at top speed. As they rose, the Bladeses began swinging violently below the chopper. Tunks could see how Cmdr. Whiddon, climbing frantically in the H-3, was doing everything possible to make sure the precious cargo below cleared the wave tops. It turned out to be a beautiful hoist. Jim Blades and his son rose clear of the sea and ascended to the side door of the helicopter, untouched by further calamity.

As he watched them rise, Tunks was suddenly struck with a euphoric sense of accomplishment at having successfully completed one of the first high-seas rescue-swimmer operations in USCG history. "Yes!" he howled aloud.

And just as suddenly, he felt himself breaking free of the fears that had bound him. He had full confidence in his crewmates, and as Whiddon and his helicopter danced across the skies and Carl Saylor rushed to lower the basket to him again, Tunks experienced a resolute faith in the final outcome. *They'll get me,* he thought as he drifted alone over the pummeling seas and through the darkness. *I'm going to be fine.*

Inside the helicopter, Jim Blades still did not feel safe. The rattling, wind-battered machine that carried them felt no more substantial to him, he said, than "a bunch of spare parts all flying in formation." Furthermore, it was agonizing knowing that Jeff Tunks was still in the water and that they were having real trouble trying to fish him out.

As Tunks drifted in closer to the craggy, abrupt, sheer rock cliffs lining Kruzof Island, Whiddon flashed his floodlight along the shoreline. Even from the water, Tunks could see the ponderous storm waves gathering themselves in the shallows and crashing against the cliffs. He was certain that there was no way he could survive an attempt to reach shore through such a surf.

But Tunks also knew that with thirteen years of flying under his belt, Cmdr. Whiddon was probably the finest stick-and-rudder pilot at the base in Sitka. With Lt. Breithaupt seated beside Whiddon as co-pilot, Tunks could not have imagined being caught in such a predicament with better people sitting up front. Nor could he think of more competent men than Carl Saylor on the hoist and Mark Mylne on the radio.

After three or four more missed attempts to drop the rescue basket close to him, Jeff Tunks reached overhead and managed to snag it with an arm as it swung past. Sinking the basket with the weight of his body, he swam into it, wearing fins, snorkel, and all. He came to rest on his buttocks on the floor of the metal cage. Doubling over into a ball, he rose up only long enough to give Carl Saylor another thumbs-up before crouching back down again.

Abruptly, a gust of wind of a hundred miles per hour or better plowed into the hovering chopper and sent it reeling. Completely helpless to rise, barely able to keep the aircraft in the air, Whiddon struggled to regain a semblance of control.

In the mayhem that followed, the rescue basket was jerked from the water and launched into the sky like a recoiling paddle ball. With Jeff Tunks huddled down inside, the otherwise-hollow shell was jerked about on the end of the cable line like a knot on the end of a whiplash. Tunks was jerked around so violently that he nearly collided with the bottom of the helicopter itself.

As the accelerating chopper fled backward at more than sixty miles per hour, there was a "massive explosion" as the rescue basket collided with an oncoming wave. The water struck him from behind, knocking the wind from him and ripping both his mask and snorkel from his face. Tunks hadn't even seen it coming.

It was then that John Whiddon caught the unsettling vision of Jeff Tunks out his front window. His favorite rescue swimmer was being dragged along behind them. Both basket and man bounced across the water like a skipping rock, and wherever they touched down, white explosions of sea spray erupted.

Coming off the previous collision, Tunks and the basket would arch down and forward, flying through the broad wave troughs on the blunt end of a pendulum swing before hitting the crown of the next wave. Tunks plowed into three consecutive waves before Whiddon was able to instruct a climb. The third wave proved to be the culmination of his ride. Tunks hit so hard that Whiddon could actually feel the helicopter shudder.

"Oh my God! Did you see him hit that wave?" barked Carl Saylor.

I've killed him, thought Whiddon.

Jeff Tunks felt the basket start to capsize, so he clutched at the steel meshing of the floor to prevent himself from being tossed out.

"Bring him up!" screamed John Whiddon.

When Jeff Tunks was finally yanked aboard, he was choking on some salt water he'd inadvertently inhaled.

"Swimmer's in the cabin, sir. Ready for forward flight," reported Saylor triumphantly.

Tunks crawled across the heaving floor and pulled himself up onto the troop seat. Then, looking over at Jim Blades and his son Clint, he once again gave the thumbs-up sign, which they returned.

"Jeff's all right," Carl Saylor told Whiddon. "He's swallowed a lot of water, and he's bruised, but otherwise, he's all right."

With the fishing boat *Bluebird* destroyed but her shivering survivors safely on board, Whiddon turned the H-3 toward home.

At the time Jim and Clint Blades were aboard the sinking *Bluebird,* Jill Blades and her son Curt were talking quietly. Then a freakish blast of wind rocked the house. Jill could hear the cables tethering the house to the shore cinch up tight and groan under the strain as the house swung out across the water.

Jill hurried down out of the loft and threw open one of the portholes her husband had so cleverly built into the living room walls. The wind and rain were blowing straight into her face, driving against the outside walls, pelting the windows, and sending a stream of seawater up over the outside deck, under the front door, and across the cabin floor.

Oh my word, Jill thought. *Jim's out in this?*

She hurried over to the CB radio, switched it on, and tried to reach her husband, but to no avail. She was clicking through the channels when she caught the sound of her husband's voice on Channel 16. He was talking to a Coast Guard helicopter pilot. The rescue of both her husband and son, she quickly surmised, was already under way.

"Are you guys going to get here pretty soon?" she heard Jim ask the Coast Guard. "'Cause my decks are awash."

Jill refused to panic. As the wife of a man who made his living on the sea, she was acutely aware of the inherent risks such a life involved. Besides, her husband was a strong, resourceful man who could fix or repair virtually anything. Turning to her son Curt, she said, "Daddy's in trouble, honey. Got to start praying."

With her head bowed, she began. "Oh, Father God, I just ask that you be with them out there tonight. Protect my little boy. Protect my husband. And bring them back safely to me."

Then Jill Blades struck on an idea. Switching channels, she used the radio to call Laura and Ben Hubbard, members of her church, and they began a prayer chain that quickly branched out into the community of Sitka.

"Mom," said little Curt, "when Dad and Clint get back, I'm never going to let 'em go out in a storm again."

Then Jill Blades caught the voice of the Coast Guard pilot on the radio. "Okay, we're coming up over the top of you," he said. Suddenly, all communications between the pilot and Jill's husband ceased. For the next twenty minutes, nothing more was heard from either of them.

Jill Blades had been all right up until that time. But now she felt fear beginning to well up. *The helicopter has either crashed or the boat sank, and Jim and Clint are gone,* she thought. *And they're not going to tell me, because they're afraid that I'll freak out, being out here all by myself.*

Then a friend, commercial fisherman Ottie Florschutz, radioed Jill, offering to take his fishing boat out to their houseboat and get her and her son Curt to town.

"Fishing vessel *Adeline* to *Bluebird*," he began. "Jill, do you want me to come out and pick you up?"

"No, Ottie," she replied. "I don't want anybody else out in this stuff. It's really howling out here. The only thing is—I just wish they'd tell me. If they're dead, I just want them to tell me that they're dead, so I know. I just gotta know what happened."

It was then that the voice of a member of the Coast Guard came over Channel 16.

"Mrs. Blades," the man said.

"Yes?" she replied.

"We got them."

"Thank God!" she yelled, loudly enough for all to hear.

"I didn't know if God was going to make me a widow," she later told me when I visited their island home in Sitka Sound. "I didn't know what was going to happen, because I know that some people don't come back."

I wonder if Mr. Blades ever went back out to fish the waters of Sitka Sound, or if his wife followed through on her promise, and convinced him to take up a less dangerous occupation. We'll probably never know.

SNOW AND ICE

When it comes to survival, water can be hazardous no matter what form it takes. While the perils of the ocean are many and varied, ice and snow also holds its own unique set of obstacles to conquer, the most dangerous one being the life-sapping, mind-numbing cold. The lack of fuel for a fire or natural supplies for shelter (although the many stories of survivors building snow caves indicates that the white stuff has its uses as well) are two more large impediments to making it out alive. Then there is the treacherous nature of the landscape itself—with no features to mark distance or progress and an unstable surface where every step may uncover a deadly crevasse or, if on a mountain, create a powerful avalanche—which has claimed many, many lives.

Above all, surviving in an arctic environment means slogging across an endless field of white snow, trying to prevent snow-blindness from the sunlight glaring off the wind-polished snow and ice, dodging both natural and animal hazards (did we mention hungry polar bears?), digging in to weather violent storms, and trying to see if fingers and toes have succumbed to frostbite. Yet men and women have been driven to challenge these most inhospitable climates, whether trying to find a northern passage to the Pacific Ocean, or being the first to reach the North or South Poles. Some returned from their incredible ordeal, others did not, sacrificing themselves on those barren, snow-swept plains.

The following stories are no less epic, from a man trapped on an ice floe drifting out to sea to a firsthand account of surviving being buried alive in an avalanche, these are stories of those who challenged the snow and ice—and won.

ESCAPE FROM THE TOP OF THE WORLD

Fridtjof Nansen (1861–1930)
From *Farthest North*

The North and South Poles have held a special place in the hearts of adventurers ever since they learned of their existence. From Henry Hudson's ill-fated voyage to find a Northwest Passage in 1609, where he was eventually cast adrift by his mutinous crew, to various other attempts over the years, the North Pole remained an elusive goal, pursued by explorers around the world.

In 1893, Norwegian Renaissance man Fridtjof Nansen—explorer, scientist, and diplomat (in 1922 he was awarded the Nobel Peace Prize for his work as a League of Nations High Commissioner)—began his attempt to reach the North Pole. His plan was to sail his ship the Fram *as far north as possible, trying to purposely get it stuck in the ice, which would then carry it to the North Pole. When the polar ice pack didn't accede to his wishes, he set out with Hjalmar Johansen to try and reach the pole by dog sled in 1895. Bad weather forced them to turn back, and now the arduous task of retreating from the top of the world began. Among the obstacles they faced were exposure, rotten ice, hungry, marauding polar bears, and belligerent walruses.*

WEDNESDAY, JULY 24TH. At last the marvel has come to pass—land, land! And after we had almost given up our belief in it! After nearly two years, we again see something rising above that never-ending white line on the horizon yonder—a white line, which for millennium after millennium has stretched over this sea, and, which for millenniums to come shall stretch in the same way. We are leaving it, and leaving no trace behind us; for the track of our little caravan across the endless plains has long ago disappeared. A new life is beginning for us; for the ice it is ever the same.

"It has long haunted our dreams, this land, and now it comes like a vision, like fairyland. Drift-white, it arches above the horizon like distant clouds, which one is afraid will disappear every minute. The most wonderful thing is that we have seen this land all the time without knowing it. I examined it several times with the telescope from 'Longing Camp' in the belief that it might be snowfields, but always came to the conclusion that it was only clouds, as I could never discover any dark point. Then, too, it seemed to change form, which, I suppose, must be attributed to the mist which always lay over it; but it always came back again at the same place with its remarkable regular curves. I now remember that dark crag we saw east of us at the camp, and, which I took to be an iceberg. It must certainly have been a little islet of some kind.

"The ice was worse and more broken than ever yesterday; it was, indeed, a labor to force one's way over pressure ridges like veritable mountains, with valleys and clefts in between; but on we went in good spirits, and made some progress. At lanes where a crossing was difficult to find we did not hesitate to launch kayaks and sledges, and were soon over in this manner. Sometimes after a very bad bit we would come across some flat ice for a short distance, and over this we would go like wildfire, splashing through ponds and puddles. While I was on ahead at one time yesterday morning, Johansen went up onto a hummock to look at the ice, and remarked a curious black stripe over the horizon; but he supposed it to be only a cloud, he said, and I thought no more about the matter. When, some while later, I also ascended a hummock to look at the ice, I became aware of the same black stripe; it ran obliquely from the horizon up into what I supposed to be a white bank of clouds. The longer I looked at this bank and stripe the more unusual I thought them, until I was constrained to fetch the glass. No sooner had I fixed it on the black part than it struck me at once that this must be land, and that not far off. There was a large snowfield out of which black rocks projected. It was not long before Johansen had the glass to his eye, and convinced himself that we really had land before us. We both of us naturally became in the highest spirits. I then saw a similar white arching outline a little farther east; but it was for the most part covered with white mist, from which it could hardly be distinguished, and, moreover, was continually changing form. It soon, however, came out entirely, and was considerably larger and higher than the former, but there was not a black speck to be seen on it. So this was what land looked like, now that we had come to it! I had imagined it in many forms, with high peaks and glittering glaciers, but never like this. There was nothing kindly about this, but it was indeed no less welcome; and on the whole we could not expect it to be otherwise than snow-covered, with all the snow, which falls here.

"So then we pitched the tent and had a feast suited to the occasion: lobscouse made of potatoes (for the last time but one; we had saved them long for this occasion), pemmican, dried bear's and seal's flesh, and bear tongues, chopped up together. After this was a second course, consisting of bread crumbs fried in bear's grease, also vril-food and butter, and a piece of chocolate to wind up."

We thought this land so near that it could not possibly take long to reach it, certainly not longer than till next evening. Johansen was even certain that we should do it the same day, but nevertheless thirteen days were to elapse, occupied in the same monotonous drudgery over the drift ice.

On July 25th I write: "When we stopped in the fog yesterday evening we had a feeling that we must have come well under land. This morning, when we turned out, the first thing Johansen did when he went to fetch some water for me to cook with was, of course, to climb up on the nearest hummock and look at the land. There it lay, considerably nearer than before, and he is quite certain that we shall reach it before night." I also discovered a new land to our west (S 60° W magnetic) that day; a regular, shield-like, arched outline, similar to the other land; and it was low above the horizon, and appeared to be a long way off.

We went on our way as fast as we could across lanes and rough ice, but did not get far in the day, and the land did not seem to be much nearer. In reality there was no difference to be seen, although we tried to imagine that it was steadily growing higher. On Saturday, July 27th, I seem to have a suspicion that in point of fact we were drifting away from land, I write: "The wind began to blow from the SSW (magnetic) just as we were getting off yesterday, and increased as the day went on. It was easy to perceive by the atmosphere that the wind was driving the ice off the land, and land lanes formed particularly on the east side of it. When I was up on a hummock yesterday evening I observed a black stripe on the horizon under land; I examined it with the glass, and, as I had surmised, there was an ice edge or glacier stretching far in a westerly direction; and there was plainly a broad lane in front of it, to judge by the dark bank of mist, which lay there. It seems to me that land cannot be far off, and if the ice is tolerably passable we may reach it today. The wind continued last night, but it has quieted down now, and there is sunshine outside. We try by every means in our power to get a comfortable night's rest in our new bag of blankets. We have tried lying on the bare ice, on the 'ski,' and to-night on the bare ice again; but it must be confessed that it is hard and never will be very comfortable; a little chilly, too, when one is wet; but we shall appreciate a good warm bed all the more when we get it.

"Tuesday, July 30th. We make incredibly slow progress; but we are pushing our way nearer land all the same. Every kind of hinderance seems to beset us: now I am suffering so much from my back (lumbago?) that yesterday it was only by exerting all my strength of will that I could drag myself along. In difficult places Johansen had to help me with my sledge. It began yesterday, and at the end of our march he had to go first and find the way. Yesterday I was much worse, and how I am today I do not know before I begin to walk; but I ought to be thankful that I can drag myself along at all, though it is with endless pain. We had to halt and camp on account of rain yesterday morning at three, after only having gone nine hours. The rain succeeded in making us wet before we had found a suitable place for the tent. Here we have been a whole day while it has been pouring down, and we have hardly become drier. There are puddles under us and the bag is soaked on the underside. The wind has gone around to the west just now, and it has stopped raining, so we made some porridge for breakfast and think of going on again; but if it should begin to rain again we must stop, as it will not do to get wet through when we have no change of clothes. It is anything but pleasant as it is to lie with wet legs and feet that are like icicles, and not have a dry thread to put on. Full-grown Ross's gulls were seen singly four times today, and when Johansen was out to fetch water this morning he saw two.

"Wednesday, July 31st. The ice is as disintegrated and impracticable as can well be conceived. The continual friction and packing of the floes against each other grind up the ice so that the water is full of brash and small pieces; to ferry over this in the kayaks is impossible, and the search is long before we eventually find a hazardous crossing. Sometimes we have to form one by pushing small floes together, or must ferry the sledges over on a little floe. We spend much time and labor on each single lane, and progress becomes slow in this way. My back still painful, Johansen had to go ahead yesterday also; and evening and morning he is obliged to take off my boots and socks, for I am unable to do it myself. He is touchingly unselfish, and takes care of me as if I were a child: everything he thinks can ease me he does quietly, without my knowing it. Poor fellow, he has to work doubly hard now, and does not know how this will end. I feel very much better today, however, and it is to be hoped shall soon be all right.

"Thursday, August 1st. Ice with more obstacles than here—is it to be found, I wonder? But we are working slowly on, and, that being the case, we ought, perhaps, to be satisfied. We have also had a change—a brilliantly fine day; but it seems to me the south wind we have had, and which opened the lanes, has put us a good way farther off land again. We have also drifted a long distance to the east, and no longer see the most west-erly land with the black rocks, which we remarked at first. It would seem as if the Ross's gulls keep to land here; we see them daily.

"One thing, however, I am rejoicing over; my back is almost well, so that I shall not delay our progress anymore. I have some idea now what it would be like if one of us became seriously ill. Our fate would then be sealed, I think.

"Friday, August 2nd. It seems as if everything conspired to delay us, and that we shall never get away from this drift ice. My back is well again now; the ice was more passable yesterday than before, so that we nearly made a good day's march; but in return wind and current set us from shore, and we are farther away again. Against these two enemies all fighting is in vain, I am afraid. We have drifted far off to the southeast, have got the north point of the land about due west of us, and we are now in about 81°36' N. My only hope now is that this drift eastward, away from land, may stop or alter its course, and thus bring us nearer land. It is unfortunate that the lanes are covered with young ice, which it would be disastrous to put the kayaks through. If this gets worse, things will look very bad. Meanwhile we have nothing to do but go on as fast as we can. If we are going to drift back into the ice again, then—then—

"Saturday, August 3rd. Inconceivable toil. We never could go on with it were it not for the fact that we *must*. We have made wretchedly little progress, even if we have made any at all. We have had no food for the dogs the last few days except the ivory gulls and fulmars we have been able to shoot, and that has been a couple a day. Yesterday the dogs only had a little bit of blubber each.

"Sunday, August 4th. These lanes are desperate work and tax one's strength. We often have to go several hundred yards on mere brash, or from block to block, dragging the sledges after us, and in constant fear of their capsizing into the water. Johansen was very nearly in yesterday, but, as always hitherto, he managed to save himself. The dogs fall in and get a bath continually.

"Monday, August 5th. We have never had worse ice than yesterday, but we managed to force our way on a little, nevertheless, and two happy incidents marked the day: the first was that Johansen was not eaten up by a bear, and the second, that we saw open water under the glacier edge ashore.

"We set off about seven o'clock yesterday morning and got onto ice as bad as it could be. It was as if some giant had hurled down enormous blocks pell-mell, and had strewn wet snow in between them with water under-neath; and into this we sank above our knees. There were also numbers of deep pools in between the blocks. It was like toiling over hill and dale, up and down over block after block and ridge after ridge, with deep clefts in between; not a clear space big enough to pitch a tent on even, and thus it went on the whole time. To put a coping-stone to our misery, there was such a mist that we could not see a hundred yards in front of us. After an exhausting march we at last reached a lane where we had to ferry over in the kayaks. After having cleared the side of the lane from young ice and brash, I drew my sledge to the end of the ice, and was holding it to prevent it slipping in, when I heard a scuffle behind me, and Johansen, who had just turned around to pull his sledge flush with mine, cried, 'Take the gun!' I turned around and saw an enormous bear throwing itself on him, and Johansen on his back. I tried to seize my gun, which was in its case on the foredeck, but at the same moment the kayak slipped into the water. My first thought was to throw myself into the water over the kayak and fire from there, but I recognized how risky it would be. I began to pull the kayak, with its heavy cargo, onto the high edge of the ice again as quickly as I could, and was on my knees pulling and tugging to get at my gun. I had no time to look around and see what was going on behind me, when I heard Johansen quietly say, 'You must look sharp if you want to be in time!'

"Look sharp? I should think so! At last I got hold of the butt-end, dragged the gun out, turned around in a sitting posture, and cocked the shot barrel. The bear was standing not two yards off, ready to make an end to my dog, Kaifas. There was no time to lose in cocking the other barrel, so I gave it a charge of shot behind the ear, and it fell down dead between us.

"The bear must have followed our track like a cat, and, covered by the ice-blocks, have slunk up while we were clearing the ice from the lane and had our backs to him. We could see by the trail how it had crept over a small ridge just behind us under cover of a mound by Johansen's kayak. While the latter, without suspecting anything or looking around, went back and stooped down to pick up the hauling rope, he suddenly caught sight of an animal crouched up at the end of the kayak, but thought it was Suggen; and before he had time to realize that it was so big he received a cuff on the ear, which made him see fireworks, and then, as I mentioned before, over he went on his back. He tried to defend himself as best he could with his fists. With one hand he seized the throat of the animal, and held fast, clinching it with all his might. It was just as the bear was about to bite Johansen in the head that he uttered the memorable words, 'Look sharp!' The bear kept glancing at me continually, speculating, no doubt, as to what I was going to do; but then caught sight of the dog and turned toward it. Johansen let go as quick as thought, and wriggled himself away, while the bear gave Suggen a cuff, which made him howl lustily, just as he does when we thrash him. Then Kaifas got a slap on the nose. Meanwhile Johansen had struggled to his legs, and when I fired had got his gun, which was sticking out of the kayak hole. The only harm done was that the bear had scraped some grime off Johansen's right cheek, so that he has a white stripe on it, and had given him a slight wound in one hand; Kaifas had also got a scratch on his nose.

"Hardly had the bear fallen before we saw two more peeping over a hummock a little way off—cubs, who naturally wanted to see the result of the maternal chase. They were two large cubs. I thought it was not worthwhile to sacrifice a cartridge on them, but Johansen expressed his opinion that young bear's flesh was much more delicate in flavor than old. He would only shoot one, he said, and started off. However, the cubs took to their heels, although they came back a little while later, and we could hear them at a long distance growling after their mother.

"Johansen sent one of them a ball, but the range was too long, and he only wounded it. With some terrific growls it started off again, and Johansen after it; but he gave up the chase soon, as he saw it promised to be a long one. While we were cutting up the she-bear the cubs came back on the other side of the lane, and the whole time we were there we had them walking around us. When we had fed the dogs well, and had eaten some of the raw meat ourselves, and had furthermore stowed away in the kayaks the meat we had cut off the legs, we at last ferried over the lane and went on our way.

"The ice was not good; and, to make bad worse, we immediately came on some terrible lanes, full of nothing but tightly packed lumps of ice. In some places there were whole seas of it, and it was enough to make one despair. Among all this loose ice we came on an unusually thick old floe, with high mounds on it and pools in between. It was from one of these mounds that I observed through the glass the open water at the foot of the glacier, and now we cannot have far to go. But the ice looks very bad on ahead, and each piece when it is like this may take a long time to travel over.

"As we went along we heard the wounded bear lowing ceaselessly behind us; it filled the whole of this silent world of ice with its bitter plaint over the cruelty of man. It was miserable to hear it; and if we had had time we should undoubtedly have gone back and sacrificed a cartridge on it. We saw the cubs go off to the place where the mother was lying, and thought to ourselves that we had got rid of them, but heard them soon afterward, and even when we had camped they were not far off.

"Wednesday, August 7th. At last we are under land; at last the drift ice lies behind us, and before us is open water—open, it is to be hoped, to the end. Yesterday was the day. When we came out of the tent the evening of the day before yesterday we both thought we must be nearer the edge of the glacier than ever, and with fresh courage, and in the faint hope of reaching land that day, we started on our journey. Yet we dared not think our life on the drift ice was so nearly at an end. After wandering about on it for five months and suffering so many disappointments, we were only too well prepared for a new defeat. We thought, however, that the ice looked more promising farther on, though before we had gone far we came to broad lanes full of slush and foul, uneven ice, with hills and dales, and deep snow and water, into which we sank up to our thighs. After a couple of lanes of this kind, matters improved a little, and we got on to some flat ice. After having gone over this for a while, it became apparent how much nearer we were to the edge of the glacier. It could not possibly be far off now. We eagerly harnessed ourselves to the sledges again, put on a spurt, and away we went through snow and water, over mounds and ridges. We went as hard as we could, and what did we care if we sank into water till far above our fur leggings, so that both they and our 'komager' filled and gurgled like a pump? What did it matter to us now, so long as we got on?

"We soon reached plains, and over them we went quicker and quicker. We waded through ponds where the spray flew up on all sides. Nearer and nearer we came, and by the dark water-sky before us, which continually rose higher, we could see how we were drawing near to open water. We did not even notice bears now. There seemed to be plenty about, tracks, both old and new, crossing and recrossing; one had even inspected the tent while we were asleep, and by the fresh trail we could see how it had come down wind in lee of us. We had no use for a bear now; we had food enough. We were soon able to see the open water under the wall of the glacier, and our steps lengthened even more. As I was striding along I thought of the march of the Ten Thousand through Asia, when Xenophon's soldiers, after a year's war against superior forces, at last saw the sea from a mountain and cried, 'Thalatta! thalatta!' Maybe this sea was just as welcome to us after our months in the endless white drift ice.

"At last, at last, I stood by the edge of the ice. Before me lay the dark surface of the sea, with floating white floes; far away the glacier wall rose abruptly from the water; over the whole lay a somber, foggy light. Joy welled up in our hearts at this sight, and we could not give it expression in words. Behind us lay all our troubles, before us the waterway home. I waved my hat to Johansen, who was a little way behind, and he waved his in answer and shouted 'Hurrah!' Such an event had to be celebrated in some way, and we did it by having a piece of chocolate each.

"While we were standing there looking at the water the large head of a seal came up, and then disappeared silently; but soon more appeared. It is very reassuring to know that we can procure food at any minute we like.

"Now came the rigging of the kayaks for the voyage. Of course, the better way would have been to paddle singly, but, with the long, big sledges on the deck, this was not easy, and leave them behind I dared not; we might have good use for them yet. For the time being, therefore, there was nothing else to be done but to lash the two kayaks together side by side in our usual manner, stiffen them out with snowshoes under the straps, and place the sledges athwart them, one before and one behind.

"It was sad to think we could not take our two last dogs with us, but we should probably have no further use for them, and it would not have done to take them with us on the decks of our kayaks. We were sorry to part with them; we had become very fond of these two survivors. Faithful and enduring, they had followed us the whole journey through; and, now that better times had come, they must say farewell to life. Destroy them in the same way as the others we could not; we sacrificed a cartridge on each of them. I shot Johansen's, and he shot mine.

"So then we were ready to set off. It was a real pleasure to let the kayaks dance over the water and hear the little waves plashing against the sides. For two years we had not seen such a surface of water before us. We had not gone far before we found that the wind was so good that we ought to make use of it, and so we rigged up a sail on our fleet. We glided easily before the wind in toward the land we had so longed for all these many months. What a change, after having forced one's way inch by inch and foot by foot on ice! The mist had hidden the land from us for a while, but now it parted, and we saw the glacier rising straight in front of us. At the same moment the sun burst forth, and a more beautiful morning I can hardly remember. We were soon underneath the glacier, and had to lower our sail and paddle westward along the wall of ice, which was from fifty to sixty feet in height, and on which a landing was impossible. It seemed as if there must be little movement in this glacier; the water had eaten its way deep underneath it at the foot, and there was no noise of falling fragments or the cracking of crevasses to be heard, as there generally is with large glaciers. It was also quite even on the top, and no crevasses were to be seen. Up the entire height of the wall there was stratification, which was un-usually marked. We soon discovered that a tidal current was running west-ward along the wall of the glacier with great rapidity, and took advantage of it to make good progress. To find a camping ground, however, was not easy, and at last we were reduced to taking up our abode on a drifting floe. It was glorious, though, to go to rest in the certainty that we should not wake to drudgery in the drift ice.

"When we turned out today we found that the ice had packed around us, and I do not know yet how we shall get out of it, though there is open water not far off to our west.

"Thursday, August 8th. After hauling our impedimenta over some floes we got into open water yesterday without much difficulty. When we had reached the edge of the water we made a paddle each from our snowshoe staffs, to which we bound blades made of broken-off snow-shoes. They were a great improvement on the somewhat clumsy paddles, with canvas blades lashed to bamboo sticks. I was very much inclined to chop off our sledges, so that they would only be half as long as before; by so doing we could carry them on the afterdeck of the kayaks, and could thus each paddle alone, and our advance would be much quicker than by paddling the twin kayaks. However, I thought, perhaps, it was unadvis-able. The water looked promising enough on ahead, but there was mist, and we could not see far; we knew nothing of the country or the coast we had come to, and might yet have good use for the sledges. We there-fore set off in our double kayak, as before, with the sledges athwart the deck fore and aft.

"The mist soon rose a little. It was then a dead calm; the surface of the water lay like a great mirror before us, with bits of ice and an occasional floe drifting on it. It was a marvelously beautiful sight, and it was indeed glorious to sit there in our light vessels and glide over the surface without any exertion. Suddenly a seal rose in front of us, and over us flew con-tinually ivory gulls and fulmars and kittiwakes. Little auks we also saw,

and some Ross's gulls, and a couple of terns. There was no want of animal life here, nor of food when we should require it.

"We found open water, broader and broader, as we paddled on our way
beside the wall of ice; but it would not clear so that we could see something
of our surroundings. The mist still hung obstinately over it.

"Our course at first lay west to north (magnetic); but the land always
trended more and more to the west and southwest; the expanse of water
grew greater, and soon it widened out to a large sea, stretching in a southwesterly direction. A breeze sprang up from the north-northeast, and there
was considerable motion, which was not pleasant, as in our double craft
the seas continually washed up between the two and wetted us. We put
in toward evening and pitched the tent on the shore ice, and just as we
did so it began to rain, so that it was high time to be under a roof.

"Friday, August 9th. Yesterday morning we had again to drag the
sledges with the kayaks over some ice, which had drifted in front of our
camping ground, and during this operation I managed to fall into the
water and get wet. It was with difficulty we finally got through and out
into open water. After a while we again found our way closed, and were
obliged to take to hauling over some floes, but after this we had good
open water the whole day. It was a northeasterly wind, which had set the
ice toward the land, and it was lucky we had got so far, as behind us, to
judge by the atmosphere, the sea was much blocked. The mist hung over
the land so that we saw little of it. According as we advanced we were
able to hold a more southerly course, and, the wind being nearly on the
quarter, we set sail about one o'clock, and continued sailing all day till we
stopped yesterday evening. Our sail, however, was interrupted once when
it was necessary to paddle round an ice-point north of where we are now;
the contrary current was so strong that it was as much as we could do
to make way against it, and it was only after considerable exertion that
we succeeded in doubling the point. We have seen little of the land we are
skirting up to this, on account of the mist; but as far as I can make out it
consists of islands. First there was a large island covered with an ice-sheet;
then west of it a smaller one, on which are the two crags of rock, which
first made us aware of the vicinity of land; next came a long fjord or
sound, with massive shore ice in it; and then a small, low headland, or
rather an island, south of which we are now encamped. This shore ice lying along the land is very remarkable. It is unusually massive and uneven;
it seems to be composed of huge blocks welded together, which in a great
measure, at any rate, must proceed from the ice-sheet. There has also,

perhaps, been violent pressure against the land, which has heaved the sea ice up together with pieces of ice from the calving of the glacier, and the whole has frozen together into a conglomerate mass. A medium-sized iceberg lay off the headland north of us, where the current was so strong. Where we are now lying, however, there is flat fjord-ice between the low island here and a larger one farther south.

"This land grows more of a problem, and I am more than ever at a loss to know where we are. It is very remarkable to me that the coast continually trends to the south instead of to the west. I could explain it all best by supposing ourselves to be on the west coast of the archipelago of Franz Josef Land, were it not that the variation, I think, is too great, and also for the number of Ross's gulls there still are. Not one has with certainty been seen in Spitzbergen, and if my supposition is right, this should not be far off. Yesterday we saw a number of them again; they are quite as common here as the other species of gull.

"Saturday, August 10th. We went up on to the little islet we had camped by. It was covered by a glacier, which curved over it in the shape of a shield; there were slopes to all sides; but so slight was the gradient that our snowshoes would not even run of themselves on the crust of snow. From the ridge we had a fair view, and, as the mist lifted just then, we saw the land about us tolerably well. We now perceived plainly that what we had been skirting along was only islands. The first one was the biggest. The other land, with the two rocky crags, had, as we could see, a strip of bare land along the shore on the northwest side. Was it there, perhaps, the Ross's gulls congregated and had their breeding grounds? The island to our south also looked large; it appeared to be entirely covered by a glacier. Between the islands, and as far as we could perceive southeast and east, the sea was covered by perfectly flat fjord ice, but no land was to be discerned in that direction. There were no icebergs here, though we saw some later in the day on the south side of the island lying to the south of us.

"The glacier covering the little island on which we stood joined the fjord ice almost imperceptibly; only a few small fissures along the shore indicated where it probably began. There could not be any great rise and fall in the ice here, consequent on the tide, as the fissures would then, as a matter of course, have been considerably larger. This seemed remarkable, as the tidal current ran swift as a river here. On the west side of the island there lay in front of the glacier a rampart of ice and snow, which was probably formed of pieces of glacier ice and sea ice welded together.

It had the same character as the massive shore ice, which we had seen previously running along the land. This rampart went over imperceptibly with an even slope into the glacier within it.

"About three in the afternoon we finally set off in open water and sailed till eight or so in the evening; the water was then closed, and we were compelled to haul the fleet over flat ice to open water on the other side. But here, too, our progress seemed blocked, and as the current was against us we pitched the tent."

On August 10th we were "compelled partly to haul our sledges over the ice, partly to row in open water in a southwesterly direction. When we reached navigable waters again, we passed a flock of walruses lying on a floe. It was a pleasure to see so much food collected at one spot, but we did not take any notice of them, as, for the time being, we have meat and blubber enough. After dinner we managed, in the mist, to wander down a long bay into the shore ice, where there was no outlet; we had to turn back, and this delayed us considerably. We now kept a more westerly course, following the often massive and uneven edge of the ice; but the current was dead against us, and, in addition, young ice had been forming all day as we rowed along; the weather had been cold and still, with falling snow, and this began to be so thick that we could not make way against it any longer. We therefore went ashore on the ice, and hauled until ten in the evening.

"Bear tracks, old and new, in all directions—both the single ones of old bachelors and those of she-bears with cubs. It looks as if they had had a general rendezvous, or as if a flock of them had roamed backward and forward. I have never seen so many bear tracks in one place in my life.

"We have certainly done fourteen or twenty-five miles today; but still I think our progress is too slow if we are to reach Spitzbergen this year, and I am always wondering if we ought not to cut the ends off our sledges, so that each can paddle his own kayak. This young ice, however, which grows steadily worse, and the eleven degrees below freezing we now have, make me hold my hand. Perhaps winter is upon us, and then the sledges may be very necessary.

"It is a curious sensation to paddle in the mist, as we are doing, without being able to see a mile in front of us. The land we found we have left behind us. We are always in hopes of clear weather, in order to see where the land lies in front of us—for land there must be. This flat, unbroken ice must be attached to land of some kind; but clear weather we are not to have, it appears. Mist without ceasing; we must push on as it is.

"After having hauled some distance farther over the ice we came to open water again the following day (August 11th) and paddled for four or five hours. While I was on a hummock inspecting the waters ahead, a huge monster of a walrus came up quite near us. It lay puffing and glaring at us on the surface of the water, but we took no notice of it, got into our kayaks, and went on. Suddenly it came up again by the side of us, raised itself high out of the water, snorted so that the air shook, and threatened to thrust its tusks into our frail craft. We seized our guns, but at the same moment it disappeared, and came up immediately afterward on the other side, by Johansen's kayak, where it repeated the same maneuver. I said to him that if the animal showed signs of attacking us we must spend a cartridge on it. It came up several times and disappeared again; we could see it down in the water, passing rapidly on its side under our vessels, and, afraid lest it should make a hole in the bottom with its tusks, we thrust our paddles down into the water and frightened it away; but suddenly it came up again right by Johansen's kayak, and more savage than ever. He sent it a charge straight in the eyes, it uttered a terrific bellow, rolled over, and disappeared, leaving a trail of blood on the water behind it. We paddled on as hard as we could, knowing that the shot might have dangerous consequences, but we were relieved when we heard the walrus come up far behind us at the place where it had disappeared.

"We had paddled quietly on, and had long forgotten all about the walrus, when I suddenly saw Johansen jump into the air and felt his kayak receive a violent shock. I had no idea what it was, and looked around to see if some block of floating ice had capsized and struck the bottom of his kayak; but suddenly I saw another walrus rise up in the water beside us. I seized my gun, and as the animal would not turn its head so that I could aim at a spot behind the ear, where it is more easily wounded, I was constrained to put a ball in the middle of its forehead; there was no time to be lost. Happily this was enough, and it lay there dead and floating on the water. With great difficulty we managed to make a hole in the thick skin, and after cutting ourselves some strips of blubber and meat from the back we went on our way again.

"At seven in the evening the tidal current turned and the channel closed. There was no more water to be found. Instead of taking to hauling over the ice, we determined to wait for the opening of the channel when the tide should turn next day, and meanwhile to cut off the ends of our sledges, as I had so long been thinking of doing, and make ourselves some good double paddles, so that we could put on greater pace, and, in our single kayaks, make the most of the channel during the time it was open. While we were occupied in doing this the mist cleared off at last, and there lay land stretched out in front of us, extending a long way south and west from SE right up to NNW. It appeared to be a chain of islands with sounds between them. They were chiefly covered with glaciers, only here and there were perpendicular black mountain walls to be seen. It was a sight to make one rejoice to see so much land at one time. But where were we? This seemed a more difficult question to answer than ever. Could we, after all, have arrived at the east side of Franz Josef Land? It seemed very reasonable to suppose this to be the case. But then we must be very far east, and must expect a long voyage before we could reach Cape Fligely, on Crown Prince Rudolf Land. Meanwhile we worked hard to get the sledges ready; but as the mist gradually lifted and it became clearer and clearer, we could not help continually leaving them, to climb up onto the hummock beside us to look at the country, and speculate on this insoluble problem. We did not get to bed till seven in the morning of August 12th.

"Tuesday, August 13th. After having slept a few hours, we turned out of the bag again, for the current had turned, and there was a wide chan-nel. In our single kayaks we made good headway, but after going about five miles the channel closed, and we had to clamber onto the ice. We thought it advisable to wait until the tidal current turned, and see if there were not a channel running farther. If not, we must lash proper grips of wood to our curtailed sledges, and commence hauling toward a sound running through the land, which I see about WNW (true), and which, according to Payer's chart, I take to be Rawlinson's Sound."

But the crack did not open, and when it came to the point we had to continue on our way hauling.

"Wednesday, August 14th. We dragged our sledges and loads over a number of floes and ferried across lanes, arriving finally at a lane, which ran westward, in which we could paddle; but it soon packed together again, and we were stopped. The ivory gulls are very bold, and last night stole a piece of blubber lying close by the tent wall."

The following day we had to make our way as well as we could by paddling short distances in the lanes or hauling our loads over floes smaller or larger, as the case might be. The current, which was running like a mill-race, ground them together in its career. Our progress with our short, stumpy sledges was nothing very great, and of water suitable for paddling

in we found less and less. We stopped several times and waited for the ice
to open at the turn of the tide, but it did not do so, and on the morning
of August 15th we gave it up, turned inward, and took to the shore ice
for good. We set our course westward toward the sound we had seen for
several days now, and had struggled so to reach. The surface of the ice was
tolerably even and we got over the ground well. On the way we passed a
frozen-in iceberg, which was the highest we saw in these parts—some
fifty to sixty feet, I should say. I wished to go up it to get a better view of
our environment, but it was too steep, and we did not get higher than a
third part up the side.

"In the evening we at last reached the islands we had been steering
for the last few days, and for the first time for two years had bare land under foot. The delight of the feeling of being able to jump from block to
block of granite is indescribable, and the delight was not lessened when in
a little sheltered corner among the stones we found moss and flowers, beautiful poppies (*Papaver nudicaule*), *Saxifraga nivalis,* and a *Stellaria (sp.?)*. It goes
without saying that the Norwegian flag had to wave over this our first bare
land, and a banquet was prepared. Our petroleum, meanwhile, had given
out several days previously, and we had to contrive another lamp in which
train oil could be used. The smoking hot lobscouse, made of pemmican
and the last of our potatoes, was delicious, and we sat inside the tent and
kicked the bare grit under us to our heart's content. . . .

"Saturday, August 17th. Yesterday was a good day. We are in open water
on the west coast of Franz Josef Land, as far as I can make out, and may
again hope to get home this year. About noon yesterday we walked across
the ice from our moraine-islet to the higher island west of us. As I was
ready before Johansen, I went on first to examine the island a little. As he
was following me he caught sight of a bear on the level ice to leeward. It
came jogging up against the wind straight toward him. He had his gun
ready, but when a little nearer the bear stopped, reconsidered the situation, suddenly turned tail, and was soon out of sight.

"This island (Torup's Island) we came to seemed to me to be one of
the most lovely spots on the face of the earth. A beautiful flat beach, an
old strand line with shells strewn about, a narrow belt of clear water along
the shore, where snails and sea urchins (*Echinus*) were visible at the bottom and amphipoda were swimming about. In the cliffs overhead were
hundreds of screaming little auks, and beside us the snowbuntings flut-

tered from stone to stone with their cheerful twitter. Suddenly the sun
burst forth through the light fleecy clouds, and the day seemed to be all
sunshine. Here were life and bare land; we were no longer on the eternal
drift ice! At the bottom of the sea just beyond the beach I could see whole
forests of seaweed (*Laminaria* and *Fucus*). Under the cliffs here and there
were drifts of beautiful rose-colored snow.

"On the north side of the island we found the breeding place of numbers of black-backed gulls; they were sitting with their young in ledges of
the cliffs. Of course we had to climb up and secure a photograph of this
unusual scene of family life, and as we stood there high up on the cliff's
side we could see the drift ice whence we had come. It lay beneath us
like a white plain, and disappeared far away on the horizon. Beyond this
it was we had journeyed, and farther away still the *Fram* and our comrades were drifting yet.

"I had thought of going to the top of this island to get a better view,
and perhaps come nearer solving the problem of our whereabouts. But
when we were on the west side of it the mist came back and settled on
the top; we had to content ourselves with only going a little way up the
slope to look at our future course westward. Some way out we saw open
water; it looked like the sea itself, but before one could get to it there was
a good deal of ice. We came down again and started off. Along the land
there was a channel running some distance farther, and we tried it, but it
was covered everywhere with a thin layer of new ice, which we did not
dare to break through in our kayaks, and risk cutting a hole in them; so,
finally, a little way farther south we put in to drag up the kayaks and take
to the ice again. While we were doing this one huge bearded seal after
another stuck its head up by the side of the ice and gazed wonderingly at
us with its great eyes; then, with a violent header, and splashing the water
in all directions, it would disappear, to come up again soon afterward on
the other side. They kept playing around us, blowing, diving, reappear-
ing, and throwing themselves over so that the water foamed around them.
It would have been easy enough to capture one had we required it.

"At last, after a good deal of exertion, we stood at the margin of the
ice; the blue expanse of water lay before us as far as the eye could reach,
and we thought that for the future we had to do with it alone. To the
north there was land, the steep, black, basalt cliffs of which fell perpen-
dicularly into the sea. We saw headland after headland standing out northward, and farthest off of all we could descry a bluish glacier. The interior

was everywhere covered with an ice-sheet. Below the clouds, and over the land, was a strip of ruddy night sky, which was reflected in the melancholy, rocking sea.

"So we paddled on along the side of the glacier, which covered the whole country south of us. We became more and more excited as we approached the headland to the west. Would the coast trend south here, and was there no more land westward? It was this we expected to decide our fate—decide whether we should reach home that year or be compelled to winter somewhere on land. Nearer and nearer we came to it along the edge of the perpendicular wall of ice. At last we reached the headland, and our hearts bounded with joy to see so much water—only water—westward, and the coast trending southwest. We also saw a bare mountain projecting from the ice-sheet a little way farther on; it was a curious high ridge, as sharp as a knife blade. It was as steep and sharp as anything I have seen; it was all of dark, columnar basalt, and so jagged and peaked that it looked like a comb. In the middle of the mountain there was a gap or couloir, and there we crept up to inspect the seaway southward. The wall of rock was anything but broad there, and fell away on the south side in a perpendicular drop of several hundred feet. A cutting wind was blowing in the couloir. While we were lying there, I suddenly heard a noise, behind me, and on looking around I saw two foxes fighting over a little auk, which they had just caught. They clawed and tugged and bit as hard as they could on the very edge of the chasm; then they suddenly caught sight of us, not twenty feet away from them. They stopped fighting, looked up wonderingly, and began to run around and peep at us, first from one side, then from the other. Over us myriads of little auks flew backward and forward, screaming shrilly from the ledges in the mountainside. So far as we could make out, there appeared to be open sea, along the land to the westward. The wind was favorable, and although we were tired we decided to take advantage of the opportunity, have something to eat, rig up mast and sail on our canoes, and get afloat. We sailed till the morning, when the wind went down, and then we landed on the shore ice again and camped.

"I am as happy as a child in the thought that we are now at last really on the west coast of Franz Josef Land, with open water before us, and independent of ice and currents.

"Wednesday, August 24th. The vicissitudes of this life will never come to an end. When I wrote last I was full of hope and courage; and here we are stopped by stress of weather for four days and three nights, with the ice packed as tight as it can be against the coast. We see nothing but piled-up ridges, hummocks, and broken ice in all directions. Courage is still here, but hope—the hope of soon being home—that was relinquished a long time ago, and before us lies the certainty of a long, dark winter in these surroundings."

The intrepid Nansen and Johansen were forced to spend the winter in a crude hut made of rocks, moss, and walrus hides, living off walrus meat and blubber. The following spring, they headed out again, hoping to reach Spitsbergen, Norway. They traveled for another month until they met members of a British expedition camping on Franz Josef Island. Eventually Nansen returned home, having achieved the distinction of traveling the farthest north of any polar explorer up to that point.

ADRIFT ON AN ICE-PAN

Sir Wilfred Grenfell (1865–1940)

From *Adrift on an Ice-Pan*

Our next tale concerns a true humanitarian. Sir Wilfred Grenfell studied medicine at London Hospital Medical College before being assigned to improve the living conditions of the native inhabitants and fishermen along the Labrador coast of Newfoundland by the Royal National Mission to Deep Sea Fisherman organization in 1893. Conditions being what they were in the late nineteenth century, where one wrong move in the inhospitable land could mean a slow death, Grenfell had to be a survivalist and adventurer as well as a physician. As the following tale shows, he—and his team of sled dogs, several of whom provided the ultimate sacrifice for him—were more than equal to whatever task lay ahead of them, including surviving a bone-chilling night on the frigid waters off Newfoundland.

IT WAS EASTER SUNDAY AT ST. ANTHONY IN THE YEAR 1908, but with us in northern Newfoundland still winter. Everything was covered with snow and ice. I was walking back after morning service, when a boy came running over from the hospital with the news that a large team of dogs had come from sixty miles to the southward, to get a doctor on a very urgent case. It was that of a young man on whom we had operated about a fortnight before for an acute bone disease in the thigh. The people had allowed the wound to close, the poisoned matter had accumulated, and we thought we should have to remove the leg. There was obviously, therefore, no time to be lost. So, having packed up the necessary instruments, dressings, and drugs, and having fitted out the dog-sleigh with my best dogs, I started at once, the messengers following me with their team.

My team was an especially good one. On many a long journey they had stood by me and pulled me out of difficulties by their sagacity and endurance. To a lover of his dogs, as every Christian man must be, each one had become almost as precious as a child to its mother. They were beautiful beasts: Brin, the cleverest leader on the coast; Doc, a large, gentle beast, the backbone of the team for power; Spy, a wiry, powerful black and white dog; Moody, a lop-eared black-and-tan, in his third season, a plodder that never looked behind him; Watch, the youngster of the team, long-legged and speedy, with great liquid eyes and a Gordon-setter coat; Sue, a large, dark Eskimo, the image of a great black wolf, with her sharp-pointed and perpendicular ears, for she "harked back" to her wild ancestry; Jerry, a large roan-colored slut, the quickest of all my dogs on her feet, and so affectionate that her overtures of joy had often sent me sprawling on my back; Jack, a jet-black, gentle-natured dog, more like a retriever, that always ran next to the sledge, and never looked back but everlastingly pulled straight ahead, running always with his nose to the ground.

It was late in April, when there is always the risk of getting wet through the ice, so that I was carefully prepared with spare outfit, which included a change of garments, snowshoes, rifle, compass, ax, and oilskin overclothes. The messengers were anxious that their team should travel back with mine, for they were slow at best and needed a lead. My dogs, however, being a powerful team, could not be held back, and though I managed to wait twice for their sleigh, I had reached a village about twenty miles on the journey before nightfall, and had fed the dogs, and was gathering a few people for prayers when they caught me up.

During the night the wind shifted to the northeast, which brought in fog and rain, softened the snow, and made traveling very bad, besides heaving a heavy sea into the bay. Our drive next morning would be somewhat over forty miles, the first ten miles on an arm of the sea, on salt-water ice.

In order not to be separated too long from my friends, I sent them ahead two hours before me, appointing a rendezvous in a log tilt that we have built in the woods as a halfway house. There is no one living on all that long coastline, and to provide against accidents—which have happened more than once—we built this hut to keep dry clothing, food, and drugs in.

The first rain of the year was falling when I started, and I was obliged to keep on what we call the "ballicaters," or ice barricades, much farther up the bay than I had expected. The sea of the night before had smashed the ponderous covering of ice right to the landwash. There were great gaping chasms between the enormous blocks, which we call pans, and half a mile out it was all clear water.

An island three miles out had preserved a bridge of ice, however, and by crossing a few cracks I managed to reach it. From the island it was four miles across to a rocky promontory—a course that would be several miles shorter than going around the shore. Here as far as the eye could reach the ice seemed good, though it was very rough. Obviously, it had been smashed up by the sea and then packed in again by the strong wind from the northeast; and I thought it had frozen together solid.

All went well till I was about a quarter of a mile from the landing point. Then the wind suddenly fell, and I noticed that I was traveling over loose sish, which was like porridge and probably many feet deep. By stabbing down, I could drive my whip handle through the thin coating of young ice that was floating on it. The sish ice consists of the tiny fragments where the large pans have been pounding together on the heaving sea, like the stones of Freya's grinding mill.

So quickly did the wind now come offshore, and so quickly did the packed slob, relieved of the wind pressure, "run abroad," that already I could not see one pan larger than ten feet square; moreover, the ice was loosening so rapidly that I saw that retreat was absolutely impossible. Neither was there any way to get off the little pan I was surveying from.

There was not a moment to lose. I tore off my oilskins, threw myself on my hands and knees by the side of the komatik to give a larger base to hold, and shouted to my team to go ahead for the shore. Before we had gone twenty yards, the dogs got frightened, hesitated for a moment, and the komatik instantly sank into the slob. It was necessary then for the dogs to pull much harder, so that they now began to sink in also.

Earlier in the season the father of the very boy I was going to operate on had been drowned in this same way, his dogs tangling their traces around him in the slob. This flashed into my mind, and I managed to loosen my sheath-knife, scramble forward, find the traces in the water, and cut them, holding on to the leader's trace wound around my wrist.

Being in the water I could see no piece of ice that would bear anything up. But there was as it happened a piece of snow, frozen together like a large snowball, about twenty-five yards away, near where my leading dog, Brin, was wallowing in the slob. Upon this he very shortly climbed, his long trace of ten fathoms almost reaching there before he went into the water.

This dog has weird black markings on his face, giving him the appearance of wearing a perpetual grin. After climbing out on the snow, as if it were the most natural position in the world, he deliberately shook the ice and water from his long coat, and then turned around to look for me. As he sat perched up there out of the water, he seemed to be grinning with satisfaction. The other dogs were hopelessly bogged. Indeed, we were like flies in treacle.

Gradually, I hauled myself along the line that was still tied to my wrist, till without any warning the dog turned around and slipped out of his harness, and then once more turned his grinning face to where I was struggling.

It was impossible to make any progress through the sish ice by swimming, so I lay there and thought all would soon be over, only wondering if anyone would ever know how it happened. There was no particular horror attached to it, and in fact I began to feel drowsy, as if I could easily go to sleep, when suddenly I saw the trace of another big dog that had himself gone through before he reached the pan, and though he was close to it was quite unable to force his way out. Along this I hauled myself, using him as a bow anchor, but much bothered by the other dogs as I passed them, one of which got on my shoulder, pushing me farther down into the ice. There was only a yard or so more when I had passed my living anchor, and soon I lay with my dogs around me on the little piece of slob ice. I had to help them onto it, working them through the lane that I had made.

The piece of ice we were on was so small, it was obvious we must soon all be drowned, if we remained upon it as it drifted seaward into more open water. If we were to save our lives, no time was to be lost. When I stood up, I could see about twenty yards away a larger pan floating amid the sish, like a great flat raft, and if we could get onto it we should postpone at least for a time the death that already seemed almost inevitable. It was impossible to reach it without a lifeline, as I had already learned to my cost, and the next problem was how to get one there. Marvelous to relate, when I had first fallen through, after I had cut the dogs adrift without any hope left of saving myself, I had not let my knife sink, but had fastened it by two half hitches to the back of one of the dogs. To my great joy there it was still, and shortly I was at work cutting all the sealskin traces still hanging from the dogs' harnesses, and splicing them together into one long line. These I divided and fastened to the backs of my two leaders, tying the near ends around my two wrists. I then pointed out to Brin the pan I wanted to reach and tried my best to make them go ahead, giving them the full length of my lines from two coils. My long sealskin moccasins, reaching to my thigh, were full of ice and water.

These I took off and tied separately on the dogs' backs. My coat, hat, gloves, and overalls I had already lost. At first, nothing would induce the two dogs to move, and though I threw them off the pan two or three times, they struggled back upon it, which perhaps was only natural, because as soon as they fell through they could see nowhere else to make for. To me, however, this seemed to spell "the end." Fortunately, I had with me a small black spaniel, almost a featherweight, with large furry paws, called Jack, who acts as my mascot and incidentally as my retriever. This at once flashed into my mind, and I felt I had still one more chance for life. So I spoke to him and showed him the direction, and then threw a piece of ice toward the desired goal. Without a moment's hesitation he made a dash for it, and to my great joy got there safely, the tough scale of sea-ice carrying his weight bravely. At once I shouted to him to "lie down," and this, too, he immediately did, looking like a little black fuzz ball on the white setting. My leaders could now see him seated there on the new piece of floe, and when once more I threw them off they understood what I wanted, and fought their way to where they saw the spaniel, carrying with them the line that gave me the one chance for my life. The other dogs followed them, and after painful struggling, all got out again except one. Taking all the run that I could get on my little pan, I made a dive, slithering with the impetus along the surface till once more I sank through. After a long fight, however, I was able to haul myself by the long traces onto this new pan, having taken care beforehand to tie the harnesses to which I was holding under the dogs' bellies, so that they could not slip them off. But alas! The pan I was now on was not large enough to bear us and was already beginning to sink, so this process had to be repeated immediately.

I now realized that, though we had been working toward the shore, we had been losing ground all the time, for the offshore wind had already driven us a hundred yards farther out. But the widening gap kept full of the pounded ice, through which no man could possibly go.

I had decided I would rather stake my chances on a long swim even than perish by inches on the floe, as there was no likelihood whatever of being seen and rescued. But, keenly though I watched, not a streak even of clear water appeared, the interminable sish rising from below and filling every gap as it appeared. We were now resting on a piece of ice about ten by twelve feet, which, as I found when I came to examine it, was not ice at all, but simply snow-covered slob frozen into a mass, and I feared it would very soon break up in the general turmoil of the heavy sea, which was increasing as the ice drove offshore before the wind.

At first we drifted in the direction of a rocky point on which a heavy surf was breaking. Here I thought once again to swim ashore. But suddenly we struck a rock. A large piece broke off the already small pan, and what was left swung around in the backwash, and started right out to sea.

There was nothing for it now but to hope for a rescue. Alas! There was little possibility of being seen. As I have already mentioned, no one lives around this big bay. My only hope was that the other komatik, knowing I was alone and had failed to keep my tryst, would perhaps come back to look for me. This, however, as it proved, they did not do.

The westerly wind was rising all the time, our coldest wind at this time of the year, coming as it does over the Gulf ice. It was tantalizing, as I stood with next to nothing on, the wind going through me and every stitch soaked in ice water, to see my well-stocked komatik some fifty yards away. It was still above water, with food, hot tea in a thermos bottle, dry clothing, matches, wood, and everything on it for making a fire to attract attention.

It is easy to see a dark object on the ice in the daytime, for the gorgeous whiteness shows off the least thing. But the tops of bushes and large pieces of kelp have often deceived those looking out. Moreover, within our memory no man has been thus adrift on the bay ice. The chances were about one in a thousand that I should be seen at all, and if I were seen, I should probably be mistaken for some piece of refuse.

To keep from freezing, I cut off my long moccasins down to the feet, strung out some line, split the legs, and made a kind of jacket, which protected my back from the wind down as far as the waist. I have this jacket still, and my friends assure me it would make a good Sunday garment.

I had not drifted more than half a mile before I saw my poor komatik disappear through the ice, which was every minute loosening up into the small pans that it consisted of, and it seemed like a friend gone and one more tie with home and safety lost. To the northward, about a mile distant, lay the mainland along which I had passed so merrily in the morning— only, it seemed, a few moments before.

By midday I had passed the island to which I had crossed on the ice bridge. I could see that the bridge was gone now. If I could reach the island I should only be marooned and destined to die of starvation. But there was little chance of that, for I was rapidly driving into the ever widening bay.

It was scarcely safe to move on my small ice raft, for fear of breaking it. Yet I saw I must have the skins of some of my dogs—of which I had eight on the pan—if I was to live the night out. There was now some three to five miles between me and the north side of the bay. There, immense pans of Arctic ice, surging to and fro on the heavy ground seas, were thundering into the cliffs like medieval battering rams. It was evident that, even if seen, I could hope for no help from that quarter before night. No boat could live through the surf.

Unwinding the sealskin traces from my waist, around which I had wound them to keep the dogs from eating them, I made a slipknot, passed it over the first dog's head, tied it round my foot close to his neck, threw him on his back, and stabbed him in the heart. Poor beast! I loved him like a friend—a beautiful dog—but we could not all hope to live. In fact, I had no hope any of us would, at that time, but it seemed better to die fighting.

In spite of my care the struggling dog bit me rather badly in the leg. I suppose my numb hands prevented my holding his throat as I could ordinarily do. Moreover, I must hold the knife in the wound to the end, as blood on the fur would freeze solid and make the skin useless. In this way I sacrificed two more large dogs, receiving only one more bite, though I fully expected that the pan I was on would break up in the struggle. The other dogs, who were licking their coats and trying to get dry, apparently took no notice of the fate of their comrades—but I was very careful to prevent the dying dogs crying out, for the noise of fighting would probably have been followed by the rest attacking the down dog, and that was too close to me to be pleasant. A short shrift seemed to me better than a long one, and I envied the dead dogs whose troubles were over so quickly. Indeed, I came to balance in my mind whether, if once I passed into the open sea, it would not be better by far to use my faithful knife on myself than to die by inches. There seemed no hardship in the thought. I seemed fully to sympathize with the Japanese view of hara-kiri.

Working, however, saved me from philosophizing. By the time I had skinned these dogs, and with my knife and some of the harness had strung the skins together, I was ten miles on my way, and it was getting dark.

Away to the northward I could see a single light in the little village where I had slept the night before, where I had received the kindly hospitality of the simple fishermen in whose comfortable homes I have spent many a night. I could not help but think of them sitting down to tea, with no idea that there was anyone watching them, for I had told them not to expect me back for three days.

Meanwhile I had frayed out a small piece of rope into oakum, and mixed it with fat from the intestines of my dogs. Alas, my matchbox, which was always chained to me, had leaked, and my matches were in pulp. Had I been able to make a light, it would have looked so unearthly out there on the sea that I felt sure they would see me. But that chance was now cut off. However, I kept the matches, hoping that I might dry them if I lived through the night. While working at the dogs, about every five minutes I would stand up and wave my hands toward the land. I had no flag, and I could not spare my shirt, for, wet as it was, it was better than nothing in that freezing wind, and, anyhow, it was already nearly dark.

Unfortunately, the coves in among the cliffs are so placed that only for a very narrow space can the people in any house see the sea. Indeed, most of them cannot see it at all, so that I could not in the least expect anyone to see me, even supposing it had been daylight.

Not daring to take any snow from the surface of my pan to break the wind with, I piled up the carcasses of my dogs. With my skin rug I could now sit down without getting soaked. During these hours I had continually taken off all my clothes, wrung them out, swung them one by one in the wind, and put on first one and then the other inside, hoping that what heat there was in my body would thus serve to dry them. In this I had been fairly successful.

My feet gave me most trouble, for they immediately got wet again because my thin moccasins were easily soaked through on the snow. I suddenly thought of the way in which the Lapps who tend our reindeer manage for dry socks. They carry grass with them, which they ravel up and pad into their shoes. Into this they put their feet, and then pack the rest with more grass, tying up the top with a binder. The ropes of the harness for our dogs are carefully sewed all over with two layers of flannel in order to make them soft against the dogs' sides. So, as soon as I could sit down, I started with my trusty knife to rip up the flannel. Though my fingers were more or less frozen, I was able also to ravel out the rope, put it into my shoes, and use my wet socks inside my knickerbockers, where, though damp, they served to break the wind. Then, tying the narrow strips of flannel together, I bound up the top of the moccasins, Lapp-fashion, and carried the bandage on up over my knee, making a ragged though most excellent puttee.

As to the garments I wore, I had opened recently a box of football clothes I had not seen for twenty years. I had found my old Oxford University football running shorts and a pair of Richmond Football Club red, yellow, and black stockings, exactly as I wore them twenty years ago. These with a flannel shirt and sweater vest were now all I had left. Coat, hat, gloves, oilskins, everything else, were gone, and I stood there in that odd costume, exactly as I stood twenty years ago on a football field reminding me, of the little girl of a friend, who when told she was dying, asked to be dressed in her Sunday frock to go to heaven in. My costume, being very light, dried all the quicker, until afternoon. Then nothing would dry anymore, everything freezing stiff. It had been an ideal costume to struggle through the slob ice. I really believe the conventional garments missionaries are supposed to affect would have been fatal.

My occupation till what seemed like midnight was unraveling rope, and with this I padded out my knickers inside, and my shirt as well, though it was a clumsy job, for I could not see what I was doing. Now, getting my largest dog, Doc, as big a wolf and weighing ninety-two pounds, I made him lie down, so that I could cuddle around him. I then wrapped the three skins around me, arranging them so that I could lie on one edge, while the other came just over my shoulders and head.

My own breath collecting inside the newly flayed skin must have had a soporific effect, for I was soon fast asleep. One hand I had kept warm against the curled up dog, but the other, being gloveless, had frozen, and I suddenly awoke, shivering enough, I thought, to break my fragile pan. What I took at first to be the sun just rising, I soon found it was the moon, and then I knew it was about half-past twelve. The dog was having an excellent time. He hadn't been cuddled so warm all winter, and he resented my moving with low growls till he found it wasn't another dog.

The wind was steadily driving me now toward the open sea, and I could expect, short of a miracle, nothing but death out there. Somehow, one scarcely felt justified in praying for a miracle. But we have learned down here to pray for things we want, and, anyhow, just at that moment the miracle occurred. The wind fell off suddenly, and came with a light air from the southward, and then dropped stark calm. The ice was now "all abroad," which I was sorry for, for there was a big safe pan not twenty yards away from me. If I could have got on that, I might have killed my other dogs when the time came, and with their coats I could hope to hold out for two or three days more, and with the food and drink their bodies would offer me need not at least die of hunger or thirst. To tell the truth, they were so big and strong I was half afraid to tackle them with only a sheath-knife on my small and unstable raft.

But it was now freezing hard. I knew the calm water between us would form into cakes, and I had to recognize that the chance of getting near enough to escape onto it was gone. If, on the other hand, the whole bay froze solid again I had yet another possible chance. For my pan would hold together longer and I should be opposite another village, called Goose Cove, at daylight, and might possibly be seen from there. I knew that the komatiks there would be starting at daybreak over the hills for a parade of Orangemen about twenty miles away. Possibly, therefore, I might be seen as they climbed the hills. So I lay down, and went to sleep again.

It seems impossible to say how long one sleeps, but I woke with a sudden thought in my mind that I must have a flag; but again I had no pole and no flag. However, I set to work in the dark to disarticulate the legs of my dead dogs, which were now frozen stiff, and which were all that offered a chance of carrying anything like a distress signal. Cold as it was, I determined to sacrifice my shirt for that purpose with the first streak of daylight.

It took a long time in the dark to get the legs off, and when I had patiently marled them together with old harness rope and the remains of the skin traces, it was the heaviest and crookedest flagpole it has ever been my lot to see. I had had no food from six o'clock the morning before, when I had eaten porridge and bread and butter. I had, however, a rubber band which I had been wearing instead of one of my garters, and I chewed that for twenty-four hours. It saved me from thirst and hunger, oddly enough. It was not possible to get a drink from my pan, for it was far too salty. But anyhow that thought did not distress me much, for as from time to time I heard the cracking and grinding of the newly formed slob, it seemed that my devoted boat must inevitably soon go to pieces.

At last the sun rose, and the time came for the sacrifice of my shirt. So I stripped, and, much to my surprise, found it not half so cold as I had anticipated. I now re-formed my dogskins with the raw side out, so that they made a kind of coat quite rivaling Joseph's. But, with the rising of the sun, the frost came out of the joints of my dogs' legs, and the friction caused by waving it made my flagpole almost tie itself in knots. Still, I could raise it three or four feet above my head, which was very important.

Now, however, I found that instead of being as far out at sea as I had reckoned, I had drifted back in a northwesterly direction, and was off some cliffs known as Ireland Head. Near these there was a little village looking seaward, whence I should certainly have been seen. But, as I had myself, earlier in the winter, been night-bound at this place, I had learned there was not a single soul living there at all this winter. The people had all, as usual, migrated to the winter houses up the bay, where they get together for schooling and social purposes.

I soon found it was impossible to keep waving so heavy a flag all the time, and yet I dared not sit down, for that might be the exact moment someone would be in a position to see me from the hills. The only thing in my mind was how long I could stand up and how long go on waving that pole at the cliffs. Once or twice I thought I saw men against their snowy faces, which, I judged, were about five-and-a-half miles from me, but they were only trees. Once, also, I thought I saw a boat approaching. A glittering object kept appearing and disappearing on the water, but it was only a small piece of ice sparkling in the sun as it rose on the surface. I think that the rocking of my cradle up and down on the waves had helped me to sleep, for I felt as well as ever I did in my life; and with the hope of a long sunny day, I felt sure I was good to last another twenty-four hours—if my boat would hold out and not rot under the sun's rays.

Each time I sat down to rest, my big dog Doc came and kissed my face and then walked to the edge of the ice-pan, returning again to where I was huddled up, as if to say, "Why don't you come along? Surely it is time to start." The other dogs also were now moving about very restlessly, occasionally trying to satisfy their hunger by gnawing at the dead bodies of their brothers.

I determined, at midday, to kill a big Eskimo dog and drink his blood, as I had read only a few days before in *Farthest North* of Dr. Nansen's doing—that is, if I survived the battle with him. I could not help feeling, even then, my ludicrous position, and I thought, if ever I got ashore again, I should have to laugh at myself standing hour after hour waving my shirt at those lofty cliffs, which seemed to assume a kind of sardonic grin, so that I could almost imagine they were laughing at me. At times I could not help thinking of the good breakfast that my colleagues were enjoying at the back of those same cliffs, and of the snug fire and the comfortable room, which we call our study.

I can honestly say that from first to last not a single sensation of fear entered my mind, even when I was struggling in the slob ice. Somehow it did not seem unnatural; I had been through the ice half a dozen times before. For the most part I felt very sleepy, and the idea was then very strong in my mind that I should soon reach the solution of the mysteries that I had been preaching about for so many years.

Only the previous night (Easter Sunday) at prayers in the cottage, we had been discussing the fact that the soul was entirely separate from the body, that Christ's idea of the body as the temple in which the soul dwells is so amply borne out by modern science. We had talked of thoughts from that admirable book, *Brain and Personality*, by Dr. Thompson of New York, and also of the same subject in the light of a recent operation performed at the Johns Hopkins Hospital by Dr. Harvey Cushing. The doctor had removed from a man's brain two large cystic tumors without giving the man an anesthetic, and the patient had kept up a running conversation with him all the while the doctor's fingers were working in his brain. It had seemed such a striking proof that ourselves and our bodies are two absolutely different things.

Our eternal life has always been with me a matter of faith. It seems to me one of those problems that must always be a mystery to knowledge. But my own faith in this matter had been so untroubled that it seemed now almost natural to be leaving through this portal of death from an ice-pan. In many ways, also, I could see how a death of this kind might be of value to the particular work that I am engaged in. Except for my friends, I had nothing I could think of to regret whatever. Certainly, I should like to have told them the story. But then one does not carry folios of paper in running shorts, which have no pockets, and all my writing gear had gone by the board with the komatik.

I could still see a testimonial to myself some distance away in my khaki overalls, which I had left on another pan in the struggle of the night before. They seemed a kind of company, and would possibly be picked up and suggest the true story. Running through my head all the time, quite unbidden, were the words of the old hymn:

My God, my Father, while I stray
Far from my home on life's dark way,
Oh, teach me from my heart to say,
　　Thy will be done!

It is a hymn we hardly ever sing out here, and it was an unconscious memory of my boyhood days.

It was a perfect morning—a cobalt sky, an ultramarine sea, a golden

sun, an almost wasteful extravagance of crimson over hills of purest
snow, which caught a reflected glow from rock and crag. Between me
and the hills lay miles of rough ice and long veins of thin black slob that
had formed during the night. For the foreground there was my poor,
gruesome pan, bobbing up and down on the edge of the open sea, stained
with blood, and littered with carcasses and debris. It was smaller than last
night, and I noticed also that the new ice from the water melted under
the dogs' bodies had been formed at the expense of its thickness. Five dogs,
myself in colored football costume, and a bloody dogskin cloak, with a
gay flannel shirt on a pole of frozen dogs' legs, completed the picture. The
sun was almost hot by now, and I was conscious of a surplus of heat in my
skin coat. I began to look longingly at one of my remaining dogs, for an
appetite will rise even on an ice-pan, and that made me think of fire. So
once again I inspected my matches. Alas! The heads were in paste, all but
three or four blue-top wax ones.

These I now laid out to dry, while I searched about on my snow-pan
to see if I could get a piece of transparent ice to make a burning-glass.
For I was pretty sure that with all the unraveled tow I had stuffed into
my leggings, and with the fat of my dogs, I could make smoke enough to
be seen if only I could get a light. I had found a piece which I thought
would do, and had gone back to wave my flag, which I did every two
minutes, when I suddenly thought I saw again the glitter of an oar. It did
not seem possible, however, for it must be remembered it was not water,
which lay between me and the land, but slob ice, which a mile or two
inside me was very heavy. Even if people had seen me, I did not think
they could get through, though I knew that the whole shore would then
be trying. Moreover, there, was no smoke rising on the land to give me
hope that I had been seen. There had been no gun flashes in the night,
and I felt sure that, had anyone seen me, there would have been a bonfire
on every hill to encourage me to keep going.

So I gave it up, and went on with my work. But the next time I went
back to my flag, the glitter seemed very distinct, and though it kept disappearing as it rose and fell on the surface, I kept my eyes strained upon
it, for my dark spectacles had been lost, and I was partly snowblind.

I waved my flag as high as I could raise it, broadside on. At last, beside the
glint of the white oar, I made out the black streak of the hull. I knew that,
if the pan held on for another hour, I should be all right.

With that strange perversity of the human intellect, the first thing I
thought of was what trophies I could carry with my luggage from the

pan, and I pictured the dog-bone flagstaff adorning my study. (The dogs actually ate it afterward.) I thought of preserving my ragged puttees with our collection of curiosities. I lost no time now at the burning-glass. My whole mind was devoted to making sure I should be seen, and I moved about as much as I dared on the raft, waving my sorry token aloft.

At last there could be no doubt about it: the boat was getting nearer and nearer. I could see that my rescuers were frantically waving, and, when they came within shouting distance, I heard someone cry out, "Don't get excited. Keep on the pan where you are." They were infinitely more excited than I. Already to me it seemed just as natural now to be saved as, half an hour before, it had seemed inevitable I should be lost, and had my rescuers only known, as I did, the sensation of a bath in that ice when you could not dry yourself afterward, they need not have expected me to follow the example of the apostle Peter and throw myself into the water.

As the man in the bow leaped from the boat onto my ice raft and grasped both my hands in his, not a word was uttered. I could see in his face the strong emotions he was trying hard to force back, though in spite of himself tears trickled down his cheeks. It was the same with each of the others of my rescuers, nor was there any reason to be ashamed of them. These were not the emblems of weak sentimentality, but the evidences of the realization of the deepest and noblest emotion of which the human heart is capable, the vision that God has use for us his creatures, the sense of that supreme joy of the Christ—the joy of unselfish service. After the handshake and swallowing a cup of warm tea that had been thoughtfully packed in a bottle, we hoisted in my remaining dogs and started for home. To drive the boat home there were not only five Newfoundland fishermen at the oars, but five men with Newfoundland muscles in their backs, and five as brave hearts as ever beat in the bodies of human beings.

So, slowly but steadily, we forged through to the shore, now jumping out onto larger pans and forcing them apart with the oars, now hauling the boat out and dragging her over, when the jam of ice packed tightly in by the rising wind was impossible to get through otherwise.

My first question, when at last we found our tongues, was, "How ever did you happen to be out in the boat in this ice?" To my astonishment they told me that the previous night four men had been away on a long headland cutting out some dead harp seals that they had killed in the fall and left to freeze up in a rough wooden store they had built there, and that as they were leaving for home, my pan of ice had drifted out clear of

Hare Island, and one of them, with his keen fisherman's eyes, had seen something unusual. They at once returned to their village, saying there was something alive drifting out to sea on the floe ice. But their report bad been discredited, for the people thought that it could be only the top of some tree.

All the time I had been driving along I knew that there was one man on that coast who had a good spyglass. He tells me he instantly got up in the midst of his supper, on hearing the news, and hurried over the cliffs to the lookout, carrying his trusty spyglass with him. Immediately, dark as it was, he saw that without any doubt there was a man out on the ice. Indeed, he saw me wave my hands every now and again toward the shore. By a very easy process of reasoning on so uninhabited a shore, he at once knew who it was, though some of the men argued that it must be someone else. Little had I thought, as night was closing in, that away on that snowy hilltop lay a man with a telescope patiently searching those miles of ice for *me*. Hastily they rushed back to the village and at once went down to try to launch a boat, but that proved to be impossible. Miles of ice lay between them and me, the heavy sea was hurling great blocks on the landwash, and night was already falling, the wind blowing hard onshore.

The whole village was aroused, and messengers were dispatched at once along the coast, and lookouts told off to all the favorable points, so that while I considered myself a laughingstock, bowing with my flag to those unresponsive cliffs, there were really many eyes watching me. One man told me that with his glass he distinctly saw me waving the shirt flag. There was little slumber that night in the villages, and even the men told me there were few dry eyes, as they thought of the impossibility of saving me from perishing. We are not given to weeping overmuch on this shore, but there are tears that do a man honor.

Before daybreak this fine volunteer crew had been gotten together. The boat, with such a force behind it of will power, would, I believe, have gone through anything. And, after seeing the heavy breakers through which we were guided, loaded with their heavy ice battering rams, when at last we ran through the harbor mouth with the boat on our return, I knew well what wives and children had been thinking of when they saw their loved ones put out. Only two years ago I remember a fisherman's wife watching her husband and three sons take out a boat to bring in a stranger that was showing flags for a pilot. But the boat and its occupants have not yet come back.

Every soul in the village was on the beach as we neared the shore. Every soul was waiting to shake hands when I landed. Even with the grip that one after another gave me, some no longer trying to keep back the tears, I did not find out my hands were frostburnt—a fact I have not been slow to appreciate since, however. I must have been a weird sight as I stepped ashore, tied up in rags, stuffed out with oakum, wrapped in the bloody skins of dogs, with no hat, coat, or gloves besides, and only a pair of short knickers. It must have seemed to some as if it were the old man of the sea coming ashore.

But no time was wasted before a pot of tea was exactly where I wanted it to be, and some hot stew was locating itself where I had intended an hour before the blood of one of my remaining dogs should have gone.

Rigged out in the warm garments that fishermen wear, I started with a large team as hard as I could race for the hospital, for I had learned that the news had gone over that I was lost. It was soon painfully impressed upon me that I could not much enjoy the ride, for I had to be hauled like a log up the hills, my feet being frostburnt so that I could not walk. Had I guessed this before going into the house, I might have avoided much trouble.

It is time to bring this egotistic narrative to an end. Jack lies curled up by my feet while I write this short account. Brin is once again leading and lording it over his fellows. Doc and the other survivors are not forgotten, now that we have again returned to the less romantic episodes of a mission hospital life. There stands in our hallway a bronze tablet to the memory of three noble dogs, Moody, Watch, and Spy, whose lives were given for mine on the ice.

In my home in England my brother has placed a duplicate tablet, and has added these words, "Not one of them is forgotten before your Father which is in heaven." And this I most fully believe to be true. The boy whose life I was intent on saving was brought to the hospital a day or two later in a boat, the ice having cleared off the coast not to return for that season. He was operated on successfully, and is even now on the high road to recovery. We all love life. I was glad to be back once more with possibly a new lease of it before me. I had learned on the pan many things, but chiefly that the one cause for regret, when we look back on a life, which we think is closed forever, will be the fact that we have wasted its opportunities. As I went to sleep that first night there still rang in my ears the same verse of the old hymn, which had been my companion on the ice, "Thy will, not mine, Lord."

Knighted by King George V for his humanitarian work, Grenfell survived to continue his work among the indigenous people of Newfoundland. After his death in 1940, his ashes were brought back to St. Anthony in Newfoundland, where they were placed inside a rock face above the harbor.

Grenfell's story is a classic case of not panicking when all may seem lost, and using whatever equipment—even the bodies of his faithful dogs—was at hand to stay alive and signal for help.

LOOK FOR A CORPSE

Larry Kaniut

From *Danger Stalks the Land*

Alaska figures prominently in this collection of survival stories, for there are few lands that are both more beautiful and that will test a person more severely. However, few people have been pushed as far to the edge as Fred Easley, who came to our forty-ninth state to do a little mining in 1936, and ended up fighting for his life in one of nature's most dangerous challenges—an avalanche.

SLOWLY THE THREE MEN SLOGGED along in the swirling snow and billowing wind. Their destination was the mine on Lucky Chance Mountain near Sitka, Alaska. It was a Sunday in December 1936. J. Clark Sutherland, an engineer, Otto Hill, a miner, and Fred Easley eagerly anticipated what lay ahead. When the wind ceased, they realized that instead of being on the side of the mountain, they were far down the mountain, nearly at the bottom of a canyon. The air was clear. Not only was it easy to discern their whereabouts, but it was also possible to evaluate the conditions of the snow around them.

Fred immediately recognized a danger signal near him in the snow. He knew from experience that the yellow spot hid a pocket of air below the surface. He reveled in the fact that they had stopped where they had, or they might have ventured out onto the crust of snow and broken through into the cavern below. While contemplating their good fortune, they heard a *schhhwoosh*.

During that moment, the mountainside loosed part of its snowpack and jettisoned it to the canyon below. Fred was completely covered with snow. One moment the three men were talking; the next moment Fred was gone.

Clark and Otto were slammed across the snow by the same wall of snow that buried Fred. Snow covered Clark, who resigned himself to death. Just before losing consciousness he realized two of his fingers were above the snow! That's when he started clawing free.

Clark felt Otto's hand on his boot. Clark dug until he had Otto's head free and discovered that Otto was alive but unconscious. After reviving Otto, the two dug for nearly three hours until they were free from their trap.

In the meantime, Fred, who had heard nothing from his friends and assumed they were dead, figured he was going to have to make it out on his own.

The avalanche struck at 9 A.M., pitching Fred into total blackness, totally encasing him in snow. He sprawled facedown in the snow that pressed against every part of his body. He felt that he was drowning in snow. His lungs screamed for oxygen. He couldn't yell. Panic overcame him. He held his breath for as long as he could, figuring it was his last. His ears pounded. When he could hold his breath no longer and his lungs were on the verge of exploding, he gasped for air.

Perhaps some air had been trapped near his head. Whatever the reason, he gulped a mouthful. Gradually he was able to piece things together. He had been standing near a large boulder when the avalanche hit. The force of the snow knocked him onto his face where he lay at a forty-five-degree angle. His left hand was pinned near his side with his elbow bent. His right arm was straight in front of him, his hand barely touching the boulder. His head was immobile, as was his body because of the tremendous weight of the snow.

Fred experienced anxious moments thinking his back might be broken, paralyzing him, until he joyfully moved the fingers of his right hand.

A myriad of thoughts flashed through his mind. Strangely enough he wondered about the heir to his stamp collection and the prediction of a fortune-teller who had once told him he'd live to be an old man (he didn't consider his current age of twenty-eight old!). But the thought that the shock of his death might kill his mother motivated him to get out.

Slowly he freed his right hand and scooped the snow away from his face. He found his stocking cap and put it on his head. He could barely make out the dark outline of the rock. He had no way of keeping track of time as his watch had stopped.

Even though Fred's movements were severely limited, he had some things in his favor. First, he was warmly dressed. He wore long-handled underwear, blue denim jeans, a wool shirt, three pairs of heavy woolen socks, shoe packs with rubber bottoms, and an oilskin suit—pants and jacket waterproofed with oil. He also wore a pair of homemade snowshoes with long wooden frames. In addition to his stocking cap Fred wore a homemade woolen hat, consisting of two wool socks, which covered his head, extended to his shoulders, and kept his neck dry and warm. He couldn't have been better dressed for his ordeal.

Second, he carried the group's lunches. He had volunteered to carry the men's six-pound lard can containing a dozen sourdough pancakes, six sardine sandwiches, three chocolate bars, and coffee.

Third, Fred had some matches and a pocketknife.

After assessing his situation, he wondered about Clark and Otto. He knew that almost certainly his survival depended upon their welfare. Had they been buried in the slide? Were they digging him out? Had they gone for help? He didn't like the prospect of rescuers' finding their frozen bodies after the snow melted.

Fred found breathing easier, possibly because the snow had not fully compacted around him due to his proximity to the boulder—maybe there was an air pocket between him and the rock.

Although his right pant's leg had frozen to the snow where the oilskin was pulled above the jeans, Fred did not feel cold because he was dressed so warmly.

He called out. There was no answer. From time to time he repeated his cry for help. Vaguely he heard a sound in the distance, one which he did not recognize. At first he thought it was the sound of shovels biting into the snow. He exulted in the thought that his pals were digging him out. But then he realized there was no rhythm to the sound, just an irregular but steady smooshing sound. With horror Fred recognized the sound as that which results when snow settles!

As unnerving as it was to hear the steadily compressing snow above him, he reconfirmed his decision to give it a fight.

By now he had freed both his right hand and his right leg. Gradually he groped snow from beneath him and kicked it behind him with his right leg.

Sometime later, his tomb lightened as a thread of daylight shone through near the large boulder. Could it be? Then he glimpsed blue sky as the crack widened and let in fresh air.

Fred yelled excitedly over and over. He heard an answer, "Hell-ooo." It was too good to be true. He was going to be saved! Or was he hearing things? He had to remain calm. Then he heard the unmistakable voice of his pal Otto: "We'll have you out in a little while."

Soooo . . . his friends were both alive. And they were going to rescue him. Fred satisfied his longing for air with huge gulps, and he rejoiced—he'd be out of this tomb in jig time. He thanked God for air and for his friends above. While Fred rejoiced, he heard Clark tell Otto to get the shovels while he looked for Fred.

No sooner had Fred heard Clark than another *schhhwoosh* trembled his body. With the movement, his breathing hole closed. Another avalanche had covered Fred! Had his friends found him sooner, he could have escaped his doom.

Fred now breathed with greater difficulty. The settling snow began its crunching sound anew, and Fred felt the fear it presented as well as the fear for his companions' welfare. Since they knew he was alive and had a pretty good idea where he was, there was still hope for his rescue unless the second avalanche had buried them.

The second avalanche hit at noon, fifteen minutes after Clark and Otto had freed themselves and had begun searching for Fred. That second slide swept them down the canyon. Clark was tossed free, but his friend was buried a second time. When Clark looked for Otto, he saw his hand protruding from the snow. Clark hurriedly began digging him out. By the time Clark freed Otto, however, it was dark; and both men had frostbitten feet. They had to reach the shelter cabin before they froze. They wanted to inform officials of Fred's predicament so they could recover his body.

Once they reached the safety of the cabin, Clark left Otto to warm up and to regain his strength while he struck out for Sitka to raise help and to telegram Fred's mother of his demise.

Meanwhile the "corpse" was busy trying to dig himself out. Although able to dig only with his right hand the first three hours, Fred had since freed the snow around his body and managed to bend his right knee enough to reach and free the snowshoe. Using his teeth, he eventually gnawed through the wood frame until he'd broken off a piece. He used it as a paddle to shovel the snow.

In time Fred freed his entire body except his left arm, which was trapped by his pack, frozen to the top of his tomb.

In wild desperation Fred set his teeth to the leather pack strap only to give up in frustration when he met with failure. Reminded of his pocketknife, he began an effort to get it. The knife was just beyond his grasp, his fingertips barely able to touch it. The fabric of his pants pocket provided the solution—he could pull on the top of the fabric and gradually ease the pocket and thus the knife upward. Finally he retrieved it.

At length he clasped the knife between his teeth and opened the blade with his right hand. The knife fell from his nervous fingers. He found it in the snow and picked it up. Eventually he cut the strap of the pack.

By now it was late afternoon, and he was hungry. He found the metal lard container crushed and its contents squished and generously saturated with coffee. Nevertheless it was food, and it was welcome to his lips. He inhaled coffee-sodden pancakes and a chocolate bar.

Unknown to Fred, his companions were stumbling away toward safety, frostbitten and bruised, and grieving for the loss of their friend.

Fred ascertained by the darkening that afternoon had evolved into night. He took out his watch and struck a match, but there wasn't oxygen enough for the match to burn. He was unable to see the dial of his watch and discovered it had stopped. He wound it and let it go at that. The ticking provided a companion to mark time with him.

Fred's hands became cold. He had also dropped his knife and his snowshoe paddle and was unable to find either. He decided to hang on to his other paddle at all costs, knowing that its loss spelled certain death for him.

An overwhelming thirst gnawed at Fred. In spite of his surroundings he was suffering dehydration. His lips were dry and chapped. He reached ahead and secured clean snow, which he placed under his tongue. Allowing it to melt slowly into water assuaged some of his thirst.

He felt a need to remove his boots because his feet were soaked. With great effort he removed his footwear and his socks. He struggled to wring the water from his stockings. The chilling cold made his finger movements difficult, and his struggle to get his socks and boots back on was so grueling that he decided not to remove them again.

His eating paralleled his digging. He rationalized that help would arrive. Plus he needed energy to stay warm and to dig. So he ate.

Digging and moving snow became routine. He inched along his tunnel, digging, passing snow along his body, kicking it beneath his feet and scooting forward. Little by little he moled along.

Fred's efforts were compounded by the consistency of the snow. Rather than a light, fine powder, it was hard-packed, wet snow. His digging required jabbing and scraping the crystallized, icelike snow.

Scrape. Jab. Scrape. Dig. Pile. Scoop. Tamp. Inch ahead.

The routine continued hour after hour.

And always the sound of settling snow continued above. *Was it a shovel?* The sound could discourage and cause panic . . . or Fred could use it to inspire his escape.

More digging . . . moving from side to side to scrape and poke, first resting on one elbow then the other. His coffinlike cocoon gave him enough room to turn from side to side, but provided no excess room for exaggerated movement.

While Fred inched along his tunnel toward the surface, Clark Sutherland trudged toward Sitka. Twenty-four hours had elapsed since the first avalanche had struck. Early Monday morning Clark, still suffering from exposure and shock, arrived in Sitka. The town siren screamed across the bay summoning men and women from their daily tasks. Sutherland told his story. He impressed on the townspeople the urgency of assisting Otto and recovering Fred's body.

The wheels of rescue churned. U.S. Commissioner William Bahrt put together provisions and men to rescue Otto Hill and to recover Fred Easley's corpse.

A day and a half of physical confinement and determined digging coupled with the mental trauma of combating cold, fatigue, and near hopelessness had taken their toll on Fred. His strength was sapped by his effort and the cold. His body screamed for relief.

Fred's feet were numb, requiring his attention. He rubbed them to maintain circulation. Every jab at the ice demanded a conscious effort. Cold constantly chewed at his hands, numbing them and creeping up his arms. He wondered how long it would be before the cold made it too difficult to hold his snowshoe paddle. His elbows became raw from alternately leaning on first one and then the other.

Sleep teased him. His eyes became heavy. His body's need for rest battled his mind's resolve to keep digging. He knew that the siren song of sleep would doom him, that if he allowed himself to sleep, his body mechanism would not permit him to wake up. Monday afternoon dragged on. To sleep or not to sleep.

Dig. Scrape. Jab. Scoop. Tamp the snow behind. Inch ahead.

Twelve more hours crawled by. Fred had now been trapped forty-eight hours.

It was Tuesday. Hallucinations confounded his mind. He closed his eyes and beheld a large room, domed and spacious. A crack in the ceiling beckoned him. He opened his eyes and jabbed at the dome overhead, only to hit crystallized ice inches above him. His excitement faded. He was still trapped in his tomblike cavity.

Near noon on Tuesday Fred gave in. He decided to sleep. He reasoned that sleep brought comfort. It relieved his pain. There was no cold. The ache in his elbows subsided. The mental struggle ceased. It would be a peaceful, painless death. He opened his eyes for a final look at his tomb.

Again the crack in the dome captured his attention. It seemed to be widening, almost calling him to another world. He closed his eyes. He heard the compressing snow . . . *kaa-runnch* . . . *kaa-runnch* . . . *kaa-runnch*. It had become rhythmic. But the sound was different. Was he dreaming?

No. A ringing sound of a shovel against rock! Could it be?

The *chunk* of shoveled snow tossed upon snow met his ears. It *was* rhythmic!

Yes. Rescuers!

Fred shouted. His muffled, quiet voice met his ears. Adrenaline coursed through his veins. He turned around and dug feverishly in the direction he'd left.

One of the workers had heard Fred's cry and thought it was a fellow worker.

The sound of digging grew louder. Suddenly a *sschhuunk* penetrated the snow. A shovel pierced the snow before his face. The shovel withdrew, taking snow with it; and a hole opened up to the outside world.

With a thrust and a grin Fred lurched from the depths and said, "Gee, fellows, I'm sure glad to see you."

Although the brightness of his new surroundings was blinding, the sky had never looked so blue to Fred. He had never breathed purer, sweeter air. He reveled in the beauty beyond the grave. He looked across Sitka Sound and marveled at his resurrection.

Ten men had been digging for four hours, expecting to recover Fred's body. Sutherland had directed the effort, having designated a fifty-foot circle, telling the searchers that Fred would be found within that circle. Fred emerged from the circle's center. Now his rescuers were spellbound by this living creature standing before them.

Although Fred thought he could walk, his legs would not support him. He was carried on a sled to the cabin where men took turns for sixteen hours massaging him and restoring his circulation before they took him to the hospital in Sitka.

Before long, Fred was back to normal. After a monumental struggle and almost unheard-of tunneling of fifteen feet in fifty-two hours, Fred was finally saved from the jaws of death—beneath two avalanches and a combined twenty-one feet of snow.

Though the townspeople of Sitka had looked for a corpse, Fred Easley had spit in death's eye.

There is only one thing I can add to this incredible account—never give up. Fred Easley could have let death claim him at just about any time during those two days, but his will to live kept him going, and ensured that he would survive his ordeal. It wouldn't have surprised me to read that if the rescuers hadn't dug him out, Fred would have eventually reached the surface by himself.

HOW IT FEELS TO BE CRUSHED IN AN ICE CREVASSE

Michelle Hamer

From *How It Feels to Be Attacked by a Shark: And Other Amazing Life-or-Death Situations!*

Make no mistake, the snowfields of the Arctic and Antarctic are always hazardous places, where one wrong move can spell disaster. Veterinarian Raina Plowright knows this all too well, having lived through her own life-threatening experience at the bottom of the world. Here she relates her terrifying ordeal to author Michelle Hamer.

I WAS GOING to work on a penguin-monitoring program at Mawson Station in the Antarctic, but I was only there for three days before the accident. We were being trained to use the quad bikes, but the person leading the training accidentally took us through a crevasse field. The ice was very, very bumpy and very difficult to navigate, so I was really concentrating.

I saw a little patch of snow in front of me and thought I'd better be careful about how I got across it. I slowed down and suddenly my front wheels were just spinning on the ice, and then my back wheels broke through the snow—it was a snow bridge over a crevasse—and I found myself plummeting down. My body was upright and the four-wheel bike was plummeting vertically with me. Even though I must have been falling for just a millisecond, I had enough time to think, *I'm falling—this is it.*

I always thought when someone fell off a cliff it would happen so fast they wouldn't know anything before they were dead—which I thought was good, because they wouldn't have that horrific, awful feeling of knowing they were dying. But it's not true; you have enough time to know what's happening and to know it's the end.

The crevasse was at least a hundred feet deep. It was very dark. The ice was a neon blue color. After falling about twenty feet, the next thing I felt was just this enormous weight of metal crushing me as the seven-hundred-pound bike fell on me and wedged me into the ice. It was crushing my thoracic area and my abdomen, so I couldn't breathe at all.

I thought, *Well, this is definitely it now,* because I couldn't get a breath. I thought I was going to die within minutes. There is not a word to describe that feeling. It was extraordinarily unexpected—to be riding along on the ice and then two seconds later I'm dying. Here I am, halfway down this crevasse, not able to breathe, and I thought, *What a stupid way to die.*

I totally focused on figuring out some way to breathe. My chest was crushed, my abdomen was crushed, I had no mechanism to move air into my lungs. I had done a lot of meditation in the past and I don't know if it saved my life or not, but I pulled all those skills together to try to breathe, and I was able to move some air into my lungs through my throat. I'm not sure exactly how I did it.

The people above came to the edge of the crevasse and were yelling down. I couldn't communicate back, but one of them asked me to wiggle my fingers and I knew it was really important to show them that I was alive. So I did it, but I lost control and couldn't breathe again and had to regain focus.

Very soon after being crushed into the ice wall I felt my legs go numb. It was like I had two heavy logs hanging from my body, and I also lost control of my bladder. I'm a veterinarian, so I knew instantly that I might be a paraplegic. That wasn't scary for me at all, though. At the time I just wanted to live, and if I was a living paraplegic that was just fine.

When the search-and-rescue guy broke the ice above the crevasse and came down to me, the first thing he did was to check my pulse and I just thought that was such a waste of time. I was on the edge between life and death and here he was checking my pulse! I was thinking, *Just get me out of here.*

He put a rope around my chest and then attached me to his harness. They put a winch on the quad bike and started to pull it up. But the movement crushed me even more into the ice wall; I was being compressed into it. They pulled it up faster and then I got a real breath and fell into the guy's arms.

A white curtain of complete despair came over me and I lost consciousness. As I was lifted over the edge of the crevasse, I regained consciousness, and I felt this overwhelming feeling of "I'm okay, I'm going to live." I was down there for an hour and a quarter but I can only remember about three minutes of it.

They took me on the back of a truck to the medical center. My body temperature was about 90° Fahrenheit (the average body temperature is

98.6° Fahrenheit), but it was fifteen minutes before I started to feel cold. I was shaking violently and felt extraordinarily icy to the core. I heard the doctor say, "Her blood pressure is sixty over zero," and I thought that just couldn't be right.

I had overwhelming nausea and started vomiting blood. I just felt so awful; the pain was extraordinary. The next day they decided to operate. I had a crushing injury to the abdomen, bleeding vessels, a hematoma in my abdomen, which was crushing nerves in my spinal cord, and traumatic pancreatitis.

Both my legs were paralyzed but one started to come back straightaway and the other recovered in a couple of months. I had a second operation a week later and then they sent me home by ship. I was in a rehabilitation hospital for three weeks back in Australia. I don't think your body is ever the same after injuries such as those, but I'm largely recovered.

As the previous story shows, all it takes is a single instant to create a life-threatening situation. Ms. Plowright managed to keep her head and stay alive under incredible adversity—not to mention a very heavy vehicle.

THE WILD COUNTRY

Of course, as dangerous and potentially terrifying as being trapped on the open ocean or at the top or bottom of the world is, surviving in other parts of the planet poses hazards as well. The breadth of natural dangers that await the unwary traveler are countless, including dangerous terrain, inclement weather, hostile animals, and even poisonous plants. And if a person makes even one wrong decision, it is easy to accidentally compound a dangerous situation into one even more perilous.

The following excerpts span the globe, from icy mountain peaks to deep forests, presenting the people facing each survival situation an array of choices that, in the end, always comes down to one simple decision—to keep fighting to live, or to give up? How each one faces this decision, and how they go about saving their lives, are truly studies in courage and perseverance. Whether it's a man forced to race for his life against hostile Native Americans during the fur trapper's glory days or a young man coming to terms with both himself and nature on an ill-considered mountain climbing attempt, these stories reveal the depths of willpower people will draw on to live one more day.

MAROONED IN FLORIDA

Pierre Viaud (1725–?)
Translated by Robin F. A. Fabel
From *Shipwreck and Adventures of Monsieur Pierre Viaud*

After the harrowing stories of being marooned at sea and stranded in the frozen wastelands of Alaska and the Poles, one would think that survival on dry land would be easier—there is potential food and shelter to be found in more temperate areas, and depending on the season, the weather can also be more comfortable as well. However, the hazards posed by being lost or stranded on land are no less dangerous. Exhaustion, starvation, disease, navigating dangerous terrain without injury, and wild animal attacks are all obstacles that must be faced.

Pierre Viaud's sensational account of his shipwreck and fight for survival on the coast of Florida created an uproar in Europe when it was first published in France in 1768, with an English translation appearing in 1781. Having already seen other members of his party leave to find help or die, Viaud finds himself considering a course of action that many might find abhorrent, but that he considered necessary under the desperate circumstances in which he found himself.

WE STOOD ON A RIDGE. On all sides we saw a boundless skyline. On our right was the sea and our left a forest stretching as far as the eye could see. In front of us, in the direction in which we had determined to go, was a dry empty plain on which could be seen only the traces of wild beasts and nothing, which could sustain us. This sight threw us into bitter despair. Our battered spirits lost all remnants of courage. We abandoned our originally intended route because we could not see how it could end well and because it contained no promise of comfort or nourishment. Instead we walked downhill to the left, directing our steps toward the nearby forest. It was frighteningly dense. The trees were oppressively close to each other; in some places we could not pass between them. The path we had wanted to follow petered out after a few yards. We found alternative tracks, which often doubled back to where we had begun. Others would have taken us deep into the woods and left us without a chance of ever getting out, certain of dying from hunger or animal attacks.

None of these trees apparently offered what we needed to survive. Most of them had the same kind of leaves, which had made us so sick.

It's all over, I said to myself, as anguish stabbed me. *It's all over. We must die. We can't go on anymore.*

Muttering these words, I threw myself on the ground. Madame La Couture lay down next to me. My black placed himself at our feet a little distance from us. Without looking at each other, we all began to weep. Sunk in gloomy thought, we stayed bitterly silent. We understood each other's preoccupations perfectly. They exclusively concerned our frightful situation. We had no need to talk.

The gloomiest ideas occurred to me then. *Is there anyone,* I asked myself, *who has ever seen himself reduced to my extremity? What other man has found himself in a desert, lacking everything, and ready to die of hunger?* I then began to recall the adventures of some travelers driven off course by a storm. Adverse winds and dead calms had kept them in unknown waters, and they had used up their stock of provisions without the possibility of replenishing them. I remembered that, having suffered hunger to the point where they were dying of starvation, the only recourse left to those unfortunates was to sacrifice one of their number in order to save the rest of them. Sometimes it was by lot that the choice was made of a victim who, in losing his own life, prolonged his companions' by giving them his corpse to eat.

Dare I confess it to you, my friend? You are going to shudder when reading what remains for me to tell but, believe me, your horror cannot possibly be as great as mine. You will see to what excess despair and starvation can drive us and you will pity me, perhaps, for the suffering, which I had endured.

While I was remembering the harrowing experiences of other voyagers, my wandering eyes fell on my black. They lingered there with a kind of greed. *He is dying,* I said to myself madly. *A quick death would be a blessing for him. He is dying by inches and all human efforts are powerless to protect him. Why shouldn't his death be made useful to me?*

I will admit that my mind did not reject this possibility. Affected by the weakness of my body, my reason was warped. Starvation undermined me. I felt searing pangs in my innards. The urgent need to appease them completely dominated me. Alternative ways of doing it were out of the question. There was only one, it seemed. My disturbed mind could not reflect and examine coolly. It formed horrible desires and provided me with countless sophisticated arguments to justify them.

"What crime will I be committing?" I muttered. "He is mine. I brought him to serve me. Of what greater service could he ever be?" Madame La Couture had been entertaining murderous ideas similar to mine. She caught my final words. She did not know what train of thought had led up to them and the reasoning, which had preceded them but necessity made everything clear. She attracted my attention in a low voice and when I looked her way she pointed both with her eyes and hand in the direction of my black. Her eyes then turned back to me. They had a literally deadly look and she made an even more expressive gesture with her hand—which I fully understood.

To be unleashed it seems that my madness awaited only the approval of a backer. I did not hesitate for a second. Delighted to see that she thought as I did, I felt justified. I started up and, seizing a knobbly stick, which I had used to lean on during our marches, I went up to my black. He was dozing. I brought him out of his stupor by bringing the stick down with stunning force on his head. My hand trembled and I did not dare to hit him again. My heart palpitated. My latent humanity screamed an appeal, depriving me of the strength to go on.

On coming around, the black rose to his knees, clasped his hands together and, looking at me with anguish, said beseechingly and sadly, "What are you doing, master? What have I done to you? Won't you at least spare my life?"

I could not help softening. I wept and for two minutes I could not reply. I could not do anything At last my hunger pangs overcame the voice of reason. A mournful shout and another signal from the eye of my female friend reequipped me once more with frenzied resolution.

Beside myself, distraught, affected by an unprecedented delirium, I hurled myself at the wretched black and threw him to the ground. I yelled aloud, both to numb myself and so that I would not hear the black's screaming, which might have blunted my cruel determination. I tied his hands behind his back. I called for my companion, who came to my help in this savage procedure. She knelt on the head of my poor black, while I drew my knife and, with all my strength, sank it in his throat and widened the wound. He died at once.

There was a fallen tree near us. I dragged the black to it and hung him on it head down, so that his blood could drain out. Madame La Couture helped me.

This horrible act had exhausted both our strength and our determination. Our fearful eyes lingered on the bleeding body which, a moment before, had been a living being. We shuddered at what we had just done. We quickly ran to a nearby spring to wash our bloodstained hands, which we could not look at except with horror. We fell to our knees to ask God's forgiveness for the inhuman crime we had just committed. We also prayed for the poor wretch whose throat we had just cut.

Nature manages to combine extremes. Completely opposite feelings gripped us at almost the same time. Although devout sentiment followed on the heels of savagery, it was the latter that soon regained the upper hand. Urgent hunger pangs interfered with our prayers. "Lord," we exclaimed, "you know our situation, our overwhelming wretchedness, which pushed us into committing murder! Pardon us in our misfortune and at least bless the vile food we are going to eat. Make it nourish us. We have already paid enough for it."

With these words we got up, lit a great fire, and carried out our monstrous determination. I scarcely dare record the details: the very memory of them turns my stomach. No, my friend, except for this period of my life I have never been a barbarian. I was not born for it. You know me well and I have no need to apologize to you, but you must be the only reader of these words. I would suppress this part of my narrative if I imagined that there would ever be other readers. What an idea they would have of my character! Of what other atrocities would they not suspect me capable? Only by reasoning that, thanks to severe hardships, my sense of right had deserted me might they, perhaps, claim that they understood my actions. Few, however, would be fair enough to ponder my misfortunes and to realize that horrors of the kind, which I endured actually effect radical changes in a man's character and that the deviations into which they may lead him should not be classed as crimes.

As soon as our fire was ready, I immediately cut off the black's head. I impaled it on the end of a stick and set it up in front of the blaze. Although I took care to turn it frequently so that it would be thoroughly cooked, our raging hunger did not allow us to wait until it was properly roasted. We ate it quickly and, once we were full, made arrangements to pass the night where we were and to protect ourselves from attacks by animals. We rightly expected that the noise of their approach would prevent us from sleeping and therefore spent the night in dismembering the corpse of our black. We cut his flesh into suitable pieces for grilling on the embers or held them in smoke in the hope of preserving them from

decay. We had already suffered appallingly from hunger. The only insurance against it was to secure provisions, which would not spoil. We stayed
in the same place all the next day and the following night, hoarding our
food, eating only what would be difficult to preserve and which, consequently, we would be unable to take with us. We parceled the rest, wrapping it in our remaining handkerchiefs and in swatches of cloth from our
garments. We hung these packages from our bodies with the makeshift
ropes from our raft.

On April 24th or thereabouts we resumed our journey. The break we
had taken had rested us and the food we had eaten had restored our strength.
Certain of a supply for some time, we did not fear to move onto the plain,
which had seemed so frightening on the day when we killed the black. We
walked slowly and, now just the two of us, did not set out without remorse
for the companion who had previously followed us and whose grisly remains we now carried about us. For several days we walked, enduring
great strain and meeting many difficulties. Crossing through canebrakes
near the sea or in the middle of bramble patches or thorn bushes and other
equally hostile plants, we bloodied our feet and legs.

This annoyance, though less serious than hunger, frequently delayed
us. The bites of gnats, mosquitoes, and a host of other insects, which we
met on the coast so disfigured us that we became quite unrecognizable.
The bites covered our faces, hands, and legs, causing them to swell monstrously. In an attempt to avoid them, if possible, we made for the seashore, deciding to follow it thereafter, in the hope, too, of lucky finds in
the shape of edibles to supplement the provisions we carried. We were
not mistaken in this expectation. When the tide was out and the weather
fine, we sometimes found on the beach small mollusks and little flat fish,
which we speared with a sharpened stick. All the same we happened on
them very seldom and there were never enough to fill us. They were, however, not to be despised and we gratefully accepted them as a gift from God
with deep emotion.

I cannot give you the details, day by day, of the painful and apparently
endless odyssey, which we doggedly pursued. The canebrakes, with which
the shore was covered in many places, and through which we were forced
to travel, were as wicked as the brambles, which we had wanted to avoid.
Dry canes, splintered by the wind, tore at our legs, cutting them most cruelly. Wild beasts scared us every night, and even more frightening was
the frequent need to prepare and eat loathsome meals. Our murderous
madness had receded along with our hunger. Reason had resumed control

of our minds and reason recoiled at the very idea of cannibalism. We resorted to it only at times of extreme need, when we had managed to find absolutely no other food and when reborn hunger overcame disgust.

One evening, as we made our customary halt, I felt so weak that I could scarcely summon the strength to collect the wood needed for our fire. It proved beyond my power to build it in stacks around our camping place as I always did at night. My monstrously swollen legs could no longer support me. Luckily it then occurred to me that I could do the job better by burning the canes and briars in our vicinity and letting the wind spread the blaze. Not only would it keep wild animals away, but it would have the additional advantage of easing our journey. It would burn all those awkward canes off our intended path and we would be able to walk more conveniently along the shore by following the fire's traces. We found, the following day, that the fire had literally blazed our route for us. I regretted that I had not thought sooner of this expedient to save us from the leg wounds, which gave great discomfort and compelled us to cover only short distances daily.

As a bonus we found lying in our path very appetizing food: two rattlesnakes. One had fourteen joints; the other twenty-one. Thus we at once knew their age, if it is true that they grow an extra ring at the end of each year. The snakes were very fat. The fire had surprised them while they slept and its smoke had choked them. They provided us with fresh meat all that day and the one that followed. We also dried part of their flesh for later consumption and added it to our stock of provisions.

During our journey I found yet another means of increasing our store of food. One morning I spotted a sleeping alligator in a nearby pool. I went toward it for a closer look. The beast did not frighten me, although I knew how dangerous it was. The only idea in my mind was how great an addition to our rations the alligator would make, if only I could kill it. For a moment I hesitated to attack it, not because of fear, but simply from uncertainty as to the best way of killing it.

I went forward armed with my stick, which was of a hard and heavy wood. With it I struck the beast sharply on the head three times with such force that I made it capable neither of attacking nor retreating. It merely opened its frightful maw, into which I promptly sank the end of my stick, which was fairly well pointed. I probed for and transfixed his throat and pushing downward at once to the full length of my arm, I pinned the monster to the ground. He leaped and moved in such a frantic fashion that, if my stick had not been firmly and deeply driven into the sand, it would have been impossible to hold the fierce beast, and I would have become the victim of my daring.

Simply keeping the alligator where he was took all my strength. I was fixed in an awkward posture, which prevented me from adjusting my stance to improve my chances of killing the monster. I shouted for Madame La Couture, begging her to come and help. She did not dare to assist directly. She did, however, look for and bring me a piece of wood three or four feet in length. I used it to stun the alligator, wielding it with one of my hands, while I continued to grip the stick with which I had impaled it in the other, until the beast had all but ceased to thrash about. My companion, bolder now, took my place, enabling me to use both my hands, thanks to which I managed to crush the alligator's head and to cut off its tail.

My victory had taken a great deal out of me: I was shattered, and we did not even consider continuing our journey on that day. We used our time to cook a good meal and to preserve the flesh of the alligator as we had that of our black. We cut it up into pieces about the size of a man's hand. That way they would dry out more easily and we should avoid unnecessary delay. I used the hide to make moccasins for Madame La Couture and myself. We contrived leggings for ourselves from other strips of skin. By wrapping them around our legs we protected them from the bites of the insects, which had plagued us: naturally their stings could not penetrate alligator hide. Other strips of hide covered our hands and faces. We used it, too, for makeshift masks. At first we found them awkward, but by preserving us from insect bites they were worthwhile.

Such were the various types of relief, which we derived from our alligator. We spent all that day and the following night in these preparations. Wakeful, we put off until the night after that the need to snatch some rest. We did not want to prolong our trip with breaks. It was already made long enough by the unavoidable brevity of our daily marches.

The next day our progress was thwarted after a mere hour by a river, which flowed into the sea. Although not very wide, its current was very swift. I reconnoitered. Hoping to find it fordable, I undressed and waded in to test its depth. I met insuperable obstacles: first the water's depth, which made swimming unavoidable, and second, the strength of the current, which was impossible to overcome and would certainly have swept me into the ocean. Alone I might have been able to cope but Madame La Couture could never have done so. Unbearably frustrated, I returned to the riverbank. We had no choice but to walk inland, following the bank until we found either a more peaceful stretch of river or a place where a shallower bed would make fording feasible.

And so we resumed walking. Two whole days elapsed and we found nothing to inspire optimism. The farther we went, the less practicable seemed a river crossing. Our concern and desperation grew. We had already given up hope of ever leaving Florida. We chanced on nothing to eat in those two days and consequently survived on alligator meat, leaving the black's flesh as a last resort. We worried that we would exhaust all our provisions before arriving at an inhabited place where we could replenish them.

Frightened by our past experience, doubtful of the future, and uncertain of how long our run of bad luck would last, we spent our time in hoping, complaining, and then despairing. The sight of the river invariably flowing briskly seemed to increase our weariness. The seeming impossibility of ever crossing it and the consequent need to keep walking upstream, without knowing when we would strike a crossing point, robbed us of courage.

At the end of the second day on which we had followed this river, I saw a turtle, which must have weighed ten pounds, and I turned it onto its back with my stick. This new providential source of food, for a while, quelled our complaints, converting them in fact to prayers of thanksgiving. Previously we had seen a plump turkey hen, which regularly came to drink at the river, each morning and evening. It seemed to have its nest somewhere near but we looked for it in vain. The hope of finding wholesome food had caused us to make the most minute search for its eggs, but we had no luck. It was a frustration, which added greatly to our ill humor and made us curse our fate.

Discovering the turtle to some extent reconciled us to our destiny. We thought of cooking it and our hearth was ready. You can imagine what a shock it was when I could not find my gunflint! I emptied all my pockets and then turned them inside out. I undid all our packets of provisions. I rummaged everywhere with the most scrupulous attention. Madame La Couture helped. We did not find it. Our woe was proportionate to the need we had for the flint and to the help it had afforded us. Never has a loss given more grief to a man. We now thought of the turtle, over which we had gloated, with the utmost indifference. We would have willingly exchanged it for the flint. The loss of half of our provisions would have troubled us less. Without the flint, how could we protect ourselves from the cold and the attacks of wild beasts? How could we cook and preserve our food, or keep ourselves dry?

Madame La Couture's distress equaled mine. I reasoned that we must have lost the flint either in the place where we had slept the previous night or on the path, which we had subsequently taken. I felt tired and weak but did not hesitate for a second to retrace my steps to look for it. I suggested to Madame La Couture that she might either come with me or wait for me. She had no real choice. Although she was nervous about staying alone, she lacked the strength to make the journey again. At the same time she longed, no less than I, to recover the treasure we had lost. She made me promise not to abandon her and to return as soon as possible.

It was fortunate that we had covered little ground on the most recent stage of our journey. We had walked for a mere hour and a half, and night-fall was still far off. I retraced our path with the intention of returning before darkness fell, but it proved impossible. I was too feeble to move briskly. Besides, I did not take a single step without looking around for the flint. I hoped that I had lost it on the path and that I would recover it without the need to walk very far, but it proved necessary to go all the way back to the place where we had slept.

I had used up a great deal of time. Night had already fallen when I arrived. I could see almost nothing. I looked about in every place where I could discern footprints. It was a fruitless exercise. I found nothing. I lay on the ground feeling all around with my hands. They had to do duty for my eyes, which darkness had made useless. Tired of wearing myself out without result, I ran to the fire, which I had lit the previous night to see if I could find an ember which might enable me to revive it and thus give me the light needed for my search. The fire was utterly dead. I found only cinders without the least glimmer.

Overwhelmed by this latest disappointment, as though I had a right to expect anything else, I remained lying down, giving way to deep depression, despairing of deriving any good from my efforts, unable to rejoin Madame La Couture that night, and not even giving thought to doing so. The notion of going back to her without my flint was unbearable. I decided to wait until morning to resume my search, in the hope that in the end I would find it. I went to throw myself down on the pile of ferns, leaves, and various plants, which had been our makeshift bed. I thought that perhaps it was there that I had lost my flint. For a moment I debated with myself whether to wait until the following day before resuming my

search. It was clearly the most sensible course. Broad daylight was absolutely necessary. I could not expect to find anything in the dark. My
reason was fully persuaded but my mind was too agitated to put up with
delay.

I passed my hands repeatedly over every part of the surface of the bed
but they encountered nothing. My initial intention had been to stop after
doing this and to put off a more thorough search until daylight, but in my
impatience I could not resist going on. Fistful by fistful I went through
the pile of foliage. After examining each handful I put it down elsewhere.
I spent the best part of the night doing this. I was losing hope of recovering my treasure because I had been through and displaced every single
plant comprising the bed. I stretched my hands finally onto the earth, which
the plants had formerly covered. They came to rest on the object of my
longing. I snatched it up with a joy equal to the distress, which its loss had
caused me. Holding it tightly, I took all manner of precautions to avoid
losing it in future.

While occupied with these activities I was a little concerned about
wild animals. Although they came from far away, I could hear their cries
and I worried from time to time both for myself and for my unfortunate
companion. She was alone and her fear in the middle of the night must
have been acute. I thought of rushing to her side to reassure her, if that
was possible, but I admit that fear of a dangerous encounter on the way
kept me from doing anything for a long time. It finally struck me that the
care we had taken to make fires every night along our route must have
persuaded the brutes to keep their distance, causing them to retire to the
far corners of the wasteland we were crossing in order to avoid the fires.
Actually during this time they had never come near the places where we
made camp and we had heard their snarling only from a certain distance—
which had done much to minimize our fear. At last I persuaded myself
that I was unlikely to meet any beasts and with some qualms set off. Several times I was on the point of stopping to light a fire to give myself re-
assurance, but did not in fact halt. Fear lent me wings and, despite my
weak condition, I got back to Madame La Couture about two hours before daybreak. I could easily have missed her and might have wandered
far from the place I had left her, because a combination of darkness and
fear prevented me from recognizing the spot. Only a moan, which I heard
purely by chance and which made me shudder, told me that I was about
to pass her by without her seeing me. She had heard the sound of my
footsteps and, in her fright, had thought that a fierce animal was coming

toward her. It was she who had moaned. I asked at the top of my voice, "Is that you, Madame?"

"Yes," she replied almost inaudibly. "My God, how you frightened me! With you so far away and so late coming back, you have given me some bad moments! Did you hear that horrible snarling? It's been dinning in my ears. When you didn't return I thought you'd been eaten and it wouldn't be long before I was, too!"

"I'm still alive," I shouted, "and now I've found you again! Both of us have been petrified with fear but I've found my flint again! We'll have a fire! We'll be able to rest and have something to eat."

Even while uttering these words I was collecting some bits of dry wood. I struck sparks from my flint. For tinder I used a strip from my shirt, which was quite worn out and almost in rags. For a long time I had been using either it or Madame La Couture's chemise to start fires.

We soon had a great blaze going, on which we cooked part of our turtle. Its flesh was extremely tender and succulent. On cutting it open, we found in its body a quantity of little eggs which we grilled on the embers, thus enjoying a food, which was as wholesome as it was refreshing. It did wonders for us. We slept afterward. This needed rest, which lasted five hours, both comforted and strengthened us.

On waking we discussed the advisability of continuing in the direction we were going. The upper course of the river was visible and quite straight. We looked at it and despaired of finding a suitable crossing point for a long time. We decided to risk a passage where we were, for which I thought of building a raft. Solid materials convenient for the job were at hand. They were six trees, defoliated by time, which had floated downstream. They had come to rest on the riverbank near a gnarled tree, which leaned over the river, but whose roots were still embedded in the shore. I got into the water. Luckily it was shallow at this place and, using creepers, I lashed four of the trees together, making them reasonably fast. As best I could, I attached a long pole to them. It was thicker at one end than at the other and was meant to serve as both oar and rudder.

Once I had finished, we prepared to leave. We stripped off our clothes, making a bundle of them, which we bound with natural materials. We took this precaution so that we could save ourselves more readily if some accident happened. Our clothes would have got in our way if we had fallen in the water. Wrapping all our clothes in one bundle would make it easier to retrieve them if I had to go swimming in search of them. The outcome would show how right we were to take these precautions.

Our conditions made prudish conventions irrelevant. While we traveled together, we were scarcely aware that we were of different sexes. I was conscious of my companion's gender only because, like most women, she lacked muscular strength. She was conscious of mine merely from observing the firmness and courage with which I tried to inspire her, and the help, which my superior strength enabled me to give her. We were numb to other feelings. Our exhausted bodies, oblivious of all other considerations, asked only that we supply them with food.

Our fear of possible accidents was insufficient to make us part with our provisions as we had done with our clothes. Losing our garments would have been less calamitous than losing our food. We organized our food packages in such a way as to be able to hang them from our bodies. They would survive with us or we would die with them.

We got onto the raft, which I pushed off from the shore, steering as best I could with the pole. At first the current snatched at us with a speed, which made me shiver. In an instant it had borne us more than three hundred yards from the place where we had embarked. I was afraid that it would sweep us down to the sea. With the utmost difficulty I labored to cut across it. Finally I succeeded, but only at the cost of losing way and riding downstream at a monstrous rate so that I expected to reach the opposite shore a mile and a half lower than the place from which we had set out.

With considerable effort, I managed to get more than halfway over the river. The current then slackened and we had almost reached the spot where it was most placid. Suddenly the current took our raft sideways onto a tree, which was near to us at water level. The movement, which I made to avoid it brought disaster. The strain broke the lashings holding our craft together, loosing the lengths of wood of which it was constituted. We fell in the water and would certainly have drowned, had I not seized a branch of the tree with one hand. With the other I simultaneously gripped Madame La Couture's hair at the very instant when she was already sinking, no doubt never to reemerge. She was still conscious and I shouted for her not to grasp me with her arms and legs, the better to hold her up. Where we were, the water was very deep. I made her clamber onto the trunk of the tree while I swam around it. Its other end touched the bank, enabling me to lead her there. She sat on shore while I detached the packages of food hanging from me and placed them at her side. I went back to the river to see if I could retrieve our clothes and soon glimpsed them. They were caught in the branches of the tree, but the river was stirring them. At the moment when I dived in, the current had begun to carry them away. I swam in pursuit and had the good luck to catch up with them. Pushing them in front of me toward the shore, I landed them safely.

My first concern was to take the bundle to Madame La Couture who untied it, wrung the clothes and then spread them out. Meanwhile I prepared a fire to hasten their drying and to cook such pieces of turtle as we still possessed. We had actually lost nothing by being wrecked, and shed no tears over the raft which, having brought us across the river, had served its purpose. We would have abandoned it, whatever happened.

After eating a restoring meal, we dried our provisions, an occupation, which kept us busy all day. We spent the night where we were. The next day, rested and refreshed, we resumed our journey. Taking our bearings as well as we could, we tried to keep in the right direction for St. Mark's, Apalache. We were constantly worried that we had lost our way. On the east side of the river the forests were just as dense, and the briars and canes as unpleasant and dangerous as ever. Our shoes, leggings, and makeshift gloves and masks were unserviceable. Immersion in the river had ruined them. As before, brambles scratched and mosquitoes and flies tormented us: our bodies became enormously swollen from their constant poisonous biting. We found even less food than on the western shore. The remains of our black and our alligator were all we had to eat.

Suffering these hardships, which grew progressively worse, we walked for several days. Our bodies and spirits were both affected. Hope with its consoling fancies no longer lulled us. We were in a deplorable condition and looked more like walking barrels than human beings. We walked laboriously, scarcely able to place one foot before the other and rising only with difficulty after sitting down.

Madame La Couture held out longer than I. As long as I had possessed strength, I had been thrifty with hers, and had taken on all the arduous tasks that arose. Her spirits, moreover, were less depressed than mine, because she had let me do all the worrying. Until then, therefore, I had borne the brunt in all respects, but now came a time when I had to give in to sustained misfortune.

One day I was scarcely able to see because the bites of the insects I have mentioned had caused swelling around my eyes, which weakened and almost closed them. Feeling beaten and unable to go on, I threw myself down on the shore under a tree about a hundred yards from the sea. After lying there for an hour, I tried to rise to continue our journey, and found it was beyond my strength to get to my feet.

"It's all over," I said to my companion. "I can't go any farther. This spot will mark the end of my journey, my troubles, and my life. Use your remaining strength to try and reach an inhabited place. Take our provisions with you. Don't squander them by uselessly waiting here for me. I see that God does not want me to survive. My utter exhaustion is a sign of it. The courage and strength, which He has allowed you to keep means that He has other plans for you. Enjoy your blessings and think sometimes of the wretch who has shared your troubles for such a long time, who has eased them for you as much as he could, and who would never have deserted you, if he had been allowed to travel with you provided he could be useful. Let's surrender to cruel necessity, which is commanding us with its harsh laws. Leave! Try to survive and, when you are enjoying abundance again, and becoming forgetful of the privations we experienced, say sometimes: 'I lost a friend in the wastes of America.' No doubt you will be with Europeans again one of these days. You will hear of ships sailing for France. When you do, please do me a favor, the only one I want and expect from our friendship. Write to my parents describing the fate of their unlucky son. Tell them he is no more and that they can divide among themselves the sorry remains of his estate. They are to do with it what they think fit, without worrying that I shall ever come back to reclaim it. Tell them to pray for and pity me."

Madame La Couture did not reply except with tears. Her emotion touched me: it is a great consolation for the afflicted to see that they have aroused compassion. She took my hands and pressed them tenderly. I tried again to persuade her to leave me and to show her that it was necessary, but failed. "No, my friend," she said. "No, I shan't leave you. I shall give you, as far as I can, the care that I owe you, like that you gave me for such a long time. Be brave! Your strength may return. If that hope proves false I shall still have time enough to be left alone in this vast wasteland, accompanied only by my fears. If I abandoned you, I would feel sure every minute that God was going to send wild beasts to rip me apart as punishment for leaving you at a time when I could have helped you. As to our provisions, we'll try to make do with them. I'll also see what there is on the seashore. Any that I find will help restore your health. From now on I am going to begin to look after you. You can't protect yourself against insects, so take this!"

With these words, she took off one of her two petticoats. Using my knife she split it in two. With one piece she covered my legs: the other she placed over my arms and face. They gave me great relief, providing effective protection against possible stings. My companion then lit a fire and went to the beach, from which she returned with a turtle. I thought that the blood of this creature might prove soothing if rubbed into my wounds. I tried it and advised Madame La Couture to follow my example. She readily did so, for her head, neck, and arms were covered with mosquito bites. We then rested, but my feeling of weakness remained. I felt so ill that I had no doubt that death was near. A large turkey hen, which we then saw, flew back into a copse only a few yards from us, making us think she had a nest there. Naturally it inspired us to get hold of her eggs. Madame La Couture undertook to look for them. I was in no state to go myself, being totally immobile, and so remained lying by the fire.

I stayed alone like that for about three hours. The sun had just set and I was in a kind of stupid torpor, unmoving and almost without the power to think. I can compare my condition only to that deep calm one experiences between sleeping and waking. A frightening numbness pervaded my heavy limbs. I felt no pain but instead a general malaise throughout my body. At this moment, I heard shouts, which dragged me from my lethargy and aroused my attention. I strained my ears. They seemed to come from the seashore. I thought they must be from a band of Indians following the coastline and getting nearer.

"Great God!" I cried. "Does this clamor portend the end of all my hardships? Have You sent these Indians to my rescue or are they coming to stamp out the last remaining flickering spark of my life? Whatever You want, I am ready. Whether it is to strike or to save me, either will deliver me from my sorrows. I will equally accept whichever it is."

The same shouts were repeated over and over. A ray of hope lightened my heart. I tried to get myself up into a sitting position and succeeded only by dint of atrocious efforts. A doleful thought occurred then to lessen my excitement Perhaps, I reflected, these men I hear are skirting the coast in a boat. Soon they will have rowed farther on and they won't see me unless they disembark. What will become of me if they don't get out of their boat here? In the predicament I was in, how could I let them know that in this place was a wretch needing rescue?

This idea made me desperate. I tried to shout but my voice was gone. My fear, however, of letting slip the only chance of help, which had occurred in a very long while restored a little of my strength. I used it to drag myself on hands and knees as close as possible to the beach. I could distinctly see a large open boat working its way along the coast. It had not yet passed me. Rising to my knees I took my cap in one hand and tried to wave it but was constantly thwarted by my inability to hold myself up. I kept falling on my stomach. I much regretted then that I did not have Madame La Couture with me. She would have been able to go to the beach and run along it shouting for help and would certainly have attracted attention. But she was far away and surely beyond earshot of the shouts of the men in the boat. Otherwise she would have come running.

In her absence I did all that I could to make myself visible. I found a pole nearby. On it I fixed my cap and a scrap of the petticoat, which my companion in misfortune had left me. This makeshift flag, wafted in the air, caught the attention of those in charge of the boat. I realized it both from their excited shouts and from an alteration in the course of their craft, which now veered toward the shore. I dug my pole into the sand so that they would not lose sight of my signal and let myself drop onto the sand. I lay at full stretch, worn out with the efforts I had just made, but comforted by the certainty of imminent deliverance. I thanked God for the blessing, which He had been pleased to bestow on me.

Looking closely at the boat, I noticed that the men crewing it wore clothes. This observation, which persuaded me that I would be dealing with Europeans, rid my mind of fears which would certainly have troubled me had they been Indians. While awaiting my rescuers I cast my eyes toward the fireside, looking for Madame La Couture. I could not wait to see her so that I could tell her of and share with her our good luck. Without her I could not savor it fully. Her tender concern for me and her determination never to abandon me had confirmed the friendship between us, which had been engendered by our joint experience of misfortune. I could not see her and it took something from the joy of the moment; not much, because her happiness was sure to come. It could be delayed only very briefly. Her return could not be far off because it was getting late: nightfall was very close.

At that moment, the people I had been waiting for arrived. My extreme joy almost killed me. It precipitated a physical reaction so severe that, for several minutes, I could not answer their questions. I could not utter even one word. They gave me a drop of taffia to steady me and I was able to say something of my ordeal. At once they realized the danger of my condition and had the good sense not to make me talk much. I was delighted to see Europeans. I knew from the way they spoke French that it was not their native language, but did not ask their nationality. Actually it was of no importance. It was enough that I was among men who wanted to help me.

I begged them to resume their hailing while searching in the nearby copse, so that Madame La Couture might hear them. Her prolonged absence had begun to worry me but, a moment later, all my fears evaporated. She appeared, running toward me with all her might. She had caught the turkey hen and had brought its nest, too.

Although there has been spirited debate over the intervening centuries about the authenticity of Viaud's account (his battle with the alligator does seem far-fetched), and the introduction to the University of Florida edition gives an excellent account of the various translation oddities and embellishments that had been included at the time. However much of Viaud's account is real (and he certainly was shipwrecked on the Florida coast, that has been conclusively proven) and how much may have been fanciful exaggeration; there is no doubt that it was riveting reading at the time, and still is today.

ESCAPE FROM THE BLACKFEET

Thomas James (1782–1847)

From *Three Years Among the Indians and Mexicans*

The American frontier attracted a hardy breed of men and women—fur trappers, mountain men, explorers, adventurers, people able to live off the land and survive in some of the wildest environments day after day. One of the men who saw places that no European had ever seen before was John Colter. The young adventurer had already made his mark during his time on the Lewis and Clark expedition to explore the Louisiana Purchase. Afterward, he was the first white man to enter what is now Yellowstone National Park, and explored much of modern-day Wyoming.

Of course, traveling in such uncharted territory carried its share of dangers as well, not the least of which came from the various Native American tribes in the West. The Blackfeet were one such tribe that dealt harshly with interlopers coming into their territory, as Colter relates here, in this oral account written down and published by fellow mountain man Thomas James.

WHEN JOHN COLTER WAS RETURNING in 1807 with Lewis and Clark, from Oregon, he met a company of hunters ascending the Missouri, by whom he was persuaded to return to the trapping region, to hunt and trap with them. Here he was found by [Manuel] Liza in the following year, whom he assisted in building the Fort at the Big Horn. In one of his many excursions from this post to the Forks of the Missouri, for beaver, he made the wonderful escape adverted to in the last chapter and, which I give precisely as he related it to me. His veracity was never questioned among us and his character was that of a true American backwoodsman. He was about thirty-five years of age, five feet ten inches in height and wore an open, ingenuous, and pleasing countenance of the Daniel Boone stamp. Nature had formed him, like Boone, for hardy endurance of fatigue, privations, and perils.

He had gone with a companion named Potts to the Jefferson river, which is the most western of the three forks, and runs near the base of the mountains. They were both proceeding up the river in search of beaver, each in his own canoe, when a war party of about eight hundred Blackfeet Indians suddenly appeared on the east bank of the river. The chiefs ordered them to come ashore, and apprehending robbery only, and knowing the utter hopelessness of flight and having dropped his traps over the side of the canoe from the Indians, into the water, which was here quite shallow, he hastened to obey their mandate.

On reaching the shore, he was seized, disarmed, and stripped entirely naked. Potts was still in his canoe in the middle of the stream, where he remained stationary, watching the result. Colter requested him to come ashore, which he refused to do, saying he might as well lose his life at once, as be stripped and robbed in the manner Colter had been. An Indian immediately fired and shot him about the hip; he dropped down in the, canoe, but instantly rose with his rifle in his hands. "Are you hurt," said Colter.

"Yes," said he, "too much hurt to escape; if you can get away do so. I will kill at least one of them." He leveled his rifle and shot an Indian dead. In an instant, at least a hundred bullets pierced his body and as many savages rushed into the stream and pulled the canoe, containing his riddled corpse, ashore. They dragged the body up onto the bank, and with their hatchets and knives cut and hacked it all to pieces, and limb from limb. The entrails, heart, lungs, etc., they threw into Colter's face.

The relations of the killed Indian were furious with rage and struggled, with tomahawk in hand, to reach Colter, while others held them back. He was every moment expecting the death blow or the fatal shot that should lay him beside his companion. A council was hastily held over him and his fate quickly determined upon. He expected to die by tomahawk, slow, lingering, and horrible. But they had magnanimously determined to give him a chance, though a slight one, for his life.

After the council, a chief pointed to the prairie and motioned him away with his hand, saying in the Crow language, "go—go away." He supposed they intended to shoot him as soon as he was out of the crowd and presented a fair mark to their guns. He started in a walk, and an old Indian with impatient signs and exclamations, told him to go faster, and as he still kept a walk, the same Indian manifested his wishes by still more violent gestures and adjurations

When he had gone a distance of eighty or a hundred yards from the army of his enemies, he saw the younger Indians throwing off their blankets, leggings, and other incumbrances, as if for a race. Now he knew their object. He was to run a race, of which the prize was to be his own life and scalp. Off he started with the speed of the wind. The war whoop and yell immediately arose behind him; and looking back, he saw a large company of young warriors, with spears, in rapid pursuit.

He ran with all the strength that nature, excited to the utmost, could give; fear and hope lent a supernatural vigor to his limbs and the rapidity of his flight astonished himself. The Madison Fork lay directly before him, five miles from his starting place. He had run half the distance when his strength began to fail and the blood to gush from his nostrils. At every leap the red stream spurted before him, and his limbs were growing rapidly weaker and weaker. He stopped and looked back; he had far outstripped all his pursuers and could get off if strength would only hold out. One solitary Indian, far ahead of the others, was rapidly approaching, with a spear in his right hand, and a blanket streaming behind from his left hand and shoulder.

Despairing of escape, Colter awaited his pursuer and called to him in the Crow language, to save his life. The savage did not seem to hear him, but letting go his blanket, and seizing his spear with both hands, he rushed at Colter, naked and defenseless as he stood before him and made a desperate lunge to transfix him.

Colter seized the spear, near the head, with his right hand, and exerting his whole strength, aided by the weight of the falling Indian, who had lost his balance in the fury of the onset, he broke off the iron head or blade which remained in his hand, while the savage fell to the ground and lay prostrate and disarmed before him. Now was *his* turn to beg for his life, which he did in the Crow language, and held up his hands imploringly, but Colter was not in a mood to remember the golden rule, and pinned his adversary through the body to the earth in one stab with the spear head.

He quickly drew the weapon from the body of the now dying Indian, and seizing his blanket as lawful spoil, he again set out with renewed strength, feeling, he said to me, as if he had not run a mile. A shout and yell arose from the pursuing army in his rear as from a legion of devils, and he saw the prairie behind him covered with Indians in full and rapid chase. Before him, if anywhere was life and safety; behind him certain death; and running as never man before sped the foot, except, perhaps, at the Olympic Games, he reached his goal, the Madison river and the end of his five mile heat.

Dashing through the willows on the bank he plunged into the stream and saw close beside him a beaver house, standing like a coalpit about ten feet above the surface of the water, which was here of about the same depth. This presented to him a refuge from his ferocious enemies of which he immediately availed himself. Diving under the water he arose into the beaver house, where he found a dry and comfortable resting place on the upper floor or story of this singular structure.

The Indians soon came up, and in their search for him they stood upon the roof of his house of refuge, which he expected every moment to hear them breaking open. He also feared that they would set it on fire. After a diligent search on that side of the river, they crossed over, and in about two hours returned again to his temporary habitation in which he was enjoying bodily rest, though with much anxious foreboding.

The beaver houses are divided into two stories and will generally accommodate several men in a dry and comfortable lodging. In this asylum Colter kept fast till night. The cries of his terrible enemies had gradually died away, and all was still around him, when he ventured out of his hiding place, by the same opening under the water by which he entered and which admits the beavers to their building.

He swam the river and hastened toward the mountain gap or ravine, about thirty miles above on the river, through which our company passed in the snow with so much difficulty. Fearing that the Indians might have guarded this pass, which was the only outlet from the valley, and to avoid the danger of a surprise, Colter ascended the almost perpendicular mountain before him, the tops and sides of which a great way down, were covered with perpetual snow.

He clambered up this fearful ascent about four miles below the gap, holding on by the rocks, shrubs, and branches of trees, and by morning had reached the top. He lay there concealed all that day, and at night proceeded on in the descent of the mountain, which he accomplished by dawn.

He now hastened on in the open plain toward Manuel's Fort on the Big Horn, about three hundred miles ahead in the northeast. He traveled day and night, stopping only for necessary repose, and eating roots and the bark of trees for eleven days. He reached the fort, nearly exhausted by hunger, fatigue, and excitement. His only clothing was the Indian's blanket, whom he had killed in the race, and his only weapon, the same Indian's spear, which he brought to the fort as a trophy. His beard was long, his face and whole body were thin and emaciated by hunger, and his limbs and feet swollen and sore.

The company at the fort did not recognize him in this dismal plight until he had made himself known. Colter now with me passed over the scene of his capture and wonderful escape, and described his emotions during the whole adventure with great minuteness. Not the least of his exploits was the scaling of the mountain, which seemed to me impossible even by the mountain goat. As I looked at its rugged and perpendicular sides I wondered how he ever reached the top—a feat probably never performed before by mortal man. The whole affair is a fine example of the quick and ready thoughtfulness and presence of mind in a desperate situation, and the power of endurance, which characterize the western pioneer.

As we passed over the ground where Colter ran his race, and listened to his story an undefinable fear crept over all. We felt awestruck by the nameless and numerous dangers that evidently beset us on every side. Even Cheek's [a fellow fur trapper] courage sunk and his hitherto buoyant and cheerful spirit was depressed at hearing of the perils of the place. He spoke despondingly and his mind was uneasy, restless and fearful. "I am afraid," said he, "and I acknowledge it. I never felt fear before but now I feel it." A melancholy that seemed like a presentiment of his own fate, possessed him, and to us he was serious almost to sadness, until he met his death a few days afterward from the same Blackfeet from whom Colter escaped.

Colter told us the particulars of a second adventure, which I will give to the reader. In the winter when he had recovered from the fatigues of his long race and journey, he wished to recover the traps, which he had dropped into the Jefferson Fork on the first appearance of the Indians who captured him. He supposed the Indians were all quiet in winter quarters, and retraced his steps to the Gallatin Fork.

He had just passed the mountain gap, and encamped on the bank of the river for the night and kindled a fire to cook his supper of buffalo meat when he heard the crackling of leaves and branches behind him in the direction of the river. He could see nothing, it being quite dark, but quickly he heard the cocking of guns and instantly leaped over the fire. Several shots followed and bullets whistled around him, knocking the coals off his fire over the ground.

Again he fled for life, and for the second time, ascended the perpendicular mountain, which he had gone up in his former flight fearing now as then, that the pass might be guarded by Indians. He reached the top before morning and resting for the day descended the next night, and then made his way with all possible speed, to the fort. He said that at the time, he promised God Almighty that he would never return to this region again if he were only permitted to escape once more with his life.

He did escape once more, and was now again in the same country, courting the same dangers, which he had so often braved, and that seemed to have for him a kind of fascination. Such men, and there are thousands of such, can only live in a state of excitement and constant action. Perils and danger are their natural element and their familiarity with them and indifference to their fate, are well illustrated in these adventures of Colter.

Colter certainly seemed to have luck and skill to spare, escaping from the ambushes not once, but twice. However, even he knew when his luck was coming to an end, and moved back to Missouri, where he married and worked a farm. When the War of 1812 began, he enlisted and fought with Nathan's Rangers against the British. Accounts of his death are sketchy at best, with one report saying he died of jaundice in 1812, and another saying he passed away in 1813. No matter what the manner of his death, John Colter's life was filled with danger, heroism, and narrow escapes enough for two men.

SNOWBOUND IN THE SIERRA NEVADA MOUNTAINS

Virginia Reed Murphy (1833–1921)
From *Across the Plains in the Donner Party*

One of the most gruesome episodes in the settling of the American West was the plight of the Donner Party, a group of settlers that became snowbound in the Sierra Nevada Mountains in 1846–1847, and were forced to resort to cannibalism of the dead to survive. Twelve-year-old Virginia Reed was one of the few children who lived through the hellish journey. Years later she wrote a long letter that detailed much of the hardship and suffering the people faced during that long, cold winter. Rather than comment on what occurred, I'll simply let the words of one who was there speak for themselves.

THE ROAD AT FIRST WAS ROUGH and led through a timbered country, but after striking the great valley of the Platte the road was good and the country beautiful. Stretching out before us as far as the eye could reach was a valley as green as emerald, dotted here and there with flowers of every imaginable color, and through this valley flowed the grand old Platte, a wide, rapid, shallow stream. Our company now numbered about forty wagons, and, for a time, we were commanded by Col. William H. Russell, then by George Donner. Exercise in the open air under bright skies, and freedom from peril combined to make this part of our journey an ideal pleasure trip. How I enjoyed riding my pony, galloping over the plain, gathering wildflowers! At night the young folks would gather about the campfire chatting merrily, and often a song would be heard, or some clever dancer would give us a barn-door jig on the hind gate of a wagon.

Traveling up the smooth valley of the Platte, we passed Court House Rock, Chimney Rock, and Scott's Bluffs, and made from fifteen to twenty miles a day, shortening or lengthening the distance in order to secure a good camping ground. At night when we drove into camp, our wagons were placed so as to form a circle or corral, into which our cattle were driven, after grazing, to prevent the Indians from stealing them, the campfires and tents being on the outside. There were many expert riflemen in the party and we never lacked for game. The plains were alive with buffalo, and herds could be seen every day coming to the Platte to drink. The meat of the young buffalo is excellent and so is that of the antelope, but the antelope are so fleet of foot it is difficult to get a shot at one. I witnessed many a buffalo hunt and more than once was in the chase close beside my father. A buffalo will not attack one unless wounded. When he sees the hunter he raises his shaggy head, gazes at him for a moment, then turns and runs; but when he is wounded he will face his pursuer. The only danger lay in a stampede, for nothing could withstand the onward rush of these massive creatures, whose tread seemed to shake the prairie.

Antelope and buffalo steaks were the main article on our bill-of-fare for weeks, and no tonic was needed to give zest for the food; our appetites were a marvel. Eliza [their servant] soon discovered that cooking over a campfire was far different from cooking on a stove or range, but all hands assisted her. I remember that she had the cream all ready for the churn as we drove into the south fork of the Platte, and while we were fording the grand old stream she went on with her work, and made several pounds of butter. We found no trouble in crossing the Platte, the only danger being in quicksand. The stream being wide, we had to stop the wagon now and then to give the oxen a few moments' rest. At Fort Laramie, two hundred miles farther on, we celebrated the fourth of July in fine style. Camp was pitched earlier than usual and we prepared a grand dinner. Some of my father's friends in Springfield had given him a bottle of good old brandy, which he agreed to drink at a certain hour of this day looking to the east, while his friends in Illinois were to drink a toast to his success from a companion bottle with their faces turned west, the difference in time being carefully estimated; and at the hour agreed upon, the health of our friends in Springfield was drunk with great enthusiasm. At Fort Laramie was a party of Sioux, who were on the war path going to fight the Crows or Blackfeet. The Sioux are fine looking Indians and I was not in the least afraid of them. They fell in love with my pony and set about bargaining to buy him. They brought buffalo robes and beautifully tanned buckskin, pretty beaded moccasins, and ropes made of grass, and placing these articles in a heap alongside several of their ponies, they made my father understand by signs that they would give them all for Billy and his rider. Papa smiled and shook his head; then the number of ponies was increased and, as a last tempting inducement, they brought an old coat, that had been worn by some poor soldier, thinking my father could not withstand the brass buttons!

On the sixth of July we were again on the march. The Sioux were several days in passing our caravan, not on account of the length of our train, but because there were so many Sioux. Owing to the fact that our wagons were strung so far apart, they could have massacred our whole party without much loss to themselves. Some of our company became alarmed, and the rifles were cleaned out and loaded, to let the warriors see that we were prepared to fight; but the Sioux never showed any inclination to disturb us. Their curiosity was annoying, however, and our wagon with its conspicuous stovepipe and looking glass attracted their attention. They were continually swarming about trying to get a look at themselves in the mirror, and their desire to possess my pony was so strong that at last I had to ride in the wagon and let one of the drivers take charge of Billy. This I did not like, and in order to see how far back the line of warriors extended, I picked up a large field glass, which hung on a rack, and as I pulled it out with a click, the warriors jumped back, wheeled their ponies and scattered. This pleased me greatly, and I told my mother I could fight the whole Sioux tribe with a spyglass, and as revenge for forcing me to ride in the wagon, whenever they came near trying to get a peep at their war paint and feathers, I would raise the glass and laugh to see them dart away in terror.

A new route had just been opened by Lansford W. Hastings, called the Hastings Cutoff, which passed along the southern shore of the Great Salt Lake rejoining the old Fort Hall Emigrant road on the Humboldt. It was said to shorten the distance three hundred miles. Much time was lost in debating which course to pursue; Bridger and Vasques, who were in charge of the fort, sounded the praises of the new road. My father was so eager to reach California that he was quick to take advantage of any means to shorten the distance, and we were assured by Hastings and his party that the only bad part was the forty-mile drive through the desert by the shore of the lake. None of our party knew then, as we learned afterward, that these men had an interest in the road, being employed by Hastings. But for the advice of these parties we should have continued on the old Fort Hall road. Our company had increased in numbers all along the line, and was now composed of some of the very best people and some of the worst. The greater portion of our company went by the old road and reached California in safety. Eighty-seven persons took the Hastings Cutoff, including the Donners, Breens, Reeds, Murphys (not the Murphys of Santa Clara County), C. T. Stanton, John Denton, William McClutchen, William Eddy, Louis Keseburg, and many others too numerous to mention in a short article like this. And these are the unfortunates who have since been known as the "Donner Party."

On the morning of July 31st we parted with our traveling companions, some of whom had become very dear friends, and, without suspicion of impending disaster, set off in high spirits on the Hastings Cutoff; but a few days showed us that the road was not as it had been represented. We were seven days in reaching Weber Canyon, and Hastings, who was guiding a party in advance of our train, left a note by the wayside warning us that the road through Weber Canyon was impassable and advising us to select a road over the mountains, the outline of which he attempted to give on paper. These directions were so vague that C. T. Stanton, William Pike, and my father rode on in advance and overtook Hastings and tried to induce him to return and guide our party. He refused, but came back over a portion of the road, and from a high mountain endeavored to point out the general course. Over this road my father traveled alone, taking notes, and blazing trees, to assist him in retracing his course, and reaching camp after an absence of four days. Learning of the hardships of the advance train, the party decided to cross toward the lake. Only those who have passed through this country on horseback can appreciate the situation. There was absolutely no road, not even a trail. The canyon wound around among the hills. Heavy underbrush had to be cut away and used for making a road bed. While cutting our way step by step through the Hastings Cutoff, we were overtaken and joined by the Graves family, consisting of W. F. Graves, his wife and eight children, his son-in-law Jay Fosdick, and a young man by the name of John Snyder. Finally we reached the end of the canyon where it looked as though our wagons would have to be abandoned. It seemed impossible for the oxen to pull them up the steep hill [Donner Hill] and the bluffs beyond, but we doubled teams and the work was, at last, accomplished, almost every yoke in the train being required to pull up each wagon. While in this canyon Stanton and Pike came into camp; they had suffered greatly on account of the exhaustion of their horses and had come near perishing. Worn with travel and greatly discouraged we reached the shore of the Great Salt Lake. It had taken an entire month, instead of a week, and our cattle were not fit to cross the desert.

We were now encamped in a valley [Tooele Valley] called Twenty Wells. The water in these wells was pure and cold, welcome enough after the alkaline pools from which we had been forced to drink. We prepared for the long drive across the desert and laid in, as we supposed, an ample supply of water and grass. This desert had been represented to us as only forty miles wide but we found it nearer eighty. It was a dreary, desolate, alkali waste; not a living thing could be seen; it seemed as though the hand of death had been laid upon the country. We started in the evening, traveled all that night, and the following day and night—two nights and one day of suffering from thirst and heat by day and piercing cold by night. When the third night fell and we saw the barren waste stretching away apparently as boundless as when we started, my father determined to go ahead in search of water. Before starting he instructed the drivers, if the cattle showed signs of giving out to take them from the wagons and follow him. He had not been gone long before the oxen began to fall to the ground from thirst and exhaustion. They were unhitched at once and driven ahead. My father coming back met the drivers with the cattle within ten miles of water and instructed them to return as soon as the animals had satisfied their thirst. He reached us about daylight. We waited all that day in the desert looking for the return of our drivers, the other wagons going on out of sight. Toward night the situation became desperate and we had only a few drops of water left; another night there meant death. We must set out on foot and try to reach some of the wagons. Can I ever forget that night in the desert, when we walked mile after mile in the darkness, every step seeming to be the very last we could take! Suddenly all fatigue was banished by fear; through the night came a swift rushing sound of one of the young steers crazed by thirst and apparently bent upon our destruction. My father, holding his youngest child in his arms and keeping us all close behind him, drew his pistol, but finally the maddened beast turned and dashed off into the darkness. Dragging ourselves along about ten miles, we reached the wagon of Jacob Donner. The family were all asleep, so we children lay down on the ground. A bitter wind swept over the desert, chilling us through and through. We crept closer together, and, when we complained of the cold, Papa placed all five of our dogs around us, and only for the warmth of these faithful creatures we should doubtless have perished.

At daylight Papa was off to learn the fate of his cattle, and was told that all were lost, except one cow and an ox. The stock, scenting the water, had rushed on ahead of the men, and had probably been stolen by the Indians, and driven into the mountains, where traces of them were lost. A week was spent here on the edge of the desert in a fruitless search. Almost every man in the company turned out, hunting in all directions, but our eighteen head of cattle were never found. We had lost our best yoke of oxen before reaching Bridger's Fort from drinking poisoned water found standing in pools, and had bought at the fort two yoke of young steers, but now all were gone, and my father and his family were left in the desert, eight hundred miles from California, seemingly helpless. We realized that our wagons must be abandoned. The company kindly let us have two yoke of oxen, so with our ox and cow yoked together we could bring one wagon, but, alas! not the one, which seemed so much like a home to us, and in which Grandma had died. Some of the company went back with Papa and assisted him in caching everything that could not be packed in one wagon. A cache was made by digging a hole in the ground, in which a box or the bed of a wagon was placed. Articles to be buried were packed into this box, covered with boards, and the earth thrown in upon them, and thus they were hidden from sight. Our provisions were divided among the company. Before leaving the desert camp, an inventory of provisions on hand was taken, and it was found that the supply was not sufficient to last us through to California, and as if to render the situation more terrible, a storm came on during the night and the hilltops became white with snow. Someone must go on to Sutter's Fort after provisions. A call was made for volunteers. C. T. Stanton and William McClutchen bravely offered their services and started on bearing letters from the company to Captain Sutter asking for relief. We resumed our journey and soon reached Gravelly Ford on the Humboldt.

I now come to that part of my narrative, which delicacy of feeling for both the dead and the living would induce me to pass over in silence, but which a correct and lucid chronicle of subsequent events of historical importance will not suffer to be omitted. On the fifth day of October, 1846, at Gravelly Ford, a tragedy was enacted, which affected the subsequent lives and fortunes of more than one member of our company. At this point in our journey we were compelled to double our teams in order to ascend a steep, sandy hill. Milton Elliott, who was driving our wagon, and John Snyder, who was driving one of Mr. Graves's became involved in a quarrel over the management of their oxen. Snyder was beating his cattle over the head with the butt end of his whip, when my father, returning on horseback from a hunting trip, arrived, and, appreciating the great importance of saving the remainder of the oxen, remonstrated with Snyder, telling him that they were our main dependence and at the same time offering the assistance of our team. Snyder having taken offense at something Elliott had said declared that his team could pull up alone, and kept on using abusive language. Father tried to quiet the enraged man. Hard words followed. Then my father said: "We can settle this, John, when we get up the hill." "No," replied Snyder with an oath, "we will settle it now," and springing upon the tongue of a wagon, he struck my father a violent blow over the head with his heavy whipstock. One blow followed another. Father was stunned for a moment and blinded by the blood streaming from the gashes in his head. Another blow was descending when my mother ran in between the men. Father saw the uplifted whip, but had only time to cry: "John, John," when down came the stroke upon mother. Quick as a thought my father's hunting knife was out and Snyder fell, fatally wounded. He was caught in the arms of W. C. Graves, carried up the hillside, and laid on the ground. My father regretted the act, and dashing the blood from his eyes went quickly to the assistance of the dying man. I can see him now, as he knelt over Snyder, trying to stanch the wound, while the blood from the gashes in his own head, trickling down his face, mingled with that of the dying man. In a few moments Snyder expired. Camp was pitched immediately, our wagon being some distance from the others. My father, anxious to do what he could for the dead, offered the boards of our wagon, from which to make a coffin. Then, coming to me, he said: "Daughter, do you think you can dress these wounds in my head? Your mother is not able, and they must be attended to." I answered by saying: "Yes, if you will tell me what to do." I brought a basin of water and sponge, and we went into the wagon, so that we might not be disturbed. When my work was at last finished, I burst out crying. Papa clasped me in his arms, saying: "I should not have asked so much of you," and talked to me until I controlled my feelings, so that we could go to the tent where Mama was lying.

We then learned that trouble was brewing in the camp where Snyder's body lay. At the funeral my father stood sorrowfully by until the last clod was placed upon the grave. He and John Snyder had been good friends, and no one could have regretted the taking of that young life more than my father.

The members of the Donner party then held a council to decide upon the fate of my father while we anxiously awaited the verdict. They refused to accept the plea of self-defense and decided that my father should be banished from the company and sent into the wilderness alone. It was a cruel sentence. And all this animosity toward my father was caused by Louis Keseburg, a German who had joined our company a way back on the plains. Keseburg was married to a young and pretty German girl, and used to abuse her, and was in the habit of beating her till she was black and blue. This aroused all the manhood in my father and he took Keseburg to task—telling him it must stop or measures would be taken to that effect. Keseburg did not dare to strike his wife again, but he hated my father and nursed his wrath until Papa was so unfortunate as to have to take the life of a fellow creature in self-defense. Then Keseburg's hour for revenge had come. But how a man like Keseburg, brutal and overbearing by nature, although highly educated, could have such influence over the company is more than I can tell. I have thought the subject over for hours but failed to arrive at a conclusion. The feeling against my father at one time was so strong that lynching was proposed. He was no coward and he bared his neck, saying, "Come on, gentlemen," but no one moved. It was thought more humane, perhaps, to send him into the wilderness to die of slow starvation or be murdered by the Indians; but my father did not die. God took care of him and his family, and at Donner Lake we seemed especially favored by the Almighty as not one of our family perished, and we were the only family no one member of which was forced to eat of human flesh to keep body and soul together. When the sentence of banishment was communicated to my father, he refused to go, feeling that he was justified before God and man, as he had only acted in self-defense.

Then came a sacrifice on the part of my mother. Knowing only too well what her life would be without him, yet fearful that if he remained he would meet with violence at the hands of his enemies, she implored him to go, but all to no avail until she urged him to remember the destitution of the company, saying that if he remained and escaped violence at their hands, he might nevertheless see his children starving and be helpless to aid them, while if he went on he could return and meet them with food. It was a fearful struggle; at last he consented, but not before he had secured a promise from the company to care for his wife and little ones.

My father was sent out into the unknown country without provisions or arms—even his horse was at first denied him. When we learned of this decision, I followed him through the darkness, taking Elliott with me, and carried him his rifle, pistols, ammunition, and some food. I had determined to stay with him, and begged him to let me stay, but he would listen to no argument, saying that it was impossible. Finally, unclasping my arms from around him, he placed me in charge of Elliott, who started back to camp with me—and Papa was left alone. I had cried until I had hardly strength to walk, but when we reached camp and I saw the distress of my mother, with the little ones clinging around her and no arm to lean upon, it seemed suddenly to make a woman of me. I realized that I must be strong and help Mama bear her sorrows.

We traveled on, but all life seemed to have left the party, and the hours dragged slowly along. Every day we would search for some sign of Papa, who would leave a letter by the wayside in the top of a bush or in a split stick, and when he succeeded in killing geese or birds, he would scatter the feathers about so that we might know that he was not suffering for food. When possible, our fire would always be kindled on the spot where his had been, but a time came when we found no letter, and no trace of him. Had he starved by the wayside, or been murdered by the Indians?

My mother's despair was pitiful. My younger sister Patty and I thought we would be bereft of her also. But life and energy were again aroused by the danger that her children would starve. It was apparent that the whole company would soon be put on a short allowance of food, and the snow-capped mountains gave an ominous hint of the fate that really befell us in the Sierra. Our wagon was found to be too heavy, and was abandoned with everything we could spare, and the remaining things were packed in part of another wagon. We had two horses left from the wreck, which could hardly drag themselves along, but they managed to carry my two little brothers. The rest of us had to walk, one going beside the horse to hold on my youngest brother who was only two-and-a-half years of age. The Donners were not with us when my father was banished, but were several days in advance of our train. Walter Herron, one of our drivers, who was traveling with the Donners, left the wagons and joined my father.

On the nineteenth of October, while traveling along the Truckee, our hearts were gladdened by the return of Stanton, with seven mules loaded with provisions. Mr. McClutchen was ill and could not travel, but Captain Sutter had sent two of his Indian vaqueros, Luis and Salvador with Stanton. Hungry as we were, Stanton brought us something better than food—news that my father was alive. Stanton had met him not far from Sutter's Fort; he had been three days without food, and his horse was not able to carry him. Stanton had given him a horse and some provisions and he had gone on. We now packed what little we had left on one mule and started with Stanton. My mother rode on a mule, carrying Tommy in her lap; Patty and Jim rode behind the two Indians, and I behind Mr. Stanton, and in this way we journeyed on through the rain, looking up with fear toward the mountains, where snow was already falling although it was only the last week in October. Winter had set in a month earlier than usual. All trails and roads were covered; and our only guide was the summit, which it seemed we would never reach. Despair drove many nearly frantic. Each family tried to cross the mountains but found it impossible. When it was seen that the wagons could not be dragged through the snow, their goods and provisions were packed on oxen and another start was made, men and women walking in the snow up to their waists, carrying their children in their arms and trying to drive their cattle. The Indians said they could find no road, so a halt was called, and Stanton went ahead with the guides, and came back and reported that we could get across if we kept right on, but that it would be impossible if snow fell. He was in favor of a forced march until the other side of the summit should be reached, but some of our party were so tired and exhausted with the day's labor that they declared they could not take another step; so the few who knew the danger that the night might bring yielded to the man, and we camped within three miles of the summit.

That night came the dreaded snow. Around the campfires under the trees great feathery flakes came whirling down. The air was so full of them that one could see objects only a few feet away. The Indians knew we were doomed, and one of them wrapped his blanket about him and stood all night under a tree. We children slept soundly on our cold bed of snow with a soft white mantle falling over us so thickly that every few moments my mother would have to shake the shawl—our only covering—to keep us from being buried alive. In the morning the snow lay deep on mountain and valley. With heavy hearts we turned back to a cabin that had been built by the Murphy-Schallenberger party two years before. We built more cabins and prepared as best we could for the winter. That camp, which proved the camp of death to many in our company, was made on the shore of a lake, since known as Donner Lake. The Donners were camped in Alder Creek Valley below the lake, and were, if possible, in a worse condition than ourselves. The snow came on so suddenly that they had no time to build cabins, but hastily put up brush sheds, covering them with pine boughs.

Three double cabins were built at Donner Lake, which were known as the Breen Cabin, the Murphy Cabin, and the Reed-Graves Cabin. The cattle were all killed, and the meat was placed in snow for preservation. My mother had no cattle to kill, but she made arrangements for some, promising to give two for one in California. Stanton and the Indians made their home in my mother's cabin.

Many attempts were made to cross the mountains, but all who tried were driven back by the pitiless storms. Finally a party was organized, since known as the Forlorn Hope. They made snowshoes, and fifteen started, ten men and five women, but only seven lived to reach California; eight men perished. They were over a month on the way, and the horrors endured by that Forlorn Hope no pen can describe nor imagination conceive. The noble Stanton was one of the party, and perished the sixth day out, thus sacrificing his life for strangers. I can find no words in which to express a fitting tribute to the memory of Stanton.

The misery endured during those four months at Donner Lake in our little dark cabins under the snow would fill pages and make the coldest heart ache. Christmas was near, but to the starving its memory gave no comfort. It came and passed without observance, but my mother had determined weeks before that her children should have a treat on this one day. She had laid away a few dried apples, some beans, a bit of tripe, and a small piece of bacon. When this hoarded store was brought out, the delight of the little ones knew no bounds. The cooking was watched carefully, and when we sat down to our Christmas dinner mother said, "Children, eat slowly, for this one day you can have all you wish." So bitter was the misery relieved by that one bright day, that I have never since sat down to a Christmas dinner without my thoughts going back to Donner Lake.

The storms would often last ten days at a time, and we would have to cut chips from the logs inside, which formed our cabins, in order to start a fire. We could scarcely walk, and the men had hardly strength to procure wood. We would drag ourselves through the snow from one cabin to another, and some mornings snow would have to be shoveled out of the fireplace before a fire could be made. Poor little children were crying with hunger, and mothers were crying because they had so little to give their children. We seldom thought of bread, we had been without it so long. Four months of such suffering would fill the bravest hearts with despair.

During the closing days of December 1846, gold was found in my mother's cabin at Donner Lake by John Denton. I remember the night well. The storm fiends were shrieking in their wild mirth, we were sitting about the fire in our little dark home, busy with our thoughts. Denton with his cane kept knocking pieces off the large rocks used as fire irons on which to place the wood. Something bright attracted his attention, and picking up pieces of the rock he examined them closely; then turning to my mother he said, "Mrs. Reed, this is gold." My mother replied that she wished it were bread. Denton knocked more chips from the rocks, and he hunted in the ashes for the shining particles until he had gathered about a teaspoonful. This he tied in a small piece of buckskin and placed in his pocket, saying, "If we ever get away from here I am coming back for more." Denton started out with the first relief party but perished on the way, and no one thought of the gold in his pocket. Denton was about thirty years of age; he was born in Sheffield, England, and was a gunsmith and gold-beater by trade. Gold has never been found on the shore of the lake, but a few miles from there in the mountain canyons, from which this rock possibly came, rich mines have been discovered.

Time dragged slowly along till we were no longer on short allowance but were simply starving. My mother determined to make an effort to cross the mountains. She could not see her children die without trying to get them food. It was hard to leave them but she felt that it must be done. She told them she would bring them bread, so they were willing to stay, and with no guide but a compass we started—my mother, Eliza, Milt Elliott, and myself. Milt wore snowshoes and we followed in his tracks. We were five days in the mountains; Eliza gave out the first day and had to return, but we kept on and climbed one high mountain after another only to see others higher still ahead. Often I would have to crawl up the mountains, being too tired to walk. The nights were made hideous by the screams of wild beasts heard in the distance. Again, we would be lulled to sleep by the moan of the pine trees, which seemed to sympathize with our loneliness. One morning we awoke to find ourselves in a well of snow. During the night, while in the deep sleep of exhaustion, the heat of the fire had melted the snow and our little camp had gradually sunk many feet below the surface until we were literally buried in a well of snow. The danger was that any attempt to get out might bring an avalanche upon us, but finally steps were carefully made and we reached the surface. My foot was badly frozen, so we were compelled to return, and just in time, for that night a storm came on, the most fearful of the winter, and we should have perished had we not been in the cabins.

We now had nothing to eat but raw hides and they were on the roof of the cabin to keep out the snow; when prepared for cooking and boiled they were simply a pot of glue. When the hides were taken off our cabin and we were left without shelter Mr. Breen gave us a home with his family, and Mrs. Breen prolonged my life by slipping me little bits of meat now and then when she discovered that I could not eat the hide. Death had already claimed many in our party and it seemed as though relief never would reach us. Baylis Williams, who had been in delicate health

before we left Springfield, was the first to die; he passed away before starvation had really set in.

I am a Catholic although my parents were not. I often went to the
Catholic church before leaving home, but it was at Donner Lake that I
made the vow to be a Catholic. The Breens were the only Catholic family in the Donner party and prayers were said aloud regularly in that cabin
night and morning. Our only light was from little pine sticks split up
like kindling wood and kept constantly on the hearth. I was very fond of
kneeling by the side of Mr. Breen and holding these little torches so that
he might see to read. One night we had all gone to bed—I was with my
mother and the little ones, all huddled together to keep from freezing—
but I could not sleep. It was a fearful night and I felt that the hour was not
far distant when we would go to sleep—never to wake again in this
world. All at once I found myself on my knees with my hands clasped,
looking up through the darkness, making a vow that if God would send
us relief and let me see my father again I would be a Catholic. That prayer
was answered.

On his arrival at Sutter's Fort, my father made known the situation of
the emigrants, and Captain Sutter offered at once to do everything possible for their relief. He furnished horses and provisions and my father
and Mr. McClutchen started for the mountains, coming as far as possible
with horses and then with packs on their backs proceeding on foot; but
they were finally compelled to return. Captain Sutter was not surprised
at their defeat. He stated that there were no ablebodied men in that
vicinity, all having gone down the country with Frémont to fight the
Mexicans. He advised my father to go to Yerba Buena, now San Francisco, and make his case known to the naval officer in command. My
father was in fact conducting parties there—when the seven members of
the Forlorn Hope arrived from across the mountains. Their famished
faces told the story. Cattle were killed and men were up all night drying
beef and making flour by hand mills, nearly two hundred pounds being
made in one night, and a party of seven, commanded by Captain Reasen
P. Tucker, were sent to our relief by Captain Sutter and the alcalde, Mr.
Sinclair. On the evening of February 19, 1847, they reached our cabins,
where all were starving. They shouted to attract attention. Mr. Breen
clambered up the icy steps from our cabin, and soon we heard the blessed
words, "Relief, thank God, relief!" There was joy at Donner Lake that
night, for we did not know the fate of the Forlorn Hope and we were told
that relief parties would come and go until all were across the mountains.

But with the joy sorrow was strangely blended. There were tears in other eyes than those of children; strong men sat down and wept. For the dead were lying about on the snow, some even unburied, since the living had not had strength to bury their dead. When Milt Elliott died—our faithful friend, who seemed so like a brother—my mother and I dragged him up out of the cabin and covered him with snow. Commencing at his feet, I patted the pure white snow down softly until I reached his face. Poor Milt! it was hard to cover that face from sight forever, for with his death our best friend was gone.

On the twenty-second of February the first relief started with a party of twenty-three—men, women, and children. My mother and her family were among the number. It was a bright, sunny morning and we felt happy, but we had not gone far when Patty and Tommy gave out. They were not able to stand the fatigue and it was not thought safe to allow them to proceed, so Mr. Glover informed Mama that they would have to be sent back to the cabins to await the next expedition. What language can express our feelings? My mother said that she would go back with her children—that we would all go back together. This the relief party would not permit, and Mr. Glover promised Mama that as soon as they reached Bear Valley he himself would return for her children. Finally my mother, turning to Mr. Glover said, "Are you a Mason?" He replied that he was. "Will you promise me on the word of a Mason that if we do not meet their father you will return and save my children?" He pledged himself that he would. My father was a member of the Mystic Tie and Mama had great faith in the word of a Mason. It was a sad parting—a fearful struggle. The men turned aside, not being able to hide their tears. Patty said, "I want to see Papa, but I will take good care of Tommy and I do not want you to come back." Mr. Glover returned with the children and, providing them with food, left them in the care of Mr. Breen.

With sorrowful hearts we traveled on, walking through the snow in single file. The men wearing snowshoes broke the way and we followed in their tracks. At night we lay down on the snow to sleep, to awake to find our clothing all frozen, even to our shoestrings. At break of day we were again on the road, owing to the fact that we could make better time over the frozen snow. The sunshine, which it would seem would have been welcome, only added to our misery. The dazzling reflection of the snow was very trying to the eyes, while its heat melted our frozen clothing, making them cling to our bodies. My brother was too small to step in the tracks made by the men, and in order to travel he had to place his knee on the little hill of snow after each step and climb over. Mother coaxed him along, telling him that every step he took he was getting nearer Papa and nearer something to eat. He was the youngest child that walked over the Sierra Nevada. On our second day's journey John Denton gave out and declared it would be impossible for him to travel, but he begged his companions to continue their journey. A fire was built and he was left lying on a bed of freshly cut pine boughs, peacefully smoking. He looked so comfortable that my little brother wanted to stay with him; but when the second relief party reached him poor Denton was past waking. His last thoughts seemed to have gone back to his childhood's home, as a little poem was found by his side, the pencil apparently just dropped from his hand.

Captain Tucker's party on their way to the cabins had lightened their packs of a sufficient quantity of provisions to supply the sufferers on their way out. But when we reached the place where the cache had been made by hanging the food on a tree, we were horrified to find that wild animals had destroyed it, and again starvation stared us in the face. But my father was hurrying over the mountains, and met us in our hour of need with his hands full of bread. He had expected to meet us on this day, and had stayed up all night baking bread to give us. He brought with him fourteen men. Some of his party were ahead, and when they saw us coming they called out, "Is Mrs. Reed with you? If she is, tell her Mr. Reed is here." We heard the call; mother knelt on the snow, while I tried to run to meet Papa.

When my father learned that two of his children were still at the cabins, he hurried on, so fearful was he that they might perish before he reached them. He seemed to fly over the snow, and made in two days the distance we had been five in traveling, and was overjoyed to find Patty and Tommy alive. He reached Donner Lake on the first of March, and what a sight met his gaze! The famished little children and the deathlike look of all made his heart ache. He filled Patty's apron with biscuits, which she carried around, giving one to each person. He had soup made for the infirm, and rendered every assistance possible to the sufferers. Leaving them with about seven days' provisions, he started out with a party of seventeen, all that were able to travel. Three of his men were left at the cabins to procure wood and assist the helpless. My father's party (the second relief) had not traveled many miles when a storm broke upon them. With the snow came a perfect hurricane. The crying of half-frozen children, the lamenting of the mothers, and the suffering of the whole party was heartrending; and above all could be heard the shrieking of the Storm King. One who has never witnessed a blizzard in the Sierra can form no idea of the situation. All night my father and his men worked unceasingly through the raging storm, trying to erect shelter for the dying women and children. At times the hurricane would burst forth with such violence that he felt alarmed on account of the tall timber surrounding the camp. The party were destitute of food, all supplies that could be spared having been left with those at the cabins. The relief party had cached provisions on their way over to the cabins, and my father had sent three of the men forward for food before the storm set in; but they could not return. Thus, again, death stared all in the face. At one time the fire was nearly gone; had it been lost, all would have perished. Three days and nights they were exposed to the fury of the elements. Finally my father became snowblind and could do no more, and he would have died but for the exertions of William McClutchen and Hiram Miller, who worked over him all night. From this time forward, the toil and responsibility rested upon McClutchen and Miller.

The storm at last ceased, and these two determined to set out over the snow and send back relief to those not able to travel. Hiram Miller picked up Tommy and started. Patty thought she could walk, but gradually everything faded from her sight, and she, too, seemed to be dying. All other sufferings were now forgotten, and everything was done to revive the child. My father found some crumbs in the thumb of his woolen mitten; warming and moistening them between his own lips, he gave them to her and thus saved her life, and afterward she was carried along by different ones in the company. Patty was not alone in her travels. Hidden away in her bosom was a tiny doll, which she had carried day and night through all of our trials. Sitting before a nice, bright fire at Woodworth's Camp, she took dolly out to have a talk, and told her of all her new happiness.

There was untold suffering at that Starved Camp, as the place has since been called. When my father reached Woodworth's Camp, a third relief started in at once and rescued the living. A fourth relief went on to Donner Lake, as many were still there—and many remain there still, including George Donner and wife, Jacob Donner and wife, and four of their children. George Donner had met with an accident, which rendered him unable to travel; and his wife would not leave him to die alone. It would take pages to tell of the heroic acts and noble deeds of those who lie sleeping about Donner Lake.

Most of the survivors, when brought in from the mountains, were taken by the different relief parties to Sutter's Fort, and the generous hearted captain did everything possible for the sufferers. Out of the eighty-three persons who were snowed in at Donner Lake, forty-two perished, and of the thirty-one emigrants who left Springfield, Illinois, that spring morning, only eighteen lived to reach California. Alcalde Sinclair took my mother and her family to his own home, and we were surrounded with every comfort. Mrs. Sinclair was the dearest of women. Never can I forget their kindness. But our anxiety was not over, for we knew that my father's party had been caught in the storm. I can see my mother now, as she stood leaning against the door for hours at a time, looking toward the mountains. At last my father arrived at Mr. Sinclair's with the little ones, and our family were again united. That day's happiness repaid us for much that we had suffered; and it was spring in California.

Words cannot tell how beautiful the spring appeared to us coming out of the mountains from that long winter at Donner Lake in our little dark cabins under the snow. Before us now lay, in all its beauty, the broad valley of the Sacramento. I remember one day, when traveling down Napa Valley, we stopped at noon to have lunch under the shade of an oak; but I was not hungry; I was too full of the beautiful around me to think of eating. So I wandered off by myself to a lovely little knoll and stood there in a bed of wildflowers, looking up and down the green valley, all dotted with trees. The birds were singing with very joy in the branches over my head, and the blessed sun was smiling down upon all as though in benediction. I drank it in for a moment, and then began kissing my hand and wafting kisses to Heaven in thanksgiving to the Almighty for creating a world so beautiful. I felt so near God at that moment that it seemed to me that I could feel His breath warm on my cheek. By and by I heard Papa calling, "Daughter, where are you? Come, child, we are ready to start, and you have had no lunch." I ran and caught him by the hand, saying, "Buy this place, please, and let us make our home here." He stood looking around for a moment, and said, "It *is* a lovely spot," and then we passed on.

Virginia Reed Murphy lived for many years after her harrowing brush with death, eloping at sixteen with John Marion Murphy, and assisting him with running his real estate and insurance businesses. When he died, she became the first woman on the Pacific Coast to handle business insurance. She passed away in 1921 at the age of eighty-seven.

TRIAL BY BALLOON

Maria Bovsun and Allan Zullo

From *The Greatest Survivor Stories Never Told*

───────────

Often when things go wrong, they go wrong very quickly, as in this case, where a Navy hydrogen balloon carrying three men encounters a storm that blows them hundreds of miles off course deep into the Canadian wilderness. When they finally land, their struggles are just beginning. What happens next is a hard-fought tale of survival against the elements.

CONDITIONS WERE GOOD FOR THE FLIGHT of Navy Balloon A-5598 when it floated off in the late afternoon of Monday, December 13, 1920, from the U.S. Naval Air Station at Rockaway Beach, New York. Skies were clear and winds were mild. There was no sign of the vicious storm that would soon blow the three pilots into an icy death grip.

Carrying Lts. A. J. Kloor, Walter Hinton, and Stephen Farrell in a rattan basket, the rising 35,000-cubic-foot hydrogen balloon headed north in a test flight. The men had rations for a day: a couple of bottles of coffee, eight sandwiches, chocolate bars, and packages of crackers. It was more than enough for the trip. Or so it seemed.

The men expected an ordinary little balloon hop. For directions, they brought along a railway map provided by the Quebec Central Railroad. They planned to figure out their location by following the tracks. The plan was to hook on to an air stream that would carry them north over the Adirondack Mountains of upstate New York. They were wearing their flying suits; they hadn't bothered to put on electrically heated protective clothing.

When they took off, they had twenty-one thirty-pound bags of sand to use as ballast. They also were carrying a cage of four carrier pigeons to use for sending messages back to the naval station.

As they climbed above New York City, they marveled at the sight of the Brooklyn Bridge and released one of the pigeons over the Brooklyn Navy Yard. Soon, however, there were no more sights to see because thick, gray clouds had formed a floor under them, blocking their view of the world below. With no visibility, they had to determine their position solely by compass.

Although not the ideal way to navigate, it wasn't particularly worrisome to the three aeronauts. All were Navy aces with countless dangerous journeys by balloon or airplane under their belts. In fact, Hinton, who was flying in a balloon for the first time, had been a member of the crew of the NC-4 Flying Boat, which had made the world's first transatlantic flight in 1919.

About 8 P.M., after about three hours of traveling through the fog and darkness, the three balloonists descended to get their bearings and found themselves near a little town. They moored their huge floating craft to the top of a tree and startled a man who was walking below them.

"Hello!" Kloor called out. "Where are we?"

"Wells, New York," the surprised stroller yelled back, peering up into the cloudy night sky at the massive whitish shape above him.

The fliers had never heard of the town. "Where's the nearest city?" Kloor asked.

"Don't know, I can't really say for sure," the man replied.

For a moment they considered setting down in Wells, but decided against it. Kloor, the youngest and greenest of the group, was in command on this trip and was eager to complete his mission. He wasn't about to let a little fog get in his way. So they untied their balloon and lifted off again.

Spirits were light as they skimmed at around thirty miles per hour over the earth through the clouds in the silent craft. Christmas was on their minds. Both Hinton and Farrell were married men with children and were looking forward to spending the holidays at home with their families.

Kloor, dubbed "The Kid" by his fellow crew members, was twenty-two and the only bachelor member of the trio, although he had recently decided to embark on a journey perhaps more perilous than anything he could encounter in the air. Just weeks earlier he had become engaged to the lovely Alexandra Flowerton, who lived on Manhattan's Upper East Side.

The balloonists had begun munching on their food and were trading jibes in the dark, when suddenly an unexpected gust slammed into the balloon, practically pushing it on its side and changing the frail craft's course. The gust turned into a steady, hard wind that blew in a driving rain. Icy droplets tasting of salt stung the aeronauts' eyes and caked their clothes.

The cold rain fell for hours as the wind shoved the balloon at more than sixty miles an hour.

Around midnight, the craft dipped briefly under the clouds just long enough for the men to see the lights of what looked like a large town. Again they debated setting down but again decided against it, figuring the worst was over and the rains would end in a few hours. They ate more sandwiches and drank more coffee as they brought the balloon higher and continued to lurch through the storm.

By daybreak the rains had let up and the clouds cleared enough for the men to get a bird's-eye view of the landscape below them. They looked out over an expanse of forests, lakes, and snow but saw no sign of human life. The balloonists had no idea where they were.

The temperature started to drop, and the balloon, kept aloft by hydrogen, started to descend quickly as the hydrogen's volume contracted.

"Get light! Get light!" Kloor shouted as their rattan basket scraped noisily against the tops of the trees. "Dump the sand!"

Frantically, the three men hoisted bag after bag of the ballast overboard, until the craft started to gain a little altitude. But it wasn't enough, so the men quickly looked around the tiny basket for more things to toss out. First to go was the heavy, long drag rope, essential to let the balloonists know when they were getting too close to the tree tops. Because the rope was the heaviest thing on board, they cut it up and dumped it out. Next went thermos bottles, seats, carpets, even the lining of the basket. The compass, altimeter and other instruments were about to go over when Farrell thought better of it and decided to hold on to them for just a bit longer. The delicate instruments might come in handy.

"We're in bad," Farrell murmured. The other two men glanced at him but said nothing. Then their predicament took a turn for the worse. At that moment, the sun burst out from behind the clouds, and now the hydrogen gas in the balloon started to warm and expand. With nothing to hold it down, the balloon quickly soared to 6,500 feet, and drifted in a northwesterly direction.

As far as the men could see there was still no sign of human life until half past noon when they spotted what they thought was a little shack, and perhaps salvation. But they couldn't be sure, flying at that height and at that speed. It might just as well have been a big boulder.

Then a faint sound reached the craft. "Do you hear that?" Hinton whispered. They listened again.

"It's a dog," Kloor declared. The others nodded. Even at such a great height, they were sure they had heard a barking dog. "Where there's a dog, there's often a man and a chance for survival. We're going to set down."

The only way to do it was to release hydrogen and risk a crash landing. Over the next half hour Kloor released hydrogen three times and the balloon descended. It slammed into the tops of trees, dragging the rattan basket for twenty feet and smashing it to bits. Fortunately, none of the men was thrown out or hurt by the time it came to rest.

They climbed down the tree onto the snow-packed ground. To their relief, the temperature was an unseasonably balmy thirty degrees. However, there was no sign of human life. The aeronauts realized they were completely on their own. Since the Navy didn't know where they were, no one would be able to rescue them. They had to rescue themselves.

They had no supplies and no water. But they did have matches and their three caged pigeons. The men set off at a fast clip, heading toward the southeast in hopes of finding the barking dog—and, hopefully, civilization. They traveled until dusk and then built a fire of rotten wood and pine brush for the night. Silently, the three downed balloonists stared into the crackling flames, wondering what fate awaited them.

Hearing what he thought was a stream, Hinton decided to look for it. They desperately needed water. After trudging through the dense forest for a while, Hinton became overheated, so he took off his heavy flight suit and laid it on the ground. He continued his search for fresh water but the woods closed in on him. Soon he didn't know where he was or where he had left his flight suit. He started walking faster and faster but it all seemed to be taking him down the wrong path.

Finally he noticed the smell of burning pine and followed his nose back to his companions. Through the night the men huddled together for warmth. Kloor's feet were so close to the fire that his boots were singed.

After a fitful sleep the shivering men killed one of their pigeons, roasted it, and ate it for a meager breakfast. For water they resorted to dipping into *moose licks,* small holes made when moose lap up snow.

They set out Wednesday morning, weak from lack of food and drink. On they trudged, heading east, toward the sound of the barking dog, which they heard from time to time. They finally reached a creek and drank their fill. They decided to follow the creek downstream, but soon a fierce winter storm blew in, bringing heavy ice and snow and plunging temperatures. The men could walk for only about two hours before their feet became so cold that they had to stop and build a fire. In fits and starts, they pressed on until nightfall.

After a dinner of caribou moss, the men made camp along the banks of the creek. The storm had stopped but the temperature had plunged below zero. Except for the crackling of the fire, the rustling of the trees, and the occasional howl of a wolf, it was oddly silent.

"Where do you suppose we are?" Kloor asked.

"Somewhere in New York," offered Hinton.

"Nah, I say Canada, the woods," Farrell said. "Think we'll ever find that dog?"

No one answered. For a long time, they fell into a glum silence, staring into the flames.

"Something will turn up tomorrow," Hinton said. "I know it. It'll be the third day."

They all nodded their heads, as if Hinton had just uttered some great words of wisdom. As hope faded and superstition took hold, the men were clinging to the old seaman's belief that the third day of a journey will bring good luck. "Something will turn up," Hinton repeated.

Kloor and Farrell dozed off while Hinton stayed up for several hours watching the fire. They slept in shifts to make sure that the flames didn't die out. Still, none of the men managed to get much shut-eye, and that deepened their misery.

The third morning, Thursday, brought them nothing that felt like good luck, just hunger, weakness, and nausea. Worst of all was the uncertainty. They had no idea whether they were one mile or one hundred miles from the nearest human. Because they had kept the compass, they knew for sure that they had not been walking in circles. But that was small consolation.

"I think we should write farewell letters to our loved ones and put them in our pockets," Farrell suggested. "That way, if they ever find us, they'll know our last thoughts were of them."

"There'll be plenty of time for that later—if we ever give up," Kloor replied.

For breakfast they killed and ate one of their two remaining pigeons. The men decided it would be bad luck to kill the third pigeon. Besides, the little birds yielded no more than two ounces of meat per man, not much to travel on. They set the surviving bird free because they didn't want to continue toting its cage. Everything was becoming unbearably heavy. Through the day as they walked, more slowly and painfully with each passing hour, it became clear that the pigeon cage was the least of their problems.

Farrell had started to lag behind, and Hinton suggested it might be wise for him to ditch the heavy flight suit, which he did. Under his flight suit Farrell had only his long underwear, and he continued the trek in nothing but that garb. Walking was so strenuous that it kept him from freezing. Hinton had of course lost his suit and Kloor had cast off his heavy suit earlier in the journey; both were traveling in only thin shirts and jackets. The cold was hard to endure, but the suits were just too heavy to wear.

At one point, Farrell stumbled over a log, fell headlong, and slashed his shins. Helping Farrell up, Hinton heard the flier murmur words he couldn't quite believe he was hearing. "I'm not going to make it," Farrell muttered. "Cut my throat, take my body for food. Let me die."

"Don't talk like that," said Hinton. "You're just fatigued. We have to stick together, and if that time comes, then we'll die together."

"We have to keep moving," Kloor said. "We're getting closer to the dog."

After staggering along the creek bank, they came to a clearing and finally found the barking dog that had fueled their belief a house was near. But instead of shelter they found irony. They had come upon a stray husky caught by the leg in a beaver trap—and it was sending out its own call for help. They freed the dog.

Despite their hopeful superstitions, their third day in the frigid wilderness was ending in much the same way as the previous days—with hunger, agony, and the looming realization they might not get out alive.

On the fourth day, they reached a frozen river and discovered that they could make much better time walking on the ice than through the snow along the bank. But making better time to where? They decided to head east.

While they slowly trudged through the bitter cold, Kloor spotted something that revived their spirits: sled tracks.

The three desperate aeronauts quickened their pace and soon covered about five miles, until the tracks came to a frozen lake about two miles wide. Then they saw a heartening sight. Off in the distance, about a mile ahead of them, they could barely make out the form of a man. Mustering all their strength, they shouted, hooted, waved, leaped, and tossed their arms above their heads, hoping to catch the eye of the stranger.

They finally succeeded. The man, a local Cree Indian trapper named Tom Marks, took one look at the tattered trio—especially Farrell in his torn, baggy long underwear—and their frenzied dance, and then he did what he thought was the only sensible thing to do. He bolted, thinking that he was seeing spirits.

They shouted in English and French for him to come back. Although he knew only a few words of those languages, something in their tone made him believe they were in trouble and not dangerous. He turned and warily walked toward them. Through hand signs, grunts, and the offer of cigarettes, Kloor managed to convey their desperate situation. The Indian gestured for them to follow him. Kloor took a few steps, then turned to discover that neither of his companions was behind him.

"I can't go on," Farrell groaned, as he tried to stand. "I just can't."

"I'm played out, too," muttered Hinton.

They were so close to rescue, yet they couldn't move. Reluctantly Kloor went on alone to follow the Indian and promised help would return.

For two hours Kloor and the Indian trudged through snow and ice. Finally, to Kloor's elation and relief, they arrived at a cluster of rustic cabins with smoke curling from the chimneys. It was a small settlement of white and Indian fur traders who spoke English.

"Are we in New York?" Kloor asked his hosts.

"No, Canada," one of the trappers grunted. "This is the settlement of Moose Factory."

It was an old, remote Hudson Bay trading post in the wild northwestern region of Ontario. The winds had carried the balloon 1,200 miles from its base to an area just south of James Bay. The fliers were about 600 miles off course.

The luck that seemed to desert the three men when the wind pushed them so far into Canada could actually have been worse. Had the wind taken them a little farther northeast, they would have been carried over Hudson Bay and would likely have come down in an even more desolate, deadly area.

Soon a rescue party was dispatched to retrieve Farrell and Hinton, and now the famished Kloor devoured plates of bacon and moose meat. Soon his fellow balloonists, ragged and starving, staggered through the door and sat down to eat their first real meal in nearly a week.

With their bellies full and their bodies in warm clothes, they penned quick messages to their loved ones. Kloor told his fiancée that the experience had been like "passing through the tortures of hell." He also wrote a note to the Naval Air Station that they were safe. A messenger at Moose

Factory then left to deliver the messages to the nearest telegraph office in Mattice, Ontario, 200 miles away.

Meanwhile, the men stayed at Moose Factory for ten days, building up their strength and writing more and longer letters to their relatives. Their letters were taken to Mattice by Indian runners who wound up suffering frostbitten faces in the ever-worsening weather. When the outside world heard of their ordeal, it was inevitable that the press would eagerly pursue their story. More than a dozen reporters headed to meet them in Mattice.

Back in Moose Factory, the aeronauts celebrated Christmas with the traders who made them presents of bags of candy, a tiny British flag, and a Canadian pin. Three days later, the trio had regained their strength and were ready for the next part of their journey—mushing out of the wilderness via the Missinaibi Trail to Mattice, where they would get on a train for the trip home.

But if they thought their worries were over, they were wrong.

They were severely tested again when they and their three guides left the trading post on dog sleds. By now the snow was four feet deep and the temperatures had plunged to forty degrees below zero. On the treacherous Missinaibi Trail, they slogged through blinding whiteouts and stinging blasts of wind-whipped ice particles while three teams of eight sturdy huskies pulled the supply sleds. Three times, the fury of a blizzard forced the men to bury themselves in snow caves and wait out the storm.

Despite being clad in thick fur, they battled the horrible tortures of deadly cold that searched for any exposed flesh. With each breath the super frigid air seared their lungs. Adding to their misery, the balloonists suffered *snowshoe sickness,* a condition that painfully attacks the nerves of the legs. It's caused by lifting the weight of the snow-caked snowshoes mile after mile. It tormented Hinton so badly that the only way he could walk was to tie a piece of rope to the back of each snowshoe and lift it at each step with his hands.

During the arduous walk, the aeronauts uncharacteristically bickered with each other over the slightest irritation, their tempers triggered by the hardships and grueling struggles that they had to endure. But as quickly as the quarrels flashed they subsided.

The trail was unbroken almost the whole way, so the men had to go ahead and tamp it down as hard as they could. Legs burning and feet blistered, the weakening trio had to keep up a steady pace with their guides or be left behind. For fourteen grueling, punishing days, they trekked in the bleak, barren snowscape, until finally on January 11th they reached Mattice.

Incredibly, within fifteen minutes of their arrival, a bitter argument erupted between Hinton and Farrell. Ignoring their friendship, which had grown stronger through the escapes from death they had shared, Farrell launched into an obscenity-laced tirade against Hinton in front of shocked newspaper reporters who had traveled to Mattice to interview the survivors. Then Farrell struck Hinton in the jaw, knocking him over a table before reporters could restrain him. Farrell's fury had been ignited by a reporter's revelation that Hinton had written letters claiming Farrell was the weakling of the group. The letters had been published in the press. Further agitating Farrell was his belief that Hinton had violated an agreement that the three of them had made back in Moose Factory to sell their story to the highest bidder. (Yes, even back then survivors were savvy about checkbook journalism.)

A few hours later Farrell and Hinton, who was sporting a shiner, patched up their differences and Kloor issued a statement claiming the fight was "a passing flare-up attributable to overwrought minds and over-wrought bodies."

The following day they boarded a train for New York, where they were greeted by hundreds of well-wishers who released tiny balloons in tribute to the aeronauts' survival.

Kloor told the public that the secret of the trio's survival was their collective strength. "We have sacrificed for each other mutually and without partiality and have fought the battle out as one composite group of shipmates. In accordance with the best traditions of the great United States Navy, we did all we could to uphold our own dignity, and will forever be brothers and the best of friends."

Whenever a group is stranded in a survival situation, cooperation becomes paramount to ensure that everyone survives. In this case, the three men supported each other as best as they could, even when one said he couldn't go any further. The last quote by Lt. Kloor bears this out, the incident between Lts. Farrell and Hinton notwithstanding (despite the fact that Farrell had told the other two to go on without him). The determination of Kloor and Hinton to ensure that all three men made it out of the Canadian woods alive is a testament to the bonds that can be forged in life-or-death situations.

THE SIERRA SURVIVOR

Maria Bovsun and Allan Zullo

From *The Greatest Survivor Stories Never Told*

Whether trapped in the Sierra Nevada Mountains in the nineteenth century, as the Donner Party was, or more than a century later, as the subject of our next story is, it seems that other than the way First Lt. Steeves ended up there (jet crash), the time of year (spring instead of winter), and the clothes he was wearing, not much else had changed in the area since the 1840s.

MR. AND MRS. HAROLD STEEVES'S HEARTS SANK when they heard the grim news on May 9, 1957. Their twenty-three-year-old son, Air Force Lt. David A. Steeves, and his jet had disappeared somewhere over California's rugged Sierra Mountains and he was now considered missing. The couple began to pray and hope.

After two anxiety-ridden weeks, during which 191 search missions combed the area without discovering a hint of the whereabouts of the pilot or the wreckage of the plane, the couple received word that the Air Force had called off the hunt for their son. Although disconsolate, his parents refused to give up hope.

Days later, right before Mother's Day, the telegram that every serviceman's parent fears arrived at the Steeveses' home in Trumbull, Connecticut. In it, the Air Force informed the couple that their son's status had been changed. No longer was he considered missing. Now he was declared dead.

Still the couple clung to hope. David was strong, athletic, and resourceful. Why, hadn't he hitchhiked from California to Alaska by himself when he was only seventeen? And hadn't he always remained calm in difficult situations? They just couldn't believe he was gone, although the strength of their conviction was weakening.

Then on May 28th, the day before Memorial Day, they received an official Air Force letter telling them it was hopeless to think that their son could have survived in that wild terrain. The Steeveses knew they couldn't deny the bleak facts much longer.

Finally, right before Flag Day, the death certificate of their son arrived in the mail. Only then did the couple accept that their strapping, handsome, blue-eyed boy was officially dead.

But they were dead wrong.

At that moment, their son was waging a dire struggle for survival alone in the untamed, harsh wilderness.

First Lt. David Steeves's adversity began when he took off in his two-seat Lockheed T-33 jet trainer from Hamilton Air Force Base, near San Francisco, for a flight to Craig Air Force Base, near Selma, Alabama. As he reached 33,000 feet, he radioed his position and settled back for what he thought would be smooth flying to his home base.

About seventy-five miles east of Fresno, California, he suddenly found himself fighting for his life.

Steeves heard a loud crackling sound in the cockpit and then a deafening, explosive boom that momentarily knocked him out cold. When he regained consciousness, he faced a scene of horror. Fire was ravaging the cockpit, singeing his face and devouring the controls. His helmet was melting in the heat as smoke consumed the cockpit, stinging his eyes and throat. Blood was trickling down the back of his neck.

Trying to keep his cool, Steeves feverishly worked the controls, but it was a futile effort. The plane refused to respond. As the cockpit continued to burn and fill with swirling, dense smoke, the jet began lurching from side to side and was losing altitude.

I'm going down! he thought. *Time to bail out—now!*

There was no time to send out a Mayday, no time to send up a prayer. Blindly, he fell back on the skills he had honed during his cadet training and two years in the service. He activated his ejection seat and blasted out of the fiery jet as it continued its erratic flight.

His parachute billowed open, yanking him sharply, then dropping him with unusual speed in a spinning spiral toward earth. *Why am I falling so fast?* he wondered. He looked up to see rips in two panels of the light fabric. Glancing down, he saw he was over a vast primitive wilderness of formidable snow-capped granite peaks.

With limited control of his parachute, he whizzed by snowy slopes and headed for the only rock outcropping that was void of snow. *I'm coming in too fast*, he thought. *Stay loose, don't tense up. This is it.*

Steeves slammed into the rock so hard he knocked himself out. After regaining consciousness hours later, he tried to stand. But the pain around his ankles was too great and he slumped to the ground. Dazed, he tried to get up again but faltered. After loosening his boots, Steeves put his hands around his ankles and found that they were red and swollen. The jarring landing had badly sprained them and, he would later learn, had torn several ligaments. He loosened the laces of his boots and started to take them off but then stopped. *I might not get them on again,* he said to himself.

He then checked his body for other injuries. He had sustained several bumps and bruises and a nasty laceration on the back of his head, but otherwise he was okay—except, of course, for his ankles.

He felt his pockets, knowing that whatever was in them now was his survival gear. When the plane exploded, he had bailed out so quickly that he hadn't had time to grab a survival kit. In one pocket he found his pipe, some loose wooden matches, and a half-used matchbook. "No tobacco," he muttered with a bitter smile.

From another pocket he pulled out his identification papers, some cash, and two photographs. One was of his pretty twenty-one-year-old wife, Rita, in her wedding dress; the other was of his fifteen-month-old daughter, Leisa. He smiled and tucked them gently back in his pocket.

The only other things he had were a fountain pen, a mechanical pencil, and the .32-caliber revolver that he carried in an ankle holster.

"Oh, great," he lamented. "Not even a chocolate bar or anything to eat."

He shivered and hugged the parachute tightly around himself but he was still freezing. His clothing wasn't much help. He was wearing thin, warm-weather overalls that would have been fine if things had gone as planned and he had landed in Alabama. But they wouldn't help much in the wintry, wind-whipped Sierra Nevada Mountains.

He had fallen onto a rocky depression at about 11,000 feet, just above the timberline in a desolate area near Lake Helen in Kings Canyon National Park. Up above him, 12,000-foot-high snow-lined ridges ringed backcountry that even the hardiest, best-equipped hikers wouldn't tackle except in the brief summer months.

Steeves, who had never gone camping in his life, was poorly prepared to endure the rigors of such frozen heights at a time of year when much of the region was impassable. But the downed pilot did have several traits in his favor. He possessed a hardy physique (six feet tall, 195 pounds), ingenuity, faith, and a will to live. And he also was wearing a new pair of high lace-up combat boots.

But with no food and no water around him, there was no hope unless he got off the large snowless outcropping. *I've got to start walking down the mountain,* he told himself. With the parachute wrapped firmly around him to ward off the chilly wind, he slowly stood up and took one step. He nearly fainted from the pain. *There's no way I'm going to make it. But if I stay here, I'll die.*

For more than an hour he sat despondently on the cold rock. Then he pulled out the photos of Rita and Leisa. *I've got to get up. I've got to keep moving.* He tried to do so repeatedly, but each time he tumbled to the ground after just a step or two. "Keep moving!" he shouted to himself.

Realizing that he was in no condition to stand up and walk, he began crawling on his hands and knees. *This is weird,* he thought. *Here I am crawling on the ground while little Leisa is walking all over the house. I wonder what she's doing right now. I wonder if the Air Force has told Rita that I'm dead.*

At times when the rock was steep, Steeves found it easier to roll. Sometimes he took a long rest, then painfully rose and walked a few steps before falling again. After a whole day of this agonizing progress, he had traveled only about a quarter of a mile. But it was enough to reach a lifeline—a patch of snow that he could melt in his mouth for water.

Nearby was a stand of trees where, on his hands and knees, he gathered twigs and dead branches. *I've got wood and matches so I'll build a fire to stay warm. Hopefully someone will see the smoke and find me. God, I hope they haven't given up on me.* His chest heaving with excitement, he rested against a boulder and tried to light his bundle of sticks. But after several attempts nothing caught. *The wood is too wet. I could sit here and strike every match I have and it'll never catch.*

A nippy wind swept down as the sun dipped behind the ridge. Steeves pulled the parachute tautly around him and crawled to the lee side of the boulder, where he spent his first night in the wilderness. When morning came, he knew staying there meant death, so he pushed onward. During the succeeding days he crawled and at night he huddled behind a boulder.

On the fourth night he burrowed into a rotted hollow log to sleep. Although he felt weak from hunger, Steeves was encouraged the next day because the swelling in his ankles had started to go down, allowing him to walk gingerly. The going was slow, about a mile a day.

For the next week he sometimes had to roll down steep embankments, claw his way over fields of jagged ice-covered rocks, and slide on cold mud. Although he was shivering, he dumped his parachute because it was becoming a drag to wear.

For twelve days, he had nothing but snow water to sustain him. Not a single morsel of food crossed his lips. Famished and fatigued, Steeves was losing hope that he could survive much longer. *Oh,* he thought, *what I wouldn't give for a peanut butter and jelly sandwich.*

Then he came upon a green meadow. He stopped in amazement and rubbed his eyes at the blessed sight in front of him. There stood a tiny log cabin. Thoughts of food, supplies, and warmth whirled around in his head. Although each footfall sent pain through his body, he loped to the door and knocked. There was no answer. After peering through the windows and seeing it was unoccupied, he broke the glass and climbed inside.

The place was a forest ranger's structure filled with tools and equipment for measuring and clearing snow. Everything inside was neatly arranged and cared for, although it seemed the cabin hadn't been used in many months.

Steeves rushed to a cabinet and flung open the doors. "Yes! Yes! Yes!" he shouted gleefully, looking at shelves displaying a treasure trove of cans of beans and ham and other staples, packets of soup flakes and sugar. "Food!" Rather than wait to collect kindling and start a fire, he ravenously feasted on beans and ham, the first meal to soothe his empty, shrunken stomach in almost two weeks.

After he gobbled his food, he decided to make a fire, but the wood he gathered wouldn't light. So he used the papers in his pocket. *I've got money to burn,* he thought as he held a match to several dollar bills. Next went his ID, but not the pictures in his wallet.

He found a map of the area and figured out that he was in Simpson Meadow. Stashed in a corner of the cabin were magazines, books, and records of campers. Over the next two weeks, he used them to make fires, but only after he read them first. Unfortunately, in all the publications, large sections of pages were torn out so he never got to read a complete magazine. However, he read one intact article offering tips on how to survive in the Arctic. But he no longer needed the information. He was down under the frost line, at 6,000 feet, where the days were getting warmer as June approached.

The only book containing all its pages was a cookbook, which was a blessing and a curse. Thumbing through it made his mouth water and he dreamed of a banquet of sumptuous food, but it also made him yearn for the wonderful meals Rita made for him. The pages in the cookbook were among the last sacrificed to make his fires.

He spared a few sheets of paper on which he scribbled notes about his ordeal from the time he bailed out until he arrived at the cabin. *If they find me dead, at least they'll know what happened to me,* he thought.

But he didn't plan on dying. Although not a religious person, he began to talk to God and gain faith that he would survive. After all, what were the odds that in this vast wilderness he would stumble upon this cabin? He was beginning to believe a higher power had guided him there.

By the tenth day at the cabin, much of his strength had returned and his ankles continued to heal. But he also had polished off most of the canned food, so he knew he needed to find new food sources.

To his joy, he discovered some fishing line and a couple of rusty hooks that he had overlooked earlier. Steeves hobbled out to the banks of a tributary of the Kings River, dug some grubs out of a tree for bait, tossed in the line, and enjoyed fresh trout that evening. A couple of days later, he decided to try for bigger game. Although his sore ankles prevented him from tracking a deer, he devised an ingenious trap. He tied his revolver to a sapling next to a salt lick and rigged a trip wire. A couple of nights later in the dead of night he heard the unmistakable.

An animal obviously had tripped the wire, firing the gun. Steeves wanted to check it out, but the darkness kept him inside the cabin. At first light, he hobbled toward the salt lick and let out a triumphant shout when he saw from a distance that he had dropped a deer. *Fresh venison tonight!* he thought. *I'll have enough meat for days!*

But his joy was tempered when he reached the dead deer. Mountain lions had beaten him to the prize, which was already half eaten. Using a knife he found in the cabin, he cut off what he could, then cooked it.

It was gone within a few days, but by then he discovered new sources of food, including green snakes. Wild strawberries and dandelions were sprouting as temperatures warmed up and spring showers melted the snow higher up on the mountain.

About a month after he had bailed out of his stricken jet, Steeves felt he was strong enough to hike out. He spread out the park map and charted a course that would take him to a little stream, a minor tributary of the Kings River. He would wade across it and head to a road that, according to the map, would lead him to civilization.

After walking several miles through deep gorges, he came to what was supposed to be the placid little brook. To his dismay, he discovered it was a raging river swollen by snow melt and several recent cloudbursts. *I have no choice,* he thought. *I have to chance it.* He stepped into the frigid rushing water, trying to feel his way along the rocky bottom. Suddenly he slipped, fell, and was pulled under. He surfaced, gasping for air, but the powerful torrent swept him under again. Thrashing wildly as he slammed against the rocks, he grabbed hold of a fallen tree and lifted himself out of the water and onto a muddy bank.

He was shivering and catching his breath when he thought, *The pictures! Oh, God, I hope I didn't lose them.* He dug his hand into his pocket and pulled out the photos of Rita and Leisa. They were wet but still intact. With a deep sigh of relief, he picked himself up and headed back to the cabin. Five days later, after another unsuccessful try at the river, he abandoned his idea to reach the other side and returned to the cabin to figure out another game plan. The two attempts had sapped his strength, so he stayed at the cabin for another three weeks eating trout and wild greens and dreaming of returning to his family.

In the six weeks since the accident, his usually clean-shaven face had become covered with a thick, grizzled, reddish beard. *What will Rita think of my new look if she ever gets to see me again?* It was especially distressing to him when June 23rd came and went. He had spent his second wedding anniversary away from his beloved wife.

Missing out on his anniversary strengthened his resolve to get out. *There doesn't seem to be an easy way down from here. How do people get into here?* He stared at the map until he figured a new way out—a mountain pass several miles away that led to a valley called Granite Basin and a road to a ranger station. *Of course! Instead of going down, I have to go up and over.* To get to Granite Basin, he had to climb up the 10,600-foot Granite Pass and then hike down, a total distance of twelve grueling miles.

Steeves set out early Sunday morning, June 30th. The going was rough and slow and his ankles ached with each step, but he kept a steady pace. By the time he had hiked through the pass and was heading down toward Granite Basin, dusk was settling in. He was looking for a spot to spend the night when he saw a light flickering a few hundred yards ahead. *Is it what I think it is?* he wondered. His heart pounding in anticipation, he plodded on until he broke through a thick stand of pines. *Yes! It's a campfire!*

Two wilderness lovers, Albert Ade of Squaw Valley and Dr. Charles Howard, a dentist from Fresno, had pitched a tent and were sitting around their campfire when they were startled by a tall, gaunt, bearded figure emerging from the darkness. For the first time since he fell out of the sky fifty-three days earlier, Steeves finally had made human contact.

After telling them of his astounding odyssey, Steeves was treated by the campers to a dinner of steak grilled over the open fire. As much as he wanted to get to the ranger station, Steeves was dog-tired and fell into a deep, contented sleep. *I made it,* he told himself before nodding off. *I'm going to survive.*

The following morning Steeves arrived at the Cedar Grove Ranger Station, riding on Dr. Howard's horse and guided by Ade. Forest rangers estimated Steeves had walked about thirty miles through brutal terrain. Even men as experienced as the rangers were amazed that he survived. Although he had lost thirty pounds, he was in good condition.

The first thing he did was phone home. He tried Rita, but no one answered. So he had the operator dial his mother. "Would you accept a collect call from Lieutenant David Arthur Steeves?" the operator asked.

On the line, Steeves heard his mother gasp. "I most certainly will," she said somewhat hesitatingly because she wasn't sure if this was a sick joke. But when she heard his voice, she knew that her prayers had been answered. Her son David had come back from the dead.

When Rita was given the fantastic news she went into shock because she had already accepted his death. After she had been informed officially on May 28th that she was a widow, she immediately had sold their mobile home in Selma, Alabama, stored their furniture, and enrolled at Bridgeport University in Connecticut with plans to become a teacher.

Meanwhile, reporters flocked to the young flier with the movie star looks, wanting to know how he survived. "At the beginning, I didn't know if I was going to make it," he told them. "As time went on I began to develop faith. I'd never been a very religious man, but this faith in God grew stronger and stronger. That, plus love for my wife and child drove me."

A few days later, Steeves flew east to be reunited with his loved ones. At the emotional reunion, Rita took one look at his beard, which he had not touched since his ordeal ended, and joked, "Dave, you look horrible!"

Horrible or not, David Steeves became an overnight sensation. He accepted offers to appear on TV with the biggest names of the era—Arthur Godfrey, Dave Garroway, Art Linkletter, and Ed Sullivan. He went on a game show and received $1,250 from an electric shaver manufacturer for shaving off his beard in front of the cameras. He signed a book contract with Henry Holt & Co. and a $10,000 deal for his story with the *Saturday Evening Post.*

But as difficult as it was to survive in the wild, Steeves faced another test of survival—the survival of his good name.

When not a single piece of wreckage from his T-33 could be found, the cheering stopped. Rumor and innuendo surrounded him, fueled, in part, by Americans' Cold War fears that Communists were infiltrating the country. He'd sold the plane to the Russians. He'd shipped the jet piecemeal to Mexico. He'd concocted his story to make money off it. He was a traitor, a liar, a con man. It was all a hoax.

Steeves insisted that his tale of survival was true. "I told the story as it happened. They can't disprove my story," he told the press. "How can they? Are they going to interview the animals?"

As doubts mounted, his life went into a tailspin. The Air Force became suspicious and launched an inquiry. They grilled Steeves for hours and forced him to undergo psychiatric examinations. He asked for, and was granted, a discharge, which ended his dream of making a career in the Air Force.

Abruptly, both his lucrative book and magazine deals were canceled. But the worst blow of all came when Rita filed for divorce and took their daughter with her.

His reputation all but ruined, Steeves moved to Fresno, where he remarried, worked as a commercial pilot, and designed planes. Whenever he found extra money and time, he rented a plane and scoured the Sierras in search of the wreckage. But it was all in vain. His jet was either still hidden deep in the wilderness or it somehow had flown on its own before crashing into the Pacific Ocean.

In 1963, the breach of contract suits that he had filed five years earlier against the book publisher and magazine were settled out of court. But that did little to clear his name. He knew the only way to do that was to find the wreckage or even a small piece of it. Despite repeated efforts, he never found the proof he needed to back up his story.

In 1965 at the age of thirty-one, Steeves was killed when the single-engine cargo plane he had modified crashed during takeoff in Boise, Idaho.

The strange case of the Sierra survivor was all but forgotten until 1977, twelve years after his death. Two Boy Scouts were hiking in Kings Canyon National Park in an extremely rugged area that few people had ever traversed when they came upon a large piece of Plexiglas. Rangers later recovered it and identified it as a cockpit canopy. It bore the serial number 52-92-32, the same serial number as the missing jet of Lt. David A. Steeves.

First Lt. Steeves's story had a rather tragic ending, particularly in light of everything he'd endured to stay alive in the first place. It's too bad Steeves never got to see the proof of his incredible story turn up until almost twelve years after his death, and that trying to clear his name was, ironically, what ended up killing him. It's a sobering lesson that sometimes the struggle for survival is only the beginning, and the real test may come after a person finds themselves back in civilization.

I'M ON MY WAY TO SAN JOSÉ

Yossi Ghinsberg

From *Jungle*

In 1981 a wandering Israeli named Yossi Ghinsberg was touring South America when he fell in with a small group of adventurers, led by a geologist named Karl Ruchprecter, looking for gold in the Bolivian mountains. At first the trip went well, but when their leader's promises of an Indian village didn't materialize, the group split up. Yossi and his friend Kevin Gale tried to ride a balsa-log raft out of the jungle, only to encounter the San Pedro Canyon rapids, which destroyed their raft and separated the two men. Now Yossi was alone and lost in the Amazon rainforest with scant supplies and no food. Now his real test of survival begins, and, as described in the following excerpt, the next several weeks would push him to the very limits of his mental and physical endurance.

MY HOPES FOR CLEAR WEATHER WERE DISAPPOINTED; it was pouring rain, but I didn't let that stop me. I packed up my things, slung my pack on my back, tightened the belt and shoulder straps, took up my newly acquired walking stick, and off I went.

Although the trail began wide and well marked, within a few minutes' walk it narrowed considerably, and I had to search for machete marks on the trees in order to follow it. It did run parallel to the Tuichi, however, and whenever I strayed from the trail, I simply had to progress along the bank until I picked it up again.

I got used to walking in the rain and was in a great mood. I thought I was keeping a steady pace and, barring any unforeseen setbacks, I would cover the distance to the village in four days. As I strode along, I composed a marching song, far from original or inspiring, but at least it kept time. I took a popular Israeli tune, "I'm on My Way to Beit Shean," changed the destination, and sang out loud:

> I'm on my way to San José
> On my way, yeah, yeah, my way
> I'm on my way to San José.

So I walked on through the lush jungle in good spirits.

The ground was fairly level. Every now and then a few hills rose up, but they weren't steep. The streams posed a greater obstacle. I passed over a great many that emptied into the Tuichi, forming basins too wide to be passable at the junction. I was forced to follow each one upstream into the jungle until I came upon a convenient fording place. The machete gashes were fantastic signposts. They led directly to the places where the streams were fordable. They sometimes took me far from the river, but I eventually discovered this to be a shortcut.

At one point I came upon a wide, sandy beach, just the kind of place for a picnic and a little romance. The sand was soft and clean and shaded by trees. Logs were piled up on the shore, deposited there by the current. I had an idea. Rescuers might come looking for me by airplane or by helicopter, so I should contrive some kind of signal that could be seen from the air. I started hauling logs and large rocks about, placing them in the shape of an arrow pointing downstream. Next to it I formed the letter *Y* for the first initial of my name, and after it I wrote *12* for the date. I was pleased with my ingenuity and sure the signal would be spotted from above. The truth is I still thought I would be disappointed if someone came to rescue me. I was convinced that I was so close that it would be a shame not to do it on my own.

Toward late afternoon I came upon a stream that flowed in a shallow defile. I quickly descended the rock wall, but the opposite side was an arduous climb, and the walking stick proved a hindrance. I hurled it to the top and, clutching at bushes and protruding rocks, struggled my way to the top. There I retrieved my walking stick and went on. Soon, on a fallen tree, I saw a nest holding four brown spotted eggs. They were only a little smaller than chicken eggs and still warm. The mother must have just left the nest. I was thankful to have happened upon nourishing food. I cracked open one of the eggs and was about to pour its contents into my mouth when I noticed the tiny baby curled up inside. Should I eat it or not? No, I couldn't bring myself to do it. I put the broken egg back in the nest with its brothers and sisters.

If someone above is watching over me, I thought, *He'll surely provide me with other sustenance.*

Not five minutes passed before I came upon a large fruit tree. The fruit, called *trestepita,* is round and yellow and, broken open, divides into three equal parts. Each contains about twenty pits, similar to the pits of a lemon but covered with a sweet, slippery membrane. The fruit doesn't provide a great deal of meat, but I savored the juice it contained.

I leaned up against the trunk of a fallen tree and took out the tins, emptied a few tamarinds out of one, and used it to gather up trestepitas. The tree was low, and by bending its branches, I could reach the fruit. I didn't leave a single one.

I continued on my way to San José with renewed vigor. This time the trail led me deep into the jungle. I was so far from the river that its roar was not even faintly audible. After walking for a very long time I found myself surrounded by towering trees. I had lost all sense of direction. I didn't know which way was north or where the river was. The trail looked strange. It was extremely narrow; I had to go very slowly for fear of losing it. It was often blocked by wild undergrowth or fallen trees. It didn't make any sense, for only a few months ago people should have been using it. I plodded on, still convinced that it would lead me back to the river at any moment, but two hours had passed, and it was growing dark. Then I finally heard the familiar rush of the river. I was extremely relieved to learn that I could rely on the trail.

I met back up with the river just where one of the springs emptied into it. It was a narrow spring that flowed down a narrow ravine. I stood there gaping; there was a large footprint in the mud. The sole of the shoe that had made it was just like mine. God, it must be Kevin! He was alive! Kevin had big feet and wore the same kind of shoes that I did. And who besides him could have left the print? I was overcome with joy. I stared again at the print in the mud. How was it that the rain hadn't washed it away?

The climb up the other side of the ravine was difficult. The wall was almost vertical. I had to throw the walking stick up ahead of me, but regardless of how tired I was after a day of walking I felt myself endowed with superhuman strength. Pushing with my knees and dragging myself up with my arms, I made it to the top. But something seemed funny. Five minutes later I came upon a fallen tree. Next to it lay heaps of tamarind and trestepita peels and pits. Then I knew. I collapsed, broken-spirited, to the ground and almost burst into tears. It wasn't Kevin. It was me. I had wasted more than three hours walking in a circle. The trail had led me back to where I had started.

Desperation began to gnaw at me. I considered giving up and heading back to Curiplaya. I was only two or three hours' walk from there. I could go back to my hut and my bed. But the thought of the village that must be nearby with food and people overcame my momentary weakness. So I had made a mistake. It wasn't the end of the world. I would learn from it. I would use the trail only when it followed the course of the river. If it wandered into the jungle, I would abandon it and make my own way until I met back up with it on the riverbank.

I was exhausted and famished and took the fruit out of my pack. It was a pathetic match for my appetite. A few fleshless pits remained. I gritted my teeth and strode back in the direction of the ravine. There I found what I was after. The mother must have abandoned the nest, for the eggs had grown cold. I broke them open one at a time and gulped down every last bit of the unborn birds. I expected them to make me nauseated, but they were quite tasty.

The sun had gone behind a cloud and now came out and shone brightly. I could still make some progress today. I had gone astray, but the entire day was not wasted; it wasn't so bad.

"It's no big deal. It's no big deal," I started to sing.

We used to sing a song like that in the Boy Scouts, and, silly as it sounds, it stuck in my mind:

> Oh, Mama, in what a fix am I.
> I'll have a baby by and by.
> Please tell me it's a lie.
> Please tell me I won't die.
> Please say it's no big deal.

I sang the tune over and over. Then I started dramatizing it, creating characters and a silly dialogue. *You're going to have a baby, and you think it's no big deal. All right, you won't die, but just you wait until your father gets his hands on him. You'll live, but tough luck for your boyfriend. Your father will kill him.*

I worked on a drama and lost awareness of my hardships and the passing time.

After that song I remembered another:

> Please say that you agree.
> He wants to marry me.
> If you say yea or you say nay,
> We're going to marry anyway.
> Please say that you agree.

I dramatized that one in my imagination as well, with a young boy, a young girl, and a nasty old aunt. I made up a silly story and wrote dialogue for them as well.

I was tired and drenched to the bone. I started looking for a campsite but saw no crags, boulders, or fallen trees to huddle under. Finally I selected a large tree whose roots protruded from the ground in every direction at irregular intervals. I chose a space between two roots that was just as wide as my body, cleared away the wet leaves on the ground, put my pack down, and went off with my walking stick to gather bedding.

There were bushes, trees, and plants of every kind. The foliage was astounding in its variety and beauty. I gathered up large leaves, similar to banana leaves, and spread them out between the sheltering tree roots. I also found a few palms. Without a machete the fronds were hard to remove. I cracked them close to the stump and then twisted them around and around until I could wrench them from the tree. I gathered about twenty large fronds that way and arranged them symmetrically over my sleeping place one on top of the other, all facing in the same direction and crawled under.

There was no way I could light a fire. My feet were damp. I took off my shoes and wrung the water out of my socks. I took the waterproof rubber bag out of the pack, put my feet inside it, and covered my legs up to the knees. Then I covered myself as usual with the mosquito nets and the poncho. Before I covered my head, I ate a few trestepitas.

I was troubled by thoughts of Kevin. I realized that there was no reason to assume that he was dead. Actually he stood a better chance than I did. Fire and food were my advantages, but I had spent many nights without a fire and had used but little of the rice and beans. There were eggs and fruit in the jungle, and Kevin had a machete. With it he could cut down fruit trees and find palm hearts. Even if that was all he ate, he wouldn't go hungry. I had them all around me and couldn't taste a bite. If I tried to get a palm heart, I would waste more energy than it would provide. Kevin was also stronger and tougher than I was. He was used to solitude, used to difficult walking; he had a weapon, and he wasn't carrying the weight of the pack on his back. Hell, he had a much better chance than I did. I wouldn't be surprised if he had already made his way to an inhabited area and been rescued. The more I thought about it, the more convinced I became that Kevin was alive. I just hoped that nothing had happened to him in the river.

The palm fronds made an impenetrable cover. The rain fell on them and ran off to the sides. I even managed to warm myself under their shelter. My feet were comfortable in the bag. My only source of discomfort was stones digging into my back, but I couldn't do anything about them. The walking stick lay at my side. At night it could serve as a weapon along with the tin can, the spoon, and the pitiful flashlight. I said a short prayer to God and asked forgiveness for eating the unborn birds. Then I gave myself over to fantasies until the break of dawn.

The pack was on my back, the staff was in my hand, and I was on my way. My feet were damp and raw, but there was no rash. The rain had cleared up and then started falling again. I didn't let it bother me and set straight out on my course. While I walked, I sang the same songs as the day before, and when I had gone through my entire repertoire, I had long conversations with members of my family and daydreamed again.

Suddenly something jumped out, right from under my feet. My heart jumped with it, but I regained my composure as soon as I saw that it was only a wild chicken. Its wings were weak; it barely raised itself off the ground. It fled from me in skips and jumps. I started chasing after it through the underbrush, holding my spear in readiness. We ran around, me wearing an expression of grim concentration, the chicken crackling and screeching. I didn't catch it, of course, but it occurred to me that I might find a nest with eggs nearby. I went back to where I had first encountered the bird, and there on the ground behind a bush was a large nest and six lovely eggs. They were bigger than domestic hen's eggs and turquoise in color. They were still warm to the touch. I carefully cracked one open and poured the contents into my mouth. It tasted so good that I couldn't help polishing off three more. The two that remained I carefully padded with leaves and put into the tin with the fruit.

What a lucky guy I am! Six eggs! Thank you, God, thank you.

I also spotted fruit trees on my way. As usual the fruit was out of reach, but occasionally I found a piece that had just fallen and was not yet rotten or devoured by ants and worms. The monkeys were having a banquet in the treetops, staffing themselves and then tossing down the scraps, peels, and pits, screeching and chattering as if they were making fun of me. I cursed them, hoping one would fall on its head. The curse worked— but on me, not them.

It was almost noon. I was descending a steep hill, and the grass underfoot was wet. I slipped and tumbled, landing on my backside right on a big, dry branch that lay on the ground. My weight snapped the branch in two, and its sharp, broken end penetrated my backside, cut through my underwear, up the anus, and deep inside. I was paralyzed by the pain. I screamed in agony and then raised myself up, groaning. The pain was excruciating. I lay back, writhing on the ground, my eyes brimming with tears. My underwear was drenched with blood. I screamed when I pulled the spear out, then felt around the wound, and tried to stop the bleeding. It was impossible to bandage. I lay there for another half hour, and after the bleeding stopped, I began walking slowly with clenched teeth in anguish and enraged.

I both scolded and consoled myself. *You hurt yourself, you idiot. You weren't careful enough, jerk. You're lucky you didn't break anything. That really would have been the end of you. Oh, Mama, if you could only see me now, how you would weep. Oh, Mama . . .*

The next time I stopped to rest, I ate the other two eggs, which miraculously hadn't been broken when I fell. I ate the remaining fruit. That was the last of my food, but I was sure that something would turn up before evening.

The trail turned away from the river once again, and I hesitated to follow it. Since the last time had led me astray, I had abandoned the trail whenever I noticed that it was taking me away from the river. I did so this time as well.

Without a cleared trail or even machete slashes to guide me, walking was not easy. I ran into many dead ends, impassable bushes and branches, an impenetrable thicket of bamboo, or a boulder blocking the way. My clothing was again in tatters, the improvised threads holding it together split apart one after another. I came to a thick clump of bushes and bent the branches down to clear my way, disturbing a hornet's nest. They swarmed upon me in frenzied attack. I was stung on my face countless times. I was stuck in the bushes and couldn't get away quickly. I could feel my lips puffing up and my eyes swelling shut. After a while I managed to blunder my way out in hysteria and ran, almost blinded, into more branches, stumbling, falling. I went down to the river, drank, and bathed my face. This wasn't my day. First my lousy ass and now my face. I went on my way, bitter and angry.

Then I picked up the trail again happily and followed it. Evening was gathering, and I suddenly noticed a group of animals not more than five yards ahead of me. I quickly hid behind a tree and peeked out at them.

There were six wild boars, four adults and two shoats. They pranced about, wiggling their backsides, heading away from me.

"If only I had a gun, I would finish them off one by one," I muttered to myself.

I was safe as long as they didn't notice me, didn't pick up my scent. I watched them getting farther away, and then they stopped and started playing. They chased after one another and frolicked.

"Get lost, you idiots. I can't hang around here all day."

I took off my pack, got out the spoon, and started rapping it against the tin can. They heard the dull noise, pricked up their ears, and then ran off. I hoped I wouldn't find them waiting for me around the bend.

I stepped up my pace, anxious to get out of the boars' territory before nightfall. I found another wild chicken's nest with five turquoise eggs. I ate two of them and saved the rest for the next morning. I chose a nearby tree with protruding roots and made the same sleeping arrangements that I had had the night before: a mat of soft leaves on the ground and twenty palm fronds for cover.

I was glad to get into my bed, put my feet in the rubber sack, and give my tired body, my injured backside, and swollen face a rest. I had one medicine for it all, a magic potion: fantasy.

The night put me at ease. I was no longer frightened by wild animals, this due only to apathy, for I had no means of protecting myself other than the walking stick. I sometimes heard rustling and footsteps in the dark, but I paid no attention and went on with my dream. My cover of leaves warmed me in lieu of fire. I had no dry twigs or logs. In any case I wanted to save the few matches that I had left. I suffered most from the loneliness. It made me create imaginary friends who dropped in for chats. I often found myself talking aloud. When I caught myself doing so, I panicked and scolded myself, *That's far enough, Yossi. Don't go out of your mind.*

It was difficult to grasp that I had been in the jungle two weeks. Two weeks alone. I couldn't bear much more of it. I was physically weak and liable to lose my senses. Two days had already gone by since I had left Curiplaya. That meant I should be coming to San José the next day. Tomorrow I would be seeing people. I didn't want to delude myself. To make myself believe that and to count on it. What if I didn't make it tomorrow? I had been walking slowly, had lost my way, had wasted a lot of time. Anyway the Indians made the walk during the dry season. And they probably were better hikers than I. Maybe a four-day walk for them

is like a seven- or eight-day walk for me. It made sense. I stopped thinking about the next day, but deep in my heart I fervently hoped that I would
find the village. What a wonderful surprise that would be.

It had stopped raining, but the dampness of the last few days had taken its
toll. The rash was beginning to spread over my feet, and my inner thighs
were red and raw. There was an irritating inflammation between my
buttocks as well, and I still suffered the tormenting pain of the deep gash
in my backside.

*I mustn't coddle myself, have to be tough. I have to ignore the pain and keep
going,* I reminded myself.

During breakfast, which consisted of two eggs, I swallowed an amphetamine. It was the second time I had taken one since the accident. It
wasn't long before it took effect, and I sprinted through the jungle as if I
had the devil on my tail, assaulting the overgrown trail, breaking through
branches, skipping up hills, and hopping over fallen trees. I lost the trail
again and stayed stubbornly near the river, always careful to keep it within
sight or at least within hearing.

The first animal I met up with this day was a snake, a brown snake
about six feet long but not particularly big around. It was slithering through
the grass, and I only noticed it when it sped off at my approach. Without
a second thought I grabbed a rock and chased after it like crazy, trying
to get close enough to have a fair shot. But the snake was faster than I
was and disappeared into the underbrush. I was sorry. If I had caught it, it
would have been nourishing, even raw. I would have eaten it salted. For
the past few days I had eaten only eggs and fruit.

Later I encountered a pair of tapirs, a mother and her young. They were
massive, and the earth quaked under their tread. When the poor things
noticed me, they ran off in fright.

I didn't actually see the third animal, but I knew it was there. It was
before noon. I had emerged from the jungle and found myself standing
on a lovely beach, the largest I had come upon since we had left Asria-
mas. The sand was so white, it was blinding. The river lapped pleasantly
at the shore. The scorching sun was directly overhead. At long last some
sunshine. I thought I would be able to dry out and heal the rawness of my
skin. I bent over to remove my pack, and that's when I noticed the jaguar
tracks on the shore, lots of tracks of different sizes. There was no doubt
that this was not a solitary jaguar, but an entire pack.

I followed the paw prints in the sand. Under a shady tree I found small piles of feces, at least six separate piles. I stepped on one of them. Though no tracker or Indian guide, I knew enough to recognize that they were fresh; they were soft and didn't crumble. There had been a lot of jaguars on this shore. It seemed to serve as their meeting place, but I didn't want to leave, and the truth is that I wasn't really afraid. I just couldn't believe that I would be eaten by jaguars in broad daylight. I felt safe.

I made myself comfortable near the water and spread out all of my wet belongings on the warm sand. I gathered up a huge stack of kindling and used only two matches lighting a fire. I kept the fire well fed and placed a tin of water in it. I stripped off my wet clothing and spread it out near the poncho and the mosquito nets. I stretched out on the sand in my birthday suit, spreading my legs wide to expose my raw inner thighs to the sunlight. The flies and mosquitoes swarmed over me, and I was forced to cover myself with one of the nets. The sun shone through it, however, and gently caressed my body.

I lay there for about an hour and then got up to prepare soup. This time I put in two tablespoons each of rice and beans, intending to prepare them as solid food and take along on my way. I dipped the water out of the tin and drank it, until all that was left at the bottom of the tin was an oatmeal-like residue. The rice was all right, though it didn't smell fresh, but the beans had not cooked long enough. On top of that I had added too much salt. It tasted awful, but even so it was difficult to follow my resolve and save the bulk for later.

Since I had a good fire, I wanted to catch a fish and cook it. It looked like a good place for fishing. The river could have been as much as several hundred feet wide—from the bank it was hard to tell—and the current was not strong. I had no difficulty swatting a few big flies and tried to use them to catch a minnow. I stood on the riverbank, draped with the mosquito net, making sure the line had enough slack. The sun beat down on my head, and suddenly everything went black, and I lost consciousness. The cool water brought me to immediately. I leaped from the river, wet and frightened. I couldn't let that happen again. It was both terrifying and dangerous.

I stretched out again for a while, then donned my dry clothing and gingerly put my socks and wonderfully sturdy shoes back on. Before leaving this fabulous beach I invested a great deal of effort in marking it. There were heavy stumps lying about, and I laboriously pushed and rolled them until they formed an arrow pointing in the direction I was going. As before, I made a letter Y and the date: 14.

The map had also dried, and I studied it at length. The distance between Curiplaya and San José appeared to be twenty-five miles by river, or about thirty miles by the path alongside the river. I had been walking almost twelve hours a day. There was no reason to believe that I wouldn't arrive in San José within a day or two. Only one thing worried me. San José was on the left bank, the opposite side of the river. The only landmark before the village was a large river that emptied into the Tuichi from the left. Karl had told us that it was the village's source of water. He had said that San José lay not on the bank of the Tuichi but a few miles up that other river. On the right bank, the one I was on, there wasn't a single landmark to tell me where I was. So I couldn't depend entirely on the map. I was concerned that I might not notice the village and mistakenly pass it by. Then I would be lost. For good. Between San José and Rurrenabaque there were no other villages, and it would be impossible to walk the entire distance. The only really safe thing to do would be to cross the Tuichi and walk along the other side. That way I wouldn't miss the village. I went on, looking for a good place to cross.

Farther on I came to a dead end. A stream fed into the Tuichi in a deep, impassable wadi. I had to change course and march upstream into the jungle until the wadi flattened out and I found an easy place to cross it. This detour took several hours. I doubled back on the other side of the stream, straight and to the left, in the direction of the Tuichi. Another stream cut across my path, but this one I could ford easily, skipping from stone to stone, careful not to lose my balance and fall in. Beyond the stream was a field of thorns. There were no trees at all, only bushes and thistles as tall as I was. Having no other choice, I plodded into it, trying to clear a path.

I experienced a new kind of hell in the field of thorns. I lost my sense of direction, and my entire body was scratched and mauled. Scathing nettles stabbed into me, and I shook with pain and fear. At long last I made it back to the jungle and to the lost path. The trail here did not look as if it had been in use, however. It was unreliable and led me astray for a long while. It was frequently covered over completely with jungle foliage. *It couldn't be that men marched over this path every year,* I told myself, but no sooner had I done so than I suddenly heard, in the distance, human voices. There were speaking, and someone called out something. I started running and shouting, "Help! Hey, hey! Wait for me! *Espera! Espera!*"

I ran as if possessed. I shouted myself hoarse. I struck out at the branches that blocked my way. Then stopped to listen. Not the slightest whisper was to be heard. It must have been my imagination playing tricks on me.

My idiotic pride had long since worn thin. Now I prayed for someone to rescue me. Let people say that I was a wimp, that I should have been able to make it out of the jungle on my own. I just wanted to be saved.

It was now the fourteenth of December. Someone had to do something—Lisette, the embassy. Marcus must be back by now. Or Kevin perhaps. I was certain that I would soon hear the drone of a plane overhead. They couldn't help but see me. I had left unmistakable signs on two beaches. They would easily spot the markings. But maybe, just maybe, I would still make it on my own. I must be so very close to San José.

Toward evening I thought that I had found a good place to cross. The river was wide, but the current seemed mild. Furthermore, there were four substantial islands strung out between one bank and the other. I could go from island to island until I reached the other side. Still, I thought, it might not be as easy as it looked, and I decided to take some precautions.

I was loath to get my clothing wet again, especially my socks. I stripped, shoved my clothing into the rubber bag, and closed it inside the pack. I took out the fishing line and tied it to the shoulder straps. I set the pack in the river; it floated satisfactorily. I pulled it back in and set in on the edge of the shore. Then I jumped barefoot into the water, holding the line. The water was shallow. I could walk, wading farther out, slowly but surely.

The current was stronger than it had looked, and the sharp stones on the river bottom cut into the soles of my feet. Only the walking stick came to my aid. I leaned heavily upon it, taking one cautious step after another. As I went, I gradually let out the fishing line, until I made it to the first island, about seventy-five feet from the shore. Now I would pull the pack over and go on to the next island. That was my plan. But it didn't work out that way.

I gave the fishing line a yank, and the pack slipped into the river. The undertow sucked it beneath the surface, and though I tugged with all my might, I couldn't pull it to me. I decided to change plans and tied the end of the line to a small tree on the shore of the island. I would walk back across to the riverbank and carry the pack on my back, but first I wanted to check out the second island.

I walked quickly to the far side of the first island. As I walked, mosquitoes swarmed all over me. I was black with them. I swatted myriads of them with my hands, but they didn't leave me alone. I rushed to the water but discovered it to be deep. I couldn't touch bottom and almost lost my faithful walking stick to the current. I threw it up on the bank and tried swimming to the second island, but the current was so strong that I headed back to the first while I was still able.

I would never make it across the river, at least not with the weight of the pack on my back. Perhaps I should leave the pack behind? No, I still needed it. I returned to the bank of the Tuichi, picking up the pack on my way. I dried myself on a mosquito net as best I could and put my clothes back on. I was covered with mosquito bites and clawed at them in a frenzy. My only consolation that day was a new nest of wild chicken eggs. I gulped down four warm, delicious eggs and saved two for morning.

It was growing dark, and I had not yet set up camp. I didn't find a tree that offered any shelter. Either the roots didn't protrude far enough out of the earth, or the tree wasn't standing on level ground. The sun had almost set before I found a place to settle.

The rain started coming down again in the middle of the night, not a drizzle but a downpour, which seeped through my thatch of fronds. I shivered and curled up into a ball. I pulled the rubber bag high up over my knees and tucked the red poncho in all around me. I had three fantasies that by this time I had worked into long scenarios. Each was set in a different place. I put the hood over my face and went to visit Las Vegas, São Paulo, and my home in Israel, drifting from one to another all night long.

In the morning I ate the salty rice-and-bean paste together with two eggs. A real feast.

If anyone is looking down on me, He is absolutely heartless.

It was pouring rain, and all my efforts to keep my clothes dry were wasted. I was supposed to find San José today. Maybe I would spend this night in the company of other men. That thought drove me out of my mind. I didn't want to pin all my hopes on it. *Well, if not today, then surely tomorrow,* I thought, trying to convince myself.

Walking was difficult. I was soaking wet, heavy, and clumsy. I could feel the water in my shoes and knew only too well what it was likely to do to my feet. The ground was muddy and slippery, and the wind chilled me to the bone. The longer I spent here, the more likely I was to sink into despondency. Even marching songs were of no avail, so I decided to flee to São Paulo, Brazil, a city I had heard much about.

My uncle lives here, and I am visiting him. I like it here. Why not stay for a while? I make elaborate plans for putting down roots in the city. I meet a few people my own age, all of them students. I spend a lot of time with them and discreetly inquire which is the wealthiest family in town. Do they have a young daughter? They do, of course, and of course she is both intelligent and beautiful. But how can I meet her? How can I ask her out? I have to find a way. Maybe I should take my uncle's car and crash into hers. That sometimes works in the movies. Maybe I should just hang around waiting for her and win her over with sincerity? Maybe she won't be able to resist my charms? Finally I come up with a plan. I will get to the daughter through the mother. My first thought is to have her run me over, just a little, like in *Being There*, but that would be risky. Plan B is to save her from muggers. And that's what I do.

Hey, you, kid! Come over here a minute.

I'm no kid. You'd better watch it, or else . . .

He was a street urchin who always hung around the neighborhood.

Take it easy, pal. I didn't mean to insult you. I just wanted to know if you'd like to make a few bucks.

You bet, but it depends how.

This is going to sound weird, but . . . and I tell him my plan.

The kid drives a hard bargain, and I end up agreeing to pay him more than I had intended, but for this it's worth it. I just worry that he might double-cross me.

You'd better not keep on running. Don't try to con me.

You don't know us, señor. We never go back on our word.

The mother goes out to a large shopping center, wearing a fancy dress and carrying a fancy bag. She is elegant, aristocratic. She walks down the street like she owns it, oblivious to the admiring glances of everyone she passes. Then something happens: something that forces her down from Olympus. A short, dark-skinned boy brushes up against her, pushes her roughly, grabs her purse out of her hands, and runs off.

Thief! Thief! Stop him!

Now she turns to the crowd for help, but the dark-skinned boy knows his business; he has vanished into the crowd, quick as an eel.

This is where I come in. Around the corner the boy hands me the purse as we had agreed. I bend over and let him give me a punch in the nose before he takes off.

I return the fancy bag. She smothers me with gratitude and takes out a clean handkerchief to staunch the bleeding. Then she takes out a wad of bills and offers them to me. I look her straight in the eye and refuse to take her money. She begins questioning me.

Speak more slowly, señora. I don't speak the language that well.

We chat. I know I am making a good impression.

Perhaps you'd care to join us for dinner this evening, she says. My husband and daughter would be so pleased to meet you.

Well, I don't know. I . . .

Please do come.

The evening is unforgettable. I am introduced to her daughter. It's a special moment, charged with expectations of things to come. I know that she will someday be my wife.

We seat ourselves around the table. Liveried servants serve a magnificent repast: salads, soufflés, skewered meats, vegetables, baked potatoes. The table is laden with every kind of delicacy, and I do not pass up a single dish. I taste everything, trying to do so without a rude display of gluttony.

When it is time to take my leave, I have the nerve to invite the mother and daughter to visit me in the apartment I have rented in the city. On the appointed day, after poring over recipes, I decide to serve a pizza, the very best pizza ever prepared. I knead the dough and toss it into the air like a professional. I don't settle for tomato paste seasoned with oregano, but sauté onions in a deep skillet together with whole, peeled tomatoes. I add green peppers and numerous cloves of garlic. I spice the sauce and ladle it over the crust. I sprinkle aromatic grated cheese in a thick layer. The cheese melts even before I put the pizza into the oven.

Dinner is a great success. We drink a lot of wine. It doesn't take long from there to the wedding . . .

My belly was howling. Brazil had been swell, but I had gotten my digestive juices all worked up for nothing. No matter, one day the dream would come true. For now I had to find something to eat.

Walking was intolerably difficult. The rain poured down. The jungle was dark and gloomy, and I walked slowly. It wasn't much better on the path. It was often blocked and frequently left me abandoned, helpless, in the jungle. The little streams were brimming over and difficult to cross.

Scaling the walls of the wadis and climbing steep hills was treacherous. My shoes were caked with mud, and I slipped often. I was exhausted. I leaned heavily on my walking stick. I was weak and famished but afraid to take another amphetamine. Fate mocked me: I came upon a fruit tree whose inaccessible branches were laden with manzanas de monte. The rain and wind had knocked a few of them down into the mud. I picked out and ate the best of them. Most already had fat worms crawling through them. If only I could climb the tree or chop it down, I would have enough food for two days.

You know, Kevin, if you were here with the machete, with your muscles that tree would have been down in less than an hour. And you know what else, Kevin? If you were here, you'd be the one carrying this cruddy pack, not me.

But I was alone, and the fruit was out of reach. The pack was burdensome, and the rain still poured down.

I no longer felt that someone was watching over me, but still I prayed. *Make the rain stop. Make me get to San José. Make a plane come and find me. Do something.*

Nothing happened, and I kept walking mechanically forward, but I couldn't stand it anymore. I decided to hop a plane for Las Vegas.

I arrive at night. A hot desert wind is blowing. At the hotel I take a shower and freshen up, then go down to the casino, smooth-shaven and well dressed. I had last been here on my way back from Alaska and had left a contribution of a thousand dollars on the blackjack table. But Judgment Day is here; I have come for my revenge.

Lord, what cards I hold this evening! I am dealt blackjack on almost every round. I increase the amounts I bet and tip the dealer generously. I play recklessly, paying no attention to the dealer's cards. I have fourteen, and he has six showing.

Hit me, I tell him.

The other players at the table give me disapproving looks but are astounded when I am dealt a seven. What can I say?

Everyone gathers around to watch the big-time young card shark. I start betting two hands at once and wipe out every dealer in the place.

The pit boss comes to my table and watches anxiously. His face is blank, but I can read his thoughts. I could swear I hear him say, *Go on, sweetheart, keep playing. I know your type. You don't know when to get up and leave the table. You'll end up depositing all your money here.*

He's wrong, of course. My luck never runs out. The pot gets bigger and bigger, astronomical sums of money. They have to call the manager to raise the limit. The manager has been watching me through one-way mirrors in the ceiling. He signs the authorization, and the game goes on.

Waitresses showing a lot of cleavage try to ply me with drinks.

Not right now, honey, no thanks. Only coffee for me. Sure, you can put a little Grand Marnier in it, but just a little.

A gorgeous kitten materializes behind me, massaging my shoulders, brushing her breasts against my back.

I know why you're here, sweetie. I say to myself. It's not because of my charming smile, but it's all right with me. I'm no prude. Just a few more hands, and then we'll have a good time.

I get up from the table with $300,000 in chips. The manager signs the check personally. I have to admit that they are gracious losers. He shakes my hand and informs me that my luggage has already been moved to the VIP suite. He gives me a card entitling me to free use of all of the hotel's facilities. And this hotel has everything: floor shows, bars, restaurants, girls. You name it. They have it. I promise that I will be back tomorrow to triple my winnings. We are both happy.

Now I get down to business. I take my well-endowed bunny and go into the casino's fanciest restaurant. The credit card works wonders. The special treatment we receive is fantastic. Everyone has already heard about me. The table is surrounded by waiters.

Sweet-and-sour ribs, sir? Waldorf salad? Would you like to try a new kind of crepe? Wine? Fish in garlic and butter? A T-bone steak with french fries? What kind of dressing would you like on the chef's salad? Roquefort? Yes, sir, right away. A banana split or ice cream? Chocolate and strawberry ice cream? Yes, of course, sir. You know just what to order.

The flattery pays off for the waiter. I don't leave anyone out. They all ask me to return. If I was a big hit at the blackjack tables, that was nothing compared with the restaurant.

You can rest assured, my friends, that I'll be back very soon . . .

In the late afternoon I was surprised by another river cutting across my path. It was quite wide—one hundred feet at least—but most of it was a desiccated riverbed. Down in a relatively narrow channel a placid flow of water ran into the Tuichi. The Tuichi itself looked treacherous. Its waters were black with the mud it churned up. Logs, branches, and uprooted bushes were carried along by the current, which was extremely swift. I wouldn't have liked to have fallen into those waters.

I stood there frightened, staring helplessly at the two rivers. I was certain that the map hadn't indicated another river emptying into the Tuichi on this bank before San José. I knew the map by heart, and according to it, the next river on the right-hand bank was far beyond San José. Could I have passed the village without realizing it? San José was located up in the hills and was not visible from the Tuichi. I was supposed to have spotted it by the wide path and the balsa rafts on the shore. I might not have noticed and passed it when I was walking in the jungle, not along the bank.

Perhaps this river simply wasn't charted on the map. But how was that possible? The Ipurama and the Turliamos were marked, and they were no bigger than this river. The map wasn't dependable. Maybe this river had been overlooked because it was so shallow. I didn't know what to think, whether to backtrack and look for the landmarks on the opposite bank or go on, not knowing where I was. I finally decided to go on walking for one more day. Since I hadn't reached the village, I was bound to get there tomorrow. If not, then I would have no choice but to turn around and go back.

The remains of a path through the jungle lent credence to my assumption that I hadn't yet passed the village. The path continued, a narrow, difficult trail that took me about fifty yards from the Tuichi. What I found there surprised me and restored my hopes: traces of a campsite: two poles tied together with vines and a few palm fronds resting upon them. It was an old campsite. The vines were withered and dry, as were the fronds.

I couldn't have passed San José yet if there was a campsite here, I reassured myself. It also meant that San José couldn't be as close as I had assumed. Why would anyone bother setting up camp if it was only a few more hours' walk? I concluded that I must have at least another full day's hike ahead of me. It made sense. This was the path the villagers used on their way upriver to Curiplaya. It was reasonable to assume that they set out in the morning and set up camp after a day's walk. That put me a day from San José. I figured that this must be the first camp that they used on their way.

My spirits rose. I was sure it was the first camp; hadn't I been walking for four days already? So, I'd be there tomorrow.

You did it, Yossi. Congratulations. You made it. Tomorrow night you won't be sleeping alone in the jungle. You'll eat your fill. You won't be exposed to the rain and other dangers. One more day, Yossi, one more day.

It had stopped raining. The path led a little way past the camp and

then dwindled and vanished altogether. I figured that this must be where
the natives crossed the Tuichi. It was a convenient place to cross. The
wadi was muddy. The stream ran through its center and was only about a
foot deep. I crossed to the other side.

The land here was completely flat and well forested. There were no
hills or steep inclines. The jungle was dense, and vines were draped from
the trees amid bushes and reeds. I could neither go forward nor find
traces of the path. I kept on looking for broken branches or machete
strokes, with no luck. I returned to the riverbank, searching for signs of
where the natives had resumed their march, where the path would be.
Sudden claps of deafening thunder set the jungle quaking. Hell, it was
going to start pouring again. I had better find shelter. I could use the remains of the camp back on the other side of the river. It would mean wasting the two hours of walking time I had left that day, but the rain slowed
me down anyway. Tomorrow the weather would surely be more benign,
and I would hurry on.

I crossed back to the camp. Thunder clapped, and lightning lit up the
sky. The wind came up. It was going to be a terrible storm. I hurriedly
set about reinforcing the remains of the camp. I replaced the vines with
fresh ones and went into the jungle to look for palm fronds. It had already started raining. I had never seen such a downpour. The drops came
down with a sharp sting. I tore off about twenty fronds. The effort wore
me out, but I didn't give up. I arranged the fronds so that they were closely
overlapping one another across the poles. I covered every crack through
which the rain might seep. I knew that it would take a thick layer to keep
the wet out. The jungle outside was well flooded over, as if the end of the
world were approaching. From a distance the Tuichi looked turbulent
and gloomy.

I hurried into my shelter. Water leaked through in several places, but
I didn't dare go back outside. I tried to rearrange the fronds from inside. I
got out my nighttime necessities: the rice-and-bean pillow, the rubber
sack to cover my feet, the nets to use as blankets, and the poncho to wrap
around everything else. I took off my shoes and wrung out my socks. Up
until now I had managed to keep my feet in fair condition. I had only one
more day to go. I prayed that they wouldn't let me down now.

Drops fell steadily through the leaks in the roof onto the poncho and
dripped down to the ground. Outside I could hear the raging storm. In a
very short time the ground became muddy, then soggy. I lay drenched in

my shelter, miserable, trembling with both cold and fear. There was nothing I could do but pray to God.

The storm grew worse, and my shelter began to blow away, leaving open spaces through which the water streamed down upon me. I wanted to cry, to wail. I wanted away from this horror.

Why, why, did this have to happen to me? Please, God, help me. I'm afraid of dying.

Each minute seemed an eternity, and I had nowhere to flee. It required fierce concentration to immerse myself in fantasy. This time I went home.

I am married and have small children. My brother, Moshe, and I start a ranch on huge tracts of land we have bought in the Upper Galilee. We stock it with cattle I bought in Bolivia and Argentina of a quality not to be found in Israel. Most of Israel's meat is imported from Argentina, but we have a good climate and unused open spaces for grazing. Why shouldn't we raise our own cattle?

My brother and I work hard. The ranch prospers. We erect a huge house and all live together: my brother, his wife Miri, his daughter Lilach, and his other children, and of course me and my wife and our children.

We send our children to the regional school in a nearby kibbutz . . .

"Ahhh!" I came out of my fantasy with a scream. There was an earsplitting din, and the ground shuddered. The trees around me, their roots left with nothing to hold on to, were crashing down one after another. When a tree of that size falls, it takes a few other trees with it.

God, help me! Save me! God . . .

The uproar died down, and the ground under me grew still. I heard only the rain and the roar of the Tuichi. Drenched and clammy with sweat, I forced myself back to the Galilee.

My brother and I rise at six, have our coffee in large mugs with thick slabs of cake. We leave early for the range on horseback. We check the fencing, take a count of the herd, check on a pregnant cow. At nine we head back home. The kids have already eaten and gone to school, and now the cook devotes herself to us. She prepares omelets, salads, cheeses. Thick bread and butter, cream of wheat or rice pudding, hot chocolate, and her own special marmalade.

I don't know the source of our misfortune, but our fabulous cook leaves our employ. We place an ad in the newspaper: "Wanted: gourmet cook. Residence on ranch in Galilee. Good terms and pay."

We receive a great many applications and set up interviews. I am in charge. I sit in the office at the ranch and meet the prospective cooks. Each describes in detail the delicacies she or he knows how to prepare. I interview them one after another, listening to descriptions of every imaginable kind of food. This was my favorite among my fantasies since I could stretch it out and go into the minutest details of every dish and its preparation: Moroccan, European, hot and spicy, Polish dishes, Chinese food, and exotic concoctions. There is no end to the variety of food and no end to the line of applicants.

Outside it seemed that all the biblical prophecies of doom had been fulfilled, and there I was, by myself, the only human in this vast jungle. No other people, no settlements. Only San José, somewhere up there in the hills on the other side of the river, and I might at any instant be crushed to death by a falling tree. Yes, it could happen at any second, and it's the only thing that will pacify this jungle, let it settle peacefully back into its former calm. It wants to expel this arrogant interloper, this man who dared to think he could survive here alone.

I went on fantasizing until dawn. From time to time I was startled out of my daydreams in a panic, thinking my end had come, but despite everything someone was still watching over me. The morning rays cast their light on nothing good. The rain still came down in torrents. The wind kept howling against my shelter, rattling its rickety poles, but they held fast. My breath under the poncho kept my wet body warm, and my fantasies kept my mind occupied, but I wanted to get up and start marching. I had to get out of the jungle, no matter what. Kneeling, I packed my things, slung the pack on my back, snatched up my walking stick, and dashed outside.

Good Lord! Rain flooded down. I turned to start in the direction of the river and stood rooted to the ground. The wadi was flooded. The entire riverbed was brimming with water, as deep as ten feet, I guessed. Incredible. A shallow stream, a wadi that had been almost dry, had overnight become a wide river, almost overflowing its banks. The Tuichi, which flowed by about fifty yards from where I stood, looked threatening. Its waters were black, and the current so swift it seemed that someone had filmed the river and was showing it at double speed. So many enormous trees floated downstream that the water itself was barely visible. The river had washed over its shores, gathering up all that booty. I assumed that the signposts that I had so laboriously erected, indicating my presence and the direction in which I was going, had also been washed away. I cursed the day.

How was I going to make it across the river? I started away from the Tuichi following the course of the unknown river upstream, but I didn't get far. There was no path nor hope of finding a place to cross. I had to go back to my shelter.

I was furious with myself. If I were to stay put, that meant spending another entire day in the jungle, and I wouldn't be sleeping in San José that night. I had had such high hopes of making it. There was nothing that I could do about it, however. There was no choice but to wait for the storm to blow over, for the river to recede so that I might cross it and be on my way.

I lay back down. My empty stomach was beyond grumbling or growling. I now felt the hunger with my entire body, a primordial need to eat, but all I had were the fruits of my imagination.

I suppose close to half an hour had passed when I became aware of water running down my back and shoulders. How could that be? I had a thick roof of leaves. Cold water reached my buttocks and feet. Then I grasped what had happened and had no time to spare. Both rivers were flooding, and I, fool that I was, hadn't seen it coming. The ground was level and flooded in a flash. I hurriedly knelt and shoved everything into my pack, including my socks and shoes. I didn't have time to close the rubber sack but rushed outside in my bare feet and began running. The water was already up to my ankles and would soon be knee deep. I ran in a panic but realized almost immediately that I had forgotten my walking stick in the shelter. I wasn't about to abandon my trusty walking stick. I set my pack down on a little rise and ran back.

By the time I had reclaimed the stick and had returned to the pack, the water was already past my waist, and the rise was flooded. The pack was floating, and I rushed toward it before it could be carried away. I put my arm through one of the shoulder straps and grabbed hold of a tree. I could feel the water tugging me toward the river. If I lost my hold on the tree, I would drown. I started swimming away, kicking hard, and succeeded in grabbing onto the next tree. All of my muscles ached, and I was afraid that they would give out on me, but the palpable fear of death lent me new, unfamiliar stores of energy. I pushed myself away from the tree with a great thrust, reaching from tree to tree. Once I missed my grasp and was swept away, but the jungle was dense, and I was rammed into trees until I caught hold of one of them. There was no chance of my climbing a tree and, anyway, I might have been stuck up there forever. I would be better off trying to make it to higher ground.

For once I was oblivious to pain. I was quite simply fighting for my life: pushing away, grabbing, pulling, snatching instants to catch my breath. I went on like that for half an hour until I came upon a hill that wasn't flooded. I stood there panting, water pouring out of the holes in my pack, my clothing drenched and torn, rain beating down upon me mercilessly.

I got my socks and shoes out and pulled them onto my battered feet. The red rash was spreading, and I knew only too well what was in store for me. I was bitter, despondent, and furiously angry that the whole world— all the mighty elements of nature—had ganged up on one solitary man.

On the other side of the hill the jungle had flooded only waist high. Walking was a torment. I sank into the mud, and each step was excruciating, for the mud had seeped into my shoes and socks and had begun to abrade the skin. Places I had passed so easily yesterday presented dangerous obstacles today. Every tiny wadi had become a stormy deluge. Every broad expanse was now a treacherous swamp. The area was suddenly overrun with frogs. Where had they all come from? Their croaking made a din, but, strangely, I didn't see a single one. The storm had left its traces everywhere. Broken trees lay like corpses on the ground, leaving gaping, flooded craters where they had been uprooted.

I went on as best I could, walking away from the Tuichi, fleeing to the hills. I went on for miles, hours passed, but nothing changed. I walked immersed in mud, without knowing where I was putting my feet. I got stuck in bushes and pulled myself free. I stepped on sharp rocks and bit back the pain. I was frequently forced to swim. When I had to haul myself back out of wadis, I slipped and slid, crawling on my hands and knees. When I tried to get a grip on a root or a bush, I fell backward, clutching the uprooted plant in my hand. I had no idea where I was or where I was going, I only wanted to find a resting place for my battered body. I wanted to get to someplace where I would be able to lie down and wait for the storm to pass. Finally I climbed a hill and looked for a tree with thick roots. I didn't want to lie down under a tree that was likely to fall over and crush me. Completely exhausted, I tore off a few palm fronds and lay down on the ground under what appeared to be a reliable tree.

The rain hadn't stopped but seemed to have abated somewhat. I took off my shoes and shoved my feet into the sack. They were so raw that I was afraid to take my socks off, fearful that I wouldn't be able to put them back on the next day. Both the mosquito nets and the poncho were dripping wet. I was shivering cold. The wind was still blowing, and I was afraid that I would come down with pneumonia. If I became sick, I would die.

I began praying. I prayed to God with all my heart. *Please forgive me for ever having doubted you and not putting all my faith in you. I know that you are always watching. Please don't let me get sick. Let me make it back to safety. Please God.*

I considered taking a vow, promising something, but I didn't want God to think that I was haggling. I took out Uncle Nissim's book for moral support. The plastic bag had not kept it dry. I kissed the book and slipped it into my pocket.

It was the seventeenth morning of my solitude. The storm was over. I was in sad shape. I was far from my destination and doubted that I would be able to go on. My feet were infected. From now on walking would be torture. How could my body take any more? I was weak with hunger. I had eaten nothing for the past two days. Now how would I find eggs or fruit? The storm had washed everything away. Was I going to die of hunger or injury? Morbid thoughts filled my mind; there was no chance of my escaping into fantasy. I was distressed to the point of despondency. All my hopes of reaching San José faded away. I hadn't yesterday. I apparently wasn't going to today. Who knew if I ever would?

What an idiot I was. I should never have left Curiplaya. I could have waited there in my hut. I could have survived there for at least a month, and by then surely someone would have come looking for me. Someone would have done something.

Now what would I do? Where should I go? I no longer believe there was much chance of my reaching San José. I doubted that I would be able to cross the river. Though the storm had died away, the whole jungle was submerged. I was bitter and on the edge of absolute despair, almost ready to give up. I started back to Curiplaya.

Overcome by self-pity, I hobbled painfully on until I came to a trestepita tree. The tree was bent low, almost touching the ground. It still had fruit on it, and I eagerly sucked the sweet-sour pulp from the pits. The small quantity of nourishment tormented my aching belly, but it helped restore my hopes.

Someone is still watching over me. Uncle Nissim's book will protect me. I won't die as long as I have it in my pocket. I shouldn't underestimate its powers. I mustn't lose hope. I am stronger than I think I am. If I have been able to survive this far, I can go on.

I gave myself a good talking-to and turned toward San José once again. I was going on, no matter what. I trod through flood waters, swam across streams, climbed up wadi walls. I don't know where I got the energy. While I was wading through the mud, I made believe that I was one of the Zionist pioneers, draining the swamps. A long black snake passing near my foot startled me. I threw my walking stick at it but missed.

"Wait a minute," I called, chasing after it. "Wait a minute. I want to eat you."

My shirt caught on a branch and tore. The sharp branch slashed my upper arm down to the elbow. Blood spurted from the wound. I fought back tears of desperation.

It doesn't matter. I'll get over it. I'm going on.

I could neither see nor hear the river but followed the streams that cut in front of me. I knew that they would lead me to the Tuichi. It wasn't raining, but the wind was blowing, and it was very cold. The humidity formed a heavy mist.

Suddenly I heard a sputter, a drone, the sound of an engine . . . an airplane.

Don't be a fool, Yossi. It's only your imagination.

But the sound grew louder. It was an airplane!

They're looking for me! Hooray! I'm saved!

The sound grew louder, and I ran like a lunatic, ignoring my tattered feet. I had to get to Tuichi. I had to signal the plane. The sound was right overhead. I stopped, panting, and looked up. Between the treetops I saw a few gray clouds, and amid them, at a moderate altitude, a small white plane glided past.

"Hello, here I am! Help! I'm down here." I waved my arms frantically. "Don't go. Don't leave me here. Here I am."

The plane vanished from the sky, its drone fading away.

Now I became aware of my feet. The frantic running had torn the flesh from them, and I felt as if they were on fire. I collapsed to the earth, my face buried in the mud. I lay sprawled there and wanted to cry, but the tears wouldn't come.

I can't take any more. I can't budge another inch. That's it.

From the bottom of my heart I prayed, not for rescue, not even for survival. I prayed for death. *Please, good God, stop this suffering. Let me die.*

And then she appeared. I knew it was all in my mind, but there she lay, next to me. I didn't know who she was. I didn't know her name. I knew we'd never met, and yet I knew that we were in love. She was weeping despondently. Her fragile body trembled.

"There, there, stop crying," I tried to comfort her.

Take it easy. It's all right. Get up, Yossi, I urged myself, *you have to lead the way, keep her spirits up.*

I plucked myself up out of the mud and very gently helped her up. Tears still poured down her cheeks.

"The plane didn't see us. It just went by," she wailed.

"Don't worry, my love. It will surely be back this way. It didn't see us through the jungle trees. We can't be seen from the air. If we could get a fire going, the smoke might be spotted."

But everything was soaking wet.

When I heard the drone of the plane's engine once again, I knew we had no hope of being found that day.

I had made it back to the Tuichi, but there was no bank. I stood on the bluff, about twenty feet above the river, its rapids tumbling beneath me. I took out the poncho and waved it frantically, but I knew there was no chance of being spotted through the trees. The plane was flying too high and too fast. I watched it go past with longing eyes.

She looked up at me forlornly.

"Don't worry. They'll be back tomorrow," I promised. "Look, we were almost saved today. I'm sure that that's Kevin up there. It has to be Kevin. I just know it is. He must have gone to my embassy for help."

I still did not recognize her: where she was from, why she was here. I just kept comforting her.

"They knew they'd have a hard time finding us today since the weather is so cloudy, but I'm sure they'll come back tomorrow and won't give up until they find us.

"You know, once in a while some guy gets lost in the Judeaen desert, and they call out the army and volunteers and trackers. Sometimes they have to keep looking for a whole week before they find the guy, dead or alive. They never just stop looking.

"What we have to do is help them find us. We have to find a shore to stand on, so they'll be able to see us."

I remembered the beach where the jaguars had been. I had better head back there.

"Yes, that's a great idea. It's a huge beach."

I had marked it clearly, and while I assumed that the markings had all

been washed away, the beach itself must still be there. It was so wide. I
quickly figured the distance. I had first arrived at Jaguar Beach on the
afternoon of the fourteenth. I had wasted the rest of that day trying un-
successfully to ford the river. On the fifteenth, as well, I had stopped walking relatively early. That meant that a day's walk was between me and the
beach. I could still get in a good few hours' walk today. Tomorrow I would
start walking at dawn and perhaps make Jaguar Beach in the morning
hours.

I explained my plan to her.

"Come on, love. Another day's walk, maybe less, and we'll be there,"
I said encouragingly. "There they will spot us easily. First the plane will
go over and see us. The pilot will signal us with a tilt of the wings and go
back to base. Within a few hours a helicopter will arrive, land on the
beach, and pick us up. We'll be saved. It'll all happen tomorrow. We have
to stick it out one more day. Come on, let's get going."

I changed direction for the third time that day. This time without
hesitation. I knew that I was doing the right thing.

My feet barely obeyed my will, almost refusing to carry my weight.
They couldn't stand much pressure. Every time I stepped on a rock or
root, terrible pains pierced through me. When I had to climb a hill and
descend the other side, it seemed an impossible effort. I had to get down
and crawl, drag myself along with my elbows. But I kept my suffering to
myself. She was with me. She was also injured, weak, and hungry. It was
harder for her than for me. If I wasn't strong, she would break.

I have to push myself harder, hide my own feelings, and keep her morale up.

When we were climbing upward, I would bite my lip and plead with
her, "Just a little farther, my love. Yes, I know how much it hurts. Here,
I'll give you a hand. One more little push. That's all. You see? We made
it. We're at the top. Now we have to get down. Sit like this and slide.
Slowly, take it easy. Watch out. Be careful you don't slip."

Rocks and thorns sliced into my buttocks. I noticed with concern that
the rash had spread to other parts of my body. Red dots had broken out
under my armpits and around my elbows. The cut on my arm hadn't
formed a scab. The edges were white. My fingers and the palms of my
hands were also lily-white. I had been constantly wet for several days.

My body is rotting.

We walked until late evening. I didn't stop talking for a minute, chattering all day long, trying to keep her spirits up, trying to keep her from
losing hope. When she stumbled or slowed down, I offered her my hand,

caressing her sad face. I was so anxious to cover as much ground as possible that I didn't even notice that the sun had almost set. I had to hurry and find a place to rest our heads before darkness fell.

I tore off some palm fronds and spread them over some muddy tree roots. I didn't bother trying to get comfortable; my body was inured to discomfort. I covered myself with the wet nets and the poncho. Taking my shoes off had been agony. I didn't remove my socks. They would just have to remain wet and dirty with mud, blood, and pus. I pulled the sack over my feet very carefully, knowing how tormenting the slightest contact would be. I didn't change position all night long in order to give my feet a rest.

I believed with all my heart that tomorrow would be my last day of hardship. Tomorrow a plane would find me.

"Thank you, my love. Thank you for being here. Tomorrow you'll get the kid-glove treatment. Don't cry. Try to shut your eyes, to get some sleep. Tomorrow we still have a few more hours to walk. We have to get there early, before the plane comes.

"Good night, my love."

At the break of dawn a heavy rain began pouring down. My prayers and pleas were to no avail. She was awakened by the first drops.

"Today is the big day, the last day," I told her. "We aren't going to let a little rain stop us. Don't let it get you down. It's not so bad. When we get to Jaguar Beach, I'll build you a strong shelter. You'll be able to rest, to sleep, until the helicopter comes.

"You're hungry? Yes, I know you're hungry, but we don't have anything left for breakfast. Don't worry, I'll find something to eat in the jungle. You can count on me."

I couldn't stand. My feet were soft and mushy, as if a skinless mass of raw, bloody flesh had been poured into my shoes. I couldn't take a single step, but I knew that my only chance for survival was to walk. I had to get to the shore. If I stayed in the jungle, no one would ever find me. I stumbled forward like a zombie. I discovered traces of the path, but it vanished after a while.

Walking through the dense growth was like marching through hell. I tried to stay as much as possible on soft, muddy ground, to ease the pain of every step I took. I tried to keep my weight on my trusty walking stick and often pulled myself forward by clutching at bushes and branches. When I came to an incline, even a gentle slope, I got down on all fours and crawled, my face caked with mud, my clothes torn and weighing me down. I was weak and afraid of losing consciousness. All I had was water. Water had become the enemy. Other than water nothing had passed my lips. The girl was my only consolation.

We walked on together for a few hours, but Jaguar Beach was nowhere to be seen. I tried to locate it by looking for the four islands that had been strung across the river. I remembered them as being very close to the beach, but I saw only one solitary island in the river. I feared that the current had swept the islands away but found that hard to believe. The islands had been large and well forested. They couldn't have vanished without a trace.

I trudged on and on through the mud and finally came upon a fruit tree. It was tall, a species of palm. At its top were large clusters of dates. A family of monkeys were up there having a noisy feast. A few pieces of fruit were strewn on the ground. They were squashed into the mud and rotting. My body quivered, twitched with craving, an age-old primordial instinct. I was hungry like a wild beast. I pounced upon the dates in the mud. I didn't care if they were rotten. The worms did not disgust me. I put the fruit into my mouth, rolled it around with my tongue, cleaned it off with my saliva, spat it out into the palm of my hand, and then spat out the residue of mud in my mouth before putting the fruit back. Soon, however, I lost patience and swallowed the fruit together with the mud. I didn't leave a single piece on the ground. Even the worms were a source of protein. The monkeys started throwing half-eaten dates down at me. They laughed and tossed pits down on my head. I was grateful to them, for the monkeys didn't take more than one bite out of each piece and discarded a thick layer of edible pulp. I could see their teeth marks on the dates before I ate them.

I went on for several hours without stopping to rest. It required effort, a supreme and painful effort. Jaguar Beach was nowhere to be seen. I began to worry, though I didn't think that I could have missed it. It had been the widest strip of shore along the entire length of river. I must be moving more slowly than I thought. I was injured, and walking through the mud was slow and laborious. I can't give up. *I have to make it back there before the plane passes overhead again.*

Then I lost my head for a moment. It wasn't her fault. The hill was just too steep. I knew that I wouldn't make it to the top without a great deal of suffering and pain. Here I collapsed. She burst into tears and refused to go on. I was sick of speaking to her kindly and lovingly.

What the hell does she think? I wondered, enraged. *That I'm having a picnic?*

"Stop coddling yourself," I shouted. "I'm sick of you and your whining, do you hear? Who needs you anyway? I don't have enough problems without schlepping a crybaby along? You don't help with anything. All you do is cry. Would you like to trade places with me for a while and carry this lousy pack on your back? I've had it with your bawling. You can cry your eyes out, for all I care, but you'd better not stop walking, because I'm not going to wait for you anymore."

I behaved cruelly but felt relieved to have let off steam. Afterward I felt ashamed of myself. I went over to her, gave her a hug, stroked her hair gently, and told her that I was sorry for having lost my temper and hadn't really meant any of it. I told here that I loved her, that I would protect her and bring her back to safety, but she had to make the effort and walk.

I had by now grown faint and dizzy, become weaker and weaker. When I came across a fallen tree that blocked my path, I had to walk around it. I couldn't lift my legs over it.

I have to make it to Jaguar Beach. Have to, have to, have to!

I could hear the plane's engine in the distance. I waited as it drew near. I knew that the plane wouldn't be able to see me, but I at least wanted to see it. The sound was dull and distant, then faded altogether. Had I imagined it? Maybe they were looking for me somewhere else. But Kevin was there, I was sure of that, and he knew where I was.

Toward evening I came to an area where a puddle of water floated on the mud. I walked on, oblivious, and before I had a chance to comprehend what was happening, the earth swallowed me up. I sank swiftly. Shocked and in a panic. I found myself up to my waist in bog. I went into a frenzy, like a trapped animal, screaming, trying to get out, but the mud was thick and sticky, and I couldn't move. My walking stick cut through it like a hot knife through butter and was of no help at all. I reached out to some reeds and bushes, stretching my body and arms in their direction. I tried pulling myself out by them, but they came loose in my hands. I continued sinking slowly.

I came out of my convulsive throes and calmed down. I tried to act rationally. I stuck my hands down deep into the mud, wrapped them around one knee and tried to force one leg up out of the mud. I pulled with all my might, but to no avail. It was as if I had been set in concrete. I couldn't budge. I wanted to cry again but felt only a thick lump in my throat.

So this is it, death. I end my life in this bog.

I was resigned. I knew that I didn't have the strength to get myself out, and no power in the world would reach down and pluck me out of the swamp.

It would be a slow, horrible death. The mud was already up to my belly button. The pack rested on the mud, and I was relieved of its weight. Suddenly I had a brilliant idea. I would commit suicide. I took the pack from my shoulders and rummaged through it hurriedly until I found the first-aid kit. There were about twenty amphetamines and perhaps thirty other, unidentified pills. That was it. I would take all of them. I was sure they would kill me or at least make everything good and hazy before I drowned. First I opened the tin of speed. I held a few of them in the palm of my hand.

You're being selfish, Yossi, really egotistical. It's easy enough for you to die, just swallow the pills, and you're off to paradise. But what about your parents? Your mother: what will this do to her?

You can't die like this. Not after all you've already been through. It wouldn't be so bad if you had died on the first day in a sudden accident. But now, after all this suffering? It isn't fair to just give up now.

I put the pills back in the tin. I strained forward, leaning my torso out across the mud and moved my arms forward as if I were swimming. I moved my arms back and forth, pulling and wriggling in the mud. I kicked my legs in fluttering movements. I fought with every ounce of strength. Fought for my life.

It took about half an hour, maybe more. As soon as I got my legs free of the mud, I crept forward without sinking. I left neither the pack not the walking stick behind. After I'd advanced another six feet, I was out of the quagmire.

My entire body was caked with a thick layer of black, sticky mud. I cleared it out of my nostrils, wiped my eyes, and spat it out of my mouth.

To live. I want to live. I'll suffer any torment, but I'll go on. I'll make it to Jaguar Beach, no matter what.

Yossi made it to Jaguar Beach, where he was saved by his friend Kevin, who had been rescued himself and returned by boat to look for Yossi. No trace was ever found of Karl and Marcus.

Today, Yossi Ghinsberg is an accomplished public speaker, and has been working diligently to help protect the Amazon rainforest. His book about the experience, entitled Jungle, *was a worldwide bestseller, and sparked a mini-tourism boom to the area he struggled through and wrote about.*

THE DEVILS THUMB

Jon Krakauer (1954–)

From *Eiger Dreams*

Unlike many authors in this anthology, the next one needs little introduction. Jon Krakauer is the internationally bestselling author of Into Thin Air, *his account of two disasterous 1997 expeditions to climb Mount Everest, and* Into the Wild, *his re-creation of the last days of Christopher McCandless, who traveled to Alaska to live in the wild, and ultimately died there.*

Krakauer himself is no stranger to feats of wilderness derring-do, as shown in this excerpt from his book Eiger Dreams, *a collection of mountaineering stories. Among them is this tale of trying to solo the Devils Thumb in Alaska. The twenty-three-year-old Krakauer who undertakes what many would call a fool's mission is full of both guts and gumption, and he'll need both to survive the attempt before the mountain is through with him.*

BY THE TIME I REACHED THE INTERSTATE I was having trouble keeping my eyes open. I'd been okay on the twisting two-lane blacktop between Fort Collins and Laramie, but when the Pontiac eased onto the smooth, unswerving pavement of I–80, the soporific hiss of the tires began to gnaw at my wakefulness like ants in a dead tree.

That afternoon, after nine hours of humping 2 × 10s and pounding recalcitrant nails, I'd told my boss I was quitting: "No, not in a couple of weeks, Steve; right now was more like what I had in mind." It took me three more hours to clear my tools and other belongings out of the rust-stained construction trailer that had served as my home in Boulder. I loaded everything into the car, drove up Pearl Street to Tom's Tavern, and downed a ceremonial beer. Then I was gone.

At 1 A.M., thirty miles east of Rawlins, the strain of the day caught up to me. The euphoria that had flowed so freely in the wake of my quick escape gave way to overpowering fatigue; suddenly I felt tired to the bone. The highway stretched straight and empty to the horizon and beyond. Outside the car the night air was cold, and the stark Wyoming plains glowed in the moonlight like Rousseau's painting of the sleeping gypsy. I wanted very badly just then to be that gypsy, conked out of my back beneath the stars. I shut my eyes—just for a second, but it was a second of bliss. It seemed to revive me, if only briefly. The Pontiac, a sturdy behemoth from the Eisenhower years, floated down the road on its long-gone shocks like a raft on an ocean swell. The lights of an oil rig twinkled reassuringly in the distance. I closed my eyes a second time, and kept them closed a few moments longer. The sensation was sweeter than sex.

A few minutes later I let my eyelids fall again. I'm not sure how long I nodded off this time—it might have been for five seconds, it might have been for thirty—but when I awoke it was to the rude sensation of the Pontiac bucking violently along the dirt shoulder at seventy miles per hour. By all rights, the car should have sailed off into the rabbitbrush and rolled. The rear wheels fishtailed wildly six or seven times, but I eventually managed to guide the unruly machine back onto the pavement without so much as blowing a tire, and let it coast gradually to a stop. I loosened my death grip on the wheel, took several deep breaths to quiet the pounding in my chest, then slipped the shifter back into drive and continued down the highway.

Pulling over to sleep would have been the sensible thing to do, but I was on my way to Alaska to change my life, and patience was a concept well beyond my twenty-three-year-old ken.

Sixteen months earlier I'd graduated from college with little distinction and even less in the way of marketable skills. In the interim an off-again, on-again four-year relationship—the first serious romance of my life—had come to a messy, long-overdue end; nearly a year later, my love life was still zip. To support myself I worked on a house-framing crew, grunting under crippling loads of plywood, counting the minutes until the next coffee break, scratching in vain at the sawdust stuck *in perpetuum* to the sweat on the back of my neck. Somehow, blighting the Colorado landscape with condominiums and tract houses for three-fifty an hour wasn't the sort of career I'd dreamed of as a boy.

Late one evening I was mulling all this over on a barstool at Tom's, picking unhappily at my existential scabs, when an idea came to me, a scheme for righting what was wrong in my life. It was wonderfully uncomplicated, and the more I thought about it, the better the plan sounded. By the bottom of the pitcher its merits seemed unassailable. The plan consisted, in its entirety, of climbing a mountain in Alaska called the Devils Thumb.

The Devils Thumb is a prong of exfoliated diorite that presents an imposing profile from any point of the compass, but especially so from the north: its great north wall, which had never been climbed, rises sheer and clean for six thousand vertical feet from the glacier at its base. Twice the height of Yosemite's El Capitan, the north face of the Thumb is one of the biggest granitic walls on the continent; it may well be one of the biggest in the world. I would go to Alaska, ski across the Stikine Icecap to the Devils Thumb, and make the first ascent of its notorious nordwand. It seemed, midway through the second pitcher, like a particularly good idea to do all of this solo.

Writing these words more than a dozen years later, it's no longer entirely clear just *how* I thought soloing the Devils Thumb would transform my life. It had something to do with the fact that climbing was the first and only thing I'd ever been good at. My reasoning, such as it was, was fueled by the scattershot passions of youth, and a literary diet overly rich in the works of Nietzsche, Kerouac, and John Menlove Edwards—the latter a deeply troubled writer/psychiatrist who, before putting an end to his life with a cyanide capsule in 1958, had been one of the preeminent British rock climbers of the day.

Dr. Edwards regarded climbing as a "psycho-neurotic tendency" rather than sport; he climbed not for fun but to find refuge from the inner torment that characterized his existence. I remember, that spring of 1977, being especially taken by a passage from an Edwards short story titled "Letter from a Man":

> So, as you would imagine, I grew up exuberant in body but with a nervy, craving mind. It was wanting something more, something tangible. It sought for reality intensely, always if it were not there . . .
>
>   But you see at once what I do. I climb.

To one enamored of this sort of prose, the Thumb beckoned like a beacon. My belief in the plan became unshakeable. I was dimly aware that I might be getting in over my head, but if I could somehow get to the top of the Devils Thumb, I was convinced, everything that followed would turn out all right. And thus did I push the accelerator a little closer to the floor and, buoyed by the jolt of adrenaline that followed the Pontiac's brush with destruction, speed west into the night.

You can't actually get very close to the Devils Thumb by car. The peak stands in the Boundary Ranges on the Alaska–British Columbia border, not far from the fishing village of Petersburg, a place accessible only by boat or plane. There is regular jet service to Petersburg, but the sum of my liquid assets amounted to the Pontiac and two hundred dollars in cash, not even enough for one-way airfare, so I took the car as far as Gig Harbor, Washington, then hitched a ride on a northbound seine boat that was short on crew. Five days out, when the Ocean Queen pulled into Petersburg to take on fuel and water, I jumped ship, shouldered my backpack, and walked down the dock in a steady Alaskan rain.

Back in Boulder, without exception, every person with whom I'd shared my plans about the Thumb had been blunt and to the point: I'd been smoking too much pot, they said; it was a monumentally bad idea. I was grossly overestimating my abilities as a climber, I'd never be able to hack a month completely by myself, I would fall into a crevasse and die.

The residents of Petersburg reacted differently. Being Alaskans, they were accustomed to people with screwball ideas; a sizeable percentage of the state's population, after all, was sitting on half-baked schemes to mine uranium in the Brooks Range, or sell icebergs to the Japanese, or market mail-order moose droppings. Most of the Alaskans I met, if they reacted at all, simply asked how much money there was in climbing a mountain like the Devils Thumb.

In any case, one of the appealing things about climbing the Thumb— and one of the appealing things about the sport of mountain climbing in general—was that it didn't matter a rat's ass what anyone else thought. Getting the scheme off the ground didn't hinge on winning the approval of some personnel director, admissions committee, licensing board, or panel of stern-faced judges; if I felt like taking a shot at some unclimbed alpine wall, all I had to do was get myself to the foot of the mountain and start swinging my ice axes.

Petersburg sits on an island, the Devils Thumb rises from the mainland. To get myself to the foot of the Thumb it was first necessary to cross twenty-five miles of salt water. For most of a day I walked the docks, trying without success to hire a boat to ferry me across Frederick Sound. Then I bumped into Bart and Benjamin.

Bart and Benjamin were ponytailed constituents of a Woodstock Nation tree-planting collective called the Hodads. We struck up a conversation. I mentioned that I, too, had once worked as a tree planter. The Hodads allowed that they had chartered a floatplane to fly them to their camp on the mainland the next morning. "It's your lucky day, kid," Bart told me. "For twenty bucks you can ride over with us. Get you to your fuckin' mountain in style." On May 3rd, a day and a half after arriving in Petersburg, I stepped off the Hodads' Cessna, waded onto the tidal flats at the head of Thomas Bay, and began the long trudge inland.

The Devils Thumb pokes up out of the Stikine Icecap, an immense, labyrinthine network of glaciers that hugs the crest of the Alaskan panhandle like an octopus, with myriad tentacles that snake down, down to the sea from the craggy uplands along the Canadian frontier. In putting ashore at Thomas Bay I was gambling that one of these frozen arms, the Baird Glacier, would lead me safely to the bottom of the Thumb, thirty miles distant.

An hour of gravel beach led to the tortured blue tongue of the Baird. A logger in Petersburg had suggested I keep an eye out for grizzlies along this stretch of shore. "Them bears over there is just waking up this time of year," he smiled. "Tend to be kinda cantankerous after not eatin' all winter. But you keep your gun handy, you shouldn't have no problem." Problem was, I didn't have a gun. As it turned out, my only encounter with hostile wildlife involved a flock of gulls who dive-bombed my head with Hitchockian fury. Between the avian assault and my ursine anxiety, it was with no small amount of relief that I turned my back to the beach, donned crampons, and scrambled up onto the glacier's broad, lifeless snout.

After three or four miles I came to the snowline, where I exchanged crampons for skis. Putting the boards on my feet cut fifteen pounds from the awful load on my back and made the going much faster besides. But now that the ice was covered with snow, many of the glacier's crevasses were hidden, making solitary travel extremely dangerous.

In Seattle, anticipating this hazard, I'd stopped at a hardware store and purchased a pair of stout aluminum curtain rods, each ten feet long. Upon reaching the snowline, I lashed the rods together at right angles, then strapped the arrangement to the hip belt on my backpack so the poles extended horizontally over the snow. Staggering slowly up the glacier with my overloaded backpack, bearing the queer tin cross, I felt like some kind

of strange *Penitente*. Were I to break through the veneer of snow over a hidden crevasse, though, the curtain rods would—I hoped mightily—span
the slot and keep me from dropping into the chilly bowels of the Baird.

The first climbers to venture onto the Stikine Icecap were Bestor
Robinson and Fritz Wiessner, the legendary German-American alpinist,
who spent a stormy month in the Boundary Ranges in 1937 but failed to
reach any major summits. Wiessner returned in 1946 with Donald Brown
and Fred Beckey to attempt the Devils Thumb, the nastiest looking peak
in the Stikine. On that trip Fritz mangled a knee during a fall on the hike
in and limped home in disgust, but Beckey went back that same summer
with Bob Craig and Cliff Schmidtke. On August 25th, after several aborted
tries and some exceedingly hairy climbing on the peak's east ridge,
Beckey and company sat on the Thumb's wafer-thin summit tower in a
tired, giddy daze. It was far and away the most technical ascent ever done
in Alaska, an important milestone in the history of American mountaineering.

In the ensuing decades three other teams also made it to the top of the
Thumb, but all steered clear of the big north face. Reading accounts of
these expeditions, I had wondered why none of them had approached the
peak by what appeared, from the map at least, to be the easiest and most
logical route, the Baird. I wondered a little less after coming across an article by Beckey in which the distinguished mountaineer cautioned, "Long,
steep icefalls block the route from the Baird Glacier to the icecap near
Devils Thumb," but after studying aerial photographs I decided that Beckey
was mistaken, that the icefalls weren't so big or so bad. The Baird, I was
certain, really was the best way to reach the mountain.

For two days I slogged steadily up the glacier without incident, con-
gratulating myself for discovering such a clever path to the Thumb. On
the third day, I arrived beneath the Stikine Icecap proper, where the long
arm of the Baird joins the main body of ice. Here, the glacier spills abruptly
over the edge of a high plateau, dropping seaward through the gap between two peaks in a phantasmagoria of shattered ice. Seeing the icefall
in the flesh left a different impression than the photos had. As I stared at
the tumult from a mile away, for the first time since leaving Colorado the
thought crossed my mind that maybe this Devils Thumb trip wasn't the
best idea I'd ever had.

The icefall was a maze of crevasses and teetering seracs. From afar it
brought to mind a bad train wreck, as if scores of ghostly white boxcars
had derailed at the lip of the icecap and tumbled down the slope willy-

nilly. The closer I got, the more unpleasant it looked. My ten-foot curtain rods seemed a poor defense against crevasses that were forty feet across and two hundred fifty feet deep. Before I could finish figuring out a course through the icefall, the wind came up and snow began to slant hard out of the clouds, stinging my face and reducing visibility to almost nothing.

In my impetuosity, I decided to carry on anyway. For the better part of the day I groped blindly through the labyrinth in the whiteout, retracing my steps from one dead end to another. Time after time I'd think I'd found a way out, only to wind up in a deep blue cul-de-sac, or stranded atop a detached pillar of ice. My efforts were lent a sense of urgency by the noises emanating underfoot. A madrigal of creaks and sharp reports—the sort of protests a large fir limb makes when it's slowly bent to the breaking point—served as a reminder that it is the nature of glaciers to move, the habit of seracs to topple.

As much as I feared being flattened by a wall of collapsing ice, I was even more afraid of falling into a crevasse, a fear that intensified when I put a foot through a snow bridge over a slot so deep I couldn't see the bottom of it. A little later I broke through another bridge to my waist; the poles kept me out of the hundred-foot hole, but after I extricated myself I was bent double with dry heaves thinking about what it would be like to be lying in a pile at the bottom of the crevasse, waiting for death to come, with nobody even aware of how or where I'd met my end.

Night had nearly fallen by the time I emerged from the top of the serac slope onto the empty, wind-scoured expanse of the high glacial plateau. In shock and chilled to the core, I skied far enough past the icefall to put its rumblings out of earshot, pitched the tent, crawled into my sleeping bag, and shivered myself to a fitful sleep.

Although my plan to climb the Devils Thumb wasn't fully hatched until the spring of 1977, the mountain had been lurking in the recesses of my mind for about fifteen year—since April 12, 1962, to be exact. The occasion was my eighth birthday. When it came time to open birthday presents, my parents announced that they were offering me a choice of gifts: According to my wishes, they would either escort me to the new Seattle World's Fair to ride the Monorail and see the Space Needle, or give me an introductory taste of mountain climbing by taking me up the third highest peak in Oregon, a long-dormant volcano called the South Sister that, on clear days, was visible from my bedroom window. It was a tough call. I thought the matter over at length, then settled on the climb.

To prepare me for the rigors of the ascent, my father handed over a copy of *Mountaineering: The Freedom of the Hills,* the leading how-to manual of the day, a thick tome that weighed only slightly less than a bowling ball. Thenceforth I spent most of my waking hours poring over its pages, memorizing the intricacies of pitoncraft and bolt placement, the shoulder stand and the tension traverse. None of which, as it happened, was of any use of my inaugural ascent, for the South Sister turned out to be a decidedly less than extreme climb that demanded nothing more in the way of technical skill than energetic walking, and was in fact ascended by hundreds of farmers, house pets, and small children every summer.

Which is not to suggest that my parents and I conquered the mighty volcano: From the pages and pages of perilous situations depicted in *Mountaineering: The Freedom of the Hills,* I had concluded that climbing was a life-and-death matter, always. Halfway up the South Sister I suddenly remembered this. In the middle of a twenty-degree snow-slope that would be impossible to fall from if you tried, I decided that I was in mortal jeopardy and burst into tears, bringing the ascent to a halt.

Perversely, after the South Sister debacle my interest in climbing only intensified. I resumed my obsessive studies of *Mountaineering.* There was something about the scariness of the activities portrayed in those pages that just wouldn't leave me alone. In addition to the scores of line drawings—most of them cartoons of a little man in a jaunty Tyrolean cap—employed to illustrate arcana like the boot-axe belay and the Bilgeri rescue, the book contained sixteen black-and-white plates of notable peaks in the Pacific Northwest and Alaska. All the photographs were striking, but the one on page 147 was much, much more than that: it made my skin crawl. An aerial photo by glaciologist Maynard Miller, it showed a singularly sinister tower of ice-plastered black rock. There wasn't a place on the entire mountain that looked safe or secure; I couldn't imagine anyone climbing it. At the bottom of the page the mountain was identified as the Devils Thumb.

From the first time I saw it, the picture—a portrait of the Thumb's north wall—held an almost pornographic fascination for me. On hundreds—no, make that thousands—of occasions over the decade and a half that followed I took my copy of *Mountaineering* down from the shelf, opened it to page 147, and quietly stared. How would it feel, I wondered over and over, to be on that thumbnail-thin summit ridge, worrying over the storm clouds building on the horizon, hunched against the wind and dunning cold, contemplating the horrible drop on either side? How could anyone keep it together? Would I, if I found myself high on the north wall, clinging to that frozen rock, even attempt to keep it together? Or would I simply decide to surrender to the inevitable straight away, and jump?

I had planned on spending between three weeks and a month on the Stikine Icecap. Not relishing the prospect of carrying a four-week load of food, heavy winter camping gear, and a small mountain of climbing hardware all the way up the Baird on my back, before leaving Petersburg I paid a bush pilot a hundred and fifty dollars—the last of my cash—to have six cardboard cartons of supplies dropped from an airplane when I reached the foot of the Thumb. I showed the pilot exactly where, on his map, I intended to be, and told him to give me three days to get there; he promised to fly over and make the drop as soon thereafter as the weather permitted.

On May 6th I set up a base camp on the icecap just northeast of the Thumb and waited for the airdrop. For the next four days it snowed, nixing any chance for a flight. Too terrified of crevasses to wander far from camp, I occasionally went out for a short ski to kill time, but mostly I lay silently in the tent—the ceiling was too low to sit upright with my thoughts, fighting a rising chorus of doubts.

As the days passed, I grew increasingly anxious. I had no radio, nor any other means of communicating with the outside world. It had been many years since anyone had visited this part of the Stikine Icecap, and many more would likely pass before anyone did so again. I was nearly out of stove fuel, and down to a single chunk of cheese, my last package of ramen noodles, and half a box of Cocoa Puffs. This, I figured, could sustain me for three or four more days if need be, but then what would I do? It would only take two days to ski back down the Baird to Thomas Bay, but then a week or more might easily pass before a fisherman happened by who could give me a lift back to Petersburg (the Hodads with whom I'd ridden over were camped fifteen miles down the impassable, headland-studded coast, and could be reached only by boat or plane).

When I went to bed on the evening of May 10th it was still snowing and blowing hard. I was going back and forth on whether to head for the coast in the morning or stick it out on the icecap, gambling that the pilot would show before I starved or died of thirst, when, just for a moment, I heard a faint whine, like a mosquito. I tore open the tent door. Most of the clouds had lifted, but there was no airplane in sight. The whine returned, louder this time. Then I saw it: a tiny red-and-white speck, high in the western sky, droning my way.

A few minutes later the plane passed directly overhead. The pilot, however, was unaccustomed to glacier flying and he'd badly misjudged the scale of the terrain. Worried about winding up too low and getting nailed by unexpected turbulence, he flew a good thousand feet above me—believing all the while he was just off the deck—and never saw my tent in the flat evening light. My waving and screaming were to no avail; from that altitude I was indistinguishable from a pile of rocks. For the next hour he circled the icecap, scanning its barren contours without success. But the pilot, to his credit, appreciated the gravity of my predicament and didn't give up. Frantic, I tied my sleeping bag to the end of one of the crevasse poles and waved it for all I was worth. When the plane banked sharply and began to fly straight at me, I felt tears of joy well in my eyes.

The pilot buzzed my tent three times in quick succession, dropping two boxes on each pass, then the airplane disappeared over a ridge and I was alone. As silence again settled over the glacier I felt abandoned, vulnerable, lost. I realized that I was sobbing. Embarrassed, I halted the blubbering by screaming obscenities until I grew hoarse.

I awoke early on May 11th to clear skies and the relatively warm temperature of twenty degrees Fahrenheit. Startled by the good weather, mentally unprepared to commence the actual climb, I hurriedly packed up a rucksack nonetheless, and began skiing toward the base of the Thumb. Two previous Alaskan expeditions had taught me that, ready or not, you simply can't afford to waste a day of perfect weather if you expect to get up anything.

A small hanging glacier extends out from the lip of the icecap, leading up and across the north face of the Thumb like a catwalk. My plan was to follow this catwalk to a prominent rock prow in the center of the wall, and thereby execute an end run around the ugly, avalanche-swept lower half of the face.

The catwalk turned out to be a series of fifty-degree ice fields blanketed with knee-deep powder snow and riddled with crevasses. The depth of the snow made the going slow and exhausting; by the time I front-pointed up the overhanging wall of the uppermost *bergschrund,* some three or four hours after leaving camp, I was whipped. And I hadn't even gotten to the "real" climbing yet. That would begin immediately above, where the hanging glacier gave way to vertical rock.

The rock, exhibiting a dearth of holds and coated with six inches of crumbly rime, did not look promising, but just left of the main prow was an inside corner—what climbers call an open book—glazed with frozen melt water. This ribbon of ice led straight up for two or three hundred feet, and if the ice proved substantial enough to support the picks of my ice axes, the line might go. I hacked out a small platform in the snow slope, the last flat ground I expected to feel underfoot for some time, and stopped to eat a candy bar and collect my thoughts. Fifteen minutes later I shouldered my pack and inched over to the bottom of the corner. Gingerly, I swung my right ax into the two-inch-thick ice. It was solid, plastic—a little thinner than I would have liked but otherwise perfect. I was on my way.

The climbing was steep and spectacular, so exposed it made my head spin. Beneath my boot soles, the wall fell away for three thousand feet to the dirty, avalanche-scarred cirque of the Witches Cauldron Glacier. Above, the prow soared with authority toward the summit ridge, a vertical half-mile above. Each time I planted one of my ice axes, that distance shrank by another twenty inches.

The higher I climbed, the more comfortable I became. All that held me to the mountainside, all that held me to the world, were six thin spikes of chrome-molybdenum stuck half an inch into a smear of frozen water, yet I began to feel invincible, weightless, like those lizards that live on the ceilings of cheap Mexican hotels. Early on a difficult climb, especially a difficult solo climb, you're hyperaware of the abyss pulling at your back. You constantly feel its call, its immense hunger. To resist takes a tremendous conscious effort; you don't dare let your guard down for an instant. The siren song of the void puts you on edge, it makes your movements tentative, clumsy, herky-jerky. But as the climb goes on, you grow accustomed to the exposure, you get used to rubbing shoulders with doom, you come to believe in the reliability of your hands and feet and head. You learn to trust your self-control.

By and by, your attention becomes so intensely focused that you no longer notice the raw knuckles, the cramping thighs, the strain of maintaining nonstop concentration. A trance-like state settles over your efforts, the climb becomes a clear-eyed dream. Hours slide by like minutes. The accrued guilt and clutter of day-to-day existence—the lapses of conscience, the unpaid bills, the bungled opportunities, the dust under the couch, the festering familial sores, the inescapable prison of your genes—all of it is temporarily forgotten, crowded from your thoughts by an overpowering clarity of purpose, and by the seriousness of the task at hand.

At such moments, something like happiness actually stirs in your chest, but it isn't the sort of emotion you want to lean on very hard. In solo climbing, the whole enterprise is held together with little more than chutzpa, not the most reliable adhesive. Late in the day on the north face of the Thumb, I felt the glue disintegrate with a single swing of an ice ax.

I'd gained nearly seven hundred feet of altitude since stepping off the hanging glacier, all of it on crampon front-points and the picks of my axes. The ribbon of frozen melt water had ended three hundred feet up, and was followed by a crumbly armor of frost feathers. Though just barely substantial enough to support body weight, the rime was plastered over the rock to a thickness of two or three feet, so I kept plugging upward. The wall, however, had been growing imperceptibly steeper, and as it did so the frost feathers became thinner. I'd fallen into a slow, hypnotic rhythm—swing, swing; kick, kick; swing, swing; kick, kick—when my left ice ax slammed into a slab of diorite a few inches beneath the rime.

I tried left, then right, but kept striking rock. The frost feathers holding me up, it became apparent, were maybe five inches thick and had the structural integrity of stale cornbread. Below was thirty-seven hundred feet of air, and I was balanced atop a house of cards. Waves of panic rose in my throat. My eyesight blurred, I began to hyperventilate, my calves started to vibrate. I shuffled a few feet farther to the right, hoping to find thicker ice, but managed only to bend an ice ax on the rock.

Awkwardly, stiff with fear, I started working my way back down. The rime gradually thickened, and after descending about eighty feet I got back on reasonably solid ground. I stopped for a long time to let my nerves settle, then leaned back from my tools and stared up at the face above, searching for a hint of solid ice, for some variation in the underlying rock strata, for anything that would allow passage over the frosted slabs. I looked until my neck ached, but nothing appeared. The climb was over. The only place to go was down.

Heavy snow and incessant winds kept me inside the tent for most of the next three days. The hours passed slowly. In the attempt to hurry them along I chain-smoked for as long as my supply of cigarettes held out, and read. I'd made a number of bad decisions on the trip, there was no getting around it, and one of them concerned the reading matter I'd chosen to pack along: three back issues of the *Village Voice,* and Joan Didion's latest novel, *A Book of Common Prayer.* The *Voice* was amusing enough—there on the icecap, the subject matter took on an edge, a certain sense of the absurd, from which the paper (through no fault of its own) benefited greatly—but in that tent, under those circumstances, Didion's necrotic take on the world hit a little too close to home.

Near the end of *Common Prayer,* one of Didion's characters says to another, "You don't get any real points for staying here, Charlotte." Charlotte replies, "I can't seem to tell what you do get real points for, so I guess I'll stick around here for awhile."

When I ran out of things to read, I was reduced to studying the ripstop pattern woven into the tent ceiling. This I did for hours on end, flat on my back, while engaging in an extended and very heated self-debate: Should I leave for the coast as soon as the weather broke, or stay put long enough to make another attempt on the mountain? In truth, my little escapade on the north face had left me badly shaken, and I didn't want to go up on the Thumb again at all. On the other hand, the thought of returning to Boulder in defeat—of parking the Pontiac behind the trailer, buckling on my tool belt, and going back to the same brain-dead drill I'd so triumphantly walked away from just a month before—that wasn't very appealing, either. Most of all, I couldn't stomach the thought of having to endure the smug expressions of condolence from all the chumps and nimrods who were certain I'd fail right from the get-go.

By the third afternoon of the storm I couldn't stand it any longer: the lumps of frozen snow poking me in the back, the clammy nylon walls brushing against my face, the incredible smell drifting up from the depths of my sleeping bag. I pawed through the mess at my feet until I located a small green stuff sack, in which there was a metal film can containing the makings of what I'd hoped would be a sort of victory cigar. I'd intended to save it for my return from the summit, but what the hey, it wasn't looking like I'd be visiting the top any time soon. I poured most of the can's contents onto a leaf of cigarette paper, rolled it into a crooked, sorry looking joint, and promptly smoked it down to the roach.

The reefer, of course, only made the tent seem even more cramped, more suffocating, more impossible to bear. It also made me terribly hungry. I decided a little oatmeal would put things right. Making it, however, was a long, ridiculously involved process: a potful of snow had to be gathered outside in the tempest, and stove assembled and lit, the oatmeal and sugar located, the remnants of yesterday's dinner scraped from my bowl. I'd gotten the stove going and was melting the snow when I smelled something burning. A thorough check of the stove and its environs

revealed nothing. Mystified, I was ready to chalk it up to my chemi-
cally enhanced imagination when I heard something crackle directly
behind me.

I whirled around in time to see a bag of garbage, into which I'd tossed
the match I'd used to light the stove, flare up into a conflagration. Beating on the fire with my hands, I had it out in a few seconds, but not before a large section of the tent's inner wall vaporized before my eyes. The
tent's built-in rainfly escaped the flames, so the shelter was still more or
less weatherproof; now, however, it was approximately thirty degrees
cooler inside. My left palm began to sting. Examining it, I noticed the
pink welt of a burn. What troubled me most, though, was that the tent
wasn't even mine—I'd borrowed the shelter from my father. An expen-
sive Early Winters OmnipoTent, it had been brand new before my trip—
the hang-tags were still attached—and had been loaned reluctantly. For
several minutes I sat dumbstruck, staring at the wreckage of the shelter's
once-graceful form amid the acrid scent of singed hair and melted nylon.
You had to hand it to me, I thought: *I had a real knack for living up to the old
man's worst expectations.*

The fire sent me into a funk that no drug known to man could have alleviated. By the time I'd finished cooking the oatmeal my mind was made
up: the moment the storm was over, I was breaking camp and booking for
Thomas Bay.

Twenty-four hours later, I was huddled inside a bivouac sack under the
lip of the *bergschrund* on the Thumb's north face. The weather was as bad
as I'd seen it. It was snowing hard, probably an inch every hour. Spindrift
avalanches hissed down from the wall above and washed over me like
surf, completely burying the sack every twenty minutes.

The day had begun well enough. When I emerged from the tent,
clouds still clung to the ridge tops but the wind was down and the icecap
was speckled with sunbreaks. A patch of sunlight, almost blinding in its
brilliance, slid lazily over the camp. I put down a foam sleeping mat and
sprawled on the glacier in my long johns. Wallowing in the radiant heat,
I felt the gratitude of a prisoner whose sentence has just been commuted.

As I lay there, a narrow chimney that curved up the east half of the
Thumb's north face, well to the left of the route I'd tried before the storm,
caught my eye. I twisted a telephoto lens onto my camera. Through it I
could make out a smear of shiny grey ice—solid, trustworthy, hard-frozen
ice—plastered to the back of the cleft. The alignment of the chimney

made it impossible to discern if the ice continued in an unbroken line from top to bottom. If it did, the chimney might well provide passage over the rime-covered slabs that had foiled my first attempt. Lying there in the sun, I began to think about how much I'd hate myself a month hence if I threw in the towel after a single try, if I scrapped the whole expedition on account of a little bad weather. Within the hour I had assembled my gear and was skiing toward the base of the wall.

The ice in the chimney did in fact prove to be continuous, but it was very, very thin—just a gossamer film of verglas. Additionally, the cleft was a natural funnel for any debris that happened to slough off the wall; as I scratched my way up the chimney I was hosed by a continuous stream of powder snow, ice chips, and small stones. One hundred twenty feet up the groove the last remnants of my composure flaked away like old plaster, and I turned around.

Instead of descending all the way to base camp, I decided to spend the night in the 'schrund beneath the chimney, on the off chance that my head would be more together the next morning. The fair skies that had ushered in the day, however, turned out to be but a momentary lull in a five-day gale. By midafternoon the storm was back in all its glory, and my bivouac site became a less than pleasant place to hang around. The ledge on which I crouched was continually swept by small spindrift avalanches. Five times my bivvy sack—a thin nylon envelope, shaped exactly like a Baggies brand sandwich bag, only bigger—was buried up to the level of the breathing slit. After digging myself out the fifth time, I decided I'd had enough. I threw all my gear in my pack and made a break for base camp.

The descent was terrifying. Between the clouds, the ground blizzard, and the flat, fading light, I couldn't tell snow from sky, nor whether a slope went up or down. I worried, with ample reason, that I might step blindly off the top of a serac and end up at the bottom of the Witches Cauldron, a half-mile below. When I finally arrived on the frozen plain of the icecap, I found that my tracks had long since drifted over. I didn't have a clue how to locate the tent on the featureless glacial plateau. I skied in circles for an hour or so, hoping I'd get lucky and stumble across camp, until I put a foot into a small crevasse and realized I was acting like an idiot—that I should hunker down right where I was and wait out the storm.

I dug a shallow hole, wrapped myself in the bivvy bag, and sat on my pack in the swirling snow. Drifts piled up around me. My feet became numb. A damp chill crept down my chest from the base of my neck, where spindrift had gotten inside my parka and soaked my shirt. If only I had a cigarette, I thought, a single cigarette, I could summon the strength of character to put a good face on this fucked-up situation, on the whole fucked-up trip. "If we had some ham, we could have ham and eggs, if we had some eggs." I remembered my friend Nate uttering that line in a similar storm, two years before, high on another Alaskan peak, the Mooses Tooth. It had struck me as hilarious at the time; I'd actually laughed out loud. Recalling the line now, it no longer seemed funny. I pulled the bivvy sack tighter around my shoulders. The wind ripped at my back. Beyond shame, I cradled my head in my arms and embarked on an orgy of self-pity.

I knew that people sometimes died climbing mountains. But at the age of twenty-three personal mortality—the idea of my own death—was still largely outside my conceptual grasp; it was as abstract a notion as non-Euclidian geometry or marriage. When I decamped from Boulder in April 1977, my head swimming with visions of glory and redemption on the Devils Thumb, it didn't occur to me that I might be bound by the same cause-effect relationships that governed the actions of others. I'd never heard of hubris. Because I wanted to climb the mountain so badly, because I had thought about the Thumb so intensely for so long, it seemed beyond the realm of possibility that some minor obstacle like the weather or crevasses or rime-covered rock might ultimately thwart my will.

At sunset the wind died and the ceiling lifted one hundred and fifty feet off the glacier, enabling me to locate base camp. I made it back to the tent intact, but it was no longer possible to ignore the fact that the Thumb had made hash of my plans. I was forced to acknowledge that volition alone, however powerful, was not going to get me up the north wall. I saw, finally, that nothing was.

There still existed an opportunity for salvaging the expedition, however. A week earlier I'd skied over to the southeast side of the mountain to take a look at the route Fred Beckey had pioneered in 1946—the route by which I'd intended to descend the peak after climbing the north wall. During that reconnaissance I'd noticed an obvious unclimbed line to the left of the Beckey route—a patchy network of ice angling across the southeast face—that struck me as a relatively easy way to achieve the summit. At the time, I'd considered this route unworthy of my attentions. Now, on the rebound from my calamitous entanglement with the nordwand, I was prepared to lower my sights.

On the afternoon of May 15th, when the blizzard finally petered out, I returned to the southeast face and climbed to the top of a slender ridge that abutted the upper peak like a flying buttress on a gothic cathedral. I decided to spend the night there, on the airy, knife-edged ridge crest, sixteen hundred feet below the summit. The evening sky was cold and cloudless. I could see all the way to tidewater and beyond. At dusk I watched, transfixed, as the house lights of Petersburg blinked on in the west. The closest thing I'd had to human contact since the airdrop, the distant lights set off a flood of emotion that caught me completely off guard. I imagined people watching the Red Sox on the tube, eating fried chicken in brightly lit kitchens, drinking beer, making love. When I lay down to sleep I was overcome by a soul-wrenching loneliness. I'd never felt so alone, ever.

That night I had troubled dreams, of cops and vampires and a gangland-style execution. I heard someone whisper, "He's in there. As soon as he comes out, waste him." I sat bolt upright and opened my eyes. The sun was about to rise. The entire sky was scarlet. It was still clear, but wisps of high cirrus were streaming in from the southwest, and a dark line was visible just above the horizon. I pulled on my boots and hurriedly strapped on my crampons. Five minutes after waking up, I was front-pointing away from the bivouac.

I carried no rope, no tent, or bivouac gear, no hardware save my ice axes. My plan was to go ultralight and ultrafast, to hit the summit and make it back down before the weather turned. Pushing myself, continually out of breath, I scurried up and to the left across small snowfields linked by narrow runnels of verglas and short rock bands. The climbing was almost fun—the rock was covered with large, in-cut holds, and the ice, though thin, never got steep enough to feel extreme—but I was anxious about the bands of clouds racing in from the Pacific, covering the sky.

In what seemed like no time (I didn't have a watch on the trip) I was on the distinctive final ice field. By now the sky was completely overcast. It looked easier to keep angling to the left, but quicker to go straight for the top. Paranoid about being caught by a storm high on the peak without any kind of shelter, I opted for the direct route. The ice steepened, then steepened some more, and as it did so it grew thin. I swung my left ice ax and struck rock. I aimed for another spot, and once again it glanced off unyielding diorite with a dull, sickening clank. And again, and again: It was a reprise of my first attempt on the north face. Looking between my legs, I stole a glance at the glacier, more than two thousand feet below. My stomach churned. I felt my poise slipping away like smoke in the wind.

Forty-five feet above the wall eased back onto the sloping summit shoulder. Forty-five more feet, half the distance between third base and home plate, and the mountain would be mine. I clung stiffly to my axes, unmoving, paralyzed with fear and indecision. I looked down at the dizzying drop to the glacier again, then up, then scraped away the film of ice above my head. I hooked the pick of my left ax on a nickel-thin lip of rock, and weighted it. It held. I pulled my right ax from the ice, reached up, and twisted the pick into a crooked half-inch crack until it jammed. Barely breathing now, I moved my feet up, scrabbling my crampon points across the verglas. Reaching as high as I could with my left arm, I swung the ax gently at the shiny, opaque surface, not knowing what I'd hit beneath it. The pick went in with a heartening *THUNK!* A few minutes later I was standing on a broad, rounded ledge. The summit proper, a series of slender fins sprouting a grotesque meringue of atmospheric ice, stood twenty feet directly above.

The insubstantial frost feathers ensured that those last twenty feet remained hard, scary, onerous. But then, suddenly, there was no place higher to go. It wasn't possible, I couldn't believe it. I felt my cracked lips stretch into a huge, painful grin. I was on top of the Devils Thumb.

Fittingly, the summit was a surreal, malevolent place, an improbably slender fan of rock and rime no wider than a filing cabinet. It did not encourage loitering. As I straddled the highest point, the north face fell away beneath my left boot for six thousand feet beneath my right boot the south face dropped off for twenty-five hundred. I took some pictures to prove I'd been there, and spent a few minutes trying to straighten a bent pick. Then I stood up, carefully turned around, and headed for home.

Five days later I was camped in the rain beside the sea, marveling at the sight of moss, willows, mosquitoes. Two days after that, a small skiff motored into Thomas Bay and pulled up on the beach not far from my tent. The man driving the boat introduced himself as Jim Freeman, a timber faller from Petersburg. It was his day off, he said, and he'd made the trip to show his family the glacier, and to look for bears. He asked me if I'd "been huntin', or what?"

"No," I replied sheepishly. "Actually, I just climbed the Devils Thumb. I've been over here for twenty days."

Freeman kept fiddling with a cleat on the boat, and didn't say anything for a while. Then he looked at me real hard and spat, "You wouldn't be givin' me double talk now, wouldja, friend?" Taken aback, I stammered out a denial. Freeman, it was obvious, didn't believe me for a minute. Nor did he seem wild about my snarled shoulder-length hair or the way I smelled. When I asked if he could give me a lift back to town, however, he offered a grudging, "I don't see why not."

The water was choppy, and the ride across Frederick Sound took two hours. The more we talked, the more Freeman warmed up. He still didn't believe I'd climbed the Thumb, but by the time he steered the skiff into Wrangell Narrows he pretended to. When we got off the boat, he insisted on buying me a cheeseburger. That night he even let me sleep in a derelict step-van parked in his backyard.

I lay down in the rear of the old truck for a while but couldn't sleep, so I got up and walked to a bar called Kito's Kave. The euphoria, the overwhelming sense of relief, that had initially accompanied my return to Petersburg faded, and an unexpected melancholy took its place. The people I chatted with in Kito's didn't seem to doubt that I'd been to the top of the Thumb, they just didn't much care. As the night wore on the place emptied except for me and an Indian at a back table. I drank alone, putting quarters in the jukebox, playing the same five songs over and over, until the barmaid yelled angrily, "Hey! Give it a fucking rest, kid! If I hear 'Fifty Ways to Lose Your Lover' one more time, *I'm* gonna be the one who loses it." I mumbled an apology, quickly headed for the door, and lurched back to Freeman's step-van. There, surrounded by the sweet scent of old motor oil, I lay down on the floorboards next to a gutted transmission and passed out.

It is easy, when you are young, to believe that what you desire is no less than what you deserve, to assume that if you want something badly enough it is your God-given right to have it. Less than a month after sitting on the summit of the Thumb I was back in Boulder, nailing up siding on the Spruce Street Townhouses, the same condos I'd been framing when I left for Alaska. I got a raise, to four dollars an hour, and at the end of the summer moved out of the job-site trailer to a studio apartment on West Pearl, but little else in my life seemed to change. Somehow, it didn't add up to the glorious transformation I'd imagined in April.

Climbing the Devils Thumb, however, had nudged me a little further away from the obdurate innocence of childhood. It taught me something about what mountains can and can't do, about the limits of dreams. I didn't recognize that at the time, of course, but I'm grateful for it now.

Krakauer learned some valuable lessons risking his life on the Devils Thumb. Alaska seems to be full of those lessons, and will share them with people whether they want the experience or not, as the couple in our next story learn.

NEARLY TOO LATE

Larry Kaniut

From *Danger Stalks the Land*

Denise Harris and Roger Lewis thought they were going to have a once-in-a-lifetime wilderness adventure—collecting ore samples in a gold mine near Nuka Bay. But when their supplies ran low, and they tried to leave by boat in December, their problems were just beginning.

DENISE HARRIS WAS WORKING at the park chalet in Glacier National Park when she met Roger Lewis. They shared outdoor interests. She had worked with the U.S. Forest Service and he with the National Park Service. They became better acquainted and decided Alaska offered a challenge that was worthy of their attention. They might even have an adventure in the Great Land.

In the spring of 1979 they headed north. They gravitated to Seward, Alaska, where Jack Cogland offered them a job collecting ore samples at his gold mine. They accepted and were flown to Nuka Bay, fifty miles from Seward. The couple took a stray husky-shepherd pup that they named Nuka. John Kenney, a powder man, went along and settled three miles away in a trailer.

On October 31st they arrived at the remote mine site on the Gulf of Alaska side of the Kenai Peninsula.

After collecting samples in Surprise Bay for two months, they realized they were running low on food. One night John invited them to dinner, but they were unable to conquer the thickening ice in the bay to get to his quarters.

They'd had no contact with the outside world. No plane was scheduled to pick them up. Their concerns mounted. Denise and Roger didn't think anyone knew they were out there and were pretty sure no one would be looking for them.

After five days of fighting the ice and realizing their food was nearly gone, the couple decided to leave. They planned to paddle to Portlock, the closest town/logging camp, seventy-five rugged, cliff-hugging miles away by boat. They would load up and leave on December the eighteenth.

That morning the couple left an undated note for John, expressing hope of reaching Portlock or Seldovia by Christmas. They loaded their camp supplies, food, and a .30-30 rifle aboard their two-person Folbot, a collapsible kayak. Next they stowed Nuka. Then they got aboard and, with three inches of freeboard, waddled away from Surprise Bay.

The next day they pulled onto a beach and awaited better weather.

They renewed their journey on the twentieth and paddled steadily, encountering fair to heavy seas. They paddled on and on, hoping to stay afloat and endure the grueling voyage.

Nearing Gore Point at dawn on the twenty-second, they encountered eight-to-ten-foot seas, a howling wind, and riptides. This thin strip of land jutting/slicing into the Gulf of Alaska is home to some of Alaska's fiercest weather. Like much of the gulf coast, the steep cliffs offer little shelter from the elements.

Since continuing on would invite disaster, they landed a quarter mile from Gore Point. Halfway between Surprise Bay and Portlock, they established a camp at the foot of the cliffs 150 yards from the ocean. They were amazed as thirty-to-forty-foot waves hammered the beach.

During the day they moved their kayak farther from the water, then returned to their tent to wait out the storm. Early in the afternoon Roger looked from the tent and saw waves pummeling the beach only eight feet away. Their very survival depended on getting to higher ground.

Denise and Roger flew into action, dismantling the tent and jamming their sleeping bags into stuff sacks before scampering fifteen feet higher up a trough. They sheltered under a cliff in a cavelike opening with rain dropping through a hole above.

Roger placed a foam pad beneath them, wrapped blankets about them, and they huddled together. They kept vigil on their tent, packs, and gear on the beach below. They prayed. As rain continued to fall, Roger elected to cover the opening in the ceiling. He dropped down to the beach to get a piece of plastic from the pack.

Instantly he found himself swimming. He'd been swallowed by a giant wave. Struggling to stay afloat and gagging on salt water, he swam to Denise. He shoved her up through the hole and yelled, "Get out of here."

Roger chucked blankets up to Denise and pulled himself up to her. He was soaked from head to foot; and they had no fire or shelter. Fearing hypothermia, they spread the pad, lay down on it, pulled the wet wool blanket over them, and tugged the plastic over the top as a shield from the rain. They cuddled together.

It was difficult to breathe so Roger made a small hole. They spent a cold, wet night shivering.

The following morning two cold, stiff people emerged from their cocoon. During the night the waves had receded fifty to sixty feet. They saw half of the Folbot below. Along with the other half, the sea had robbed them of flares, a mirror, and binoculars.

Although they'd lost signaling devices, they still had their food pack (dry soup, rice, and beans); gas stove and a quart of fuel; the rifle and five bullets; clothing in the form of pants, sweaters, sweatpants, down and wool hats; wool blankets; and their tent. Their sleeping bags remained, but they were useless balls of ice.

Without the kayak, their only way out was on foot. They knew the country between them and Portlock was punctuated by steep cliffs and an icy, rock-covered shore (there was no such thing as beach as we perceive it). John had told Roger of a logging road coming into Port Dick, a bay just west of their location on Gore Point. Maybe they could find the road to reach Portlock or Seldovia.

The rock-covered and ice-swathed landscape was devoid of any trace of wood. They desperately needed to find other shelter.

Their only escape route was a snow-covered, steep hill behind them. It seemed insurmountable. They inched their way up the slope. At last, the couple pitched their tent on a thirty-degree slope, bathed in spraying mist from the pounding surf below. Nuka was unable to climb the cliff and they were forced to leave her below. Denise and Roger were happy at daylight the next morning when Nuka bounded into camp.

Their new home provided them with shelter and time to reflect. They rested and planned for four days. Their daily ritual included mixing snow and dried soup, allowing it to soak. Each night they started the camp stove to heat their soup lukewarm. They also tried to dry their socks (holding them over the heat). To save fuel they only used the stove five minutes. That five minutes provided them the only external heat they enjoyed. They cherished and looked forward to that time of the day.

Early in their misadventure their toes began freezing. Because they were unaware of the danger of thawing frozen flesh, they continued trying to warm their feet. They cut their space blanket into bootie-pouches for their feet. They also made mittens of their blanket.

On the twenty-seventh Roger's hopes rose when he saw a wolf. A good omen, it represented food and a way out. Roger reasoned if the wolf reached them, they could follow its trail off the beach to safety. Raising the rifle to his shoulder and aiming behind the wolf's shoulder, Roger fired. At the crack of the rifle, the wolf bolted. Roger had only wounded it.

Following the wolf, Roger waded through tide pools. A dilemma confronted the man as he pursued the animal. The tide was coming in, and he didn't want to use another bullet to shoot the animal. Afraid of losing the wolf, Roger rushed back to the tent for his sheetrock ax and knife.

When he returned, the wolf was very much alive. Roger threw rocks until he hit the wolf and it turned its head. Then Roger rushed in and hit the animal with his ax. He held the wolf underwater for two minutes until he was sure it was dead.

The young male wolf weighed no more than sixty pounds, nevertheless it was food. Roger skinned the wolf and took the hindquarter to the tent. He seasoned and fried it until it was brown. They ate what they wanted, and Denise stored the remainder in a jar.

They had seen no search planes. In their weakened and worsening physical condition, convinced that their rescue depended upon them, the couple decided to travel inland over the wolf's trail on the twenty-eighth.

Before leaving, they divided their gear. Denise carried the pack with their food, matches, stove, foam pad, and tent. Roger took the duffel bag with blankets, maps, compass, rifle, wolf hide, and Swede saw.

Their first obstacle was a steep hill thirty yards high.

Denise was wearing knee-length rubber boots, which provided little warmth and were very slippery. As she struggled up the slope, she slipped and fell. She lost her grip on the small pack, and it started tumbling away from her.

Roger ran to recover the bouncing pack. Before he could reach it, the pack took a final bounce off the boulders and plummeted straight down into the ocean.

It was all Roger could do to keep from diving in after it. He reasoned, however, that he would probably not be able to get back to shore even if he got the pack; and even if he did, he'd be soaked again. It was gone— and with it they lost their food, matches, stove, blanket, mattress pad, and tent.

Standing around feeling sorry for themselves would help none. They started up 1,400-foot Gore Peak, slogging upward one step at a time.

The cliffs ahead became even steeper. In a tight spot while gripping a ledge by two fingers, Roger lost control and fell. Thirty feet below he started sliding. Gaining speed, he rocketed toward a precipice that dropped fifty feet to the rocks below. Charged by his will to live and determination not to leave Denise behind, he spun onto his back, dug his heels into the snow, and ground to a stop.

After carefully inspecting his body, he crawled back to Denise. It was a joyful reunion.

From there they worked their way along a cliff all day—travel, rest twenty minutes, move on.

At nightfall they stopped and propped themselves against the steep, timbered slope.

With their remaining mattress pad under them and a blanket over them, they tried to sleep. But there was no sleep. They were wet. They were hungry. They were in too much pain. They removed their boots, noting that their feet continued swelling, sloughing, and turning purple.

Denise used the wolf pelt for a foot covering; Roger used his space-blanket booties and two pairs of socks (which he alternated from his feet to his body trying to keep one pair dry).

The next day was another test of their wills. They encountered hip-deep snow. They'd take a step and fall through . . . sometimes four to five feet. They'd done about all anyone could to survive.

That night they camped under a scrub spruce tree. They dug snow from around its base. Roger cut boughs with the saw to be used as bedding and a windbreak.

They repeated their nightly ritual: removing their boots and placing their feet against Nuka's fur as she lay down.

The temperature dropped to minus ten degrees that night.

The following day they descended Gore Peak and camped on a snow-less, driftwood-laden beach. Since they had no matches, they had no fire! A cold, miserable night kept them company.

The next day Roger and Denise walked but a quarter of a mile before encountering a waterside cliff. Their only course was a frozen waterfall fifty yards high and four inches thick at the base.

With the duffel bag slung from his wrist and his belt knife in hand, Roger chiseled footholds, one by one.

It took them until 1 P.M. to cover a hundred feet. As it warmed up after noon, the sun melted the ice surface. The higher they went, the thinner the ice became.

The going was very slick. Near the top Roger sought a stable spot. As he inched toward a bush twenty feet away, he heard, then saw, Denise fall, sliding and bouncing all the way to the beach a hundred feet below.

Denise examined herself. Aside from a scratched hip she was all right. However Denise didn't think she could get back up to Roger. He told her she'd have to—that he couldn't come to her.

She pleaded with him to come down to her; but he refused. He kept working toward the bush, exhorting her to climb back up.

Reluctantly Denise began climbing. She had covered half the distance to him when she slipped and fell again down the same path.

This time she was determined to stay where she was. She yelled to Roger to toss her clothes down. She decided to return to their last camp-site and die on the beach.

He refused to respond to her request.

Half an hour passed. Would she try again? Would Roger help her? Finally she started up again. It was more painstaking than ever. She had lost her mitts. She slowly removed ice from a hole and eased upward one hole at a time. Her hands throbbed, but she had no other prospect. Roger urged her on.

Nuka could not climb the ice and went off seeking a different route.

At last Denise was nearing Roger. He extended his hand in joy and re-lief and guided her to safety. They set up camp for the night. Nuka barked from the distance and wolves howled off and on till daylight. They feared the wolves would kill Nuka.

The next morning they marveled when they heard Nuka bark. Nuka not only survived the night but also found a route to them.

After that the days blurred together. Theirs was a continuous struggle physically. Barriers confronted them—mostly steep ground and ice-covered cliffs. Still Takoma Cove, Sunday Bay, and Taylor Bay lay ahead. The mental anguish also took its toll. The geography, the weather, and their condition eroded their hope for survival.

Their toes and feet turned black with frostbite. The most they slept was twenty minutes. Then they awoke in agony and prayed.

Roger's color left him. He looked lifeless, as though he were dying. They were too weak to talk normally; their conversation was slow, quiet verbalization.

Roger figured nobody would find them before it was too late. Unbe-lievably, it had been two months since they'd seen another human being. They had seen no search planes. After a week without food they talked about shooting the dog and themselves.

But Denise's determination to see her mother again gave birth to her reasoning, "I'm going to get out of here if I have to crawl all the way."

Roger was shamed by his lack of determination compared to Denise's. He resolved to go on, but his faith was gone.

Some days Roger cut handholds in the ice with his buck knife and progressed a mere fifty feet. Their best day yielded two miles, but their average was a half mile a day. They encountered seven-foot drifts and howling wind, yet miraculously continued on.

At night Roger slept with his arms crossed over his chest and his hands inside his clothes. Denise slept curled up with her back to his.

Some mornings they awakened covered by frozen ocean spray caked to their bedding. They had trouble getting out of bed in the mornings. Cramped and cold, they fought their aching joints, hands, and feet. Often it felt as if their bodies were on fire and they hurt all over. Supreme willpower was needed to force frozen feet into cold, hard, and sometimes snow-covered boots.

After the grueling task of leaving the bed, they slowly repacked the saw, rifle, and bedding into the duffel bag and lurched on till darkness fell.

By the eighth of January they'd gone without food for a week. As a last resort Roger decided to kill Nuka for food. Denise agreed. He did not want to use a bullet and decided to use his knife. Roger called the dog. Nuka wagged her tail while he felt for her heart. Then he jabbed the knife into her chest.

Although Roger's knife broke, Nuka died. The couple skinned and gutted the dog, saving the skin to use as a foot cover. Roger took a bite of the heart, assuming the meat would provide him energy.

He gagged on the raw meat. He couldn't deal with having killed their canine companion and went off to be by himself.

Denise quietly cut off the dog's hindquarter meat and placed it in a plastic jar. She then carried the dog's remains to the surf.

Later the couple ate part of the dog and felt stronger.

By this time Denise had dark circles under her eyes. Dark frostbite splotches covered her hands. Her normal 125-pound, five-foot-six-inch frame was now reduced to a hundred pounds. Her curly, long auburn hair was matted and dirty. This twenty-year-old wondered if she'd ever see civilization again.

Meanwhile thirty-one-year-old Roger had lost thirty-five pounds from his normal 170 pounds. His five-foot-ten-inch frame was stooped.

His brown hair was browner and his blue eyes hollow. Surely his former Marine and police experience had helped them get this far.

The ninth of January dawned clear and cold. Eagles wheeled overhead. Wolves howled in the distance.

Roger looked toward Taylor Bay. As much as he wanted to focus on the job at hand, his constant pain made it difficult. He saw sheer cliffs to the water's edge. There was no way they could walk the beach. While contemplating their physical agony and the mental anguish, Roger heard, then saw, a Coast Guard helicopter.

It flew over them less than 150 feet away. His joy and excitement was shortlived, as it clattered on by. Emotionally it was worse having it go by than if he hadn't seen it at all. It was 4 P.M. Dusk fell. And with it fell his hopes.

For nineteen days they'd struggled. They'd fought steep, icy walls, roaring seas, and wind. They'd struggled through deep snow. Their stomachs pinched their spines in hunger. They'd endured the frigid fingers of frost. They'd battled mental torment.

He wouldn't quit now!

As hurriedly as he could, Roger put together the saw. He cut spruce boughs and placed three letters in the snow ten feet across . . . SOS. It was grueling work in the deep snow. But he did not quit.

He tied a red sweatshirt on a fifteen-foot pole and jammed it in the middle of the O. At that moment he saw a plane fly over. It was a Grumman Widgeon. His duffel bag was twenty feet away. Roger hobbled to it for the rifle. He fired three times into air and fell backward, wanting to keep his eyes on the plane. The pilot tipped a wing toward Roger.

Roger shouted to Denise that they'd been found. The plane circled and climbed higher. The Widgeon's lights blinked. Periodically the plane flew out of sight but returned. Denise and Roger's anxiety grew as they wondered why the pilot didn't signal them. They wondered if they had, in fact, been spotted.

Cold and discouraged, Roger suggested they crawl under the cover to get warm. Denise refused, saying she wouldn't until the plane left or did something.

Roger reasoned the pilot wouldn't waste fuel flying in circles unless he had spotted them.

For an hour and a half the plane circled.

Distant purring grew louder until Roger realized and shouted to Denise that a helicopter was coming for them. The chopper came in straight and low, almost in slow motion, blades fanning the water and churning snow and branches, lights flashing. The light from a huge spotlight snaked along the landscape until it focused on them.

The helicopter hovered above them as a basket lowered earthward. Both tried to get into it. By quickly hoisting the basket, the rescuers signaled that they wanted one at a time to climb aboard.

Roger got into the basket and was lifted up. He could not conceal his joy as he hugged and kissed the state trooper on board.

Before the crew could attempt to rescue Denise, they needed to burn off extra fuel and lighten the load. As they circled, Denise's first reaction was that they were leaving her to die. She didn't know what to do and started crying.

Finally the helicopter picked her up. She was as excited and thankful as Roger had been. She grabbed a coastguardsman, hugged him, and repeatedly said, "Thank you."

Later they met their rescuer, Bill DeCreeft (Kachemak Air Service), to express their gratitude. Roger and Denise spent over a month in the Homer hospital. During this time they lost some of their toes. They felt it was a small loss compared to having their lives and each other. While in the hospital they began making plans to be married. A perfect ending to their miracle journey!

Denise and Roger were fortunate—although they made some mistakes (such as trying to thaw their frozen feet, as restoring blood circulation can cause intense pain, making it difficult to walk), they did everything they could to keep moving and survive. Above all, Denise's determination to live after she had climbed the ice cliff was stunning to see—typically people do not gain a determination to live in the midst of such hardship, so her resilience in the face of such suffering was an incredible feat of willpower.

ALONE AT THE SUMMIT
Stephen Venables (1954–)

From *Everest: Alone at the Summit*

—————————

I'm not sure whether the year 1954 holds some kind of mystical connection for mountain-climber writers (Jon Krakauer was also born in the same year), but it certainly didn't hurt the last portion of this book. I am pleased to be able to present an excerpt from British climber and writer Stephen Venables's book about reaching the summit of Mount Everest by himself in 1988, after the other members of his party had stopped for various reasons. His ten minutes at the top pales in comparison to the sixteen-hour climb from their camp to reach the summit, and now he is faced with an even more difficult trek—coming back down as night is falling fast.

I ALLOWED MYSELF TEN MINUTES on the summit. Now, writing three months later, I find it almost impossible to recall the emotions of those precious moments. Even at the time, I found it hard to know exactly what I was feeling. There was a dreamlike sense of disbelief at being in this special place, sitting so utterly alone beside the three yellow French oxygen cylinders, which the Asian expedition had left upright in the snow. The empty cylinders were labelled CNJ for China-Nepal-Japan and were decorated with the prayer flags that I had mistaken for hats. The cylinders and bits of discarded radio equipment were the only signs that people had ever been here. When I could find the strength to stand up again I looked down the West Ridge, which disappeared into swirling clouds. There was no sign of the British Services Expedition. Then I turned to the right, where the Northeast Ridge—the Mallory Route— also dropped away into the clouds. I could not see the Rongbuk Glacier, nor the Kama valley and to the south there were yet more clouds, completely hiding Lhotse from view. It was like being alone on the apex of some huge gray roof. At this point on the ridge the ground drops away slightly to the giant cornices overhanging the Kangshung Face, so that one can keep well clear of danger, yet stand right on the crest of the ridge, on a real unequivocal summit.

I had work to do. First I had to photograph myself. I took off the camera belt, removed the big camera, cocked the self-timer, and, gasping with the effort, knelt down to prop it on its case about three meters from the summit. I was too tired to lie right down and frame the picture in the viewfinder, so I just put the zoom on wide-angle and pointed it in the general direction of the summit. Then, as the self-timer whirred, I stepped back up and sat by the ornamental oxygen bottles. I thought that I heard the shutter click. I knew that I should take more frames, bracketing the exposures for safety, but I did not have the mental or physical energy to reset the camera.

Robert had the summit flags and trinkets from Norbu, but there was one small ritual for me to carry out. I reached into one of my inside pockets and pulled out a tiny polythene bag. Inside it were the two miniature envelopes given to me in Bombay by Nawang and Sonam. I carefully took out the flower petals and scattered them in the snow, then placed the two envelopes beside the oxygen bottles. Then, panting with the effort of concentration, I took two pictures on the compact camera.

The film in the SLR with the self-portrait was either not wound on properly or was lost on the journey home, for I was never to see the photo of myself on the summit. However, I do have a picture showing the little envelopes. Each envelope is decorated with the face of one of the teachers at Geeta's ashram in Pondicherri, staring up from among the radio boxes, yellow cylinders, and wisps of prayer flag on the summit of Everest.

I rested again, slumped in the snow. The air temperature in this second week of May had been getting steadily warmer and even at 8,848 meters there was still very little wind. I felt comfortable and I was almost tempted to linger, for I was aware that this was a terribly important event in my life and I wanted to savor that precious moment, storing away what memories I could in my feeble oxygen-starved brain. It would be nice to say that it was the happiest moment of my life and that I was overwhelmed by euphoria, but that would be a gross exaggeration, for at the time there was only a rather dazed feeling of—"Isn't this strange? You really have done it, after all those weeks of watching and waiting and worrying. It would have been better if everyone had made it but at least someone has actually reached the summit—and a rather special summit. . . . So this is what it's like."

It was a turning point. Even in my befuddled state I knew that this would inevitably alter my life. But I also knew that it was far more urgently critical as a turning point in the climb, the point where I no longer had to struggle upward but had to start down immediately fleeing from this bewitching dreamlike place and hurrying back down to Earth before it was too late. It was now 3:50 P.M., Nepalese time. I was just ahead of schedule, but the clouds were closing in fast and in three hours it would be dark. I stood up, took the ice ax in my mittened hand, had one last look down Mallory's ridge, then hurried away back south.

After descending a short way I stopped for my final summit task. Just below the top there was an exposed outcrop of shattered rock where I knelt down to collect some pieces of limestone and stuff them in a pocket.

The wind was mounting now, starting to blow spindrift in my face. I hurried on, using gravity to speed myself back toward the Hillary Step. As I came over the last hump the clouds enveloped me completely. Suddenly I realized that I was heading too far to the right, down toward the Southwest Face. I headed back up to the left, peering through my iced-up sunglasses at the swirling grayness. I was utterly alone in the cloud and there was no sign of the South Summit. I felt disorientated and frightened, remembering the tragedy of 1975 when Mick Burke, the last person to complete the Southwest Face, went alone to the summit and never came back. Somewhere up here, in conditions like this, blinded behind iced glasses, even more myopic than I was, he had made an unlucky mistake, probably falling through one of those fragile cornices overhanging the Kangshung Face. I suddenly noticed the dim outline of one of those bulbous overhangs just in front of me and veered back right. For God's sake don't do a Mick Burke. Just concentrate. You've gone too far left now. Head for that rock—must be solid ground there. Now I could pick out some tracks—my tracks almost filled with spindrift already, but tracks nonetheless. This is right. But it's so difficult. Must have a rest. I sank down and sat in the snow. Then I continued wearily, too slowly, legs sagging, head bowed. I stopped after only a few paces but forced myself not to sit down, leaning instead on my ice ax. Then I took a few steps again, willing my legs not to sag and crumple.

It was snowing now, stinging my face and encrusting my glasses. I had to wipe them with a clumsy mitten, clearing a hole to peer through, searching for landmarks. I recognized clumps of rock and followed them to the pinnacle above the Hillary Step. Then came the hard part, taking off mittens, pulling up some slack in the fixed rope and clipping it into my waist belt carabiner with an Italian hitch. I pulled mittens back on and started to abseil down the cliff. Even though I was moving downhill it was exhausting. Possibly the waist belt was pulling up and constricting my diaphragm, for I had to slump and rest during the twenty-meter abseil, gasping for breath. I continued in a frantic blind struggle to the bottom of the Step where I fell over and collapsed on the side of the ridge, hyperventilating furiously.

It had never happened before and I was terrified. This was quite new—this ultra-rapid panting, like a fish out of water incapable of getting oxygen into its gills. I panted harder and harder, clutching at the air, frantic to refill my lungs. But nothing seemed to get beyond my throat and for a ghastly moment I thought that I was going to suffocate. Then the air started to get through, and I gasped great sobs of relief as my breathing slowed to normal again.

I had to move. Get off that rope and continue. Take mittens off and unclip from the rope. Now, quickly get those mittens back on again. The first one is always easy but the second one won't go. I can't grip it—can't make those useless numb fingers work. It's all too difficult, I'll never get it on and my fingers will freeze solid. No more piano playing. But I must get that mitten on or I'll never get down. Concentrate. That's it, ease it up the wrist.

I slumped over again, gasping with exhaustion. The wind was flinging snow at me and I was starting to shiver. I was completely blind and tore at my sunglasses, letting them hang down around my neck by their safety leash. At least I could see a little now, only blurred shapes, but better than nothing. There's a bit of a clearing. That's the South Summit up there on the far side of the bridge. No sign of Robert or Ed. They must have gone down by now. Crazy to continue to the top in these conditions and no reason to wait for me. There's no one to help me. Either I get myself down or I die. It would be so easy to die—just lie down here and rest and soon the wind would kill me. It would be the easiest thing in the world but I'd look so bloody silly. No use to anyone climbing Everest then lying down to die. No, pull yourself together and move. It's not possible to get out the other pair of glasses without taking off mittens again, so we'll just have to move very carefully on half vision.

My invisible companion, the old man, had reappeared and together we moved forward, determined not to die. We stumbled half-blind along the ridge, crouched over the ice ax, peering anxiously through the driving snow, almost on all fours, laboriously dragging ourselves across the rocks, clinging carefully to avoid the death slide down the Southwest Face. Fear and instinct kept me moving over the rocks. Then I recognized the dry hollow by the overhanging rock where Boardman and Pertemba had waited in vain for Mick Burke to return. I wondered briefly whether I should bivouac there, but decided to continue, determined to get right back across the bridge to the South Summit. That was the critical point beyond which I was confident that I could survive.

The visibility was still atrocious and I strayed too close to the crest on the left. Suddenly my left leg shot down into a hole and I collapsed in another fit of hyperventilation. I may have trodden on the cornice fracture line, but I think it was just a deep snowdrift. Whatever it was, the jolt almost suffocated me; but I regained my breath and forced myself on up the fifteen-meter climb to the South Summit. I collapsed again and this time, as I regained my breath in great anguished gasps, I was filled with pity for the poor old man who was finding it all a bit too much.

We floundered eventually up to the crest of the South Summit where my mind must have gone almost blank, for I can only recall blurred images of snow and cloud and the gloom of dusk. I can remember nothing of the descent of the knife-edge ridge, I only have the vaguest recollection of slithering back over the *bergschrund* and then I was back on the big snow-slope, sitting down to slide, because it is easier to sit than to stand.

We were racing the darkness, using gravity to hurry down toward the safety of the South Col. But even sliding is hard work, because you have to brace your legs and brake with your ice ax. It was somewhere down here that Peter Habeler, during his phenomenal one-hour descent from the summit to the South Col, spurred on by his fear of permanent brain damage, almost flew out of control down the Kangshung Face. I was anxious about the big slope below me and kept stopping to walk further right toward the ridge. Then on one slide the old man became very frightened. We were gathering speed in a blinding flurry of powder snow. The surface underneath felt hollow and unstable and seemed to be breaking off in avalanches. We were sliding faster and faster down to the east and the old man was hating it. He had suddenly become a musician. Musicians hate this. The composer is sliding on his cello, riding the avalanche to his death. Please stop! Now!

I dug my heels in and leaned over hard on my ice ax, dragging the ferrule deep into the snow, and came to a halt. We were about to collapse and had to rest as soon as possible, but we could not sit down here. Too steep and insecure. Quick, cut a ledge. Ice ax and burrowing hand—that's it. Quick. Just enough of a hollow to sit down. Must rest. Must have a pee. The old man says do it in your pants—it'll keep you warm.

I could wait no longer and with one last frantic effort I plunged the ice ax deep into the snow and used it to heave myself up onto the ledge. Then my strength gave out and I collapsed, wetting myself and suffocating in another fit of hyperventilation.

Poor old man . . . that's better now, he's breathing again. He just needs to rest. What was all that business about music—cello music? What has that got to do with avalanches? Who is this composer? Dvorak wrote a cello concerto. Kate plays the cello—but she's a woman. It's all too confusing. Better to concentrate on reality—on me sitting here on this precarious ledge in the snow. And why did I believe that nonsense about peeing in my pants? All wet now. It must have been the shock.

I was getting chronically exhausted and it was now virtually dark so I decided to stay where I was. I sat there for about an hour, shivering as the cold pressed through from the snow. Then I decided that my precarious perch was too dangerous and that I should try to continue down to the South Col where Ed and Robert would be waiting in the tents. I lowered myself to my feet, faced into the slope and started kicking steps carefully across the snow, back toward the crest of the ridge. There I tried to orientate myself, climbing backward and forward over the rocks, trying to recognize individual outcrops from the morning. But it was dark, there was no moon and, although the afternoon storm had blown over, there were still drifting clouds to confuse my vision. Even after putting on glasses and switching on my headtorch, I found it very difficult to judge shapes and distances. I started to worry that perhaps my glissade had taken me lower than I thought and that I was now below the point where I had to turn right into the couloir.

After about half an hour of wandering about, the old man suggested that we should stop here for the night and wait for daylight to re-orientate ourselves. I decided that he would be warmest sitting on a rock and soon I found a ledge on the ridge where we could sit down. But it was precarious and sloping and we both longed to lean back properly, so we traversed back out onto the snow and dug a horizontal ledge where we could lie down properly. At about 9 P.M. we settled down for the night.

The emergency bivouac had many precedents. During the American traverse of Everest in 1963 Willi Unsoeld and Tom Hornbein completed the first ascent of the West Ridge, reaching the summit just before dark at 6:15. Two companions had reached the summit by the normal route the same afternoon and were waiting near the South Summit when Unsoeld and Hornbein started to descend the Southeast Ridge. When they met, Hornbein tried to persuade the other three to continue down to the top camp but they soon became lost in the dark and had to resign themselves to a night out in the open at about 8,500 meters. They survived the intense cold and descended safely the next day, but afterward Unsoeld had to have nine frostbitten toes amputated and one of the Southeast Ridge duo, Barry Bishop, lost all his toes.

In 1976 two British soldiers, Bronco Lane and Brummie Stokes, were also forced to bivouac on the same slope just below the South Summit, descending in bad weather. Twelve years later in Kathmandu, Stokes was to show me his mutilated toeless feet. Lane had to have fingers as well as toes amputated, but at least both of them were alive, unlike the German climber, Hannelore Schmatz, who in 1979 insisted on stopping to bivouac before dark, even though her Sherpas were urging her to carry on down to the safety of their top camp. She died sitting in the snow and for several years her frozen body was a grisly landmark on the Southeast ridge, until it was recently buried or swept away by an avalanche. I also knew about the Bulgarian climber who had died while descending the difficult West Ridge in 1984. Meena Agrawal, who had been doctor to another Everest expedition that year, had later told me how she had talked to the Bulgarian on the radio, trying to comfort him and persuade him to live through the night; but eventually the man had been unable to hold up the receiver any longer and had presumably died soon afterward.

I had no intention of dying that night. I was alone just above 8,500 meters (about 28,000 feet) but the wind, which had frightened me so much by the Hillary Step had now died away and the air temperature was probably not much lower than minus twenty degrees centigrade. I was lucky with the conditions and I knew that I could survive in the excellent clothes I wore, but I had to resign myself to the probable loss of toes. Six months earlier, caught out high on Shisha Pangma, Luke and I had dug a snowhole and crawled inside to take off boots and warm each other's toes. But now I was nearly 1,000 meters higher, I was alone and I barely had the strength to cut a ledge, let alone a proper cave where I could safely take off boots. I had climbed with the specific intention of not bivouacking, so I had no stove to melt snow. Only a trickle of half-frozen juice remained in my water bottle and in the last twenty-four hours I had drunk less than a liter. Dehydration was thickening my blood, already viscous with the concentration of red blood cells necessary to survive at altitude, and circulation was sluggish to the remote outposts of the vascular system, particularly my toes.

If the weather had been worse, I would probably have found new reserves of strength, either to dig a snowhole or to search harder for the correct descent route. But as the air was calm I lay inert, huddled up in the snow with my spare mittens providing meager insulation under my hips and my ice ax plunged into the slope in front of me, like a retaining fence post.

I was not really alone. The old man was still with me and now there were other people as well, crowding my tiny ledge. Sometimes they offered to look after parts of my body. At one stage during the long night the old man became rather patronizing toward a girl who was keeping one of my hands warm. Perhaps it was then that Eric Shipton, the distinguished explorer so closely involved with the history of Everest, took over warming my hands. At the end of the ledge my feet kept nearly falling off where I had failed to dig a thorough hollow in the snow. I was aware of several people crowding out the feet, but also trying to look after them. They were being organized by Mike Scott.

I had never met Mike Scott but I knew his father, Doug, who had bivouacked even higher than this, right up on the South Summit in 1975. He and Dougal Haston had been half-prepared for an emergency bivouac, carrying a tent sack and a stove. When they emerged from the Southwest Face late in the day, they had started digging a cave and had made a hot brew before climbing the final ridge to the summit. After photographing the magical sunset from the summit they returned to the snowcave where their oxygen ran out and they settled down for the highest bivouac ever. Scott had no down gear—only the tent sack and a rucksack to sit on, yet on that bitterly cold autumn night he had the strength not only to survive but to concentrate on "the quality of survival," warming and talking to his feet throughout the night. When he and Haston descended to the haven of Camp 6 the next day, neither of them had any frostbite.

I drifted in and out of reality, occasionally reminding myself that I was actually alone, before returning to my confused hallucinations. Toward dawn, as I started to long for warmth, my companions teased me by announcing that there were some yak herders camping just around the corner with tents and food and hot fires. They left me alone with the old man and went to investigate. It was good to be left in peace for a while and I reminded myself that yak herders could not possibly be living up here at 8,500 meters; but later the people returned to tell me that while the insidious cold of the snow had been creeping through my body they had been enjoying hot baths and food. Now I longed even more desperately to be warm.

At some stage during the night I stood up to enlarge my ledge. After that I felt slightly more comfortable and less precarious. Eventually I think that I must have slept, for I remember an actual awakening and sudden realization that the long night was finally over.

I sat up shivering. There was pastel light in the sky and only a soft blanket of gray cloud remained in the valley far below. All the people, even the old man, had gone but I had survived my night out. My body was stiff and my feet were dead, but my fingers were still alive inside their down mittens. The hairs on my eyebrows, moustache, and beard were stuck together with great lumps of ice and a frozen film encased my wooden nose. My iced sunglasses still hung useless around my neck, but my other glasses were clear, so that I could see the route down.

I could not believe that it had all seemed so strange in the dark, now that I could see the shoulder just below me, with the little dip where one had to turn right into the couloir. If only I had seen better in the dark I could perhaps have descended to Camp 3 and saved myself all that shivering!

The sun was rising over Kangchenjunga as I stood up shakily, picked up my ice ax and set off wobbling and sliding down the slope. Soon I was back in the couloir, daring myself to sit down and slide wherever possible. Once I went too fast and gave myself another alarming attack of hyperventilating, but after that I stayed in control. The world was sparkling in morning sunlight and life was wonderful. I was alive and warm again, I had climbed Everest and soon I would be back in the valley.

Suddenly I saw two people in the couloir, down by the Dunlop tent. It took a while for my dulled mind to realize that they must be Ed and Robert, who had also failed to reach the South Col in the dark and had taken shelter in the Asians' abandoned tent. They turned around and saw me sliding toward them and a few minutes later we were reunited. I cannot remember what we said. Only a few words were spoken and they were probably banal; but I remember vividly Ed and Robert's relief at seeing me alive and a deep warmth of friendship as the three of us roped together for the final descent to the South Col.

It takes a special kind of person to retain their sanity in conditions such as what Stephen Venables went through during his long night on Mount Everest. It is one thing to willingly put yourself in harm's way, knowing the risks and that you may not survive the adventure you're about to undertake.

But it's quite another thing to end up seriously injured in the middle of no-where, and have the mental and physical fortitude to stay alive until help can arrive. Our next story tells of such a man who did just that.

MIRACLE MAN

Larry Kaniut

From *Danger Stalks the Land*

I know of very few men who could survive what Gary Franklin went through after his plane crashed in the wilds of Alaska. His story is one that I will always remember as a testament to the power of the human condition and the will to stay alive, especially after the victim got back to civilization.

GARY FRANKLIN CALLED ME during the winter of 1993–1994 and wanted my help getting published. When I met him at a book signing at Loussac Library in Anchorage, he wore a clear plastic face mask with holes for nostrils, eyes, and mouth. His face was ruddy. As he extended his left hand, I noticed his right arm was crooked as if in a sling. I could not see his right hand and learned that it was sewn into his midsection to provide a warm, moist environment for his skin graft to heal.

He was recovering from third-degree burns over 52 percent of his body. He died six times in the hospital. He and his wife, Dorothy, eagerly shared their story with me in hopes we could find a publisher for a book about their incredible experience with death . . . and life.

Kaleidoscopic reds and yellows splashed the valley. Dark green tongues of black spruce licked up the sides of the Talkeetna Mountains from the valley floor, and golden-leafed aspen, birch, and willow bushes pockmarked the landscape.

The green Arctic Tern, tail numbers 64AT, lifted off the sandbar in the middle of the Talkeetna River and lumbered into the ominous sky. Pilot Gary Franklin had taken meticulous measures to lighten his plane because of the short takeoff distance.

Gary had been told the strip was 700 feet long; but on walking it he discovered the usable runway was only 550 feet in length. He opted to leave all his personal gear behind, found three metal gas cans, and drained as much fuel from the tanks as the containers would hold. Gary had considered his fuel weight and the length of the strip before determining he could safely get his plane off with him and his hunting buddy Scott Weber on board.

Just to be safe, Gary walked three-fourths of the distance down the sandbar and placed a stick to mark a go/no-go decision point on the strip—he would taxi for takeoff under full power to that point. If he didn't think the plane would lift off in the remaining distance, he would pull power and jump on the brakes to abort takeoff.

By 11 A.M. the rainstorm they'd waited to avoid had passed. It was now time to get back to Talkeetna. Scott crawled into the backseat of the tandem two-seater, and Gary took the front seat. With the plane pointing downstream, brakes on, carb heat off, mixture rich, and power at full throttle, Gary released the brakes. The plane bounced along the shore for a couple hundred feet, gaining speed. As the Tern reached and then passed the go/no-go point, Gary felt his speed was good enough to get them off.

At the end of the strip Gary pulled back on the stick and the airplane left the ground. The bush pilot's joy was complete—they were airborne. A few seconds later, however, the airplane settled back toward earth.

The Tern dropped, murky waters rising to meet it. The men had little time to think but hoped the bird would regain altitude. It was not to be. Almost instantly the Tern bounced off the water below, momentarily skipped skyward, then veered into the opposite three-foot, gravel cut bank, shearing its right landing gear. The Tern slammed onto the softball-sized rocks on the bar, striking the belly fuel tank. The tank exploded.

The plane skidded across the rough ground thirty feet before stopping in a ball of fire. The intense heat was unimaginable. Still inside the fuselage, the men were surrounded by flames. Gary threw his hands over his face and screamed. Seconds later he came to his senses, realizing he had to get out of the plane.

He reached for his seat belt and released it. He rolled from the plane and hit the ground rolling. Instantly he realized this maneuver would not work to douse the flames. He ran for the river and dived in headfirst. The cold water doused the fire and provided instant relief.

Rising from the water, Gary's immediate thoughts were of Scott. He looked back at the plane and saw it was totally engulfed in flames. He could not see Scott. Gary's heart died.

Then he saw Scott behind the plane, his clothes and body aflame. Gary ran to Scott and yelled, "Scott! Get into the water!"

Scott was in shock. He stood there with his head down staring at the ground and burning alive. Gary reached Scott, noticed a small puddle of water, and pushed Scott into it. Gary got on Scott's back and forced him down into the water. After Scott rose from the water, Gary determined the fire was out and Scott was more lucid . . . somewhat okay for the moment.

Gary then went back to the river and jumped in to feel the coolness of the water as it soothed his burned flesh.

The men took stock of their wounds while watching the plane burn like an inferno. Scott's hands began bleeding. His face and legs were the most greatly injured.

Gary felt his own skin begin to tighten on his arms, face, back, and chest.

The men discussed their situation. Gary suggested they try to reach a cabin four miles downriver, although Scott was a little leery. Both realized that Scott's injuries were much worse than they'd previously thought; worse than Gary's.

Just then the plane's fire ignited bullets from their rifles, and the men crossed the river to put distance between them and their wrecked plane. They became wet and started cooling off and sought comfort by retrieving clothes from their packs.

Gary told Scott that the soonest a rescue attempt would be made would be the following day. They decided to go to Scott's cabin.

They crossed the river three more times to reach shore, as the sandbar they'd taken off from was in the middle of the river. They reached the cabin and discovered it was locked, and the keys had been lost in the fire. Gary searched for a way into the cabin, ultimately deciding to break in.

Gary noticed Scott standing and shaking in the sunlight in front of the cabin trying to get warm. Realizing his pal was in deep shock, Gary asked Scott where the ax was. Scott told him it was in the shed near the cabin. The storage shed was also locked, and the only other way into it was to crawl under the cabin for twenty feet, drop three feet into the shed, and return the same way. Gary retrieved the ax and approached the front window.

Three-quarter-inch plywood covered the windows. Gary swung the ax at a section of plywood. The ax smashed into the wood, barely denting it due to the ax's dullness. Gary's hands cried out in pain. He looked at his hands for the first time and found the insides were nothing but blisters. The pain was so great that it almost brought him to his knees. He thought, *I cannot do this.*

Gary turned and saw Scott still standing in the sunlight shaking violently and realized, "I had no other choice." With the ax he started chopping at the window until he broke through.

Gary cleared the window, helped Scott inside the cabin, and laid him down in a sleeping bag on one of the bunk beds. Hoping to warm Scott, Gary started a fire in the stove. As he worked, he thought of the irony of having a fire nearly take their lives only to have to rely upon heat to keep them alive.

Gary wrapped Scott's hands in towels to retard the flow of blood. Recalling his survival training that a person in shock be given water, Gary gave Scott a drink every so often.

Four agonizing hours passed, then Scott started vomiting. Gary thought Scott was in bad shape. He decided to leave Scott to try to reach the downstream cabin. Scott wondered if Gary had the strength to make the trip, and Gary reassured him, "I think so. My legs feel good." Gary left around four in the afternoon.

The first mile and a half wasn't too bad. Although there was a fast current, the river was only midthigh-deep. Every hundred feet or so Gary crossed another ribbon of the stream. Two miles downstream, however, the river presented a drastically different face. Here the ribbons ran together to form one large, deep river.

Gary tried to cross the river but its depth and swiftness were too great. The water was at his armpits, and the current swept him downstream. He was halfway across, his clothes quickly became heavy, and in no time he was waterlogged.

He struggled to keep his head above water. At length he reached the far side and struggled onto the bank exhausted. Gary knew that he was in trouble—he was a long way from either cabin, and it was getting dark. Gary pondered his situation. The river was impassable in his condition. It was getting colder. He needed shelter and heat. There was great danger in continuing; but there was also great danger returning across the channel he'd just survived. He felt his only hope now was to retrace his steps to the cabin.

Gary struggled to reach the distant bank, which took nearly all his strength. He rested on the other side for a while before heading back to his pal. Gary was very weak.

When he finally reached the cabin, he was shaking and the fire was out.

Gary checked Scott, who appeared okay. Gary restarted the fire, then searched for bedding to warm Scott and himself. He found a foam pad, which he put over himself—it wasn't warm but provided some comfort.

Gary spent the rest of the time resting and keeping the fire going. When they ran out of water, Gary toted a five-gallon bucket to the stream for more. It was only fifty feet, but in Gary's condition, it seemed interminably longer.

The next day they ran out of wood, and Gary decided to chop more. His hands still hurt from the beating they'd taken breaking through the window shutter; but he gritted his teeth and chopped.

Gary spent a great deal of time thinking about his family, wondering about their suffering.

Around 4 P.M. the next day, Gary heard the first plane fly over. The plane overflew the crash site several times, convincing Gary the wreckage had been spotted. Shortly the plane left. Gary began doubting. Three hours dragged by before Gary heard a C-130 aircraft overhead. It was circling. Gary knew then that they'd been found.

Nearly three hours later Gary made out the chopping staccato of helicopter blades and knew they'd be rescued.

Approximately twenty-four hours earlier, at 5:45 P.M., Tuesday, September 6, 1993, Gary's wife, Dorothy, had arrived home to an answering machine maxed out with phone messages. Dorothy walked into her kitchen and listened to the first message, left at 10:45 A.M. It told her that Gary's airplane was overdue into Talkeetna and the caller wondered whether she had any information on the whereabouts of the cabin where Gary and Scott stayed during their hunting trips.

She knew that Scott had to be back to work on the evening of the seventh. Gary had also told her he'd call her to check on the family when he reached Talkeetna. Since she hadn't heard from Gary Tuesday, Dorothy almost called Scott's wife to see if he had made it back for work. However, not wanting to alarm Scott's wife, Dorothy did not call. Now she was confused. She knew weather was always a factor and could negate their return. Since Gary wasn't due in Anchorage until the fifteenth, she wasn't too concerned; but she was a bit confused as to why he'd filed a flight plan to be in Talkeetna the night of the seventh.

She waded through all the messages and called the Rescue Coordination Center at Elmendorf Air Force Base north of Anchorage. She gave them the latitude and longitude of the hunting cabin (made easier since Gary always left her a map of his hunting area in case of emergency).

Next Dorothy called her friend Lin Mallonee to let her know that she wouldn't be going to work the next day. Lin drove to Dorothy's to be with her. Dorothy spoke reassuringly to Cory, her daughter. Dorothy called Kulis Air National Guard, Gary's place of employment, to see if anyone there knew any more news.

While Gary and Scott agonized physically and emotionally because of their predicament and while Dorothy sought answers, a rescue was under way. News of an overdue aircraft spread among the flying community. The Rescue Coordinaton Center at Elmendorf notified Kulis Air National Guard that they were initiating a search, even though there were no correlated emergency locator transmitter (ELT) reports by satellites or aircraft in the area and no crashed planes had been seen or reported. Based on Gary's flight plan and communication with his friends and coworkers, the search was focused around Scott Weber's family cabin northeast of Talkeetna.

Maj. Al Olsen of the 210th RQS, who was also qualified in the C-130H, volunteered to fly a training mission for the 144th contingent upon procuring someone to perform search and rescue duty officer (SARDO) duties. Col. Dan Nice volunteered to fulfill this duty. Maj. Olsen and his crew, Capt. Lyle Langston, M. Sgt. John Forbes, and T. Sgt. Gary Lanham, took off in aircraft #473 ("Scars" 73). They received an update about the search site. Maj. Olsen diverted from his training flight to the search area, arriving around 17:00 hours.

While overflying the area thirty minutes later, Maj. Olsen spotted something below on the gravel bar that had been scouted several times previously. It looked like driftwood from his altitude of 1,500 feet. However, he reckoned it could be an aircraft frame.

Olsen alerted the Civil Air Patrol, requesting a Beaver to assist. Those aboard the Beaver spotted the wreckage and concluded it might be a burned plane. There was no suitable landing site for the Beaver, so "Scars" 73, the aircraft Gary Franklin normally flew in, which was now piloted by Maj. Olsen, climbed to make radio contact with RCC requesting a helicopter.

PJs (pararescue jumpers) were contacted; arrangements were made; and 345 departed to the crash site at 19:33 hours. Aboard were CW4 Charlie Hamilton, Capt. Jerry Kidrick, Sgt. Tracey Hartless, SMSgt. Hickson, and M. Sgt. Mahoney. The chopper carried no extra fuel and the sun was descending, which intensified the risk.

Within thirty minutes 345 cruised into the search area. A number of cabins dotted the riverbanks below. They spotted the charred remains of

Gary Franklin's Arctic Tern and landed near the river. They found no survivors. Upon searching further they observed footprints leading from the wreckage from either wingtip. Next they found a burned glove near a channel of the river where the tracks ended.

Their consensus was that healthy survivors would have responded to the clatter of the helicopter and the ensuing activity. Since no survivors had made an appearance, and rather than leaving empty-handed, the rescuers decided to approach the several cabins in the area in hopes of finding the survivors.

Maneuvering over uneven terrain PJs Hickson and Mahoney took less than ten minutes to reach the nearest cabin. They knocked on the cabin door and heard what sounded like a groaning old woman. One thought the groan said "Come in" and the other thought it was "Go away." They did not wish to arouse a homesteader's ire. Looking at each other and shrugging, they entered the cabin.

Their discovery was horrifying. The rescuers saw what appeared to be two lumps of grayish black, charcoaled something. They had found the grotesquely burned crash victims.

Gary and Scott were in extreme pain. They'd been vomiting for half a day.

Hickson ran to the chopper for assistance. He informed the others that the crash victims were "load and go" candidates—so critically injured that they could not be treated in the field. The chopper had limited fuel, but Hickson assured Hamilton that they could load the survivors in time.

Hamilton manned the machine. Hickson, Kidrick, and Hartless grabbed a Stokes litter and sleeping bags and headed for the cabin.

While the others worked with Franklin and Weber, Hamilton moved the chopper closer to the cabin to facilitate moving the victims and to save time. Hamilton sat the chopper down within fifty yards of the cabin, one wheel on the riverbank and the other above the river.

An expert medic, Mark Mahoney worked quickly while alone. When the others arrived, they positioned Scott in a sleeping bag and placed him on the litter. All four rescuers grabbed hold of the litter and began their trip to the chopper. Uneven terrain pockmarked by small ravines and gullies and the fading daylight compounded their efforts.

They returned for Gary and completed a second difficult trip.

Chopper 345 lifted off on bingo fuel (with little fuel to spare). They had just enough light to navigate the river valley. As the pilot maneuvered his craft through the mountains to Talkeetna, the PJs took their patients' vital signs and administered oxygen. The cabin was too dark and crowded, and the patients' swelling (edema) made it too difficult for the PJs to administer IVs. Experience taught them that their efforts were an exercise in futility—these burn victims were on their way to another world.

Upon arriving in Talkeetna in pitch darkness, the men were hurriedly transferred to the Providence Life Guard craft and rushed to Anchorage.

Since crashing around noon on the seventh nearly thirty-six hours had elapsed before the survivors arrived at Providence. They were immediately admitted into the burn unit.

Probably the cool temperatures on the river, the moisture of the air and towels, along with drinking the proper amount of water, greatly enhanced their chances of survival.

Around 7 P.M. Dorothy was given some misinformation about the missing plane. A guardsman aboard the C-130 that had spotted Gary's plane told Dorothy the plane was not damaged. Dorothy, Cory, and Lin got excited.

Later Dorothy called RCC and was informed that a helicopter was at the crash site. Dorothy was livid. Because of the misinformation given to her earlier, she was not aware of the crash site. After being on hold for ten minutes, she was told to hang up and that someone would get back to her. Hours later Kenai Flight Service called Dorothy asking for an update on her husband.

Since Dorothy hadn't heard from RCC, she called Gary's work first and was told two burn victims were being transported to Talkeetna (giving rise to the assumption that, since Talkeetna was a small town without a hospital, the victims were not in serious condition). She then called Command and Control at Kulis Air National Guard Base, speaking with Gene Ramsey and begging him to tell her what he knew of the crash site.

Not until Bob Gastrock of Kulis Air National Guard Base called her back did she know that Gary and Scott were being transported via life flight to Providence Hospital in Anchorage.

Bob Gastrock called Dorothy's next-door neighbor Carolyn Wells requesting she drive Dorothy to the hospital. In turn, Dorothy called her friend Teri Osterkamp and asked her to meet her at Providence. Lin Mallonee stayed with Cory.

When they reached the hospital, Dorothy was met by Keith Douglas and Mike Heller, both of whom worked at Kulis Air National Guard with Gary. The duty nurse kept them informed about the life flight aircraft's position.

Later the nurse came to the waiting room to tell the group that Gary had arrived. She gave Dorothy his gold necklace and wallet. Once Gary and Scott were stabilized, the nurse informed the group what to expect and that they could see Gary and Scott.

Gary seemed alert. He asked Dorothy if he could get the boat he'd been wanting for some time. He also asked her if she'd hung the picture he gave her before his trip. He wanted her to retrieve his watch from his shirt's left pocket—she dug the shirt from the garbage to find his watch (the discarded shirt had been cut away to treat his wounds).

Gary wanted to see the other visitors, so they filed by one at a time. He made jokes and told everyone he would be okay.

Gary wanted to see his daughter Cory and told Dorothy to ask the doctor when that would be possible. He suggested waiting a few days to assess Gary's recovery.

Dorothy felt Gary would be fine. She did not share the same hope for Scott, whose face was black and who trembled constantly.

Dorothy sat with Gary for an hour before the smell of burned flesh overcame her. Whenever she became nauseated, she put her head between her knees and the nurses gave her juice to keep her from passing out.

On the morning of the ninth Dorothy left the hospital around 4 A.M. From her home she contacted the family members. She told Cory the truth about her father.

Even though Cory wanted to see her father badly, it wasn't time. Dorothy took Cory to school and encouraged her to make a get-well card for him, hoping it would help her feel that she was doing something for her father. Dorothy returned to the hospital.

Gary's body was so swollen that she barely recognized him. He asked her where she had spent the night, and she broke down. She felt so helpless and scared. Her first husband had died in a small-airplane accident seven years earlier. While she cried, a nurse put an arm around her and comforted her (as many other nurses would do in the days to come).

On the ninth of September, Gary's medical attendees inserted a feeding tube through his nose to his lower intestine. Somehow the tube got coiled up around the back of Gary's throat, causing him to cough and gag. It was difficult for Dorothy to witness Gary's gasping for air, convulsing.

On the tenth the medical attendees removed Gary's breathing tube, allowing him to speak. He requested food and plenty of chocolate milk. Dorothy was thrilled to hear him. Gary told Dorothy to take a hundred dollars from his wallet and get chocolate milk.

Gary wanted to be with Scott so much that he requested he be able to room with Scott, who was scheduled for his first surgery the thirteenth of September.

When Dorothy arrived at the hospital with daughters Cindy, twenty-five, and Tina, twenty-three, on the thirteenth, Gary had eaten most of his breakfast and was resting well. He sent Dorothy to the store for ice cream and more chocolate milk. He talked and joked with his daughters.

Later that day Gary had his first skin graft. The surgery lasted nearly eight hours and went well. Dorothy and Tina stayed with Gary until 10:30 P.M., when they left for Anchorage International Airport to pick up Dorothy's father. (Tina and Cindy were scheduled to leave early the next morning.)

When Dorothy arrived at the hospital the next day, she was surprised to learn that the doctor had had to insert a tube to Gary's stomach to remove some excess from the feeding tube. Gary was upset about another tube.

Dorothy's father saw Gary in the hospital for the first time on the fourteenth. When he entered Gary's room, Gary's parents were present. It was so difficult seeing Gary in his condition that Dorothy's father left immediately.

Gary's next scheduled surgery was for his left arm on the seventeenth. Dorothy went to be with him at 4 A.M. and on the way to the hospital observed the northern lights brighter than she'd ever seen them. Burn nurses Kathy and Scott took Gary at 6:15 for his tubing before his 8:30 surgery. Kathy (from the surgery unit) debrided (peeled skin) from Gary's face while he was in surgery. Gary did have some fluid in his lungs after surgery, but it was nothing to be alarmed about, they said. In recovery they removed the breathing tube.

The next day Gary told Dorothy, "Get me out of here. They are doing nothing but making me worse." He did not remember the surgeries he had been through nor what was going on around him (was he hallucinating?). He was combative with the nurses, although he rested well when Dorothy was in the room.

Gary's mother, Della, noticed that his left foot was very swollen. When a burn nurse, Ruth changed the dressing on his leg, she noticed the extent of the swelling.

They called in a specialist to do an ultrasound of Gary's left leg. They then discovered that Gary had a blood clot in his leg caused by the femoral arterial line's having been in his leg for too long. They immediately started him on heparin (blood thinner). This started a whole other chain reaction.

Dorothy was upset that day and called her friend Lin to come sit with her while Gary had his dressing changes. In the meantime burn nurse Ruth came to the waiting room after changing the dressings and told Dorothy that Gary had kicked her to keep her away from him. She knew something was really wrong. Gary had been a good patient up to that point.

At 4:30 P.M. that afternoon Dorothy went into Gary's hospital room with their oldest daughter, Tracy. Gary was having difficulty breathing and wanted Dorothy to take the oxygen mask from his mouth in order to tell her something.

The nurses would not allow anyone to remove the oxygen mask. Then Dorothy noticed that Gary's oxygen level was low. Dorothy asked his nurse Ruth what to look for if a piece of a blood clot had broken off and lodged in Gary's lungs. Ruth replied, "Shortness in breath, lowering of blood pressure."

Gary displayed those very symptoms. His blood pressure was 71/50. Ruth started to administer dopamine, a drug to elevate blood pressure. She called in a few other nurses and escorted Dorothy and Tracy from the room. Within a few minutes the loudspeakers declared, "Code 99. Room 2026."

The implications were clear to Dorothy and Tracy. Gary had stopped breathing. Dorothy sat on the waiting-room floor praying. She couldn't understand why God would bring Gary back to her only to take him away ten days later.

The nurses revived Gary, then called the head doctor, Dr. Hood, who was in surgery with another burn patient. He went into the waiting room and put his arm around Dorothy, assuring her that he would do all that he could for Gary. After reviving Gary, the first thing that they did was to insert a line in his heart to measure the pressure of the blood flow. Dr. Hood had called in four specialists to confer about Gary.

At first the attendees thought a piece of a clot had broken off and traveled to Gary's lungs. They spoke of open-heart surgery to remove the clot, giving him a fifty-fifty chance for survival if they operated. He had hard plastic forms on his arms to keep him from disrupting the skin grafts. Because he was trying to hit people with his arms, they had to tie down his arms for his own safety. They had given Gary a paralyzing drug to counteract his fighting them should they put him in a ventilator.

Dr. Hood had called a "bug" doctor, who had given Gary antibiotics to counter septicemia. Another doctor reviewed the chest X rays, and a third, Dr. Hummel, reviewed Gary's adrenal level. He noticed the level was low and administered a large dose of cortisone.

At 1 A.M. Dr. Hummel approached the family in the waiting room and told them there was nothing more they could do for Gary. Hummel told Dorothy that Gary's stomach and kidneys had shut down and that he was assisted in breathing by a ventilator. Hummel told Dorothy that Gary's blood pressure was falling rapidly.

Tracy and Dorothy went to Gary's room to see him. It was sad. He looked so fragile, far from the big, burly Gary Franklin his friends and family knew. Tubes hung from him and machines were hooked to him. He was completely surrounded by medical personnel. They worked without speaking. Dorothy's heart broke; she thought she would die.

One of the nurses went to Dorothy and told her to say her good-byes to Gary. The nurse said there was nothing more they could do . . . that you could not talk, wish, or pray a man as sick as Gary back to health. She said that the only thing that could save him would be a miracle. She single-handedly crushed all the hopes that the family had.

Tracy went to work on her dad. She was not about to give up on him without a fight. She hollered at him telling him not to leave her. She reminded him of the father-and-daughter Brownie Banquet that he had flown into town to attend with her. His blood pressure was 75/43 when Tracy entered the room with Dorothy. Within an hour it began to rise.

Whether it was the medication or the coaching of his daughter or all the prayer groups that were called in the middle of the night to pray for Gary, a miracle transpired.

When Dr. Hood arrived the next morning, even he was surprised to see that Gary was still alive. Tracy was still talking to her father; she and Gary's father had stayed with Gary all night.

A few days later Gary was improving remarkably. Fellow workers from Gary's office stopped by to see him. Charlie Brenton and Lloyd Ruiz sat with Dorothy for hours at Gary's bedside one afternoon. On the afternoon of the twenty-second of September the nurses removed the air tube from Gary's right nostril.

Over the next few days Gary became quiet and would not speak. On the morning of the twenty-seventh Dorothy's father and Dorothy went into the hospital early. Dorothy's father was leaving Alaska and wanted to say good-bye to Gary. Dorothy had a really bad feeling.

Gary didn't wake up to speak to them as he had whenever they had come into the room previously. Dorothy took her father to the airport to catch his plane. When she returned to the hospital, she looked at the monitor machine; Gary's heart rate was dropping from one hundred down to the fifties and sixties. She called the nurses, who in turn called in Dr. Hood.

They all tried to get Gary to open his eyes, but he wouldn't. The family minister stopped by to pray with them. He is a retired doctor. Based on Gary's symptoms, he suspected a subdermal hematoma. He suggested a CAT scan be done.

Dr. Hood took Gary down to the CAT scan unit. Incredibly, the blood thinner had started a blood clot on the brain to bleed, creating a buildup of blood and fluid and causing the left side of Gary's brain to swell.

Dr. Kralick was called to perform emergency brain surgery.

The doctors told Dorothy that Gary would probably not be able to speak or that he might enter a coma as a result of the bleeding. They cautioned her that he might be "a little slow."

They drilled two holes about the size of a quarter, one in the front on the left side and the other in the back of the left side of his head. The drainage tube was in the back hole. The other hole was stapled shut.

The families were called in once again to sit in the waiting room. The surgery was a success. Tracy and Dorothy went to see Gary. Tracy held Dorothy's hand and told her she had a good feeling about the surgery. The nurses told Dorothy that Gary would be sedated for up to twenty-four hours and suggested she go home to rest. Dorothy left to visit Cory, calling throughout the night and the next morning to check on her husband.

The next morning when Tracy and Dorothy arrived, the first thing Gary did when he saw them was to give them the thumbs-up sign. Dr. Hood advised Dorothy that Gary might have problems speaking. She asked him if it made a difference that Gary was sounding out words and writing them on a dry erase board. Dr. Hood smiled and told her that Gary was going to be fine.

Since Gary had to have the surgery for the blood in his head, they had to take Gary off the blood thinner to try to stop any further bleeding. On the twenty-ninth they installed a drainage bulb in his head to try to get out as much of the blood as possible. Dorothy elected to have a bird's nest installed in the main vein from the leg into the stomach, which would intercept any clots and keep them from the heart or lungs.

Gary was awake during this procedure and told Dorothy he was watching a cool movie (causing her to wonder if he knew what was going on).

On the thirtieth they performed an echo on Gary's heart through his esophagus, to see if the heart was affected by the bacterial spray. The echo was normal. Dorothy's reaction was to "thank the Good Lord."

On October 3rd Cory turned six years old. It was the first time she was to see her father since his accident. Dorothy tried hard to prepare Cory for what she was to see. When Cory walked into the room, she put her arm around her father. Gary told her that he had gotten a little sick but that he was going to be fine.

Cory kissed his cheek and told him she loved him. There was not a dry eye in the room, including Gary's.

EPILOGUE

A few years after I met Gary, I read the April 1998 issue of *Guideposts* magazine, which included a one-page expression that Gary's hunting partner and accident companion, Scott Weber of Anchorage, had written. Titled "The Divine Touch," it is reprinted below.

> The night before Gary and I flew back to Talkeetna, Alaska, from a hunting trip, my mother had a disturbing dream. Had I known about her dream, I would never have gotten into Gary's two-seater Arctic Tern the next morning.
>
> Gary Franklin and I worked as aircraft mechanics at Kulis Air National Guard Base. We had taken a few days off to hunt moose up the Talkeetna River, in the remote interior of Alaska, where I had use of a friend's cabin.
>
> Seconds after we lifted off the makeshift wilderness airstrip that September morning in 1993, headed for home, an incredible jolt slammed the plane back down. Wind shear! We smacked the surface of the river, losing our landing gear, then skipped like a stone before hurtling across a gravelly sandbar at sixty miles an hour. The belly fuel tank erupted in flames. Instantly the plane was engulfed. As we skidded to a stop, Gary screamed, "Get out! Get out!" and dove out of the door.
>
> Seated behind him, I struggled with my safety belt. I saw my hands catch fire, my skin burning like paper, as I fumbled frantically with the red-hot buckle. *Jammed!* Pain tore through

me and I heard myself scream. Hot smoke seared my lungs. I wasn't going to make it out! *Dear God, forgive me my sins . . .*

Suddenly a firm hand took hold of my left shoulder. Gary! The next thing I knew I was standing outside, a short distance from the blazing wreckage. I threw myself on the ground, trying to smother the flames. Gary dragged me to the river and made me lie in the freezing water. Finally he helped me up. We stared at each other, our clothes burned away, our skin charred and raw. We were in desperate need of help.

It would be another day before a rescue helicopter reached us, and months of agonizing treatment before we could resume normal lives. But something Gary told me made the terrible pain more bearable. When I thanked him for helping me out of the plane, he insisted it hadn't been him.

"I was thirty feet away, rolling on the ground," he said. "I never went near the plane."

And while I was in the hospital, my mother told me about her dream. "Scottie," she said, her voice tight with emotion, "I dreamed you were in danger. I didn't know what had happened, but I knew you needed help. I woke up, knelt by my bed, and prayed for God to protect you."

At last I knew whose hand had pulled me from the flames.

Gary Franklin's determination to see that his friend Scott and he not die in the Alaskan wilderness was simply amazing. But his struggle to live even after he was rescued is more amazing. Despite the most up-to-date technology and skilled doctors, the only thing that often makes a difference between life or death is how badly the person wants to see another day.

MISTAKES CAN KILL

Larry Kaniut

From *Danger Stalks the Land*

Our final tale of survival, comes, like many others did, from Alaska. Discover what happens when an experienced bush pilot makes a few simple mistakes . . . and ends up fighting to survive in a desolate stretch of wilderness because of them.

WHEN I READ ABOUT MIKE LEGLER in the newspaper, I knew I had to meet this guy and get his story. We met at the all-American store with the big golden arches on Tudor Road near Lake Otis on January 24, 1994. Mike is not a big man, but his sparkling eyes revealed some inner strength. He handed me his typed story and proceeded to tell it to me.

Marilou Slaughter settled in for the night. She read her Bible and began her evening prayer. She thanked God for His goodness and her comfortable and warm, clean sheets and satin pillow. She immediately had a vision. She saw a cabin with a man inside. God spoke to her, "Yes, Marilou, you *are* fortunate. Look at this poor man here. He's freezing."

How was she to know that her vision was a reality? That she was seeing Mike Legler, a pilot who had been reported missing four days earlier and fought daily for survival. He was down near Seward, Alaska; and she was in Eugene, Oregon, over 2,000 air miles away.

That is one of the interesting sidelights to the story Mike Legler told me.

Monday, September 13, 1993, was a sunny day in Eagle River, Alaska. Fall in our part of America usually lasts only a few short weeks. Delighting in the beauty and planning my day off while making my morning coffee, I resolved it was a great day to go flying.

I would have the entire day to enjoy before coming home to the family and fixing dinner—a family tradition on my day off. My wife, Bev, an elementary teacher, was at work. My son, Jake, and daughter, Kris, were both at Chugiak High School.

I took care of a couple of business calls, then grabbed my Thermos of coffee, lunch, and flight gear on my way out the door.

I was comfortable in my New Balance running shoes, jeans, chamois shirt, and light nylon warm-up jacket. My trusty Leatherman tool (like a Swiss Army knife) hugged my hip in its sheath on my heavy leather belt.

My Taylorcraft airplane was tied down at Fire Lake, just a few miles from our home. On the way I stopped to purchase extra aircraft fuel, filling three five-gallon, plastic containers. The lake was calm and the air a cool forty degrees Fahrenheit.

As I pulled into the lake parking lot, I noticed a Ketchum Air 206 land and taxi to the fuel dock. I wondered what the pilot was doing on Fire Lake, a small lake not used by commercial operators.

I topped off my tanks and preflighted my little BC-12D. After loading my pistol, lunch, and coffee into the plane, I turned the plane around and drifted it back between the docks (using the rope attached to the tail for that purpose). I jumped in, turned on the mags, and hit the starter.

She ran a little rough due to the cool night air and the fifty-weight oil. I added primer to smooth out the idle, then taxied to the north end of the lake to warm up the engine. I checked air traffic and applied takeoff power. She quickly jumped on step and accelerated. I broke water and began a seventy miles per hour climbout. Again I noticed Ketchum's Cessna 206 below, whose pilot was looking up at me.

At two hundred feet I discovered the reason for the pilot's gaze—ground fog covered most of Cook Inlet and Anchorage, spreading north to Palmer. "No sweat," I thought, "I'm going south up Eagle River Valley." I turned left over town and continued my climb after reducing my rpm to 2,500 and lowering the nose to hold eighty miles per hour.

Shortly after reaching 4,200 feet I passed through Crow Creek Pass, east of Anchorage in the Chugach Mountains. I turned southeast toward the headwaters of the Twenty Mile River en route to Carmen Lake, where I wanted to check out a campsite for use on my next days off from Alaska Airlines, where I am an aircraft mechanic.

Cruising at 4,000 feet I picked out distant Prince William Sound, one of my favorite places to fly. It was clear with no fog. Climbing to 5,000 feet, I tried to raise flight service on my handheld VHF radio. I received no response on any of the frequencies they monitor. I knew I should not be flying without a flight plan, but the gorgeous day won out over my common sense, and I continued on.

A short time later I set down to wait while the ground fog burned off. After watching a couple of black bears awhile, I was airborne toward Bainbridge Passage. I flew on to Puget Bay, where the 1964 earthquake had lifted land, turning two bays into freshwater lakes—one on either side of the bay.

Deciding to land on the east lake, I made a low pass over the ocean beach and spotted several objects. *Looks like good beachcombing.*

After landing and before taking a stroll down the beach, I dumped five gallons of fuel into my tank. I picked up a nearly new crab-pot buoy and stuck it in the back of the plane. With a slight ocean breeze coming up, I sat down on one plane float and drifted to the back of the lake. I ate my sandwich, drank some coffee, and savored the thrill of being outdoors in this great setting. It was my kind of day—just drifting along without a care in the world.

After a while I decided to fire up and check the west lake across the bay before heading home. After an uneventful takeoff, I crossed the five miles of bay to the lake. It has no name and is well hidden and separated from the ocean by a 200-yard stretch of gravel and driftwood.

I flew past the lake and made a descending 180-degree turn. The lake was glassy smooth without a whisper of wind and surrounded by a steep mountain ridge on three sides. Tall fir trees covered the last 1,500 feet, reflecting back into the lake, making depth perception difficult.

Lining up on the southwest corner of the mile-and-a-half approach, I set up for a glassy water landing and began a long, slow descent. Several seconds passed as I noticed small ripples on the lake off to my left. My altimeter read 200 feet. My rpm read 1,800. Since my plane wasn't equipped with a vertical-speed indicator, I thought, *I'll just correct a little left; I should then see the ocean and the horizon, which will enhance my depth perception. Now a little left rudder, a little aileron—*

Bang! There was a tremendously loud crash. I had slammed onto the lake without realizing I was close to touchdown. I lifted my head and could see nothing out of my right eye. I put my right palm to my eye and pulled it back covered with blood. I looked down to discover I was chest deep in ice-cold water.

Crashed aircraft often have jammed doors, so I was surprised when my door opened freely. I pulled the release on my seat belt and swam out under the left wing, which rode on the water. I pulled the auto-inflation handle on my float vest, but nothing happened. Panic and confusion grabbed me. One more try and I felt the vest inflate. I was reminded and glad that Gary McDaniel, my float instructor, had taught me never to fly floats without a Stearn flotation jacket (which contained my survival gear).

I swam to the tail of the plane and grabbed the tail rope. My only thought was, *You're not going to sink on me; you're my only way out of here.*

Trying to pull the plane, I held the rope in my left hand and kicked my feet and swam with my right arm for quite a while before realizing I was wasting my energy. The plane hardly moved in relation to the quarter mile I was from shore.

Letting go of the rope, I swam back to the left wing, reached down, opened the door, and groped inside for my VHF hand radio. I removed the external antenna cable and pulled the radio from its rack, stuffing the radio into the lower pocket of my float vest.

My next action was to retrieve my Emergency Locator Transmitter. I moved around the tail to the right side. Thinking I might break the Plexiglas, I beat against the submerged rear window with my fist. The ELT was only inches away, but I could not break the window to retrieve it.

My plane was sinking fast. As long as I pulled down on the tail with the rope, trapped air seemed to keep her up. But as I released the rope, the tail rose (because of the engine's weight), and air escaped from the wings' trailing-edge drain grommets.

Water entered my mouth and shocked me. The vest was trying to come off over my head. My head went below the surface, and I realized that something held my right leg. Bracing my right hand against the top of the wing and my left against the top of the fuselage, I pushed up as hard as I could. I felt my pants rip, and I swam free.

With my heart pounding, I started for shore. Near the tail I encountered my empty gas can, which must have floated out of the large hole in the left side of the plane made by the heel of the float when it ripped off. I stopped briefly, tied it to the tail rope, and swam away. (Anyone in his right mind would have used it as a float to reach safety rather than a locator to find the aircraft later.)

The rest was like a movie. Once the wings were well beneath the water, the tail rose to near vertical and quietly slipped out of sight below the surface of the lake.

I forced myself to keep swimming without resting because I knew that time spent in cold water has catastrophic effects on people. I don't know how long I swam. It seemed like an eternity. I was able to stand about six feet from the shore, which was covered by a few small trees and weeds.

My first few steps were wobbly. My legs kept giving out and I fell several times. Seventy-five yards up the beach a breeze hit me, and I began shaking. I took cover from the wind behind a three-by-eight-foot log. My jaw quivered and my teeth chattered. I had trouble using my fingers.

I gathered a few small sticks and some dry grass tops for a fire. But my lighter wouldn't work. I blew the water away from the flint and got a small flame, but the materials were too damp to burn. Blood running from my head and dripping onto the pile didn't help matters.

I pulled out my flare gun, thinking of firing it into the sticks, but thought better of it as I envisioned the projectile bouncing off the pile, hitting the log, and ricocheting into me.

Emptying my pockets I found a pack of small cigars. I removed the cellophane wrapper, shook the water from it, and slid it under the sticks. I lit it. Thank God it burned long enough for the grass and sticks to catch fire. I built the fire up slowly by blowing on it.

I removed my clothes, wrung out the water, and hung them over the log as close to the fire as possible. I made a bandage of my handkerchief and tied it over my bleeding forehead with my left shoelace. The bandage stopped the flow of blood.

Several hours passed before I stopped shaking and my clothes were dry enough to put back on.

I walked the beach checking for anything I could use and hoping I'd find visqueen* for shelter. But I found nothing. Spotting a large fishing boat on the horizon, I fired a flare. The boat continued on until it was out of sight.

It would be dark soon, and no one would be looking for me. I stacked wood near the fire and pulled some larger logs around to form sides to my small bunker in case the wind changed during the night. Removing as many of the larger rocks as I could, I made an area between the logs and the fire to lie down. I was surprised at how weak I was, possibly from shock or hypothermia.

Just before dark I used the cross-point drive on the Leatherman tool to remove the back cover of my Icom VHF radio. An ounce of water trickled out. The inside cover and circuit board were wet. I put the radio back together and tried it an hour or so later, but it did not work.

---

* Plastic sheeting.

Well, Mike, this is a fine mess you're in. The family will be worried sick and not a soul knows where you are. Emergency locator transmitters don't work underwater. Worst of all, you dare not fall asleep. If that fire burns out on this cold, clear night, you'll never get it started in the dark.

God must protect fools like me because the wood burned with water and steam coming out both ends.

The night went by slowly at first. I could hear land otters while I watched satellites passing overhead. I dozed off around 3 A.M. and was awakened just before dawn by a wolf's howling.

I arose in the calm, cool morning air, my back and hips aching from my discomfort on the rocks. I had difficulty getting the fire going. It was a clear day, and I was full of hope expecting someone to find me. *Perhaps my ELT sounded long enough for the FCC to investigate.* I knew that was unlikely from my earlier visit to an FCC station where officials explained the satellite passes Alaska every 102 minutes. If the satellite picks up a hit on passing, a second hit must register 102 minutes later or the first hit is erased.

Another possibility was for the Ketchum pilot to tell search officials the direction he'd seen me depart the lake—that would narrow the search effort somewhat. *Maybe someone will look down here in a few days.*

Since there was nothing to keep me at the crash site, I started west down the beach, determined to walk out. Before leaving, I scanned the lake for anything that might have floated free of the plane and drank some lake water.

Even though *beach* conjures up notions of white sand, North Gulf Coast beaches are rocky. Some of the boulders are car-sized. Wave action has worn them smooth except in areas of recent rock slides, where the boulders are jagged.

I hiked five miles before encountering a rock slide 200 feet high that blocked my path. Knowing I would need my shoelace, I soaked the handkerchief with water to loosen it from my wound. I replaced the boot lace and started up the slide. At the top I viewed another slide barrier two miles down the beach; it was at least 500 feet high. Discouraged, I climbed back down to decide my course of action.

Do I go on and try to make it to Johnstone Bay, if Johnstone Bay is the next bay? A friend has a cabin at little Johnstone Bay where wheel planes practice beach landings. There is a salmon stream connecting its lake to the ocean. But do salmon run this late in the year? Are my chances of rescue better there or where the plane crashed?

I decided to return to the crash-site beach.

At the crash site the tide was just starting to come in. I noticed some black mussels on the rocks and walked closer. Most of the mussels were half the size of my little finger or smaller. I pulled one loose and split it open with my knife. I picked at it with the tip of my knife, cut off part that looked inedible, and popped the meat into my mouth. It was salty but not too fishy tasting.

I pulled more from the rocks and ate them until the tide covered the rocks. I picked up some kelp and chewed it. It was stringy and hard to chew but not bad tasting.

Near the tree line I sat and watched several boats five miles distant—on a line between Cape Resurrection and Bainbridge Passage. I flashed them with my signal mirror. No response.

Discouraged, I turned and looked toward the lake. It was concealed by dense brush. Walking toward the woods, I discovered a path. Following it deeper into the woods where it was cooler, I stopped and stared at what appeared to be a makeshift outhouse. Just beyond the outbuilding was a cabin. That was an emotional surge. I walked to the front door and pushed it open.

The plywood cabin was six by ten feet. There was no stove or windows. Two bunks were built along the back wall with a counter extending from the bunks and wrapping the corner nearly to the door. A well-used brown and tan carpet covered the floor.

My eyes darted about for food. Other than a bag of moldy, inedible peanuts, there were two rolls of toilet paper, a box of stick matches in a plastic baggy, a pan of rusty nails, an old hatchet, a rusted and dull ax, a Coleman lantern, three-quarters of a gallon of fuel, some Styrofoam cups, a Fish and Game area goat-permit map, and two ink pens.

Now I have a map. Little Johnstone Bay is twenty-two miles by beach. It is the next bay west around the corner north. If I go overland, I'll have to climb to 3,400 feet and cross a glacier . . . not impossible. This cabin will be my shelter while I'm deciding my options.

I cut some of the carpet and formed it into an envelope the size of a sleeping bag. I cut another piece to lay over the bag as an extra layer. Using a chunk of wood and some nails, I nailed the bottom to the bunk as a seal. *Maybe I'll be warm tonight.*

Afternoon found me back at the ocean beach. I saw two large commercial fishing boats about six miles across the mouth of the bay. I flashed at them with the mirror with no response. *Should I use another flare?* Depression began to set in as I watched.

To my right I heard rustling in the dry leaves and saw a large, brown, sleek land otter bounding over logs and leaves. He stopped long enough to study me before disappearing into the woods.

To keep my mind occupied I took the radio, attached the antenna, and turned it on. Parts of the LCD display appeared for the first time. I removed the back cover and the circuit board to expose another board. I set the radio in the sunlight to dry and walked east down the beach in search of anything I might have missed earlier.

Large, puffy clouds half filled the sky. In the distance I heard an airplane. As its engine noise increased, I saw it break from behind a cloud. It was a C-130 military plane heading south at about 8,000 to 9,000 feet. It disappeared into the cloud directly above me and reappeared going east. *Rescue plane on a search . . . maybe listening for weak ELT signals. But they won't hear mine. Man, I wish that radio worked!*

I started for the lake to get a drink of water. I saw my floats across the lake, washed up against the bank. About a hundred yards beyond the floats was a person standing near the bank, apparently fishing. Next to him in the brush was a backpack. I yelled to him, but he did not reply. *Maybe it's a hunter who just came down from the mountains. He may be at his pickup point.* Halfway between the hunter and the floats was a rowboat. I waved my arms and hollered to the hunter, but he did not respond. *Maybe he just doesn't want company!*

Walking to the corner of the lake, I found an old metal float with fifteen to twenty feet of line on it. I removed the line and took it along toward the hunter. There was no lakeshore, just trees to the water's edge punctuated by rock outcroppings. I walked fifty yards into the woods and paralleled the lake.

Six-foot-high devil's club and thorn bushes covered the entire area making it difficult to walk. I stopped often to eat blueberries and black currants that grew in abundance. At length I reached the area where I'd last seen the hunter.

I made my way to the shore and found the hunter—"he" was an oddly shaped tree trunk. The "rowboat" was two fallen tree trunks; and the "backpack" was reddish wood from a tree a bear had ripped open. Tired and frustrated, I sat down to rest. *I must have hit my head harder than I thought. I have no energy for chasing illusions.*

I wished I hadn't removed the emergency lightweight survival food I'd always carried in my floats in an aft compartment. Thinking I might find something I'd left in the floats, I used the line I'd brought as a lasso.

On the third try my line plopped over the water rudder on the left float. It was half-sunken and difficult to maneuver. I tired quickly while trying to free the float. A remaining portion of the spreader bar hung up on a half-sunken log near shore.

In frustration I tied it off to a tree. The right float was twenty-five feet out and too far for the rope to reach.

After resting I began my trip to the cabin. Depression set in as I walked. My legs were shaky and I tripped a few times on the rocks. *A concussion, no sleep last night, my attempt to walk out, and the hike through the brush chasing illusions have taken their toll.*

Back at the ocean beach the tide was out. I filled a large Styrofoam cup with mussels, eating some, and pulled some of the larger kelp leaves off a half-submerged rock, placing them in another cup.

Walking back to the cabin in the twilight, I heard the turbine whine and blades of a helicopter. Dropping the cups on the beach, I pulled out the flare gun. On the southwest horizon flew an Alaska Guard Rescue Blackhawk. It was on a line between Cape Junken and Resurrection Bay, five to eight miles out.

I didn't think the helicopter would get any closer, so I fired a flare. *Surely they'll see it against this dark backdrop; they are only 1,500 feet off the water.* Oh, how I wanted that chopper to turn. Then a part of me seemed to die as I listened and watched it disappear beyond the cliffs to the west.

In total despair I walked to the cabin and put the cups of mussels and kelp away. I had no appetite. Things seemed as hopeless as ever. It was getting dark so I tried the Coleman lantern. It seemed to work fine without its glass shield, even producing a little heat. I closed the door, took off my shoes, and slipped into the carpet sleeping bag. Words could not describe the depths of my depression and emptiness.

Heavy rain woke me early the next morning. I got up and opened the door. The ceiling was down to 500 feet. I turned off the lantern and the mantle crumbled to powder. *No more night-light!* I returned to the carpet bag and slept till 9 A.M.

I awoke and ate some mussels. I planned to get two cups of water from the lake. However, it was raining so hard that I feared getting wet and cold and being unable to dry out. I decided not to go.

Having nothing to do in the cabin played on my mind. I'm an active person, and sitting and listening to my own head was depressing. I chose to make a vest of the remaining carpet. I cut another piece of carpet about two feet wide and left it the full length, about six feet. I folded it in half lengthwise and used some wire as a needle and fishing line for thread, sewing the sides together.

It was entertaining trying different stitches, pulling the wire needle through jute backing with the Leatherman (tool) pliers. I cut out a side hole for each arm and one in the top for my head. I cut an opening up the front. I put it on and tied a rope around the middle to keep it closed. *Not too bad, and warm, too.* Best of all it took most of the day to complete. I went to bed early using my new vest as a pillow.

It was still raining on day four. Some choice I thought: *Stay in and starve or go out to find food and die of exposure.* At 10 A.M. the rain let up a little, allowing me to go to the beach for more shellfish and kelp. I decided to store a lot of kelp in the cabin in case the next storm was longer. The kelp seemed to keep well when not exposed to the sun or air.

Wandering around the cabin, I noticed mushrooms, most of which had started to decay. I picked a couple of small ones from logs and ate them. *Hope they're not poisonous.* Behind the cabin was debris from an old cabin. Then I saw something white under one of the logs. *Oh, jeez, it's a propane bottle.* It felt as if it was half-full.

I rigged the percolation tube from an old camp coffeepot to the tank with plastic from the Styrofoam-cup bag. I opened the valve slightly and lit the flared end of the coffeepot tube. Flame shot out two feet. At least now I'd have heat. I carried it into the cabin knowing that it had the potential of becoming a bomb. But I figured, *Who cares? The most it could do is put an end to this miserable existence out here.*

I thought about ending it all. I could swing a rope over a rafter in the cabin and jump off a bucket. I was on a mental roller coaster, very unhealthy.

Back on the beach I found three fishing floats and a piece of driftwood wrapped in pink surveyor's tape. I unwrapped the tape and laid it on the beach in the shape of a six-foot arrow pointing toward the cabin. I set the buoys in a triangle around the arrow. Above the buoys I tied a red, four-foot-square piece of cloth to a six-foot stick and wedged it between two logs. I sat on the logs and watched till dark. Nothing!

In the cabin I lit my propane heater and closed the door. The cabin warmed up quickly but something was wrong. It seemed to be getting darker in the cabin. I opened the door and detected from the minimal light coming into the cabin that the air was filled with soot. I'd have to closely monitor my use of the propane tank.

Friday was nice and sunny. But still there were no boats or planes. I thought that strange. *I'm getting weaker by the day.* Finding a spot out of the wind, I lay on the rocks in the sun until my body warmed up completely. By now I was eating beach plants—most were bitter and I spit them out, but one type had a long, white runner root that tasted a little like celery.

When I saw the land otter again, I followed it to a slide in the woods above the cabin and figured a way to snare him. *Some meat Protein might give me the strength to walk out of here.*

In the afternoon when the cabin area was in shadows and getting cooler, I walked the mile to the far side of the lake and ate berries. Warmth and something in my stomach reduced my suicidal thoughts.

Day six dawned as another nice day. Still no boats or planes. *Hard to believe no one is looking for me.* Then I noticed standing lenticular clouds drifting south out of Prince William Sound. *I'll bet it's blowing hard out of the north over Anchorage and in the Chugach Mountains. No one would risk his plane and life in that kind of turbulence.*

It was noon before I got warm in the sun. *It's too late to walk out today. I'm too weak anyway. My tennis shoes could prove fatal if I break an ankle or leg. I'll have to do something different tomorrow or I'll die here!*

I experienced more suicidal thoughts. They were most prevalent in the late afternoon and into dusk. The thoughts may have been caused from watching another day slip by with no sign of rescue . . . or by the thought of another cold night. My reasoning was affected by lack of food. Another factor was the thought of the plane I'd rebuilt with my own hands. I recalled a favorite picture of it taken at Togiak Lake. Every time I looked at it, I was reminded that we'd been over most of the state; I got teary eyed.

I sat on the beach all morning and most of the afternoon on Sunday. It was my seventh day. It was a little windy but sunny. I gathered more mussels and kelp when the tide was out. I saw one boat way in the distance. Still no planes!

Depression returned. Being cold with no one to talk to made it hard to focus on the big picture—I constantly thought about short-term things. Near the cabin I found a white paper plate that was fairly dry. I set out to write my last will and testament on it. What I wrote turned out to be more of a personal good-bye to my wife and children. I ran out of room quickly, so I closed with "To all my friends and relatives, may God keep you in peace till we meet in the hereafter."

I put the plate in a plastic baggy and hung it on the wall in the cabin. I was so ovewhelmed with grief that I began to sob like a baby. The feeling of absolute hopelessness made me feel even weaker. I closed the cabin door, took off my shoes, and slid down into the carpet covering. A heavy rain pounded the cabin.

My sleep was restless that night. My shaking from the cold continually awakened me. The air inside the cabin was damp and colder than it had been the previous nights. In the darkness of the cabin I distinguished a doglike animal calling my name. "Are you hungry, Mikey? Are you cold enough yet, Mikey? No one will ever find you here alive, Mikey!

"I can help you, Mikey! What's your God doing for you now, Mikey? Let me help you."

The creature looked like a drooling rottweiler. I spoke to it: "I should have known you were part of this—you can leave. I will never renounce God, even if it's His will that I die here."

Within thirty seconds the creature left and the cabin seemed to warm up. It suddenly wasn't as dark. The rest of the night I slept like a baby and was never cold again.

I was experiencing a battle between good and evil. I was really being watched out for. Too many things happened that convinced me that my experience was not a coincidence.

On the twentieth, rain continued. The afternoon before I had written on my daily notes on the back of the map, "Left for Johnstone Bay Sept. 20th." I crossed it out now because it was still raining hard. From the doorway I could see the lake had risen about three feet. The wind had blown leaves and bark to my corner of the lake, making it impossible to get clean water. I sat in the cabin and ate kelp I'd gathered the day before.

The rain eased up around 10 A.M. and I headed for the beach. It was windy and the clouds started breaking up. In between waves I dashed toward the surf and snatched mussels from the rocks. On one trip I slipped on the rocks, fell, and almost broke the flare gun, which I had tied on a cord around my neck so I wouldn't be without it. I accepted the injury with little concern—by now I felt that it didn't matter anyway since my chances of surviving were nil.

The next day was my ninth day since leaving home. It was clear and windy. I headed for the beach in my routine search for food. My state of mind made computing low tide difficult. The mussel-covered rocks never showed because the seas were ten to twelve feet and pushed by strong winds. The winds never let the tide go out as it had the previous eight days.

Is it possible I've been here eight days! One minute it seems the time has gone quickly, the next minute it's been an eternity. I might be here for a long time. My calorie intake is low because my jeans are loose and the vest is getting larger. I may be losing my sanity. The signs are all there, lighthearted and giddy one moment, too depressed to get up and move the next. I wonder if I'll still be alive when the first snowfall comes.

I slept late on Wednesday the twenty-second. I had little energy. I ambled to the beach around 9 A.M. The tide was still in, but the surf was smaller than on Tuesday. It was nice and sunny with a light northeast wind. I ate some roots and tried some new ones, which I spit out because they were bitter.

I sat on a log to renew my daily vigil for boats and planes, ready to signal with my mirror and flare gun. Nothing. It was almost 11 A.M. before the large rocks with mussels began to appear. I gathered all the mussels I could find and put them into a plastic bag. I ate half, storing the remainder in the cabin along with some kelp.

At noon I climbed up the hill to assess my chances of crossing the glacier. It was difficult going because of the deadfalls and moss-covered ground. One step was solid, the next I sank up to my waist. I stopped every fifteen minutes to rest. It took two hours to get above the tree line at 1,500 feet. The next 500 feet was easier, but the view was discouraging.

The top of the ridge was another 1,000 feet. I didn't have the energy to go straight up. A rock slide blocked my way around the mountain. I saw Montague Island, Day Harbor, and Cape Resurrection; but not a boat was in sight. *Maybe tomorrow . . . if the weather's good and I eat lots today and I get a good night's rest, I'll have the strength to walk it.* I returned to the cabin.

At 4 P.M. I sat on the cabin steps eating my remaining mussels. I heard an airplane and thought, *Well, there it is again. My mind at work.* There was an instant roar as the plane passed over the cabin.

I dropped the mussels and ran to the beach, watching the tail of the Cessna 500 feet above the ground and flying away from me. *Why weren't you out on the beach watching?* My heart pounded as I watched the plane bank right and head southeast across the bay. *Dang! If he'll only turn back this way, I'll shoot a flare and maybe, just maybe he'll see it.* He disappeared up a canyon, but his engine's rpm were constant, indicating he was not set up for a landing.

I ran a hundred feet to the base of a cliff in the shadows thinking it provided a dark backdrop for the flare.

Here he comes! He's over the beach now on the far side of the bay, maybe three miles away. He's turning a little. He's pointing straight at me. Now! With the flare gun pointed up as vertical as possible, I fired. *Please see it!* He seemed to come at me for a second, then turned left flying out toward the head of the bay.

I reloaded the gun. Suddenly he turned my way again. *This time I have to wait until he's closer. He must not have seen the first flare with the sun in his eyes.* When he was halfway across the bay, I could wait no longer. I fired again. I heard the power come back on the engine and saw his flaps come down.

Holy smoke! He's gonna land! I ran to the cabin to get my last two flares. Standing at the corner of the lake, I watched him land near the far shore. I reloaded the flare gun and when he taxied toward me, I fired the flare in an arc along the woods on my side of the lake.

The plane was now out of my view because of the trees and sounded as if he was taxiing to the beach I'd spent my first night on. I ran up the trail, stumbling several times and falling. I couldn't let him get out of here without me! Winded, I reached the beach. But there was no plane!

I listened closely for his engine. My blood was pounding so loudly in my ears I could hardly hear it. *Now he's heading toward the cabin.* I turned and retraced my steps. Even with adrenaline pumping I had difficulty picking up my feet. I fell a few more times, gashing my forearms and shins.

I crashed through the trees and finally saw the plane. I heard a shout: "If you're a person, you had better speak up." A man standing onshore reached for a rifle. I stopped and opened my mouth but nothing came out. I was totally winded. He looked up, saw me, put down the rifle, and resumed unloading supplies.

I stumbled to the plane, which was tailed into the bank, and I grabbed the stabilizer. Three men unloaded gear. The closest one looked at me and asked, "Oh, are you hunting here?"

"No, I've been stranded here nine days."

He then asked, "Oh, where's your plane?"

"At the bottom of the lake."

The pilot standing on the float looked at me, walked over, grabbed me, and said, "Man, sit down. I'll get you some food." When I didn't move, he said, "You can let go of my plane. I promise I won't leave without you."

The two hunters began opening boxes and handing me food. I was almost in tears. I ate one small roll and was stuffed. As I told them what had happened to me, one kept saying, "Praise God, you're all right."

The pilot, Willie Allen with Scenic Mountain Air at Trail Lakes, got me into his plane. It was a white knuckler as we were on a downwind takeoff. Willie added flaps and forced the 206 off the water and the stall-warning horn came on. *Did I survive nine days lost to die now?* Fortunately, the plane continued on.

Willie flew the coast to Seward, pointing out sheer 600-foot cliffs that barred my way up the beach and asked, "So you were going to walk this, huh?"

We touched down at Trail Lake, twenty-five miles north of Seward, and Willie's boss, Vern Kinfsford, met us with a handheld radio in one hand and a portable phone in the other. He'd been trying to call my wife, Bev, for twenty minutes; but it was busy. As I stepped off the float onto the dock, he hit redial, got a signal, and handed me the phone.

Balancing there with the phone two feet from my ear, I heard Bev's voice: "Hello." Suddenly I couldn't talk. After her third hello I managed to say, "Bev." There was a long pause, then a scream. "Mike. Mike, is that you!" I started to cry. Vern and Willie were staring at their shoes.

Before Vern could tell Bev he'd bring me to Eagle River "on the house," she hung up and was on her way with her mother and our daughter, Kris, to pick me up (a 130-mile drive). Meanwhile Vern's phone started ringing off the hook. He had three lines into his flight service and received calls from Anchorage television news channels, the FAA, NTSB. He screened calls, asking me which ones I wanted to take.

When Bev arrived, it was quite a reunion. We started back for Anchorage. We had a lot to talk about . . . and a lot to be thankful for.

EPILOGUE

A couple of days after I was rescued, I received a call from a lady who told me she had had a vision about me. She had been in Oregon during my adventure. One night at bedtime during her Bible-reading/prayer time, she thanked God for her warm bed, clean sheets, and satin pillows. God "transported" her to a cabin and said, "Yes, you are fortunate. Look at this poor man here. He's going to die."

She described items in the cabin and their location; and I had never told anyone about these things.

As Mike and I later discussed his experience, he said, "I was talking with a Lutheran minister friend who has a theory about illusions. His theory is that when you have an illusion or vision, your brain finally gets quiet enough for God to send you a message.

"I had a pretty good faith in God before my accident. During the event, I cussed him and I threw rocks and asked, 'Why are You doing this to me?' I can remember being so angry for two or three days and then finally kinda giving up. Then it slowly came around to, 'Okay, what am I supposed to learn out of this?'

"I finally surrendered and said, 'Okay, whatever You're going to do, let's do it. I'm okay with it now.' When I finally surrendered, I was at perfect peace with whatever my fate was gonna be."

In Mr. Legler's case, those little mistakes—like not filing a flight plan—can add up to grave misfortune. Fortunately, he kept his head, found shelter, and did everything he could to signal for help and stay alive. No doubt his faith was a source of comfort for him during that dark time, but an equally valid case could be made that his internal fortitude was just as important in ensuring that he survived his situation.

ACKNOWLEDGMENTS

"Alone on the Pacific," copyright © 1949 by John Caldwell. First published in *Desperate Voyage*. Reprinted by permission of Sheridan House, Inc.

"Settling in for Survival," copyright © 1974 by Maurice and Maralyn Bailey. First published in *117 Days Adrift*. Reprinted by permission of Sheridan House, Inc.

"A Family Against the Ocean," copyright © 1973 by Dougal Robertson. First published in *Survive the Savage Sea*. Reprinted by permission of Sheridan House, Inc.

"Surviving the *St. Patrick*," copyright © 1991 by Spike Walker. First published in *Working on the Edge*. Reprinted by permission of St. Martin's Press, LLC.

"Rescue on Sitka Sound," copyright © 2001 by Spike Walker. First published in *Coming Back Alive*. Reprinted by permission of the author and St. Martin's Griffin, an imprint of St. Martin's Press LLC.

"Look for a Corpse," copyright © 1999 by Larry Kaniut. First published in *Danger Stalks the Land*. Reprinted by permission of St. Martin's Press, LLC.

"How It Feels to Be Crushed in an Ice Crevasse," copyright © 2007 by Michelle Hamer. First published in *How It Feels to Be Attacked by a Shark: And Other Amazing Life-or-Death Situations!* Reprinted by permission of the publisher, Skyhorse Publishing, Inc., 555 Eighth Avenue, Suite 903, New York, NY 10018.